SYMBOLS

by the same author

We, the Tikopia
Social Change in Tikopia
Tikopia Ritual and Belief
Rank and Religion in Tikopia
(*George Allen & Unwin*)

Primitive Economics of the New Zealand Maori
(*Wellington Government Printer*)

Elements of Social Organization
(*Tavistock Publications*)

Primitive Polynesian Economy
(*Routledge*)

RAYMOND FIRTH

SYMBOLS
PUBLIC AND PRIVATE

London
GEORGE ALLEN & UNWIN LTD
RUSKIN HOUSE MUSEUM STREET
1973

First published in 1973

ISBN 0 04 573011 3

Printed in Great Britain
in 12 pt Fournier type by
Alden & Mowbray Ltd
at the Alden Press, Oxford

CONTENTS

INTRODUCTION

My anthropological interest in symbolism was aroused more than forty years ago, among the Tikopia people of Western Polynesia. Their pagan rituals embodied many symbolic actions and symbolic statements of a vivid and complex kind, and interesting questions were presented as they converted from paganism to Christianity. But my earlier attraction to Romanesque art already bore on the problem of relation between religious symbolism and structure of society in a pre-industrial phase.

The aim of this book is to help to give perspective to the anthropological study of symbolic forms and processes and the functions of symbolism. It is meant neither as a textbook nor as a comprehensive general work. I have written about a range of ideas and material that seem relevant to me in understanding the problems of symbolism, and in what I have said of symbolism in art, literature, and religion I have no specialist knowledge. As well as giving some review of the present state of knowledge in anthropological studies of symbolism, I have tried to do three things. To provide some time-dimension, I have examined some of the ideas on symbolism put forward at the end of the eighteenth century and in the early nineteenth century by mythologists, dream-philosophers, cult-analysts – some of whom might be described as proto-anthropologists – and I have continued the study as anthropological interest crystallized until the present day. To provide breadth I have brought into discussion of the nature of symbolism hints of a few selected contributions from other fields of knowledge, including philosophy, since I think anthropologists need to be more aware of the depth of such studies in symbolism. Thirdly, I have deliberately cited examples of symbolic behaviour and statements about symbols, taken from newspapers and other ephemeral sources, because to my mind they show something of the richness of material open for investigation in modern industrial society.

In all this, while not, as I have once been labelled, an 'unqualified empiricist', I have been very aware of the problem of evidence. I think speculative reasoning in anthropology is stimulating and necessary for the development of theory, but it is easy in the study of symbolism to let it pass for fact. In anthropology, our imagination will have to be welded to honest craftsmanship if in the long run it is to carry conviction.

In 1967, as the guest of Victoria University, New Zealand, I delivered the Chancellor's Lectures, beginning with 'Giving and Getting', in which I put forward some of the ideas in this book. When I was asked to become Sara H. Schaffner Lecturer at the University of Chicago for the Fall Quarter of 1970, I was stimulated to expand those themes in the direction of specific studies of symbolism, which seemed appropriate in view of the very lively interest in symbolism in the Department of Anthropology there. By the generous terms of the Lectureship, which was instituted by Mr Joseph Halle Schaffner in honour of his mother, the University was asked to give the lecturer such hospitality as would provide him with a free informal atmosphere in which to work and mingle with all members of all grades of the academic community. I am very grateful to the University authorities, and especially to Bernard S. Cohn, Chairman of the Anthropology Department, and my other colleagues there, for all the help and hospitality they gave me then and later.

I have since added to the Schaffner Lectures, and have presented parts of this book at various stages to audiences at Cornell, Case Western Reserve, Columbia, McGill, Princeton, the London School of Economics, the University of Hawaii, the University of British Columbia, the University of Toronto, and the Graduate Center of the City University of New York. I mention in particular also that a version of material on the symbolism of exchange was given as the Dr David B. Stout Memorial Lecture before the Undergraduate Anthropology Club of the State University of New York at Buffalo, in April 1970. From discussions arising from these lectures and seminars I have profited much, and am grateful for the warmth of my reception on these occasions. A substantial part of the material and general argument of Chapter 9 has appeared in another form as a contribution to a volume of essays in honour of my colleague Audrey Richards—*The Interpretation of Ritual*, edited by J. S. La Fontaine (London, Tavistock, 1972). I acknowledge with thanks the agreement of editor and publisher to my reproduction of this material.

More generally, I am indebted to many colleagues for stimulus in preparing this work, particularly to Fred Eggan, Mervyn Meggitt, Joan Metge, Jan Pouwer, David Schneider, Terence Turner, Victor Turner, Nur Yalman, for interest and encouragement at various stages. Also I should mention especially Barbara Babcock and Judith Schapiro, whose many helpful thoughts included reference to Charles Feidelson's book on symbolism in American literature, and Guy Michaud's study of the French Symbolists. Finally, clarity of expression in the first part of this work, and the thought of the whole, have benefited distinctly from talks with my wife, who blends stimulus with criticism in a way I acknowledge with gratitude.

London, August 1972 *Raymond Firth*

I

ERRATA

Page 196, line 9 read Heisenbergian *not* Heisenburgian

Page 265, line 16 from bottom read 1776, ii, *not* 1776, iii

Page 266, first line of footnote read Katharine *not* Katherine

Page 267, second line from bottom read (*Letters*, book II, iv – 1637) *not* (*Letters*, book ii, iv – 1621)

Page 271, second line of footnote should now read: and was used by Thomas Blount (*Glossographia*, 1656) – Hyacynthine, of Violet or

Symbols

Chapter 1

AN ANTHROPOLOGIST'S REFLECTIONS ON SYMBOLIC USAGE

Symbolization is a universal human process. But we still need to understand much more about it, especially in its comparative aspects, in different societies, different classes, different religions. Pervasive in communication, grounded in the very use of language, symbolization is part of the living stuff of social relationships. Western literature is shot through with references which recall to us questions of existence and identity in symbol terms. In an essay on The Poet, Emerson wrote of the universality of the symbolic language: 'things admit of being used as symbols because nature is a symbol' (but so is culture) – 'we are symbols and inhabit symbols'. In *Sartor Resartus* Carlyle held that in a symbol there is both concealment and revelation. Oriental writings show analogous views. What is it in such statements that some of us find so attractive? Is it truth or illusion about human personality? And if these are not questions for anthropologists to answer, can we at least comment meaningfully upon the forms of such statements, the conditions of their utterance, and their social effects?

In intellectual circles, symbolism in literature, art and religion has long been a subject of study; philosophers and linguists have scrutinized the concept of symbol in its more abstract significance. I show later why I think such treatment is of interest to anthropologists. But anthropologists are also concerned with the ways in which ordinary people think about symbols, behave symbolically in their daily life as members of a society, and consciously interpret what they do as having symbolic meaning.

The essence of symbolism lies in the recognition of one thing as standing for (re-presenting) another, the relation between them normally being that of concrete to abstract, particular to general. The relation is such that the symbol by itself appears capable of generating and receiving effects otherwise reserved for the object to which it refers – and such effects are often of high emotional charge.

POPULAR RECOGNITION OF SYMBOLS

Now, what is very striking about the contemporary social scene is the wide currency of the notion of symbolism, and the overt, frequent use of the term symbol to describe objects, persons, actions, relationships of public interest.* In recent years particularly, the popular press gives many examples. I pick out a few almost at random.

Countries are often spoken of as symbolized by their products. So it has been said that in the early part of this century, peat, potatoes and parish priests meant Ireland, and that these 'are still valid symbols'. But a product of one country has been taken as a symbol of some international organization because of some special quality of that product. So a Chinese animal, the rare giant panda, has been made a symbol of the World Wildlife Fund, and its image is embossed on a plaque pledging furriers not to handle skins of other endangered species. In the socio-political field, national military bases abroad have long been 'a symbol of world leadership'. Meetings of heads of state have taken on a quality far exceeding the empirical content of the occasion. A personal exchange of views of the President of France and the Prime Minister of Britain about the Common Market could, it was thought, serve a future historian of Europe as a 'symbolic turning point' in the twentieth century. President Nixon's journey to Alaska to greet the Emperor of Japan – 4,000 miles for a talk of fifty minutes – in late 1971 was interpreted as 'an essentially symbolic gesture' which it was hoped might ease some tension in Japanese-American relations; the meeting was 'of enormous symbolic importance'. The President's visit to the Peoples' Republic of China was regarded in American quarters as 'an exercise in symbolic diplomacy' – where the fact of his going to Peking would be of more diplomatic importance than any substantive agreements that might be reached while he was there. But since the

* The term has come also into the commercial field as a label, for example a London biscuit firm (of high respectability as a supplier by appointment to a member of the Royal Family) is called Symbol Biscuits Limited, with an elephant's head as its mark.

trip was 'primarily symbolic' it was recognized that it might symbolize different things in different Asian capitals, and be interpreted otherwise in Tokyo from in Peking.

In dialogue between Peking and Washington a game of ping-pong 'has been made a symbol of "people to people" exchanges'. A light-hearted if malicious act of militant Jewish youths in releasing frogs and mice in Soviet commercial agencies in New York during Passover week as part of attempts to obtain freedom of Soviet Jews to leave for Israel was described as harassment by 'symbolic plagues'. (This was thought to be parallel to the Biblical account of the efforts of God to enforce the release of the Israelites by the Egyptians.) And the recital of Psalm 83 during a Jewish service for their dead who were killed in the war was described as having 'a symbolic significance relating to the suppression of Jewish cultural and spiritual rights in the Soviet Union'. On the other hand, when the Governor of Illinois sat in his office at midnight with his aides to defy a bomb threat, he explained that it was 'a symbolic act – we're trying to tell something to the people who call and threaten and try to intimidate government.'

Intellectuals may easily agree with the President of Columbia that the university is 'the symbol and agent of the larger society' and that as such should be open to criticism, provided that 'savage symbolic attacks' do not cause it to collapse rather than reform. A more sardonic note has emerged in a description of the new massive Lyndon Baines Johnson Library at the University of Texas. 'Architecture as art and symbol is one of civilization's oldest games,' and the architect of this monumental memorial has 'made a large statement using the archives themselves for stunning symbolic and aesthetic effect'. In development operations the jabbing of a shovel into the earth 'in a symbolic earth-turning ceremony' by an Indian dressed in buckskin jacket and eagle feather head-dress marked the start of a new tribal money-making hotel-type convention centre, with the ground to be actually levelled by bulldozer. By contrast, a grand old Mississippi Gulf Coast hotel demolished to make way for a store and shopping centre was described as 'a symbol of another day'. Conceptualization of social change takes one form in the view that people opposed to the legalization of marijuana see the prohibition 'as a symbolic barrier to a culture's disintegration' in the face of almost unmanageable pressures. It takes another form when American feminists argue that the demand that a woman specify her marital status by the prefix Miss or Mrs is discriminatory and that it should be replaced by Ms – 'Ms is really just a symbol – a gesture – but it is important to many women.'

The range of objects and actions cited as symbols – from ping-pong to a panda, from shovelling earth to prohibiting marijuana – suggests that these things in themselves are not of primary significance and that the key to an understanding of their symbolic quality lies in circumstances to which they refer or of which they are a part. It is not their particular nature but their relationships which account for their selection as symbols. At the same time, one cannot ignore completely the character of an object used as symbol (for example hair, blood), because certain classes of objects tend to stand in certain types of relationship to given situations.

This is perhaps especially the case when the object is regarded as having some autonomy, some freedom of action of its own, and so can be credited with intrinsic qualities deemed appropriate to a situation. So, it is part of modern popular idiom that people can easily become symbols. A priest is said to have 'a symbolic role of being a "sign" of the church.' A devoted churchman with a social conscience – such as the controversial Brazilian archbishop Dom Helder – was described as being to his friends and admirers a saint, or 'at the very least a symbolic man' whose courageous statements at home and abroad called attention to the plight of the masses in his country. Cardinal Mindszenty of Hungary who remained for fifteen years in seclusion in protest against the regime was 'a symbol of inflexible resistance of the cold-war era'. Description of political leaders as symbols is common. P. C. Lloyd has pointed out in reference to African societies that modern symbols of national unity tend to be persons rather than objects or ideas (1967, 316). The old-guard Nationalists of China, who reject violently any idea of accommodation with the Communists, are 'symbolized' by Chiang Kai-Shek; Lon Nol of Cambodia is described as 'a purely symbolic premier' after a near-fatal stroke which immobilized him; Sheikh Mujibur Rahman, of East Pakistan (now Bangladesh), was a 'symbol of Bengali resistance'. But the same phenomenon is recognized further down the political ladder. Ernest Bevin, the British trade-union leader, was 'the symbol of the industrial side of the Labour movement' and when he was Foreign Secretary 'his roles in the creation of NATO and in the spurning of the Schumann Plan for the Coal and Steel Community were symbolic'. When ex-premier David Ben-Gurion attended the mass Israeli Labour party convention in 1971, his presence 'symbolized his *rapprochement* with the party leadership' after more than a decade of ideological disputes with it. Charles Evers, black Mayor of Fayette, Mississippi, was to his friends 'not simply a man or a small-time mayor but a precious symbol – a hero of the Southern black political renaissance'. Adam Clayton Powell, first 'negro' from the East to serve in the United States Congress, was for long 'a symbol of success to blacks'. Dr Eric Williams, Prime Minister of Trinidad-Tobago and increasingly under fire from the local black-power movement, was 'once a symbol of the blacks' struggle against British colonialism'. And in the economic field, a Scottish industrialist who was interested in purchasing a bankrupt Clydebank shipyard 'emerged from comparative obscurity to become the symbol of hope for thousands of shipyard workers on Clydeside'.

A striking example of the explicit incorporation of the notion of symbol into the relationship of a person to an abstract entity is that of the Emperor Hirohito of Japan. Previous to the defeat of Japan at the end of the Second World War, the Emperor had been regarded officially as a divine being, a direct descendant of the Sun Goddess. Deified and worshipped publicly for many years, in an imperial rescript of 1 January 1946 the Emperor renounced the idea of his divinity 'based on the fictitious idea that the Emperor is manifest god' – and became 'the Symbol of the state and of the unity of the people'. By this act the Emperor translated himself from a sacred to a secular being, from a god to a human being. In his role as an explicit symbol of the state he appears to be acceptable to a large majority of the Japanese people, and he seems also to be able to exercise a considerable if subtle influence upon political decisions made by the government. A person as political symbol may have active as well as passive functions.*

* Note that some recent consideration has been given to re-definition of the Emperor's position, to make him head of state, more in conformity with diplomatic protocol and Japanese national pride. (Cf. *New York Times*, 21 September 1971, 26 September 1971, 31 October 1971.)

Modern popular views of law and morality are rich in recognition of men as symbols. It is said that for citizens of the United States with no monarchy and no established church, the Supreme Court symbolizes the judiciary, and approaches the level of a sacred institution. It has also been stated that J. Edgar Hoover, long-time head of the Federal Bureau of Investigation, became 'symbolic of the fight against evil-doers'. On the other hand, a former Black Panther leader accused of assault on policemen and kept in jail by very high bail was held by members of his local community to be 'a symbolic victim of excessive bond' equivalent to preventive detention. Likewise, an Army officer convicted of the murder of civilian prisoners in the My Lai massacre case was regarded by many people as 'a symbol for all that was wrong with the Vietnam war'. In a general conflict over what are variously regarded as the constraints or the values of established norms, the leader of the rock group the Rolling Stones, Mick Jagger, came for many 'to symbolize and personify an entire rebellious generation with its drug-oriented, freewheeling morality'. And a recent examination of the possibility of selecting a black vice-presidential candidate for the United States elections of 1972 stressed very strongly the moral value of such a symbolic act. It was argued that a black vice-presidential candidate would have 'a tremendous symbolic impact on race relations in the United States'. Man does not live by symbols alone, but man orders and interprets his reality by his symbols, and even reconstructs it. A black moderate running for Vice-President would be 'an extremely powerful symbol of the possibility of achieving racial justice and harmony in American society'. The symbol by itself would not create justice or harmony, but it might create an atmosphere in which they might become more possible. Thus a candidate who chose a black running-mate in the name of reconciliation combined with social progress would be likely to 'touch deep wellsprings of the American political symbol system'.

This spate of examples,* culled from only a few Press sources over

* Citations concerning Ernest Bevin are from Roy Jenkins, *The Times*, 9 June 1971; those concerning the Johnson Library are from Ada Louise Huxtable, *New York Times*, 23 May 1971; those concerning a black Vice-President are from Andrew M. Greeley, *New York Times Magazine*, 19 September 1971. Other material in this set of examples has been drawn from: *Chicago Daily News*, 5 April 1971, 12, 15, 20, 26 May 1971; *New York Times*, 2, 12, 14, 18 April 1971, 23 May 1971, 2, 4 June 1971, 20, 21, 26, 27, 29 September 1971; *Newsweek*, 12, 26 April 1971, 10, 24 May 1971, 7 June 1971; *Time Magazine*, 17 May 1971, 20, 27 September 1971; *The Times*, 27 March 1971, 24 August 1971; *Guardian*, 24 August 1971.

a very limited period, illustrates the extent to which the notion of symbol has come to permeate popular thought. Little wonder then that an American publicist, Stewart Alsop, critical of modern political party trends, has written about what he calls 'symbol-think'. Members of the party 'did not have to think about the issues, or argue about them. Instead, they reacted to symbols.' People who did not react in the same way to the same symbols were not 'real' party members and thus deserved to be cast into outer darkness. Whereas formerly Republican 'symbol-thinkers' in passionate opposition to the government once exercised power, now they have been replaced by Democratic 'symbol-thinkers' . . . and so on (*Newsweek*, 26 April 1971). The social awareness indicated by such an opinion is reminiscent of the classical statement of Émile Durkheim: 'it is a well-known law that the sentiments aroused in us by something spontaneously attach themselves to the symbol which represents them.' (1926, 219). What is remarkable about such modern popular opinions is not their freedom of symbolic usage but the open way in which they recognize the usage and call it symbolic.

Yet an overt use of the term symbol may not necessarily convey clearly the kind of relation envisaged between the thing cited and whatever it is intended to represent. The idea of a sex symbol seems clear enough. But when a popular cinema star or singer is referred to as a sex symbol, as often happens, just what is meant? An epitome of sexual thoughts and longings, concretely represented in a particular body which suggests eroticism by subtle – or blatant – combinations of form and movement? Yes, but with qualifications: a sex symbol for one sex only – a man for women, a woman for men; for some people only – many are unmoved, apart from the complex question of those who reject the symbolism with anger. And apart from physical qualities, it seems as if the person so nominated usually has that indefinable quality of personal attractiveness in spirit as well as in body, so that the sex symbolism is not just the representation or suggestion of sheer brute contact and coupling, but implies some more emotional, even ethereal components as well. Perhaps it was partly for such reasons that Marilyn Monroe, labelled one of the greatest sex symbols of her time, is said to have commented that she thought symbols were 'those things that clashed together'. Beneath her wit, it may be, lay a sense of how vague such labels of symbol really are. Complications in the concept show too in a feminine protest at discrimination against educated women, by male employers with 'a secretary sex-symbol syndrome' (*Time Magazine*, 6 December 1971).

A symbol represents something else – but there may be several levels of meaning involved. President Nixon's journey to Alaska to meet the Emperor of Japan was called a *symbolic* gesture because it was thought that there was no concrete object sought – no arrangements to be concluded, no question of principle to be resolved, no treaty to be signed, which demanded his presence. What the gesture of long-distance travel stood for was presumably then a sign of the amity which existed or was hoped to exist between the countries of the two leaders. Indeed it was stated that the President's clear purpose was to demonstrate a sentiment that had tended to be lost to sight in recent controversy about economic relations between the United States and Japan, the sentiment that mature alliance with Japan was an important concern of American policy in Asia. It was also stated that he intended to indicate a symbolic counterweight to his recent friendly overtures to the Peoples' Republic of China. Yet it was one writer's opinion that while both men and both governments were 'plainly caught up in the symbolism of the occasion', 'the symbolism belonged to the past' (Max Frankel, *New York Times*, 28 September 1971).

According to this view, there was considerable resentment among the officials on both sides behind the polite façade, so the greeting symbol did not represent an existing state of affairs, but one that was past, and that it was only hoped would return. This is an illustration of how a symbol can be detached from present reality and made to stand for past reality or future contingency. Or putting it another way, what was being 'said' by the ceremonial behaviour was in effect: this greeting expresses not what we leaders – or our officials and people – feel now, but the opposite of our present feelings, or a minor not a major aspect. The idea of a symbol may then be behaviour which, if not devoid of meaning, is at least contradictory of the actual state of affairs. The connotation of symbol here is superficiality, not deepest reality. Moreover, the Japanese Emperor is by imperial rescript the symbol of the state. So his 'symbolic stop-off' for the meeting could be described as the symbolic behaviour of a person already a symbol – a kind of symbol to the second power.

The idea that 'symbol' is equivalent to 'not real' is brought out by another example – though it also raises the question whether in popular usage the term 'symbol' is often not misapplied. As part of an attempt to help control the smuggling of antique paintings out of Italy, the United States customs authorities in 1971 were stated to have 'symbolically seized' the so-called Boston Raphael, about the authenticity of which experts had been in conflict (*The Times*, 6 March 1971; *New York Times*, 11 September 1971). What is meant by the word 'symbolically' in such context? What apparently happened was that the customs authorities took charge of the painting and directed it to be removed from the wall of the Boston Museum of Fine Arts, where it hung on public exhibition, to the museum store-room. There it remained under customs seal on the claim that it had presumably been smuggled into the country without a permit. Where was the symbolism? The customs men probably did not physically lay hands on the painting, and so did not actually 'seize' it; their act might therefore be described as a *metaphorical* seizure, by which they obtained control of the picture without grasping it. To be properly described as 'symbolic' in conventional terms, it might be argued that an act of seizure should have been meant to represent something else, not that some other act represented a seizure. The expression 'symbolic seizure' may of course have been purely a newspaper invention. But from a public point of view it may be that the 'seizure' was truly symbolic in that it was not intended to grab that particular painting. The act may have been meant to show disapproval by the customs authorities (or other officials) of the practice which seems to have grown up of some museums and galleries obtaining works of art from abroad without going through the formalities of getting the appropriate licences – in other words, smuggling what may well have been stolen goods.

In another example, the ambiguity of the symbolism is more evident. When democratic elections were introduced after the war in some countries where the level of literacy was low, pictorial emblems were used to represent the different political parties seeking votes. In 1969 the Indian Congress party split into two rival factions, and a long legal battle ensued to determine which faction should have 'the party's old election symbol, the two yoked bullocks'. The issue was thought to be very important because it was held that many voters being illiterate would recognize and vote primarily for the symbol rather than for the party as such (*The Times*, 14 January 1971). When it seemed that the Supreme Court would deny this symbol of yoked bullocks to either faction, Mrs Gandhi's party was expected to adopt a symbol showing mother and child – but in the event they used a cow and calf. Some other parties to the election used analogous devices reminiscent of peasant activity – sickle and ears of grain; woman at a spinning wheel; an oil lamp (Neville Maxwell, *New Society*, 4 March 1971). Drawings of these things were described as the symbols of the political parties. Now the drawings were just conventionalized representations of bullocks, grain, etc., that is signs for them. In saying that these sketch-outline designs were 'symbols' of the various political parties it is presumably meant that they were intended to call to the minds of party leaders, members and voting public generally the nature of each party as a political entity, the ideals for which it stood, and its practical programme. Presumably too, the selection of 'naturalistic' symbols such as bullocks, cow and calf, mother and child, grain, spinning wheel, simple lamp, was meant to suggest to a significant body of voters that there was some connection between the specific party and care for the peasant way of life which these things might represent. As the legal battle over the yoked bullock device implied, it was thought that values, including those of prestige, were attached to these symbols. But what the device actually symbolized to voters remained somewhat obscure. Did they associate bullocks with the traditional Congress party so habitually that they would vote for the bullocks thinking they were still voting for that party? Did they realize that the bullocks might no longer represent the same party but still vote for that device on the grounds that people who used the bullocks as device automatically employed policies of which voters approved – that the policy went with the label, not with the party which might change label? Or did the voters not bother about such issues, but simply vote for the device which they favoured on much more literal grounds – that they preferred bullocks to a cow and calf, or they liked the sentimentalism of a device of mother and child? That this last is not at all out of the question is illustrated by the comment of an illiterate Kelantan Malay woman to the anthropologist when confronted by local political party symbols of a sheaf of rice, a fishing boat under sail, a star and crescent moon. She said she voted for the sheaf of rice because to her as a woman rice was her concern whereas a fishing boat was an affair of men, and the heavenly bodies were far away. So to describe such devices as 'symbols' of political parties ignores a possible difference in level of statement – in simplicity or directness as against complexity or indirectness of representation. To put it another way – the associations of the device might be treated by some people as agricultural and domestic, not state-wide and political as intended.

AN ANTHROPOLOGICAL APPROACH TO SYMBOLISM

I have shown the existence of a very wide range of symbolic material – things called symbols and ideas about symbols – in the current social milieu in which we all move. I have suggested too that such material can be relevant to any general anthropological study of symbols because of the problems of definition and image it raises.

But what can be a specifically anthropological contribution to the understanding of symbolism? What can an anthropologist do that has not been done already by logicians, metaphysicians, linguists, psychologists, theologians, art historians and the rest? Essentially as I see it, the anthropological approach is comparative, observationalist, functionalist, relatively neutralist. It links the occurrence and interpretations of symbolism to social structures and social events in specific conditions. Over a wide range of instances, anthropologists have observed what symbols people actually use, what they have said about these things, the situations in which the symbols emerge, and the reactions to them. Consequently, anthropologists are equipped to explain the meanings of symbols in the cultures they have studied, and to use such explanations as a means of furthering understanding of the processes of social life. Victor Turner has said of one of his studies – which have played a great part in modern developments – that it is a demonstration of the use of rite and symbol as a key to the understanding of social structure and social process. Others have explicitly examined symbolic actions in their social contexts to clarify the understanding of phenomena of political or religious change. But I think that for many of us the prime relevance of an anthropological approach to the study of symbolism is its attempt to grapple as empirically as possible with the basic human problem of what I would call disjunction – a gap between the overt superficial statement of action and its underlying meaning. On the surface, a person is saying or doing something which our observations or inferences tell us should not be simply taken at face value – it stands for something else, of greater significance to him.

I take an illustration from my own experience in the Pacific, years ago.* I remember seeing a Tikopia chief in pagan times stand up in his temple and rub the great centre post of the building with aromatic leaves drenched in coconut oil. Now you can oil wood to preserve it or give it a polish, as decoration. And in the Pacific you can oil your body and scent it with leaves, when you decorate yourself, as for a dance. But as the chief did this rubbing he murmured: 'May your body be washed with power.' Now scrubbing a baulk of timber with a hunk of oily leaves is not a very elevated intellectual act. But think of the timber as a *body* and of the fragrant oil as a decorative medium. Think too not of a material body, but of an invisible body – not necessarily with the shape of a post, but in another context, an anthropomorphic body, of a spiritual being, believed to control crops and fish and the health of men. Think too of washing as cleansing, and cleansing as a preface to adornment, and adornment as pleasing to oneself as well as to others. So you can see this act as symbolizing the anointing of the body of a god with fragrant scents to express the status relations and emotions of worship – and to render the god more amenable to the requests of his worshippers. This may seem a very faraway symbolism. Yet think further of Christ's washing of the feet of his disciples; the anointing of Christ by Mary of Bethany; the symbolic value to Christians of the Cross, with its synonyms of the Wood, the Tree; and think also of conceptions of the Eucharist (Chap. 12), of the Mystical Body of Christ, of the Glorified Body of the Virgin. It is not difficult to see that what we are dealing with in the Tikopia case is a set of symbolic counters which though superficially very

* For more details and related ritual operations see Raymond Firth, 1967a, 209–11, 218–20, 234, 245; 1970a, 117–19, pl. I.

dissimilar to the Christian ones, share some of the same basic modes of symbolic conceptualization and patterning. But the symbolic arrangement is set in a social matrix of clans, chieftainship, modes of bodily decoration, even of architectural design which need intensive study for the symbolism to become fully intelligible.

The anthropological approach, fully applied, has as its objective to provide a systematic description and analysis of such a symbolic act in its verbal and non-verbal aspects; to distinguish those parts of the action held to be significant from those which are incidental; to mark the routine or standard elements as against those which are personal and idiosyncratic; to get elucidation from actor, participants and non-participants of the meanings they attach to the act; and to set all this in its general conceptual and institutional framework, and in the more specific framework of the statuses and group relationships of the people concerned. This is a demanding task. But it has been admirably done by many anthropologists – to mention here only Audrey Richards, Monica Wilson and Victor Turner – whose work I shall be examining in later chapters. Some anthropologists have also studied change in symbolic idiom – as I myself have done in the field of Tikopia religion (Firth, 1970a).

The study of symbolism, especially religious symbolism, is fashionable now in social anthropology. There is a tendency to look on this study as a totally new development, but in fact as I show in Chapter 3, anthropological interest in symbols goes back at least 100 years, before the days of McLennan and Tylor. It is true that until recently this interest was rarely intense, systematic or sustained, and the modern interest is much more sophisticated, analytical and highly focused.* I think there are several reasons for this delayed development. Firstly, as a purely professional sequence of operations, systematic studies of symbolism have had to wait until a substantial measure of progress had been made in the more formal fields of social structure, such as kinship and politics. Now that so much groundwork has been laid we can build loftier constructions of interpretation. Secondly, developments in the theory of communication and of semantics, of signs and their meanings, have focused

* In 1956 at the Philadelphia meeting of the International Ethnological Congress I myself stated that little specific attention had been paid to symbolism by anthropologists. By contrast, Rodney Needham has recently written 'today, when there is an efflorescence of interest in all forms of symbolism' (in Hocart, 1970, xxix).

attention on the interpretation of those elements of behaviour where the meaning of the sign has often seemed most complex and obscure. Thirdly, the growing interest in culturally-defined systems of thought, and in concepts and thought-processes more generally, has stimulated inquiry in fields such as symbolism, where the relationships between elements seem above all to be of a conceptual kind. All this is part of the relatively straightforward operations of scholarship.

But I think two other reasons may be significant also. It is in keeping with the general temper of our time to be attracted to studies which concern themselves with the less rational aspects of human behaviour, which tend to reject or criticize a positivist approach, which make play with ideas of ambiguity, uncertainty, mystery. This is probably in part a counter to or a relief from the demands for rationality and precision of our industrial, machine-governed society. The other reason is more personal. Some anthropologists (and I think I should probably have to include myself here) find in working out their position on symbolism a means of examining and stating, perhaps resolving, some of their individual views about the nature and determinants of human social relationships and activity. Here I should say that while I am much impressed by a great deal of the modern anthropological work on symbolism, I do not share all the perspectives of some of its most distinguished exponents.

It seems to me to make sense, and to be relevant in the world today, that anthropologists should try to interpret symbolical language and symbolical behaviour and relate them to the range of social forms and social values. In such study political symbols are important. But I do not think that only those issues are relevant which refer to political affairs – unless one conceives of the political, as some of my colleagues do, as involving any kind of relations between persons where power is concerned, irrespective of scale. Religious symbols are important too, but I look upon them as referring to the same order of reality as the rest, categorized by the quality of attention given to them, not by the uniqueness of the objects to which they refer. So while I include both political and religious symbols in my examination in this book I deliberately take in material from ordinary daily life – such as the symbolism of ways of wearing the hair, of greeting and parting, of making and of accepting gifts, of showing flags. I deliberately also try to consider private as well as public aspects of symbolic behaviour and concepts, because I think that the inter-relationship between them has often been neglected, by anthropologists as well as by other students of symbolism. I think this relation between public and private, social and personal symbols is important to consider because certainly nowadays it seems that there are strong trends within society for the rejection of traditional symbols and for the discovery, even the invention, of new symbols – trends in which individual interests and decisions are brought to bear upon the recognition of communal symbolic forms.

Popular, unanalysed expressions of symbolism are of interest to anthropologists because they are part of the raw material for comparative study of processes of human thought and action. They reveal the direction and extent of peoples' involvement in social processes of various kinds, and the quality of abstraction applied to these processes. But at a more analytical level, specialized treatments of symbolism also have their anthropological importance. Much that philosophers, artists, art historians, literary critics, theologians, have written about symbolism is not immediately germane to anthropological studies. But I think it has distinct value for anthropological purposes. Firstly, I find it a very proper satisfaction of an intellectual curiosity to know at least the outline of the arguments put forward about symbolism by specialists in other disciplines, and the range of material they cover. Secondly, some of the illustrations they give recall obliquely some of the data anthropologists deal with, and suggest possible alternative lines of treatment. Finally, some of the hypotheses they put forward about criteria for identification of symbols, the relation between public and private symbols, the relation of symbolization to expression and communication provide parallel or challenge to anthropological views. Yet they often seem to lack that social dimension which is vital to an anthropologist, and to make assertions which seem to an anthropologist to be culture-bound, or 'ethnocentric'. So I think that no systematic theoretical exploration of symbolism by anthropologists should ignore the existence of such an interest by these other disciplines.

From this vast field of scholarly contributions I can only make a personal selection of a few examples which seem to me to have some relevance for problems with which anthropologists are primarily concerned. They may add to such limited interdisciplinary focus as anthropologists have already sought.

EXPLORATION OF SYMBOLS IN LITERATURE

Literary interest in symbols can be traced far back in history. In Chapter 3 I examine a few early-nineteenth-century examples. Propositions about symbolism in literature during the late nineteenth century, and the often polemical examination of their significance, did not precede anthropological references to symbols. But if not more sophisticated, those in literature were at least of a more highly focused quality. Unknowingly, they foreshadowed a present-day anthropological concern for the relation between social reality and models constructed to represent it. The parallel has occurred in two ways: by the symbolists' rejection of naturalistic description as a desirable even if achievable aim; and by their search for interpretation of deep forces of which the human operators themselves were unaware. But the differences were also marked. In poetry, especially, in the last decades of the nineteenth century, the aim of the symbolist movement was to replace realism by the 'idea'. But the 'idea' was evocative not analytical, emotional rather than intellectual.

All poetry relies greatly upon symbolism. In the French tradition, for instance, Francois Villon, most vigorously direct and human in so many of his ballads, often used a symbolic image. The poignant, haunting if hackneyed *où sont les neiges d'antan?* ('where are the snows of yester-year?') evokes not merely the ladies of bygone days of his poem's title, but also, one may think, the purity, calm and beauty of all that one has held most dear. But this is very different from the attitude of the proclaimed Symbolist.* The symbolism of Mallarmé and his followers aimed at the discovery of the pure poetry arising from what was thought to be the non-logical,

* Cf. Guy Michaud (1947, 637) – in every age there has been symbolism in art and literature (du *symbolisme*); but Symbolism (*le Symbolisme*) really saw the light in France in the second half of the nineteenth century. Cf. also Étiemble, who quotes Catulles Mendés to the effect that symbol is as old as the world; refers to the many meanings of symbol and to the wide variation in the definition of Symbolism; and gives an astringent critique of views which treat Rimbaud as a Symbolist (1961, 67, 68, 89–90).

irrational quality of language itself, trying, for example, to express ideas by associations of form and colour. Verlaine said of Mallarmé that he was preoccupied with the intensity of beauty, and that clarity was to him a secondary grace. Verlaine himself wrote, in *Poèmes Saturniens*:

> Le Poète, L'Amour du Beau, voila sa foi,
> L'Azur, son étendard, et L'Idéal, sa loi.

Here the *azur*, the clear blue, represented in poetic symbolic language the heaven, the infinite. But the influences involved were complex. This French symbolism was a violent reaction against the classic formalism of the earlier generations. It was also a reaction against the frustrations which followed the military defeat of France two decades before. But above all – and not unconnected with the foregoing – it was, as Alfred Poizat has put it, 'the entry of the dream into literature, it was the turning back of the view from outside inwards' (1924, 143). Or as Arnold Hauser has summed it up: 'For symbolism, the whole of empirical reality is only the image of a world of ideas' (1952, II, 896). Mallarmé was interested by 'the mystery of ideas'; he and his associates held that the only certain realities were our ideas and consequently our dreams, our imaginings. We only know the external world by images which it leaves on us and by the reactions of our sensibility. Relationships between concrete and abstract, thing apprehended and apprehender, could be created, it was believed, without overt conceptual effort. Precise direct statements of conscious formulation were regarded as less poetically revealing than vague indirectly allusive utterances which could be treated as products of unconscious impulse. Yet the romanticism of the early part of the century, in the sense of a deliberate cultivation of emotion, was rejected, especially when it used conventional metaphorical language. Shot through such claims for a purer aesthetic, in which symbols would express the true nature of relationships more adequately than would a set of descriptive terms, was a theme of spirituality, the idea of an inner incomprehensible, incommensurate quality of being of which the symbol stands as the outer representative. Hence Bowra (1943, 2–12) saw in retrospect the Symbolist movement of the nineteenth century in France as fundamentally mystical – in its intensity, its irrationality, its disregard for other beliefs and its reliance on a world beyond the senses. So, while Mallarmé spoke of art as impersonal, by concentrating on his own private visions the Symbolist stressed in effect the subjective character of his art. Michaud, with his exhaustive documentation, has pointed out the variety of Symbolist positions. But he has seen the essential message of symbolism as providing a synthesis in the simultaneous expression of different degrees or levels of reality, or expressing truths which are valuable on different planes at once. So the symbol is revelatory of an aspect of truth, of truth in its subjective aspect (1947, 414–20). And as Michaud has indicated, whatever be the judgement as to the validity of the symbolist arguments, they rendered a great service in bringing to the surface a consciousness of the symbolic process.

This classical symbolist view in literature, which had its analogue in painting (see later), made two kinds of statements about symbols which in effect challenge much of the anthropological approach to the subject. They asserted the primacy of the private recognition of the symbolic; and they claimed that the referent or reality itself, can be apprehended only through the symbol. An anthropologist is concerned primarily with the public use of the symbolic, and his aim is to separate symbol from referent so that he may describe the relation between them. But while ostensibly about poetry or art in general, such formulations have offered themes for stimulus and scrutiny to anthropology.

The influence of the Symbolist movement was wide and enduring, and in modified forms it attained a cosmopolitan status. Bowra recognized its counterpart in England in the aesthetic movement, with Rossetti, Pater and Oscar Wilde. But for Mallarmé his 'great idol' was Edgar Allan Poe, whom he translated 'admirably' and for whom he wrote a lament – 'Le Tombeau d'Edgar Poe' (Verlaine, 1884, 54, 55; Bowra, 1943, 9).

The symbolism of nineteenth-century American writers such as Poe, Melville and Henry James has been the subject of considerable analysis by literary critics. Since various cultural assumptions are built into such analysis, a confrontation between critics and anthropologists might give it a greater flexibility and sensitivity, as well as furnishing some new viewpoints for the anthropology of symbols. I give here merely a hint of an anthropological tentative in this direction.

The author of one of the most important works in this field, Charles Feidelson (1953), has argued that there is a 'family pattern' in that phase of American literature which began with Hawthorne, Emerson and Poe and ended with Melville and Whitman; that this pattern is one of symbolism; and that the concept of symbolism is not only a key to their situation but also a link between their situation and the present-day (Feidelson, 1953, 3, 5). Classed as romantics – some as transcendentalists – they were regarded as minor disciples of European masters; regarded as symbolists, even though they themselves would not have recognized the title, they can be credited with literary independence, looking forward to 'one of the most sophisticated movements in literary history'. With the general appropriateness of this classification an anthropologist is not concerned – though he may note its faintly nationalist flavour. But it is significant that in this literary context, to be credited with symbolism in his operations gives a writer a mark of distinction. Some of the studies in this field have analysed works which have been at least marginal to anthropological study; others have considered works with no direct anthropological bearing. But in both categories it is the methods used by the literary analyst which are of interest – in their identification and interpretation of symbols.

The symbolism of Herman Melville's *Moby Dick* has been a subject of study for half a century.* But Feidelson finds a latent symbolism even in Melville's *Typee*, an allegedly descriptive book, which has been used mildly for ethnographic reference on the Marquesas Islands, where Melville spent a month in 1842. For Feidelson the book is primarily a travelogue; its scene is the solid earth; and 'the language does not often *invite* a symbolistic interpretation.' Yet the stuff of Melville's experience seems to 'hover on the verge of the symbolic expansion' it was to undergo in his later works. The development of this idea is interesting from an anthropological angle. *Typee*, opening with Melville's 'basic cartography' of the division of earth and waters, stresses the circular pattern of the island encompassed by the ocean. According to Feidelson, it shadows forth the pattern of Melville's world, which in this literary critic's view, is remarkably like the spherical universe concept of Emerson. Now this raises a problem of attribution – of relation between

* It has been used for anthropological comparisons by Victor Turner, 1962.

symbolization and empirical reality – which has relevance for all anthropologists interested in symbolism and not only those concerned with Pacific islands. For Melville's *Typee* is not only one of the semi-ethnographic sources for our understanding of early culture-contact conditions in Polynesia, it is also redolent of the experience of living in a simple Pacific island environment. I can myself endorse some of his observations. As one who has lived for a long period on a remote isolated Polynesian island and who faced day-after-day on every side a blank horizon across a vast expanse of water, I too have been impressed by the 'circular pattern' of my island universe. With no thought of Melville I wrote of this island: 'in an abstract schematic way one may think of Tikopia as a circle of land bounded by the wastes of the ocean, and just within the land edge a circle of houses . . .' (1936, 79; 1969, 65). But in this analogy with Melville's conception, as interpreted by Feidelson, two points emerge. One is that the identification of an abstract pattern in a topographical field is not necessarily the same as the identification of a symbol, unless the term symbol be taken in the very broad sense of any representation of the field. (An abstract painter may strenuously deny that the patterns he produces have any symbolic quality.) An island microcosm in an oceanic macrocosm is not by itself a *symbolic* image, though it may well have led Melville towards the formulation of later symbols of such order. The second point is that while Feidelson links Melville to Emerson in symbolic development, mainly by contrasting the quality of their symbolic imagination, he seems to be misled in stressing the resemblance between the geometric patterns of their respective worlds: a circular pattern of island and surrounding ocean is only superficially akin to the sphere which was the unit of Emerson's formulation of experience. As I see it, this example of 'latent' symbolism attributed to Melville can serve as a kind of cautionary note for anthropologists concerned to identify as symbolic, primitive forms of representing the natural and social universe. But Feidelson's comments on literary symbolism in general include the very pertinent statement that the centre of symbolism is not in private feelings, but in the public medium of language (Feidelson, 1953, 51). In other words, communication is the test of a symbol that survives.

With Henry James the significance of literary symbolism for

anthropologists may be deeper. In *The Turn of the Screw* we are given the raw material for a fascinating series of questions about the nature of mental constructs, ideas of control of one personality by another, the forms which symbolization of mental force may assume, the relation of innocence to knowledge of evil. All of these emerge in different shape as problems in the anthropological study of witchcraft and related issues. But what Edmund Wilson has termed the ambiguity of James may pose an interesting problem of the relation between conscious and unconscious process in symbol formation. Edmund Wilson has been admitted by Feidelson to have been the first to remark on the affinity of nineteenth-century American writers with the symbolist aesthetic that produced much of modern literature. More than a generation ago Wilson went to some pains to elucidate the symbols in which as he saw it Henry James presented his 'chronic inhibition' – some degree of sexual impotence. One such symbolic presentation, according to Wilson, was that of the maiden innocence of immature girls violated or destroyed. In a striking example, Wilson identifies as 'one of the most curious symbols' for James's condition the wax dummy in a Parisian hairdresser's window, with which in one of the stories a man falls in love; he finally buys the dummy and takes her home to live with him. Of high significance in this interpretative analysis is the statement that the dummy was cut off at the waist.* The interest of this example for anthropologists is primarily methodological. That a sculptured figure can be a surrogate for a human being and that sexual impotence (being only 'half a man') can be represented by a figure lacking sex organs and lower limbs, are not particularly novel ideas. Nor is there much relevance for anthropology in tracing these ideas back into Henry James's fantasy. But in the prevailing climate of anthropological concern with symbolism the literary critic's methods of identification of symbols are of interest. Clearly he is using very much of an *ad hominem* argument. The conception or depiction of the upper half of the body – head, bust and torso – as representative of a person is obviously not in itself a sign of sexual impotence in an artist – otherwise a whole host of sculptors, portrait painters and

* Edmund Wilson, *The Ambiguity of Henry James* (1962, 147, 149n; the essay was originally published in 1938). It may be coincidence that among the 'symbols of the subjection of women' carried by Women's Liberation demonstrators in London in March 1971 was a tailor's dummy, cut off below the waist (*Observer*, 7 March 1971).

society photographers would be implicated, as would even the purchasers of what used to be called these 'likenesses'. The symbolic character of a portrait is well-known. But in James's story the dummy was not a portrait; the man fell in love with the figure, not with a living person; and he exercised power over it by buying it, and domesticating it. In the story the figure was a private symbol for the chief character. What the critic has done is to make a transference and interpret it as a private symbol for the author. For anthropologists, this raises the issue of the steps by which the transference was made, of the criteria by which one particular item in an author's product is picked out as symbolic of an aspect of his own personality, and others left alone as simple imaginative creations not implicating the personality of their author.

This problem is: How does one identify an object or an action as symbolic, not only for the interpreter but also for the author of it, when he provides no overt clue? It is an issue which should concern anthropologists more than it has done heretofore. In Wilson's otherwise sensitive essay I do not find much guidance on this methodological issue, though it implies that the identification of private symbols of public men can be of general interest. But one thought arises by contrast – an anthropologist faced by a problem of identification of private symbols can seek justification of his attribution because what he observes has consequences. Behaviour in regard to the hairdresser's dummy ceases at the end of James's story – 'what came after' is no more than a parlour game of guessing. But if a man in the anthropologist's field of observation bears off a female wooden figure to his home, a whole series of actions by the man and his household are bound to occur, and reflect back in confirmation or contradiction on the anthropologist's original inference about the symbolism involved. The anthropologist, though more constrained than the literary critic in his symbolic attributions, has more opportunity of testing them afterwards.

It has often been pointed out that symbolists in literature were not united under any single banner, but ranged from those proclaiming ideals of decadence through a Nietzschean brutal sensitivity to occultism and Christian mysticism. And modern French studies in this field, especially, are of great elaboration and sophistication – far more than I can indicate here. But explorations of symbolism in literature among much of general intellectual interest have raised several kinds of problem of concern to anthropologists: What phenomena are classed as symbolic and what criteria are used for identifying them? How far can the exploration go in the identification of covert or latent symbols apparently unperceived by their author? What is the relation between symbols of a public order and private symbols of the poet or other writer? And is there an irreconcilable opposition between the aesthetic, intuitive aspects of symbolic recognition and an intellectual apprehension of symbolic form and function?

SYMBOLS IN ART

Analogous processes of looking for symbols and discussing them have been important in the study of painting and other graphic arts. The interpretation of the symbolic qualities of Christian religious art of the early mediaeval period in Western Europe can be used as an illustration, since its lack of interest in naturalistic proportion and its direct relation to ritual and belief provide analogy with the 'primitive' art studied by anthropologists.

The mediaeval church was preoccupied by symbolism. The church building itself was held in structure to represent the human body, the chancel being the head and the transepts the arms. But it also represented the Cross of Christ . . . and so on (Dunbar, 1929, 403–4). Romanesque painting and sculpture presented figures which for the most part illustrated Biblical scenes. But these were not simply translations into fresco or stone of written stories which an illiterate population could not read; they also were meant to carry messages of more general import. Old Testament scenes were intended to prefigure New Testament events; animals as well as human beings symbolized abstract qualities or spiritual powers. Take for example the figure of the lion. In contrast to the leopard, which appears rarely in the mediaeval sculptural field, and is the symbol of cruelty, sin and hence of Antichrist, the Devil, the lion is very common and generally represents a noble principle. (Later I discuss the significance of Samson destroying the lion.) Following the ancient bestiaries, the lion was regarded as the king of beasts, strong and compassionate (Camerarius, 1668, II, 13). When shown fighting a dragon or serpent (as on the Percy tomb at Beverley or a tympanum at Lieding in Carinthia), it represented the power of good combating evil. According to the bestiaries, the lion had three important characteristics, which though fantasy creations, were elaborated by Christian exegesists in symbolic terms. The lion was thought to sleep with its eyes open, and so could represent vigilance – so, according to some views it was an appropriate guardian for church doors, and hence appears on many pillars.* In particular, it was an image of Christ (the Lion of the Tribe of Judah) who was awake during the night in the tomb awaiting his resurrection. The lion typified the resurrection of Jesus in another way. Its cubs were said to be born dead, but watched over by their mother for three days, after which time their father came and breathed over them, so giving them life. (A boss in Canterbury Cathedral illustrates this theme.) Again, it was held that when pursued, the lion obliterated the traces of its footprints, its spoor, by sweeping the ground with its tail – so symbolizing Christ veiling his Godhead in the Virgin's womb (T. H. White, 1960, 7–11).

But such interpretations varied according to context. When Samson was depicted in Romanesque sculpture as overcoming with nothing but his hands the young lion that had roared against him (*Judges* 14: 5) this exploit of courage and strength was given various symbolic meanings in which essentially Samson represented Christ and the lion was the Devil. (This interpretation was reinforced by *Psalm* 91: 13, by which the godly shall trample the young lion underfoot.)

* M. D. Anderson (1938, 41–2), Emile Mâle (1947, 332), Novotny (1930, pl. 65), Gantner and Pobé (1956, pl. 80). But Mâle argues that lions in confrontation, at portals and on capitals, for the most part were not symbolic but decorative. Calling on the authority of St Bernard, who said they made no sense, Mâle holds that such lion pairs simply reproduce designs of oriental fabrics. Such monsters on capitals were designed not to instruct but please (Mâle, 340–1, 437). Similarly Mâle challenges the interpretation of a male figure seated between two lions, and holding them round the neck, as being a symbolic portrayal of Daniel in the lions' den. (For example Peter Meyer, 1945, pl. 5, for cathedral of Chur; Joseph Gantner and Marcel Pobé, 1956, 55, pl. 58, for Charlieu-Loire.) Mâle is sceptical of such 'Daniel' attributions except where the figure is engaged in prayer. He argues that Daniel was not a lion-tamer, and that Romanesque artists represented the true Daniel praying between lions not daring to approach him. So according to Mâle, the pseudo-Daniel on a capital of Moissac cloister is really the Assyrian mythic hero Gilgamesh (1947, 352). The identification of a man between lion and centaur on a capital at Serrabone as Gilgamesh, by Marcel Durliat on the authority of an unpublished thesis by Mme Favre may also be due ultimately to Mâle (Durliat, 1952, 68–9). My main point in all this is to mark the uncertainty of many symbolic attributions by later generations.

Of the many sculptured presentations of this theme* one of the most spirited and aesthetically most satisfying is that on a tympanum in Gurk Cathedral, Carinthia. Samson, with long hair and flowing mantle, is towering over the lion. There is great aesthetic harmony in the sweep of line, balance of mass and repetitive ornament of the design. The sculpture gives an impression of great vitality, of force momentarily arrested as Samson has opened the lion's jaws and prepares to tear them apart while two rather astonished doves wait at the sides. The combination of these artistic qualities with religious values has tended to maintain interest in the symbolic character of the sculpture. As late as mid-1971, 800 years after the execution of the figures, I heard a sympathetic and informed interpretation given by a young student guide, to the effect that Samson represents our Saviour; the doves are souls waiting to be saved from the Devil, the lion, who would otherwise devour them; the mantle flowing out from Samson's shoulders represents power, that of the Saviour. Here is thematic development and secondary symbolism. The Samson story in the Old Testament symbolizes not just strength, but the power of virtue – a power that was lost when virtue was later seduced. The symbol of the power was Samson's hair, uncut since his youth (see Chap. 8) but the significance of this has been extended to his cloak, also flowing freely about him. And the symbolic presentation of strength through virtue of a human person has in turn been used to symbolize the spiritual power of the supreme godly person – the less symbolizes the greater.

Symbolism of this elaborate kind provided an important basis for the developments of symbolic form in religion and art of Western Europe for several centuries, and as I have shown, its effects have not completely disappeared. But study of this kind of material reveals, in addition to the rich and fascinating content and system of thought involved, a couple of points of more methodological interest. One is the quest for symbols which obviously operated in the Middle Ages

* For example on a capital of Autun Cathedral (Grivot and Zarnecki, 1961, 63, pl. 29; Künstle, I, 297 ff.); on bronze door of Augsburg Cathedral (Leisinger, 1957, pl. 42); on apse of Schöngrabern (Novotny, 1930, pl. 5); on tympanum in Gurk Cathedral (Novotny, 1930, 79–81, 83, pl. 62); on tympana in Stretton Sugwas church, Herefordshire and Highworth church, Wiltshire (A. W. Clapham, 1934, 138, 142, pl. 34; C. E. Keyser, 1927, figs 84, 85 – who interprets the Highworth figure as David (lii)).

For Samson as a type of Christ, see F. E. Hulme (1899, 126), who cited the lion (ibid, 4) as an instance of how a symbol may mean two entirely different, opposing things.

as it does today – a search for some concrete representation of what is not evident to the senses but is felt to be of prime meaning. The other point is the difficulty of symbolic transfer – of ensuring that the object created or selected by one person as a symbol is identified by other persons as having the same meaning. This difficulty is increased when even though the creator of the symbol deliberately set it up as such, he is long since dead and no check can be made of the inferences as to his intentions. And it exists in another form when the imputation is of unconscious symbolism, which needs most careful collateral evidence to justify. It is evident that mediaeval painters and sculptors meant more by their work than just illustration; this is clear from the bestiaries and from contemporary theological writings. But whether our modern interpretations of the symbolism, or even the contemporary interpretations of the clerics, actually conform to what the artists and craftsmen meant, seems often to be an open question. The interpretation of Samson's mantle as power is an example. As Paul Frankl has pointed out, in painting and sculpture the symbolical meaning of the representations was usually present already, in their creation; in architecture, however, it was often read into the work afterwards. For instance, Suger, Abbot of St Denis, ignoring structural considerations, argued that where there were twelve columns in a church, this signified the Apostles. Again, in church symbolism, the portal was interpreted as meaning Christ, because Christ is the way to the Father – but every church must have a door (Frankl, 1960, 213).

In my view, such mediaeval art offers distinct parallels for anthropological study. The world in which it was produced was before the advent of a machine-based industrialization, with much greater emphasis than today upon social relationships of a personalized character. Much of the art was concerned to illustrate concepts in the direct service of religion. Moreover, as in the 'primitive' societies of the anthropologist's classical field, the producer and the consumer of the art broadly shared the same set of values and interpretations of the symbolic images created. The symbolic values of art were regarded as not alien to those of society – except in so far as they portrayed ideals which all members of society, including the artists, were believed to share, but to be incapable of attaining without supernatural aid.

The avowedly symbolist movements in art in the late nineteenth and early twentieth century were of a very different order. They were not essentially religious in inspiration. Very loosely, they can be seen as in part a rejection of the achievement of that technical progress in the arts which had been a preoccupation of artists since the Renaissance, and a wish to seek achievement in other directions thought to be less hampering to the creative imagination. Both the stern discipline of the Impressionists' use of the prism in the painting of light, and the analytical structuralism of a Cézanne were alien to them. There was also an element of revulsion from the positivism which had sought to depict objective reality; a search for presentation of truths hidden behind visible external appearance. There was social stress too – overt or implied criticism of the matter-of-fact urban middle-class society which surrounded the artists; and in France a reaction to devastating political events such as the Franco-Prussian war of 1870. Led by Odilon Redon and Gustave Moreau, with others such as Puvis de Chavannes and Paul Gauguin loosely associated, such painters emphasized ideational and subjective factors in their work. They attempted to give an emotional value of suggestion to their use of colour, which they treated less analytically than did the Impressionists. They also saw a symbolic character in marked black outline, as in Gauguin's *Le Christ Jaune* – or later in the work of Rouault.

Developments in the twentieth century became even more complex, as attention focused more strongly on the significance of other than purely descriptive or 'naturalistic' values in art. In Britain a philosophic note was struck by R. G. Collingwood (1925, 27–8, 96), who in traditional idiom saw art as the pursuit of beauty, which he defined as imaginative coherence, but regarded this coherence as qualitatively different from the coherence of an object of thought. It was in his view an immediate or intuitive awareness of relations between parts of the object, involving a 'symbolic vision' which is a 'premonition' of the truth explicitly reached by science and philosophy. Independently of philosophers' formulations, many artists, despite the diversity of their aims and styles, were working in ways which corresponded broadly to such an interpretation. There were some banal attempts to portray symbolically national virtues or other idealistic motifs. But sterner, more austere or more wild promptings seemed to animate most artists, whether their major stress was laid upon abstraction – the depiction of the 'world without objects'; upon the visions of the artist's own inner self; or upon symbolic forms suggesting principles underlying nature and human existence. For instance, the work of the painters of the '*Brücke*' group was characterized by 'an atmosphere of catastrophe in the social sphere, a division of the ego in the private sphere; brooding revolt against the false, narrow morality and an ecstatic, almost religious individualism: these are the essential marks of German Expressionism' (Thoene, 1938, 49). The more articulate artists of the later '*Blaue Reiter*' group, however, much as their work and their formulations varied, also incorporated the notion of substitution of a world of essences for a world of appearances. Destroyers of convention, intent on revealing 'the hidden strata of existence' they regarded themselves not as rejecting nature but as overcoming and interpreting nature. They were trying, as Franz Marc wrote, to 'create symbols which could take their place on the altars of the future intellectual religion', or to 'create symbols which reassure' the mind, by corresponding to inwardly apprehended feelings, as Paul Klee is quoted as saying. In line with such developments, art historians and art critics began to interpret primitive art, Byzantine and Romanesque art, oriental art, as not stigmatized by lack of proportion and technical blemish, but as being more concerned with symbolism than with naturalism.

Yet as with the more popular references to symbols, there has been some obscurity or at least some complexity in the use of the term in painting. On the one hand, are the symbolic associations of the work of art in the sense of the suggestions that it offers of experiences not directly portrayed but implied in the forms presented. Yet such symbolization is often rejected as inappropriate in interpretation of the art object. On the other hand, there is the conception of symbolization as a process of reference, not to objects of the external world as ordinarily perceived, but to some other reality – whether in the mind of the artist, in that of the observer, or in the innate quality of existence in general. And cutting through such categorizations are the efforts of some modern artists to avoid all symbolization whatever, to present their creative effort as a direct confrontation with experience, in the attempt to provoke a dynamic reaction and change the situation. 'In proportion as the artist is pure, he is opposed to all symbolism,' wrote Roger Fry. Yet even abstract painting, while rejecting the traditional symbolism of conventional representational art, acquired a symbolic value in the quality of the response evoked in the viewer. Though it may be claimed that non-objective art has broken through the process of symbolization itself by confronting the viewer with a 'direct experience' of the forces involved in the creation of the painting, this claim has proved hard to maintain in its entirety. The language of identification with creative forces of nature in which some exponents of abstract art clothed their arguments; the influence of systems of mystical thought on some abstract painters (for example theosophy on Kandinsky and Mondrian); the attempt to give personal significance to formal structures – this has tended to involve symbolic forms of expresssion at some stage. Michel Seuphor states that to Mondrian femininity is symbolized by the vast horizontal receptacle of the sea; masculinity is symbolized by the wooden pilings against which the waves break and which protect the dunes from the sea. He argues that this fundamental dualism became the basis of Neo-Plasticism, an aesthetic system founded entirely upon the principle of the right angle, roughly prefigured in nature by the opposition between sea-and-horizon and dunes (1962, 37).*

Even where it is held that the conformations of non-objective art are 'symbolic only of themselves', and the term 'metasymbolic' has been introduced to discuss their achievement in analytical style, it has been argued that what has been involved has been a spiritual revolution, and 'the history of the destruction of the outer world of appearance signifies a gradual spiritualization of art, for it leads to ever more symbolic statements' (Fingesten, 1970, 113). In an early statement on the issues Herbert Read distinguished between symbolism in the ordinary sense, employing concrete imagery, and

* Cf. Kandinsky on the Spiritual in Art. 'There is no form, there is nothing in the world, which says nothing.' See also Jakob Rosenberg (1967, 225) who says of Kandinsky's *Kleine Welten* series of lithographs where: 'allusion to natural form is abandoned and geometrical shapes are patterned by colour or black and white' – one may speak of a symbolic image that conjures up a little cosmos (*kleine Welt*) filled with energy yet controlled by laws of attraction and repulsion. Compare also an opinion of de Kooning's 'Light in August', a study in white and black, as a 'symbolist abstraction'. Dissociated from a source in nature the organic shapes carry emotional charges of the same order as mathematical signs. . . . There is visual metaphor in which motifs released from specific objects are thus able to strike a broader resonance of associations (Harold Rosenberg, 1965, 115–16).

symbolism which employs abstractions without parallel in visual experience and operates by unconscious or intuitive process. One of the most articulate movements of this last type, surrealism, made an endeavour to utilize a dialectical process of artistic activity opposing conscious and unconscious, reason and unreason, deed and dream. So surrealism deliberately undertook manufacture of 'the object functioning symbolically' as part of an attempt to multiply the ways of reaching the most profound levels of the mental personality (André Breton, 1936, 86)*

There are two significant points in all this. One is that for the most part the creative symbolism of these art forms has been implicit, not explicit; the process of exploration, identification and labelling of symbolic patterns has often been done by observers and interpreters, unacknowledged by and often unknown to the artists concerned. Secondly, when such symbolic pattern has been recognized in their work, it has been part of the modern canon to claim for it a clearer autonomy, a greater dignity in the aesthetic scene. Symbolic statement has tended to be viewed as preferable to realistic statement because, it is argued, it is capable of conveying more general and more profound meanings.

Problems of the relation of private symbols to public symbols are raised especially in such art. How does the individual vision of the artist become translated into the set of symbols which win public acceptance? Does art arise from a fundamental paradox – the equal insistence on the creative effort of an individual, and on the capability of his product to be recognized and accepted by a body of other individuals – a public? Does the artist's belief that he alone must be the ultimate judge of the validity of his effort mask a parallel belief that only if the result of his effort is acceptable to some other individual can he himself accept it as valid?

A great range of views opens up here. If the artist sees art as basically a means of communication he obviously must try for a code by which what he has to 'say', that is paint or sculpt, can be interpreted by those to whom he wishes to communicate. He may try to find this code in the field of publicly recognized symbols – which is

* The first Surrealist exhibition held in London in 1936 included a mask of *mwai* type from the Sepik, New Guinea (cf. Bateson, 1958, pl. 28). For other material bearing on the discussion above see Roger Fry, 1928, 16–38, 284–302; Herbert Read, 1933, 65–71, 128–44; 1948; Arnold Hauser, 1952, II, 935; H. K. Röthel, 1960; William Gaunt, 1962.

what I take it 'pop art' has tried to do. Or he may try to enforce the recognition of a new code, perhaps of an order which putatively belongs to some generic human understanding – which is what I assume the various kinds of abstract art are trying to do.

But what some modern artists are attempting, if I construe them rightly, is to eliminate as far as possible the element of personality from the interpretation of their creations. The individual, personal component is ineradicably there, in the selective integrative act of creation. But it is the individual as creator-artist only that it is intended to be recognized; not the individual as a particular person with sex, temperament, social background. The characteristics of the individual painter or sculptor may be regarded by the artist as irrelevant to the consideration of the work, distracting to the recognition of the value of the experience provided by it. So a self-effacing painter such as Bridget Riley can treat her work as an attempt to stimulate by visual means, through combination of line and mass by circle, dot, stripe, in colour or black and white, a kind of personal experience in the viewer. The artist is the conceiving mind behind the creation – not necessarily even the executant, since such work may have been done by assistants following out the instructions minutely laid down (Robertson, 1971). Analogous mathematically derived sculptures and drawings have been produced by the American artist Sol Lewitt. This is an attempt to reduce to a minimum the *overt* involvement of the artist in the interpretative effort of the spectator. It seems to be successful in that knowledge of the precise personality of the artist, what kind of social and temperamental figure he or she represents, does not appear relevant to interpretation of the painting as part of the spectator's field of experience. Here there emerges what I feel like calling 'muted symbolism'. The artist says in effect: interpret the painting in your own way, in terms of your own experience; let the combinations of line, mass and colour convey their own message to you – or more strictly, let them suggest to you some stirring of the sensibilities which will make for you a cognizable experience, an 'event'. Symbolic meaning in the more figurative sense is not expected – may be even denied. There is a belief in a direct relation between the physical object and the appreciation of the viewer so that the forms of the painting do not 'stand for' something else than themselves. They are expected to evoke reaction without the mediation of other images. According to the fashionable 'structuralist' phraseology, the art forms 'mediate' directly, in a primary way, between the raw impulse-phenomena of human nature and the culturally-defined position of the spectator. There is also a further attempt to reduce the importance of the material art object, in favour of the mental image – hence 'conceptual art', 'minimal art', 'hyper-realism' and other varieties of concern to obliterate as far as possible the humanist elements in art.

But as I see it, the artist is not in fact eliminated as interpreter. It is recognized that we are confronted by a personal aesthetic of the artist. And even in the most advanced fields of modern art there is still curiosity on the part of art critics and public as to what the artist 'intended' by the work. The artist himself often shows no particular reticence in explaining what he has meant to do, sometimes in naive theoretical terms. Josef Albers, a Bauhaus veteran who has worked for years with monochromatic rectangular figures – for example his 'Homage to the Square' – has explained that the reason for aesthetics is ethics (a reversal of a more common position); that the colours in his work illustrate both independence and interdependence; that they submit to, help, hate, marry one another in an ethical as well as an aesthetic order. Critics too may react in symbolic terms – as one who appreciated the conceptual clarity of some mathematically-based images stated that they had come to seem uniquely valuable to him, possessed of a 'gentle but insistent moral force' (Grace Glueck, *New York Times*, 3 December 1971; Peter Schjeldahl, *New York Times*, 3 October 1971). Such explanations, whether by artists or by critics, can vary widely. Some have a great deal of 'overkill' of a theoretical or speculative kind, in which one feels that the exaggerated language is more concerned with the effect on the hearer or reader than with strict interpretation of the work of art. But they help to demonstrate the proposition which Gombrich has so elegantly defended in *Art and Illustration* – that the work of art is a complex product in a system of relationships in which artist and viewer are integrally involved.

The notion of symbol itself as a product of an integral set of relationships between fabricator and interpreter is congenial to an anthropological inquiry. At the same time there is an aesthetic problem which is outside the anthropological range – of the nature of the art forms which give the symbols their expressive power. The focus here is not on what the symbols mean, for artist, for public; but on what forms can be constructed so as to convey meaning most forcefully, or most sensitively. (Presumably, 'pop art' could be defended on the grounds that while its message may often be trivial, the forms in which it is presented are powerful in suggestion.)

SYMBOLS IN RELIGION

Anthropologists may have been able to ignore what has been said on symbolism by poets, artists or critics, but it has been harder for them to leave aside discussion of symbols in religion. Some anthropologists indeed have directly used their interest in Western religious symbolism to help them in the interpretation of primitive symbolism.

The symbolism of Oriental religions, especially Hinduism, is of an unparalleled richness, and rests upon a very clear differentiation between symbol and god, spirit being or cosmic force symbolized. But for our preliminary inquiry here, a few reflections on the symbolism of Christianity will suffice to illustrate the issues.

In the West the long and complex history of the term symbol itself is much involved with religion. In Greek, originally *sumbolos* and related words referred literally to the putting together of that which had been divided. An example would be the production of two halves of a token which had been broken and given to a pair of friends so that they would share a mark of identification. Conversely, this token served to differentiate them from other people who had no such proof. It was in such sense that the early Christian church seems to have adopted the term symbol. It came to be used for a formal authoritative statement of religious belief, differentiating Christians from non-Christians – a Creed. (It is suggested that it may have also been used in mystery religions of the period, for an exterior sign indicating the inner secrets of the cult.) In particular, the 'symbol' applied to the confession of faith recited at baptism by a convert. In the form of the so-called Symbol of the Apostles (Apostles' Creed) this formal statement of belief was believed (apparently without adequate historical evidence) to have been a joint profession of faith drawn up by the disciples of Jesus after Pentecost. This 'symbol' became then a kind of admission ticket to the new church. Now, not only was the church struggling to establish itself against paganism and against other Oriental religions, it had also to contend with its own internal power struggles. There were differences of view about who should exercise authority, about administrative jurisdiction, and also about doctrinal matters; and such disputes were often expressed in denunciations of heresy. Theologians and church leaders of the second and third century A.D. used this baptismal symbol in the name of apostolic legitimacy against gnostics and others who diverged from their authority, denying them its use, or enforcing its use against their beliefs. (For details see F. Kattenbusch, 1894, 1900, and review by Marcel Mauss, 1900–1, 298–301; Salomon Reinach, 1942, 262–3; A. C. McGiffert, 1953, 152–60; F. Creuzer, 1837–43, iv, 503–17.) So nearly 2,000 years ago, this alleged symbol was not just a sign standing for membership of a given religious body; it was also an instrument of power, of definition and separation, a polemical weapon, whereby persons could be made to conform, or be excluded from that body.*

As the concept of symbol developed in the early church it acquired a clearer abstract usage, in which the notion of a material token was linked with that of something unseen, immaterial. So the material church, of wood or stone, became a symbol of the spiritual church, the community of the saints and the faithful with the Trinity. So too in the rituals of the church, baptism symbolized purification, the first stage in the ascent of the soul to God, while the eucharist, the sacramental taking of bread and wine, symbolized the second stage, that of illumination. Such were solemn visible means of grace, calling forth ideas of the invisible power and love of God. In the fifth century, when such concepts of symbolism were put forward, the writer purporting to be Dionysus the Areopagite also held that owing to the transcendence of God, incomprehensible and inaccessible to human understanding, what the Scriptures told us of him could be only in symbolic language, suitable to our finite

* It remained so for a long period. Bishop Reginald Pocock, the first theologian to write in English since Anglo-Saxon times, was condemned for heresy in 1457 because, in part, he had expressed scepticism about the Apostles' authorship of the creed that bears their name (Myers, 1966, 167–9). In paintings and inscriptions much early Christian symbolism referred to life beyond the tomb, using symbols such as the fish for mystical union with Christ or the vine for the heavenly feast, of which the earthly pledge was the Eucharist. The cross appeared relatively late in the fourth century, the crucifix about the eighth century. But side by side with these came the development of symbolism of the regal authority of the church.

grasp. This theme, of symbol as an aid to understanding, penetrates throughout the whole treatment of Christian theology and has diffused more widely. It is assumed that symbols communicate meanings at levels of reality not accessible through immediate experience or conceptual thought – hence it is argued, they are in some sense revelatory. These meanings are often complex, and of different layers, as Dante defined the subject of his *Divine Comedy* as not simple but 'polysemous'. So, the meanings are not apparent to the uninitiated, hence instruction is needed to understand them. Moreover, as Dionysus wrote, the images used were often mean and contemptible, quite unlike what they represented, so there would be no danger of the faithful confusing them with reality. Yet some religious symbols, it is held, are 'natural symbols', because of their associations. So elements such as the water in baptism, or the bread of the eucharist are 'natural symbols' for spiritual cleansing and nourishment, respectively, just as a key is a natural symbol for authority because of its association with ownership or stewardship.

But religious symbols are not simply communication media: they are held to be affectively charged, non-neutral in their emotional and intellectual value. Moreover, they can also be envisaged as possessing a spontaneous power, in themselves 'projecting the mind towards the Absolute'. So, in the tradition of the mediaeval church, the mystic interpretation of symbols at different levels 'simultaneously true' led through literal description, allegorical instruction as to belief, tropological instruction as to duty, to anagoge, elevation towards the goal of union with the divine.*

In the modern religious field, a good illustration of a symbolist approach is the fideism (or symbolo-fideism) of some Protestant theologians in Paris at the end of the nineteenth century. The central theme of this approach was in line with symbolist views in literature and art rather earlier – that the essence of things escapes us and that we know only their outward manifestations in the form of figures, images, symbols. Hence no one can know what God is in himself; all that it is possible to know are the ideas we have of Him through our more or less anthropomorphized representations. So

* As illustration of the vast literature on this subject see Dunbar, 1929; McGiffert, 1953, esp. Chap. 16; Somerville *et al.*, 1967. One of the fullest treatments is that of the Abbé Auber (1884, 4 vols), who examined the symbolism of the Scriptures, the church, church architecture, decoration, ornaments, liturgy, etc., in great detail.

conceptions such as Lord, Father, Master and emblems such as Lion, Rock, Sun embody some part of our symbolization of what we can never fully comprehend (Eugene Ménégoz, n.d., 151–2). These theologians, obviously, were prepared to argue that such symbols are without doubt the expression of a living reality of an extra-human order, and they viewed their task as that of laying bare the eternal truth from under its contingent manifestations and its historical formulations.

Another view of religious symbolism was presented by Walter Marshall Urban, an idealist philosopher of Yale (1939). He was impressed by what he termed the 'intuitible' character of genuine symbols. He saw the 'sense' of a symbol as a similarity in the way of reflecting on the two things, symbol and thing symbolized – what he termed 'community of subjective form'. (This brings to mind mediaeval views on the doctrine of analogy, as well as Maurice Godelier's emphasis on the criterion of analogy as basic to mythic thought – 1971, 96–8.) Distinguishing strongly between sign and symbol, Urban held that a 'mere sign' was a depersonalized symbol, one that had lost its reference to the original object (1939, 413, 419). He undertook a complex inquiry into the symbolism of poetry, science and the Christian religion, and sought to formulate a general theory of the symbolizing function. He distinguished between symbolic and non-symbolic language, arguing that symbolic language is found where the intuitive elements of language function for the non-intuitive or conceptual. Drawing upon Jung, he held that any 'genuine' symbol in the primary sense must be the result of the co-operation of conscious and unconscious factors. So a feature of all symbolism is its dual character. Following Helen Flanders Dunbar, Urban classified symbols into: extrinsic or arbitrary symbols; intrinsic or descriptive symbols; and 'insight symbols'. The first, he thought, are particularly the symbols of science, the second, those of art and religion. The third category, the 'insight symbols' – really a sub-species of the second – do not really represent characters of relations but also lead to an understanding of them, as in poetry and religion. Urban cited the continuous tradition from Hellenic thought on through the Christian Fathers up to its complete statement in mediaeval times, of the 'fourfold method' of symbolic interpretation.

This idea of progressive interpretation, especially as it concerned the moral function of symbols (tropological), and their function in elevation of the mind to higher things (anagogical), applied to interpretation of statements of Scripture, including parables and miracles. But in Urban's view it had also a universal significance. He was concerned especially with religious symbols, and gave them a very definite value. He argued that a humanist theory of religious symbols was useless since it denied the objects for which the symbols stood. A purely moral theory of religious symbols was also untenable in his view, since they can only function morally by being more than moral. Unless a religious symbol is given its anagogic sense, unless it is metaphysically interpreted, its character as a religious symbol is not properly understood. So, in his view, any theory of religious symbolism must be a theory of religious cognition. If one were to accept his assumptions, one can see the force of such argument. I think that echoes of something similar are to be found in some anthropological writings on symbolism at the present time. But Urban was more uncompromising than some of his colleagues. He argued that propositions that religious symbols have human and social values are an attempt to retain the symbols without the object which alone gives them significance as values (1939, 596, 606–8).

Urban also posed the question of verification. He held that while the reference of a religious symbol is beyond our human moral and value experience, its authentication can take place only within that experience. This he saw as the element of truth in all moral theories of the religious symbol. As part of his general theory Urban pointed out that it is of the very nature of a symbol that it contains both truth and fiction, both the real and the unreal. Along this line he held that religious symbolism, much more than scientific symbolism, is in its essence metaphysical in character, and formed from the language of myth. It is always distorting the intuition in order to suggest and represent the infinite and transcendental. He called attention to the unique role which the 'element of negativity' plays in all religious symbolism, in that it is both the truth and not the truth about the object symbolized (1939, 582–5).

This idealistic theory of symbolism raises some basic questions of epistemology. But in its abstract conceptual approach, its emphasis on a dualistic principle, and its analysis of material from myth and religion, Urban's thought offers some parallels to the development of anthropological interest in later decades. There is no evidence to suggest that his ideas have had any marked influence on anthropology. But they do bear upon the controversy which in religious modernism has been called the distinction between truth of value and truth of fact, and which has emerged in anthropology in discussion about the meaning of stories of virgin birth.

So from theological writers and allied expositors, it is clear that taking the Western Christian church as example, religious symbols are regarded as largely institutionalized, as necessary aids to understanding and to action, and as a matter for intellectual and emotional commitment. For the most part also they are held to be sacred in that not only is their disturbance felt to be offensive, but the most crucial symbols are regarded as having power in their own right to lead the faithful to a more direct relationship with the divine. But here arises a problem which is present in quite a different form in literary or art symbolism – that of authenticity. With poet or painter the question may be argued as to the validity of the symbols they create – whether or not the symbols do the job claimed or hoped for them, of evoking ideas, emotions, or stimulating experiences. It is not ordinarily denied that the ideas, experiences, emotions can exist in somewhat the form envisaged. But with religious symbols the questions can take on a different aspect. The very existence of the referent is not common ground among the commentators. Some believe that there is an extra-human, divine entity or power, invisible, immaterial, even perhaps inaccessible, to be approached or at least to be referred to by symbolic means. Others believe that this is not so, and that the symbols purporting to make this reference are actually referring to some other object – say, the operations of human society or the character of human minds.

Anthropologists are in an ambiguous position here. Like a theologian or other religious person an anthropologist has learnt to treat religious symbols – anyone's religious symbols – with respect. He is not expected to give them authenticity in their own terms – except temporarily, perhaps by the people among whom he is studying them. But some anthropologists believe firmly in the authenticity of the symbols of one religious faith – for example Judaism, Christianity, Islam – while others are inclined to a kind of eclectic acknowledgement that all religious symbols have some factor in their referent which goes beyond the human sphere of comprehension. Still others are avowedly humanist in their interpretations. There is a kind of assumption of professional neutrality by anthropologists towards the subject of investigation. Some have argued that in studying religion, it makes a difference whether the anthropologist is himself a religious person or not – though they have not specified what this difference may be. For the problem of symbolic authenticity, the implications are still not clear in practice. No more than a humanist, can a Christian, Jewish or Muslim anthropologist, if a faithful believer, ascribe the *same* status to the pagan 'gods' of a people he is studying as the people themselves do. But presumably each will approach his study with sympathy and give inward as well as outward respect to those religious concepts in which the people express their deepest feelings. What should be understood is that, contrary to views such as those of Urban, a humanist anthropologist studying religious symbols is not alleging that they have no referent. He may hold that the referent is different from that which religious people attribute to the symbols, but that it lies in the field of human desires, emotions, strivings, conceptualizations, institutional relationships.*

* On this point I would remark that one of the most profound and powerful analyses of religious symbolism I have met is that by Gerschom Scholem, of the symbolism of the Kabbalah. He points out, among much else, how Kabbalists based their interpretation of Scripture on the assumption that every verse is a symbol of a stage in the divine process, an impulse in the divine life; and how the Torah is conceived as a vast *corpus symbolicum* representative of the hidden life in God. Scholem also expresses very lucidly in scholarly manner the significance he sees in such studies (1955, 38–9, 205–35 *et passim*).

Chapter 2

A QUESTION OF TERMS: SCOPE AND MEANING OF 'SYMBOL'

Most anthropological treatment of symbols has taken the meaning of the term for granted, and focused on the interpretation of the relationship between symbol and object symbolized. While in general this is justifiable, some exploration of what is meant by the word 'symbol' is needed, for several reasons.

Some anthropologists have complained that others writing about symbols have caused confusion by failing to define their terms.* More important, perhaps, is that as I have shown in Chapter 1, people in many other fields also write about symbolism in ways which invite anthropological contact and comparison, but which sometimes suggest that they are not always using the same categories. Without necessarily seeking agreement on all meanings, it is useful to indicate common ground of statement and where differences tend to arise.

In classical times Greek and Latin words related to symbol had a variety of meanings, arranged round a notion of matching entities: a sign or mark whereby one person gave another to understand something; a token; a contribution of money to a feast; a share of a reckoning; a commercial treaty between a pair of contracting cities guaranteeing security and protection to their respective merchants. The meaning of symbol ultimately developed into that of a concrete indication of abstract values. In particular, the term became associated in early Christianity with the set of beliefs forming the Creed, in the canon known as the 'Symbol of the Apostles' (p. 47).

* For instance, Melford E. Spiro commented on a symposium entitled 'Forms of Symbolic Action' that in none of the papers contributed was the term 'symbol' ever defined; the class of symbols was never distinguished from the class of non-symbols. The papers were admirable as contributions to anthropology, he thought, but it was not clear why they had been labelled contributions to the study of symbolism, nor why their authors – including some of the most distinguished names in this sphere – had imagined they were studying symbolism at all. (This critique was subjoined to the papers – see Robert F. Spencer (ed.), 1969.)

Historically, since the early period of Greek philosophy, epistemological problems have been concerned with the relation of particular to universal, sense-perception to idea or 'form', finite to infinite; and in the West have often taken a theological shape, as in theories of analogy. Symbolism was one of the fields in which such problems of knowledge were displayed, though as G. G. Coulton has pointed out for the mediaeval period (1958, Chap. 13), symbolic interpretations were apt to be very much less systematic than those of religious doctrine in general. In such interpretation, the broad aim was not only to accept the concrete as representative of the abstract but to use it as a key in two ways – to *explain* the concrete by reference to the abstract, the visible by the invisible; and to *extract* from the concrete its hidden meaning for an understanding of the abstract. As indicated in Chapter 1, such views were prominent in Christian church art, but had a high development in some other religious systems, notably that of the Jewish Kabbalah.

As part of symbolic inquiry, discussion of the relation between names and things named has involved consideration of the nature of words as symbols. This has meant, in Carnap's terms, a practical distinction between language as an object of discussion and metalanguage, in which the discussion is carried out. But it has also led to the invention of artificial languages, such as sets of symbols in mathematics and science. The use of such symbols has allowed operations to be performed with generality and brevity, in a way that would not have been possible with ordinary language. 'Words are the Signs and Symbols of Things,' wrote South in 1686 (OED). But words, which can be flexibly handled in an almost infinite variety of situations, are not precise enough to make fine distinctions in 'the technical discussions associated with special activities in a high state of development' (L. W. H. Hull, 1959, 101). Symbols are not only more economical and more abstract than words; they can also be made to conform to rules which allow of no irregularities. To quote Hull again: 'if the steps of an argument are symbolically recorded, each step corresponds to a particular rearrangement of the symbols. . . . We soon learn to recognize those symbolic arrangements which correspond to valid reasoning processes. We can then make such rearrangements automatically, without perpetually considering their significance' (1959, 102).

But there are three points of importance about such symbols in mathematics and science. They have been specifically invented to allow certain kinds of operations to be performed. Their use is much more limited than that of ordinary language. And, of special note, they do not of themselves provide any information about the conditions to which they refer. Such symbols are set in structural arrangements, with given assumptions as to their values, and with relations intended to be subject to variation. The resulting patterns of relations are not regarded as giving an actual description of any natural objects to which they may refer, but as suggesting that corresponding patterns exist for those objects. This is the function of the use of symbols in say, economic models. There is analogy here with religious symbols when they are used in a sophisticated way, as in reference to a transcendental God. But as a rule users of religious symbols tend to imply that such symbols do actually provide some information about the object of belief, or have power to generate the acquisition of such information. In the paintings in the Roman catacombs, for example, while the symbols of palm, ship, fish, shepherd and the like were not meant for simple illustration or instruction they were intended to portray by allusion the hopes of the Christians concerned and even at times to suggest meanings that had otherwise to be concealed. Much ordinary secular symbolization too is intended as a means of communication of information and not just as an instrument of analysis and exposition.

For anthropologists interested in the study of symbolism the work of philosophers has been important because they above all have devoted attention to questions of definition of symbols – the criteria by which a symbol may be recognized, and the relation of the concept of symbol to cognate ideas. From philosophy ultimately stems the basic formulation in methodology – that our initial question should not be 'What is a symbol?' but 'What is appropriate to designate as symbol in the differentiation of processes of human thought?' Criteria selected for classification of symbols may come from the natural world, but 'symbol' is a cultural, not a natural category. This point was made clearly a century and a half ago by J. A. Dulaure, but it has been developed in this century especially by Ernst Cassirer.

In his *Philosophy of Symbolic Forms* (first published in 1923) and later in his *Essay on Man* (1944) Cassirer argued that symbolic representation is an essential function of the human consciousness, and is basic to our understanding of the operations of language, history, science, art, myth and religion. He distinguished the expression function of symbolization, seen especially in myth (which he regarded as characteristic of the early stages of human culture) from the intuition function, associated with the use of ordinary language, and the conceptual function, manifest especially in the world of science. In myth, sign and signified merge (as with Aquinas, existence and essence merge in God); in ordinary language and the world of common sense they are differentiated, producing systems of objects or substances; and in science their differentiation produces systems of relations. Cassirer postulated what amounted to a dialectical quality in symbolic patterns of culture – an opposition of tendencies towards stabilization and towards disintegration of symbolic relations.

But philosophical propositions about symbols may be of interest to anthropologists not only because they offer frameworks for handling problems of symbol definition and classification; they sometimes incorporate judgements about society, resting upon assumptions which may be unstated, but which run counter to anthropological experience. I take an example from a field in which anthropologists have made few contributions but where they do have some knowledge. This is the symbolism of dance.

In a sensitive and stimulating theory of art, built around the notion of symbolism, Susanne K. Langer has discussed the evolution of dance. Following Cassirer, she has regarded primitive phases of social development as entirely dominated by 'mythic consciousness', based on the symbolization of subjective feelings of potency, as 'potent Beings'. 'From earliest times, through the late tribal stages, men live in a world of 'Powers' – divine or semi-divine Beings, whose wills determine the courses of cosmic and human events. . . . The first recognition of them is through the feeling of personal power and will in the human body and their first representation is through a bodily activity which abstracts the sense of power from the practical experiences in which that sense is usually an obscure factor. This activity is known as 'dancing'. The dance creates an image of nameless and even bodiless 'Powers' filling a complete autonomous realm, a 'world'. It is the first presentation of the world as a realm of mystic forces . . .' (1953, 189–90). Langer has argued that dance is the most serious intellectual business of savage life – the envisagement of a world beyond the moment of one's animal existence, the first conception of life as a whole. So the prehistoric evolution of dancing is the very process of religious thinking, which begets the conception of 'Powers' as it symbolizes them.

Now while anthropologists can learn much from Langer about the theory of symbolism and the theory of art, and find fruitful material for discussion in her views about the relation of 'public' to artist, these statements about the symbolism of dancing will seem superficial and romantic to many anthropologists. In the most primitive societies we have studied, dancing is a highly social activity, and not just an individual abstraction of a sense of power. It is very often of grave religious import, but parallel to the ritual dances are commonly other dances of plainly secular significance, concerned with recreation, sexual alignment, social display, status interest, property rights. And in the religious dances themselves, any concern with 'nameless bodiless Powers' is often subordinate to very detailed orientation towards personalized spiritual beings of complex social affiliation. (See, for example E. E. Evans-Pritchard, *The Dance* (1928) 1965a, 165–80; Raymond Firth, 1967, 281–372; A. R. Radcliffe-Brown, 1922, 128–32, 134, 246–54; Roy A. Rappaport, 1968, 186–9; Marie Reay, 1959, 154–5.) What Langer has to say in other contexts about the symbolism of the human body is very illuminating, but as an illustration to the history of symbolic thought her para-philosophic analysis of the dance is misleading.

An anthropological approach to the study of symbols should then in my view be prepared to scan philosophical treatment of the subject, primarily for elucidation of the theoretical frame, but also to be prepared to offer comment on its cultural content or assumptions.

A basic problem in the study of symbolism is the status of the relation between a symbol and that which it represents. Some have argued that there must be a natural or 'real' link between the thing recognized as a sign (*signans*) and that for which it stands (*significatum*); others have held that the relationship is only one of convention. Historically, the concept of 'natural' in a symbolic relationship has been used by anthropologists in several different senses. For

Robertson Smith (1889, 180, 189) 'natural' symbols of divinity in Semitic worship were rocks, trees, fountains – things of the external environment which had independent existence unaltered by man, as opposed to pillars or cairns of stones erected by human hands. But the 'natural symbols' of Mary Douglas (1970) have been derived not from nature in the wild but from the human body – the symbols drawn from the physical personality, with its flesh, blood, breath and orifices, ingestions and excretions. From such symbols drawn from external object or human body differ again those in the more analytical category envisaged by S. F. Nadel. For him, 'natural symbols' were those where there is a closely observable 'correspondence' between symbol and thing symbolized. Illustrations were: an 'iconic' symbol as when a sculptured representation of an animal serves as a totemic emblem (a meaning somewhat akin to that of C. S. Peirce, *v. infra*); when the symbol is also a sign, as when weeping in a play indicates mourning; and when a symbol is dynamically expressive, as when darkness symbolizes mystery (1951, 261). Of related order, though less abstractly conceived, was Edward Westermarck's view of a Moroccan marriage custom in which a bride threw a slipper at her husband, presumably to get power over him. Westermarck saw the slipper as a symbol of power because the association between slipper and domestic rule 'is so natural' that such a ceremony may well have had from its beginning the meaning ascribed to it (1914, 256–7). The notion of 'natural' in the examples of Westermarck and Nadel involves the assumptions of a cultural frame, but rests also on bases of generally observed human behaviour in situations of grief, disorientation or aggression. It embodies relations which may be deemed logical in terms of general inferences from the given assumptions.

Carl Jung has also used the notion of 'natural symbols', but for him these have their roots deep in the human psyche. One such 'natural symbol' is the Cross, representing the basic principle of order or stability, as opposed to the disorganized or chaotic character of a formless crowd; so regarded, the Cross itself may be treated as a symbol for the human body, as the self in extension. Another 'natural symbol' is the *mandala*, which the unconscious is stated to produce spontaneously, and which in Jung's view appears not only in Oriental art but also in rose windows and other circular forms in mediaeval Christian art, and even in a palaeolithic disc pattern in Rhodesia. In Jung's view such, perhaps all, symbols are 'natural' because they reach down to and express the unconscious in primitive fashion at the same time as they correspond to the highest intuitions of consciousness. But they can be seen as 'natural' in another way, which Mary Douglas's view shares, of being related to the human body. 'The symbols of the self arise in the depths of the body and they express its materiality every bit as much as the structure of the perceiving consciousness' (Jung, 1958, 138; also 318–26 and 1926, 605–7).

But on the whole in studies of symbolism the tendency has been to emphasize the lack of 'natural' links between symbol and thing symbolized – to view the symbolic attribution as a matter of cultural determination, as conventional or even as 'arbitrary'. What is implied by such expressions is that the range of possible representations of something, particularly of an abstract quality, is so great that no exclusive choice of symbol is normally feasible by someone outside the system. The reason why a specific symbol then appears in use, seems to depend upon some form of cultural condition; at the worst, since cultural components in the relationship of symbol to object are often hard to identify, the choice is termed inexplicable. But in stressing the conventionality, the 'arbitrary' character of the relationship – and in using such a criterion in the distinction of symbol from sign or signal – it is the complexity rather than the inexplicable nature of the link that is really being considered.

A firm opinion on the question of conventionality was expressed a century ago by Charles S. Peirce, a forerunner in the study of symbolic logic. A physicist and astronomer in the United States Coast and Geodetic Survey, Peirce was also a philosopher of rugged original mind. Though he held an academic post for only a brief period, through his published papers and correspondence he exercised a growing influence as a pioneer in the modern study of semiotics. (He called it *semeiotics*, the act of signifying – roughly, the theory of meaning; the term is said to have been used by John Locke.) Though Peirce said of himself that he thought in quite a different system of symbols to words – he wrote much on logic from a mathematical standpoint – he also said that he approved of inventing new words for new ideas. And as he had, or believed he had, many new ideas his writings about the classification of signs are strewn with new words. (One such is *ideoscopy*, describing and classifying the ideas that belong to experience without regard to their validity or their psychology – a term that might serve anthropologists engaged in 'cognitive anthropology' or 'ethnoscience'.) Dodging the new words and much of the detailed analysis, one can still find in Peirce several important points about symbols, first put forward in a paper in the *Proceedings* of the American Academy of Arts and Sciences in May 1867. There he defined logic as the doctrine of the formal conditions of the truth of symbols, that is the reference of symbols to their objects. Later he saw that this involved inquiry into all branches of the general theory of signs. Firstly, for such an inquiry Peirce distinguished between *index*, *icon* and *symbol*.* An index in his view was a sign directly related in fact to what it signified. If a hunter in pursuit of a lion sees a certain kind of footprint in the sand, this is an index to the passage of his game. A proper name, a symptom of a disease, are indices in Peirce's sense. An icon for him is a sign that represents its object by resembling it – which is 'determined by its dynamic objective by virtue of its own internal nature'. Peirce cited a curve of a distribution of errors; we might regard the statue of a lion as iconic in having its form and proportions determined by those of the animal. A symbol on the contrary was defined by Peirce as a sign determined by its object only in the sense that it will be so interpreted – an allocation depending on habit, convention or agreement, or natural disposition of the interpreter. Following our example, a lion is a symbol of bravery by convention. But as Peirce admitted, the characters of direct relation, resemblance and convention are not completely exclusive. So an icon – broadly equivalent to image – may have an element of conventional recognition, as we may easily see in some of the mediaeval figures termed lions at the porches of Romanesque churches.

A second point of interest made by Peirce was linked with his pragmatism – it was his view that the meaning of a concept could be completely understood only by discovering just what sort of general habits of conduct a belief in the truth of the concept would reasonably develop. This was a doctrine that truth consists in future

* Peirce, 1958, 391, 395, 402–3; (C. Harteshorne and P. Weiss (eds)) 1931–5, vols II and V; see also A. W. Burks, 1949.

serviceableness for our ends. So he held that the essential function of a sign is to render inefficient relations efficient – a view which seems to be echoed to some degree in Malinowski's treatment of symbolism (p. 141). Peirce argued that the function of the sign is not to set these relations into action, but to establish a general rule or habit whereby they will act on occasion. (Such a dynamic view of symbols seems a preferable form of statement to that which talks of symbols themselves acting – cf. Mary Douglas, 'The symbols themselves lash back at people . . .' (1970, xiv).)

A third point made by Peirce was that since symbol depends upon convention, habit or agreement, it refers not to a single instance alone, as does an index, but to a general class of instances. So for a lion to symbolize courage, there must be a general idea of the look of lions as a class and of the nature of courage as a virtue.* (Yet even with an index such as a footprint or a proper name, one may argue that for these to be meaningful there must be some general ideas – that animals leave prints, that some kinds of verbal noises can refer to persons.)

But Peirce's classification of signs, though it might have been useful for anthropologists, lay unused by them. (The first anthropological reference to Peirce's ideas I know is by E. R. Leach, 1957, 121–2.) Moreover, it left several broad questions open. Peirce's use of the notion of habit or convention in the definition of symbol offered a social component but did not take it far; in particular the problem of how the habit or convention was to be discovered and defined was not faced. Nor was it clear how far Peirce regarded the construction of symbols as an arbitrary procedure, as nothing more than the routinization of the 'natural disposition' of the interpreter by common agreement. Jean Piaget has recently criticized Peirce for not using a contrast between individual and social signifiers in his classification, and indicated his preference for Saussure's trichotomy, which does so (1971, 115n). But Piaget's own equation of symbol with individual signifier seems unduly restrictive (78–9). My own view here is that one of the main tasks of anthropology is the reduc-

* In mediaeval funerary monuments a dead knight is often portrayed with his feet on a lion, in contrast to his lady, whose feet are on a dog, symbolizing fidelity (A. R. Myers, 1966, 194). With change in symbolic idiom, were lions or knights thought not to be so brave, or was bravery thought to be less important – and ladies or dogs not so faithful or fidelity less important?

tion of arbitrariness as it appears in symbolic allocation; and that linkage of individual with social elements in symbolism is a necessary part of this task.

In the confrontation between 'natural' and 'conventional', 'individual' and 'social' as criteria in the definition of symbols, questions have arisen as to how far differences in consciousness or intention have been relevant to the process of representation. Opinion has varied on this issue.

Susan Stebbing, the logician, and S. F. Nadel, the anthropologist, both thought that for their own purposes they had best be concerned in symbols with conscious, even designed, representation. But whereas Stebbing was concerned with definition, Nadel was concerned with evidence – and I examine his view later (p. 170). Long ago Stebbing pointed out ((1930) 1948, 10, 111, 508) how in situations of everyday life our senses are being constantly stimulated by a variety of impressions, among which we have learnt to pay attention to some as being specially significant because they are *signs* of something else in which we are interested. When one thing signifies another, there is between them a connection enabling us to pass in thought from one to another. Stebbing cited waving a flag as a sign of high spirits. She argued that in some contexts it is not possible to draw a hard-and-fast line between 'sign' and 'symbol'; but made a working definition that a symbol is a sign consciously designed to stand for something. On this reading, an example of symbol would presumably be a new national flag expressly designed to be flown by representatives of a country hoping to be recognized as a political entity and admitted to the United Nations (cf. Chap. 10). Another example comes even closer to Stebbing's meaning. In 1955 a priest in the church of Pellestrina in Italy glanced at the ceiling and saw to his astonishment one of the angels in a fresco waving a red flag. This might have been taken in Stebbing's sense as a sign of high spirits on someone's part. But a young painter who had been recently hired to freshen the fading colours of the ceiling was soon afterwards sentenced to eight months in jail for 'vilifying the religion of the State' (*Chicago Daily Tribune*, 16 April 1955). It was presumably not for being just a sign of high spirits but for being a symbol with a consciously-designed political meaning that this severe punishment was awarded.

But definition of symbol in terms of conscious design has difficulties, chief of which is given by the conception of consciousness itself. If it is interpreted fairly narrowly as being equivalent to power of formulation, or at least awareness of the nature of particular experience, then much of dream symbolism would be excluded. If it is interpreted broadly as any sentient activity, equivalent to mind – 'a sort of distillate of all sensitive, teleological, organized functioning', as Susanne Langer has put it (1953, 127) then the creation of symbols becomes a very primitive human activity. Indeed, Langer has argued that the symbolic transformation of all perceptions is an endowment of the human brain which allows it to handle stimuli which otherwise would threaten the survival of the metabolic process. Some such assumption of a basic 'primitive' symbolic functioning of the human mind seems common to many anthropologists, including Malinowski and Lévi-Strauss, and the presence of unconscious elements in symbolization seems to be also admitted, though evidence for such views has rarely been systematically sought.

Another angle of approach to the problem of conscious appreciation of symbols is to consider their relation to what the symbols represent – their *significata* or referents.* It has been argued, as by Langer, that symbols differ radically from signs by their greater articulation and presentation of *concepts*. Hence a sign is comprehended if it serves to make us notice the object or situation it bespeaks; a symbol if it makes us conceive the idea it presents.† Perhaps a better way of expressing this is to distinguish the referents by their relative simplicity or complexity, since concept formation would seem to occur in both cases. If one is driving a motor car, a red flag in the middle of a road usually means an obstacle ahead, a clear sign to slow down – and this is a convention well understood internationally. We don't usually call this a symbol; the referent is a simple idea. But a red flag on a Paris barricade a few years ago, like

* The term *referent*, which in the semantic field goes back at least to Ogden and Richards, seems to me preferable to the more ponderous *significatum*. Stebbing has pointed out that *referent* has another meaning in the logic of relations, as used by Bertrand Russell for the term from which a relation proceeds. But Stebbing's own term *referend* has not found general currency, and no confusion in the use of *referent* seems to have arisen. (J. Whatmough (1956), a linguist, uses *referend*.)

† Langer, 1953, 26. Langer has explained that following Charles Morris, she has substituted *signal* for *sign* in her later work.

that of the Italian fresco painter, stood for a complex, not very specific set of ideas and actions. In an immediate general sense it stood for a simple attitude – defiance of established authority. But behind this, or side by side with it, were much more elaborate, much more vaguely delineated ideas of moral values and political freedom. It was a political symbol. Moreover, as with many symbols, strongly emotional attitudes were mingled with intellectual concepts. Here, sign (signal) and symbol can be differentiated, not by the thing doing the signifying – the same red flag was sometimes used on the barricade as had been used earlier to warn of a hole in the road – but by the degree of complication of relationships, and their quality, especially of emotion or sentiment in the thing represented. This kind of distinction is quite useful for anthropologists. So, before a Tikopia religious performance, one could see columns of smoke rising from houses where ovens were being prepared to cook the food which would be later presented as offerings in the temple. These smoke columns were signs of the particular activity of cooking; they were also signs of which particular social groups were contributing to the ritual. But they were not symbolic in that the smoke did not represent any complex set of ideas about communicating with spirit powers – as in L. H. Morgan's account of a burnt offering among the Iroquois (cf. p. 106). In Peirce's sense, it was an index to a technical and social activity. But when the chief stood up in the temple with his bunch of leaves drenched in oil, and rubbed it on the post, this was a symbol for a complex set of ideas about spirit powers and socio-political and ritual relationships. It did not take me as an anthropologist very long to learn that a smoke column on such an occasion represented not merely fire but also an oven for food, or even to identify the social group involved. But to comprehend the significance of rubbing the post demanded long and arduous exploration of Tikopia ideas. Interpretation of symbols is usually a much more difficult matter than interpretation of signs.

The variant mode of classification suggested by Charles Morris (1945), of using *sign* as the generic term (as did Peirce) and distinguishing under it *symbol* from *signal* has received much support. For Morris a symbol is a sign that is produced by its interpreter and that acts as a substitute for some other sign for which it is synonymous – as it might be, the wearing of black by a widow is a symbol of some other sign of mourning such as weeping. In Morris's terms, all signs not symbols are to be called signals – as it might be, a red flag in the road is a signal to a motorist to slow down. I think it might be argued that in ordinary usage the prime criterion of a signal is that it is a sign demanding or expecting *action* – that is, a more highly focused response is implied. Hence the difference in terminology between road signs, such as directional plaques, which are there for the motorist to take advantage of if he wishes, and road signals, such as traffic lights, which he is expected to obey.

The sign/signal and symbol dichotomy has other qualifications. What about flags, when used for communication by ships – are these signals or symbols? They are consciously designed to stand for something else, as in some definitions of symbol, and this something else can be an idea of some complexity, or a concept involving complex operations. But the hoisting of a Blue Peter flag by a vessel in port, indicating that she is to sail in twenty-four hours, is ordinarily described as a signal. This can be justified in terms of the character of the operations, which though involved, are primarily of a technical order. If the Blue Peter were to be described as a symbol then one could think of it as evoking ideas of a much vaguer order, about people sailing away, leaving loved ones behind, going out to new experiences – a symbol of parting, a symbol of adventure. So, signal tends to connote some precision of technical consequences; symbol, a much more imprecise, open-ended sequence of events and experiences.

In considering the meaning of a symbol the position of the interpreter, as stressed by Peirce, Stebbing and Morris, is very important. In the interpretation of signals, it is vital for efficient operation that fabricator and interpreter are using a common code. In the case of the Blue Peter, for instance, the flag of blue with a central white square is also the letter P in the International Code of Signals. It is essential for action that those concerned should interpret this P as meaning 'sailing soon' and not, for example, as 'paying off'! But in the interpretation of a symbol the conditions of its presentation are such that the interpreter ordinarily has much more scope for exercise of his own judgement – the alternatives in the situation may be much less circumscribed. He may be left to 'get out of it' what he can by the fabricator of the symbol, who may be concerned primarily with his own mode of expression. Hence one way of distinguishing broadly between signal and symbol may be to class as symbols those presentations where there is much greater lack of fit – even perhaps intentionally – in the attributions of fabricator and interpreter.

An aspect of great importance in consideration of all signs, including symbols, is their connectedness, with that of their referents, in series or systems. This is obviously so with many technical signs, such as the signal flags of the international code and in the distribution of colour bands in national flags (cf. p. 337). This is a matter of which anthropologists are well aware, from their functional and structural training, and I give examples later, in particular from the work of Audrey Richards, Claude Lévi-Strauss and Victor Turner. But there can be argument about the perception of system, as a matter of principle and as a matter of empirical fact. Susanne Langer has held that while language, spoken or written, is a *symbolism*, a system of symbols, art symbols do not constitute a symbolism. If I understand her view correctly, it is that each work of art is a single, unique, indivisible symbol, itself highly articulated but not capable of being resolved into components which can be reassembled in another form to make another work of art, according to given rules. But granting the autonomy, the non-repeatability, of each work of art at a primary level of creation, it would seem that we can nevertheless speak of the symbolism, say, of Romanesque art in the sense of a common body of interconnected themes, patterns, interpretations, using a set of rules provided by the sources from which the artists drew their inspiration – the bestiaries, the Church Fathers, the Scriptures. Even with modern artists trying to evade, surpass or destroy convention, there are at least common understandings, shared with a sophisticated public, if not about particular meanings of forms, about the general aims of manipulation of forms and the general kinds of response to be expected. In this sense no work of art stands completely alone, but is related to others in a system of judgement and interpretation.

The question to what degree any given set of symbols is to be interpreted systematically is a matter largely of empirical investigation, but may involve assumptions about regularity. The interpretation of the symbolism of colours offers good illustration. It has often been pointed out in Western contexts how light colours are associated with pleasure, dark colours with sadness,* while in mediaeval Japan there was a most sensitive awareness to the relationship of colours to one another according to circumstance. In modern anthropology, Victor Turner has made very effective use of colour relations in his studies of Ndembu symbolism. He has demonstrated how in the Ndembu system white stands for milk, purity, health, good luck; black for faeces and other grim things; red for blood, maleness, danger – all in complex symbolization (V. W. Turner, 1967, 59–92). Stimulated in part by Jung's notion of 'archetypes' or original models, Turner has interpreted the white-black-red triad as representing the archetypal man as a pleasure-pain process. There is much in Christian history to support such a view. For instance, in the Middle Ages black, suggestive of material darkness, was symbolical of the spiritual darkness of the soul; it was incorporated into ideas of the Devil – the Prince of Darkness; and witchcraft – the black art (F. E. Hulme, 1899, 28–9). Red and white, representing the Resurrection and Transfiguration respectively, as robes of Christ, were opposed to purple or other dark colour before these cosmic events (G. G. Coulton, 1958, 266, app. 17). Comparative ethnographic evidence of such similar symbolic colour systems can be adduced.† But the significance of the individual colours is to be interpreted primarily in terms of the relations envisaged among them in each culture, not in terms of a colour's universal value. In the West, the black shirts of the Italian Fascists and the brown shirts of the Nazis were intended as symbols of glory in contrast to the red banners of revolution; the interpretation of their colour values, as with White Russians and the Red Army after 1917, depended upon which side one was on. As we now know well, for those for whom 'black is beautiful', white has too often been the colour not of purity and the milk of human kindness but of violence and oppression. Colour terms themselves may lose their physical referent and become symbolic: in Western countries the 'Blacks' are usually brown and the 'Whites' are dirty-pink. And among the Konso of Ethiopia black appears to be auspicious and white inauspicious (C. R. Hallpike, 1971, 280–2).

* For complex association of colour with mood see Rimbaud's '*Voyelles*' and '*Bateau Ivre*'.

† A general analysis of material from antiquity, the Middle Ages and relatively recent times has been given by F. Portal, 1857.

Oriental colour symbolism tends to be markedly more systematic than does occidental, and to apply in many situations where Western colour values are relatively free of symbolic interpretation. Occidental conventions of dress until recently followed a few broad rules: bright colours were appropriate to young people and subdued colours to the elderly; black for male evening dress, with almost any latitude to women; white for confirmation and bridal dress, and black or purple according to stage for mourning. But this rough patterning, though highly sanctioned for some specific usages, was not developed at all precisely. By contrast, Chinese major colours were traditionally associated with the major compass points, the seasons and the fortunes, and these ideas were reflected quite far into dress, theatrical masks and the crises of life. Some aspects of this have been brought out in an interesting study of the significance of variation in dress colour at Chinese funerals by Arthur P. Wolf (1970; cf. Martin C. Yang, 1947, 43; and more generally, Soame Jenyns, 1935, 125–6).

An observer may see mourners at a Chinese funeral wearing garments embodying white, red or blue. White is popularly regarded in the West as *the* Chinese mourning colour, but the symbolism is much more complex. Red is the colour of joy, shown in firecrackers, good luck charms, bridal dress, and its opposite is either black or white. So at the death of the emperor, formerly, all shops covered their red signs with white or black, brides travelled in black not red sedan chairs, and so on. But red is also prophylactic, and is presented to ward off evil; it may also be incorporated into the attire of friends and kin of medium relationship when in mourning. White worn by mourners does not imply deep grief; it is a neutral colour worn as a courtesy by those who owe the deceased nothing more than a token of respect; it implies social equality. So brothers of the deceased who have been living in the same household wear white in respect; brothers who have separated and formed households of their own wear white too, but add a patch of red to their white headbands as a protective device. The colour blue is halfway on the scale between red and white, so is midway between the extremes of joy and grief. It is the colour of scholars' robes and gowns of minor officials, expressing dignified joy, a mild degree of attainment, but also not inappropriate to sorrow. Contrasted with red, blue carries negative connotations; contrasted with white, it is a positive colour. Now the mourning gowns of a man's great-grandsons, if he has been fortunate enough to have such descendants, are always dark blue. A limited degree of joy at a funeral is permissible as an expression of respect that a man has lived to witness the birth of great-grandsons and so has repaid his parents and grandparents in filial duty; so his youngest descendants wear blue to symbolize a restrained joy. As Wolf emphasizes, the meaning of a colour in the Chinese symbolic field depends not only on its place in the Chinese spectrum, but also on the use of it in particular social contexts.

Such patterning of similarity and contrast has its analogy in what Mircea Eliade has called the 'internal logic of symbols', though he has used this concept in a rather different way, in reference to the interpretation of sequences of magical operations. For instance from somewhat haphazardly selected ethnographic data he has indicated the symbolism of knotting and untying knots as means of defence of the human personality (1969, 37, 110). Such examples remind us of the insistence with which men seek to make rational pattern out of non-rationally selected material in their particular society – presumably with the aim of maintaining social communication through the possibility of predicting behaviour. (The powerful analytical instrument of structuralism, developed with great refinement by Lévi-Strauss for extracting meaning from systematic relations of symbols, is referred to in Chap. 4.)

In considering the nature of symbols the notion of representation, of one thing 'standing for' another, needs further consideration. If there is no overt identifiable relation of a direct kind between symbol and referent, no 'natural' link, how does a symbol manage to 'stand for' another object? Susanne Langer's answer in essence is that there is a formal congruence of logical structures between them, a common logical form (1953, 27). Granting this to be so, the question of why specific elements have been selected out of a range of possible logical relationships, still remains. Moreover, without pretending to any very subtle psychological or philosophical implications, one can see that other named categories such as simile, metaphor, emblem, image, allegory all share with symbol some quality of the representational operations of language, and formal congruence between *sig-*

nans and *significatum*. Symbol is not alone in the linguistic and logical field.

As regards the problem of choice among possible alternative logical structures of congruence, a plausible postulate is that this is determined by factors specific to the experience, both cultural and personal, of the actor. It is part of the job of anthropologists to identify such factors as closely as possible, particularly in the cultural field.

In exploring the problem of representation it is useful to examine briefly the categories allied to symbol, even without attempting any very formal distinctions. For working purposes we can adopt some such usage as the following. (I use as an illustration for contrast the concept of 'key'.)

Simile is a kind of comparison, indicating perception of a common, often abstract quality shared by two objects, with overt statement. The design of a carpet may embody a key-pattern, suggesting the wards of a key. *Metaphor* also makes a comparison, but implicitly, making a direct transfer of idea and substituting one term of the comparison for the other. So, the statement that the control of Gibraltar is the key to the naval strategy of the Mediterranean tacitly refers to the function of a key in controlling passage through a doorway. *Emblem* may show no discernible direct relation to its object, but may rely on some past association of ideas. The Catholic saint, St Zita, who has as her emblem a bunch of keys, is said to have been a trusted household servant and so presumably controlled locked doors. *Image*, used much in literature and public affairs* with a carry-over from pictorial art, is concerned primarily with forming a mental entity, giving shape in the 'mind's eye' to a set of qualities perceived in or attributed to the object. Wordsworth's reference to sonnet may serve as illustration: 'Scorn not the Sonnet. With this key . . . Shakespeare unlocked his heart.' *Allegory* is often described as a kind of sustained metaphor in narrative form, but its essential features include the representation of one event or series of events in a detached form (literally, 'putting side by side') to allow of separate consideration of the implications, commonly of a moral order. In the Middle Ages, the works of Virgil, like the Bible, were allegorized

* Fowler's *Modern English Usage* (1965) indicates the almost mystical value which the term 'image' has acquired in public relations.

and assigned hidden meanings not originally intended. But an open allegory, *The Romance of the Rose*, used personification of abstract figures to convey first ideas of romantic love, then of social criticism (C. H. Haskins, 1958, 106; F. Heer, 1962, 369). Pursuing the 'key' theme, an allegorical use of it occurs in Fitzgerald's rendering of Omar Khayyám's *Rubaiyat*: 'There was a Door to which I found no Key' and 'Of my base metal may be filed a Key/That shall unlock the Door. . . .'

Symbol has links with all these; but the directness or likeness of relationship to its referent is muted or attenuated. So is the relation between symbol and referent often apparently arbitrary.* The associations in a symbol are also often broader and more complex, but the action-trigger of the symbol may be more immediate, through the emotional involvement it often entails. Symbol has been contrasted especially with allegory, on such grounds. Arnold Hauser, for instance, has regarded allegory as the translation of an abstract idea into a concrete image which, however, is but one of a number of possible expressions of the idea. With a symbol, he has argued, idea and image are fused into an indivisible entity. A symbol can be interpreted in various ways (whereas an allegory usually cannot) and this variability of interpretation, this apparent inexhaustibility of the meaning of the symbol, Hauser maintained,

* Cf. J. Whatmough: 'A symbol is a surrogate. . . . But all these surrogates have one feature in common. There is nothing in the nature of things that gives them the meanings stated; that is something *we* have given them, by agreement or convention, so that the symbol acquires a certain arbitrary character' (1956, 19). Like Peirce and others, Whatmough separates symbol from sign or index on these grounds – 'a sign has a direct relation to its object.'

In the whole discussion of symbols there is a reminiscence of the mediaeval concept of analogy as put forward by Thomas Aquinas. We predicate of God qualities to which human qualities bear some resemblance, but this resemblance is always accompanied by some dissimilarity, since Godhead is inconceivable and inexpressible in human terms – such is the argument (E. L. Mascall, 1949, especially Chap. 5; F. C. Copleston, 1961, 93, 112; David Knowles, 1962, 263, 305). The analogical mode of discourse, with 'application of a concept to different beings in ways that are simply diverse from each other and are only the same in a certain respect' has appeared in some anthropological treatment of religion, notably in Evans-Pritchard's treatment of the problem of symbols (1956, Chap. 5).

Another kind of frame for discussion of the problem of representation is given by E. H. Gombrich, who uses the concept of synaesthesia, what he describes as the 'splashing over' of sense impressions from one modality to another, in his inquiry into the nature of symbolism in art (1968, 311–14). Referring incidentally to Baudelaire's *Correspondances*, and to Rimbaud's assignment of colours to the vowels, he examines the translation of sense impressions into visual forms over a rich field. Focusing on the notion of relationships in a structural matrix, he argues that what we learn from a study of symbolism is the elasticity of definitions in any attempt to indicate the nature of reality by reference to types of representation (op. cit., 85, 93). See also his discussion of ritualized gesture and expression in art (1966).

is its most essential characteristic. So, the allegory is the expression of a static, the symbol that of a dynamic process of thought, setting ideas in motion and keeping them in motion. He saw the allegory as a kind of riddle, to be solved; but the symbol as capable only of interpretation, not of solution (Hauser, 1952, 897). This is from the standpoint of art. But from the standpoint of religion a not dissimilar attitude has emerged. Gershom Scholem, as part of his massive study of Jewish mysticism, has regarded allegory as 'an infinite network of meanings and correlations' but all within the limits of language and expression. Symbol radically transcends the sphere of allegory. If allegory is a representation of something expressible by another expressible something, symbol is an expressible representation of something which in itself lies beyond the sphere of expression and communication, a hidden and inexpressible reality (Scholem, 1955, 26–7). Whether one wishes to carry the distinction to such lengths, it is clear that the notion of symbol commonly carries the meaning of a more complex, more profound representation than does that of allegory.

Referring again to our example of key image, in Christian iconography St Peter is represented by two keys, often crossed – they are his emblem, contrasted with the emblems of other saints, as, for example with the winged lion of St Mark. Historically, the emblems have at times been in political opposition, as the winged lion of St Mark, the emblem of Venice, faced the keys of St Peter, the emblem of the Papal states, in struggle for power and territory. Sometimes the opposition was mainly symbolical, representing formal rather than substantial positions. But the Christian keys can be a symbol of a more intense kind. As Matthew's Gospel has it, in return for his bold acknowledgement of Jesus as Christ the Son of the Living God, Jesus conferred upon Peter the keys of the kingdom of heaven. This metaphorical act of reciprocity has been popularly interpreted as giving jurisdiction to let souls into Paradise or keep them out. But in Catholic theology the 'giving of keys' means granting of authority, and in the light of canonical and rabbinical parallels it is held that the critical verse of Matthew's Gospel means, not that St Peter is to be the 'gate-keeper of heaven', but that Christ will confer on him vicarious authority over His household on earth, that is the church. The keys that Christ will give to Peter are the keys of the kingdom of heaven in the sense that Peter's authoritative decisions on earth, as given by his apostolic successor the Pope, will bind men in their conscience; so their entrance into the kingdom of God for all eternity will depend upon their acceptance of Peter's teaching of the Gospel and his directions for salvation. So the keys, a favourite charge in ecclesiastical heraldry and appearing in many Roman religious paintings (for example Perugino's fresco in the Sistine Chapel), can symbolize not only Jesus's assertion of His divinity and man's belief in His power, but also more personally, the anxious problem of the fate of each individual soul in the after-life – especially as determined by the representatives of Peter.* Many Protestant scholars now argue that this whole passage was a late interpolation in the Scripture to support the claims of Peter's successors in the church. But this means that the symbolism is just carried a step further, into the field of church politics and rivalries.

All this about signs and keys and modes of representation is only one way, and a compressed way, of looking for criteria in use of the term symbol, especially anthropological use. It seems to me that for anthropologists the definition of symbols has to be primarily operational. Granted their representational quality, what can be regarded as the effects associated with their use? Functional and structural inquiry is needed (giving these terms a neutral connotation without implication about the integrity of society). Inquiry is needed, too, into what I would call organizational aspects of symbolic behaviour – the ways in which use of symbols relates to interests and aims of groups and of individuals; and how symbols are involved when decisions are taken in interpersonal contacts.

From this point of view, on the question of terms, I would advocate following a treatment which recognizes *sign* as a general category, and differentiates types within it by relative emphasis upon criteria rather than by trying for completely exclusive elements. In relation to social behaviour, then, under the general head of *sign* may be differentiated:

Index – where a sequential relation is inferred, as of part to whole or precedent to antecedent, or particular to general.

* See, for example Matthew's Gospel xvi: 16–19; Donald Attwater, 1965, 274–5; *New Catholic Encyclopedia* ('Keys, Power of'), 1967; F. E. Hulme, 1899, 145. For common sexual symbolism of 'key' in dreams see Freud, 1945, 336.

Signal – where the emphasis in a sign is upon consequential action; and a relatively simple sign is a stimulus involving response of a more complex kind. Signal may be regarded as a dynamic form of index. *Signature* is a personal index which may be treated as a signal if it is to be followed by further action.

Icon – where a sensory likeness-relation is intended or interpreted. Change of scale or motion or dimension may be involved, since an icon is constructed as a physical or imaginative representation, suggesting a referent by a complex combination of elements. One can presumably admit in music iconic sound – as in Vivaldi's *Four Seasons* – as well as in pictorial art an iconic visual image.

Symbol – where a sign has a complex series of associations, often of emotional kind, and difficult (some would say, impossible) to describe in terms other than partial representation. The aspect of personal or social construction in meaning may be marked, so no sensory likeness of symbol to object may be apparent to an observer, and imputation of relationship may seem arbitrary.

Some rather formal distinctions along these lines seem necessary for anthropological usage, if only because popular phraseology seems often to ignore them. When newspapers and other public media of communication use the terms 'symbol' and 'symbolic' all that is meant seems often to be only 'index' or 'representation'. 'It may be *symbolic* of trouble ahead' that one United States presidential candidate got almost equal news coverage from telling a New York newspaper casually of his plans as another did from an expensive national telecast – 'indicative' would have been adequate here. Stories of poverty cited in a newspaper's annual appeal for the needy towards Christmas '*symbolized*' hundreds of similar cases – surely in ordinary language this could be 'represented'. A very great Soviet investment in offensive strategic weapons in 1971 was described as being '*symbolized*' by the missile silos ('holes') that the Russians had been urgently constructing throughout the year – 'demonstrated' would seem a more appropriate term, or 'hinted at' if the purpose of the silos was not clear (*New York Times*, 6 January 1972, 5 December 1971; *Newsweek*, 1 November 1971). In other expressions emphasis is laid on the disjunction of sign from object, and the unreality or lack of worth of the former. The contrast of 'symbol' with 'reality' comes out in the description of something as being 'merely' or 'only' a symbol. A pair of slippers made from glass in Cologne when it was a Roman colony in the third century A.D. were described as '*merely symbolic*' by a museum director because they couldn't be used for walking; what they were symbolic of was not made clear (*New York Times*, 17 January 1972). At the accession of Princess Margrethe to the throne of Denmark her role as Queen was termed 'a *purely symbolic* one', implying other non-symbolic aspects of the role which she would not be exercising (*New York Times*, 15 January 1972). From an earlier source, in reply to an assertion that de Gaulle was the only possible head of French resistance during the war it was alleged that de Gaulle had not a great following but '*only a symbolic* value'. The devaluation of the U.S. dollar at a time when it had been divorced from its gold basis was described as 'a *mainly symbolic* concession' (*New York Times*, 12 January 1972). While the difficulties of trade relations between Ottawa and Washington were such that it would 'take *more than symbols*' to convince Canadians that the United States was not out to improve its trade at Canadian expense (*Time Magazine*, 18 January 1972). And the concept of symbol as being equivalent to 'idea' is evident in a statement that 'the importance of China is being transmuted from *symbol to actuality* by the increasing powerlessness of the West in Asia' (Ross Terrill, *Observer*, 2 January 1972). In such examples the term 'symbolic' is almost equivalent to 'notional' or 'fictional'; the suggestion is that whatever be the feelings generated by the 'symbol' the appropriate action would not be forthcoming. Though not necessarily a reversal of a common sociological position in regard to symbols, this does imply a separability of feeling and action which can be important in symbol interpretation.

In the light of such expressions I consider the concept of symbol more closely in an action setting, from an instrumental point of view.

SYMBOL AS INSTRUMENT

A symbol is 'a device for enabling us to make abstractions', but with some end in view – a symbol has instrumental value. For brief consideration here I look at symbols as instruments of expression, of communication, of knowledge and of control.*

Expression

As instrument of expression symbols are to a supreme degree tools of the artist. It is not surprising then that in her presentation of her theory of art Susanne Langer has described symbol as 'a word around which this whole book is built' (1953, x). In many contexts an anthropologist too meets the symbolism of art – poetry, dancing, sculpture – in many different types of society, clearly expressing values regarded emotionally and intellectually as important by the people who assert them. The art of Western societies poses a problem of the expressiveness of its symbolism which is not present to the same degree in the societies normally studied by anthropologists, namely, the gap that tends to exist between artist and public. Here what the symbols express may be elite values, protest values, interest-group values. Sometimes the expression provokes and leads a social reaction, sometimes it seems to be tolerated as a kind of 'radical chic' which saves other members of the society from having to act more positively themselves.

The instrumental nature of a symbol as a means of expression is especially clear with political and religious symbols. Flag, national anthem, church painting, scriptural text, national dress, even style of headgear can evoke powerful emotions of identification with a group and be used as rallying points for group action. This can be negative as well as positive; symbols are convenient objects of hate as well as of devotion (see Chap. 10 on Flags). An example of external criticism has been the Palace of Culture in Warsaw, a building thirty-eight storeys high which was a gift to Poland from Russia after the war. It was intended to have both aesthetic and political significance. Twenty years later, it was described in an American report as 'an empty symbol', not because it was untenanted, but because of its 'hideous' outmoded Stalinist style (*Time Magazine*, 16 November 1970), and possibly because it no longer represents to the Polish recipients the same sense of solidarity as before. Architecture easily

* Questions concerning the primary character of the symbolic function in human thought, such as have been considered by Claude Lévi-Strauss as part of his inquiry into 'untamed thought' in *La Pensée Sauvage* and elsewhere, are not immediately relevant to this analysis.

becomes an expressive symbol because of its public character. Another controversial building, the Yale Art and Architecture Building, by Paul Rudolph, completed in 1963, became 'a symbol and cause célèbre in the revolution of the consciousness of man' (Ada Louise Huxtable, *New York Times*, 12 December 1971). It was first much praised by the critics; then it became 'a supersymbol' when it burnt down in 1969 after being much hated by some students as an archetype of the imposition of false values; then in reconstruction it has been described in glowing terms as a material manifestation of an ideal of human culture – 'a symbol of rebellion and revolution has been rehabilitated' (*New York Times*, 4 January 1972). In such cases the primary focus seems to be on the symbol rather than on the values it is taken to represent.

But the expressiveness of symbols can be intensified (or diminished) by circumstances. In the stresses of the last war the playing of the British National Anthem used to bring tears to the eyes of many who ordinarily treated it as rather silly verses set to uninspiring music; they now saw it as a symbol of freedom of nationhood and freedom of person largely lacking in Hitler's Europe, and under threat in Britain itself. Similarly theatres in the United States began performances with the 'Star-Spangled Banner', and gave rise to feelings of good prevailing over evil and hopes for the future (*New York Times*, 31 October 1971). In such conditions personal scepticism may be suspended, in a kind of complicity in recognition of a public symbol, in favour of the propriety of collective action. I think this is a factor which sociologists writing about public symbols, including Durkheim, have tended to overlook. (Some further issues about the relation of private to public symbols are examined in Chap. 6.)

The element of individual variation in expressive symbols may be illustrated by an experience of my own. Some time after the war Queen Elizabeth the Queen Mother was installed as Chancellor of the University of London, and delegates from many European universities were among those assembled to honour the occasion. Their formal dress was an astonishing mixture, from black morning clothes to academic robes of brilliant colour, with headgear of much diversity. Aesthetically, there was appeal in the colourful array, but there were comic combinations of ruffs and gowns and trousers and odd doctoral hats. Yet when I saw the gathering rise at the entry of the Chancellor, a lump came in my throat. As a group, in their academic robes, they became for me – and I would imagine for others too – a living symbol of Universities risen again after the dark days of suppression, a collective symbol of the search for knowledge and of the history of learning over 700 years, having kept the lamps of scholarship burning despite all manner of attack. A private symbol, created for myself out of my own interpretation – yet the materials for it were assembled independent of my volition. From other people's behaviour one might assume that they too had analogous symbolic interpretations of the occasion. The expressive value of what is called a collective symbol may lie in fact in a set of variations on a common theme rather than in any uniform conceptualization.

Communication

A major function of symbols is in facilitating communication. Utterance of words – a basic form of symbolic action – allows us to dispense with many kinds of manual and bodily actions in providing stimulus or conveying meanings (for Malinowski's views, see p. 145). In a ritual field, performance of a symbolic act allows ideas to be shared and reformulated without use of words, or with minimal verbalization. When the Tikopia chief was rubbing his temple post with scented leaves, this was a coded sign which both conveyed ideas of respect to his people and gave them a focus for their own religious acts. Symbols also serve as stores of meaning in communication. In pagan times a Tikopia temple post was a permanent reminder of religious and economic values; it commonly outlasted the lifetime of an individual worshipper, and for successive generations stood as a material symbol of an immaterial spiritual being. Among Christian Tikopia the Cross serves an analogous function.

To turn to economic symbolization, in a monetary economy coins or banknotes provide a store of public and private meanings. They symbolize past achievements and transactions; they stand for potentialities of acquisition; they can dramatize petty conquests of desire through non-spending; they are reference-points for much family conversation. In most cases it is the values or amounts rather than the actual coins or notes which are the object of interest; it is the implication of relationships symbolized by the material items, not their physical form and substance which are significant.

But the actual coins and notes, as objects of design, have symbolic significance in another way: they communicate information of an historical kind about concepts of the role of the state or its leaders in the world at large. These concepts are sometimes of a political order, sometimes of a moral order. The coins and notes of the United States of America, for instance, apart from indication of their value, portraits of presidents, national monuments and other symbols of solidarity, and supplementary data, carry two affirmations: *E pluribus unum*, and *In God We Trust*.* Both mottos must be regarded as expressions at a high level of generality; what these money tokens communicate is a historical decision to make a public profession of faith. Contemporary British banknotes, also having historical portrayals, carry no moral or religious statements. The coins, however, are more illuminating. For the last twenty years, as well as details of denomination and of design such as lion or Britannia, they have carried a portrait of the Sovereign, with two pieces of religious information. One, conveyed usually in very abbreviated form, such as D.G.REG. affirms that she is Queen by the grace of God; the other, as FID.DEF. or more familiarly F.D. indicates that she is *Fidei Defensor*, Defender of the Faith. The first is a pious assertion, meaningful to Christians and perhaps to believers in other faiths, but in a literal sense meaningless to her many sceptical or atheistic subjects, who may interpret 'the grace of God' as equivalent to 'the will of the people'. The second piece of information is a statement of an historical event – the conferment of the title of Defender of the Faith on Henry VIII by Pope Leo X as a reward for a pamphlet Henry wrote in defence of the Seven Sacraments against Luther. After Henry himself assumed the headship of the Church of England this title was withdrawn from him by the Pope, but he wished to retain it, and it was confirmed to him by Parliament in 1554. Kept on false pretences from a Roman Catholic point of view, the title of Defender of the Faith is now assumed by many British people to signalize the role of the Sovereign as head of the Established Church of England!

* I seem to remember that about twenty years ago only coins and one dollar bills carried the legend 'In God We Trust'; notes of higher value made fiduciary reference only to the Federal Reserve Bank and the United States Treasury.

What this example demonstrates is the multiple character of the referents of this symbol. A set of marks on pieces of metal represents an historical event and its sequel; a royal claim to entitlement; a view of what is important to preserve on coinage in political terms; a belief in the religious leadership of the Sovereign by many of her people. In a sense, this FID.DEF. lettering may be termed a 'condensed symbol' in that to many people the referent is incompletely known, or their premises in regard to it are mistaken.*

Symbols as stores of meaning help to cope with problems of communication over time, aiding recall and obviating to some extent a need for reformulation of ideas. As such they are a cultural asset. Condensation, the encapsulation of many forms, or many meanings, in one symbol by processes of contraction, suppression, transformation, can also facilitate communication by giving a common reference point for a variety of originally disparate ideas. But it may hamper communication by clogging the channels – by providing too many alternatives for interpretation. If a symbol is to be an effective instrument of communication, it is essential that it should convey much the same thing to people involved – or that the range of variation in their interpretations should not inhibit the action desired. How is this brought about? In such connection various writers have called attention to the ambiguous notion of what a symbol 'means'. 'There are different ways in which symbols can *mean*,' said Stebbing (1948, 14n). Even ignoring the epistemological problems here, anthropologists are very aware – perhaps more so than logicians – how many symbols in the wide range of societies they study are socially produced, if personally interpreted; that is, the meanings of the symbols are inculcated by social processes of learning – as by imitation and participatory experiment. For anthropologists, then, determination of what may be termed the level of meaning is a very important part of our inquiry.

* The notion of 'condensation symbols' in anthropology is not very clear. For Freud, condensation was a process of compression of dream-thoughts, not just by contraction and omission, but also by fusion, suppression, substitution, transformation (1945, 269–92), so that the manifest symbol was a disguise for the latent dream-thought. The meaning given by Sapir (1934) to his 'condensation symbols' seems to have been close to Freud's. But Victor Turner's conception seems to rest primarily upon the concentration of many meanings in a single symbol – 'many things and actions are represented in a single formation'. So what Turner writes of ritual symbols – that their 'simplest property is that of *condensation*' (1967, 28–9) is not necessarily true of dream symbols – or perhaps of symbols in general.

The concept of level of meaning in symbolic behaviour can operate in anthropological inquiry in both an implicit and an explicit way. Take again the illustration of the Tikopia chief rubbing the temple post. Explicitly he explained the meaning of this (symbolic) act as cleansing and decorating the body of his god, represented by the timber, on analogy with other decorative acts applied to the human body, and submissively making an appeal to the god by giving him pleasure. But implicitly the chief was also making a demonstration of power. He chose the time to perform the rite; he stood up to his full height in front of his seated followers in a temple so sacred that normally one should go on hands and knees. He scrubbed the timber in an aggressive way, emphasizing by his forceful actions that it was his privilege to do this. Implicitly the chief was showing initiative, and claiming control of a political order by a series of energetic physical behaviour patterns of a coded kind designed to secure benefit in the non-human sphere of crop fertility and the human sphere of health. This is my way of putting it as an anthropologist. But this implicit meaning of the symbolic action could have been got from the chief himself by more round-about explanation – as indeed I got it piecemeal. On the other hand, there were different levels of explicit meaning which varied according to the status and knowledge of the member of the group concerned. Some people could give much more coherent, more sophisticated, more syncretist interpretations of the symbols than could others – a kind of 'inner' meaning, though overtly expressed. It is tempting to identify such more esoteric meaning as the 'true' meaning of the symbols. But each level is valid, and must be aligned with the others for a developed analysis of the place of symbolism in social process – as Audrey Richards and Victor Turner, for instance, have shown.

Knowledge

A proposition that symbols are instruments of knowledge raises epistemological issues which anthropologists are not trained to handle. That symbolization helps us to know cannot I think be easily denied. But *what* comes to be known thereby is another question. What the process of symbolic representation presumably does is to abstract some quality common to both referent and symbol and allow one to perceive more clearly, more imaginatively, a particular type of relationship, uncluttered by details of the referent, or reduced in magnitude to comprehensible dimensions. That symbolization is a way of knowing beyond this, a mode of knowledge in itself basically different from other ways of knowledge, is a view I do not share. Éliade has argued – like some of the Symbolists (p. 31) – that the symbol reveals certain aspects of reality, the deepest aspects, which defy any other means of knowledge (1969, 12). But I think that this, like other assertions of similar order, is to be looked at in the light of the general aesthetic and philosophical position of the speaker.

Most anthropologists tackle the matter rather differently. They concern themselves more with the knower than with the known, with the social position of claimant and claim rather than with the question of the objective reality of what is claimed. Yet one strand in the complex modern interest in symbolism – even among anthropologists – is a hope of identifying 'real' underlying phenomena in an increasingly confusing world. From particle physics to personality disorders come suggestions that the 'inner knowledge is symbolic in character'. I think the issue for anthropologists here is not one of Truth or Inner Reality, but of spheres of relevance, and of effects. As an anthropologist I am sure that I am not entitled to overlook the social context of such claims. Assertions that symbols provide a unique way of knowing the truth seem to be often equivalent to defence-mechanisms. A powerful way of arguing that 'what I say is true' is to assert that 'I have a unique way of getting at the truth which is inaccessible to ordinary knowledge.' This has been the route of the mystic in all ages. A claim that symbolization offers a unique path to truth not only has no validity in itself; it invites consideration of why such a claim has been made. As anthropologists we are bound to consider such a claim in its social context if we are to comment upon its position in the theory of knowledge. And what anthropologists have done for almost a century, from the studies of James Mooney on the Ghost Dance for example, is to attempt to contextualize such claims as have come within their purview (cf. Chap. 12).

Control

Consideration of symbols as instruments of control, or more bluntly, as instruments of power, has two main aspects. Symbols may be used for reference and support when conduct is called into question; they are appealed to as repositories of values, without being actually regulated by the authority of those making the appeal. But invoking a symbol for justification – such as the Bible, the Koran, the memory of a dead parent – can be a powerful means of affecting someone else's behaviour. The other type of control is when a symbol is under the direct authority of, or capable of being manipulated by, the person wishing to affect the behaviour of others. In the struggle for a people to attain political autonomy, the selection and use of coloured materials to make a new national flag gives an important instrument for focusing and mobilizing the peoples' behaviour.

The emphasis in this instance is upon control of external behaviour by use of symbols, and anthropologists, following Wright Mills (1961) have specifically examined the significance of political symbols in power relations. An interesting treatment of symbols as action-media in this way is given by Schlomo Deshen (1971) in a study of the relation of religion to politics in Israel. In the course of an inquiry into national elections he attended a ceremony at which representatives of one of the political parties formally presented a scroll of the Law to a new synagogue. With the growth of settlement this has happened fairly often in recent years, and is a very solemn occasion. It also means great credit for whomsoever makes the gift. This particular gift concluded with an address by a representative of the political party concerned, and he ended his speech by reciting the central credo of the Jewish faith, the Hebrew verse 'Hear O Israel, the Lord is our God, the Lord is One' (*ehad*). The last word of the credo is written in the scroll with large characters, and its final letter, D, is therefore of great significance. The election symbol of this political party happened to be also the letter 'd' (*daled*). So the representative concluded, after reciting the credo: 'This is the D, the great D, the D of the party! Vote D!' This was a piece of political engineering, linking political with religious symbolism by giving a homiletic interpretation of the Hebrew character on this solemn emotional occasion. From the Mexican field an incisive analysis of the mediating role of traditional ritual fiesta symbols, and of the changes that took place in these as a reflection of political pressures, has been given by Paul Friedrich (1966). In the community he studied, changing political ideologies, in particular as expressed through the channels of agrarian politics, resulted in the decline of some of the more 'religious' symbolic practices and substitution of others with less Catholic, less general and more secular, more local meaning, with consequent reactions on social and economic behaviour of the people.

But there is a rather different sense in which symbols can be said to serve as instruments of control – that is, as instruments 'for transforming subjective experience' (Nancy Munn, 1969). Here the emphasis is not so much upon the way in which recognition of symbols affects overt behaviour, as upon the way in which it transforms or conditions the intellectual and emotional framework or basis from which that behaviour proceeds. This approach, clearly related to the more general interests of modern 'structuralist' study, has resulted in subtle analysis, as Munn has interpreted Murngin boys' circumcision myth and ritual in terms of reciprocal social relations of men and women and their joint submission to the authority of Murngin society. The drawing of blood from men and painting it on their bodies in the ritual identifies them with women's menstrual blood in myth, the symbol of female fertility; but whereas in myth women are swallowed by a snake (sexual intercourse) in the ritual it is the men who are swallowed and the women who are preserved by exclusion from the ceremonial ground. By such series of identifications, reversals and transformations, it is held, there is a coding of experiences in symbolic form which serves to organize the individual's relation to the society, and provide him with 'communalized forms of identity'.

Such type of analysis is valuable in providing fresh hypotheses about the dynamic function of symbols. It is also valuable in focusing attention upon the significance of individual perception of symbolic form and possible differences in reaction thereto. But as Abner Cohen has pointed out in a suggestive general statement on the analysis of the symbolism of power relations (Cohen, 1969) there is a constant danger that such consideration of subjective elements in the symbol field may fail to bring the analysis of thought structure to bear upon the dynamic intricacies of social organization. To put it another way, the description of subjective experience, of thought and feeling pattern, is inferential, and should be supported by systematic reference to empirical observed behaviour. And I am willing to assert that this must be so, if anthropology is to maintain its claim to deal with symbolic process on a comparative basis.

The use of symbols as instruments of control is widespread. Manipulation of symbols may be termed a domestic industry, in that it is to be found in every household, in relations between husband and wife, parent and child. Even in the relatively austere sphere of exchange of ideas in academic lecturing symbols may have a controlling effect. The philosopher J. N. Findlay has commented (Findlay, 1963, 112–13) on the effectiveness of argument: '... the emotions covered by the word "logical" are concerned with symbols and symbol structures, and this to the extent that such symbols yield us mastery over the detail offered by the senses, and reconstituted in thought. And we may say, further, that they concern such symbols as yield us another sort of mastery: that over all those minds who have access to the same empirical material, and can thereby share the same reference.'

But symbols as instruments of power and control are most prominent in the public domain, not least in the advertising industry. In the public domain the identification of what Wright Mills has called *master symbols* – to which Victor Turner's *dominant symbols* are roughly equivalent – becomes more than an academic exercise. Wright Mills pointed to the central place of master symbols in social analysis: those in authority attempt to justify their rule over institutions by linking it, as if it were a necessary consequence, with widely believed-in moral symbols, sacred emblems, legal formulae. These central conceptions may refer to a god, the 'vote of the majority', the 'will of the people', the 'divine right of kings'. Social scientists, following Max Weber, have called such conceptions 'legitimizations' or sometimes 'symbols of justification'; and Mills indicated how other thinkers have used other terms – Karl Mannheim, ideology; Durkheim, collective representations; Lasswell, symbols of authority (Mills, 1961, 36–7). Mills cast his net wide, not differentiating between major symbolic concepts such as the crown in a monarchy, or the apostolic succession in the Catholic church; and relatively minor symbolic tokens such as those of class distinction, powerfully seductive and mandatory as these may appear. But when he stated that the relations of such symbols to the structure of institutions are among the most important problems of social science, one can agree. He argued that such symbols do not form an autonomous realm within a society; their social relevance lies in their use to justify or to oppose the arrangement of power and the positions of the powerful within this arrangement; their psychological relevance lies in the fact that they become the basis for adherence to the structure of power or for opposing it. However, like Abner Cohen's argument that in social anthropology the central theoretical interest in the study of symbols is the analysis of their involvement in the relationships of power (Cohen, 1969, 218) this kind of reductionism ignores a whole range of problems concerned with men's conceptions of their social order in moral and aesthetic terms, and its relation to their conception of the natural world.

An example of the complexity of the problem of dealing with 'master symbols' is given by rites concerned with the British monarchy. Any modern sociological analysis can begin with the assumption that we are not involved in any concepts of the order of the 'divine right of kings', and many of us would regard any statement that the Sovereign reigns 'by the grace of God' as a merely symbolic affirmation. Yet many of us would also concede that a monarchy even in present conditions can have useful social and political functions, and is therefore entitled to a moderate respect, even though the monarch be quite a commonplace person. Many anthropologists would probably also concede that to assist in the maintenance of these functions, some public rituals are advisable, to mark the monarch's public role. From this point of view Kingsley Martin's comment on the coronation rites for Queen Elizabeth II is of interest. He wrote (Martin, 1963, 117–18): 'If there was some reaction afterwards that was because the claims made for the Monarch and the significance read into the ceremony were extravagant. There is a wide gap between enjoying a national holiday on which a popular young Queen is crowned, and sharing in a "national Communion service" which in the Archbishop's [of Canterbury] words, is to bring the whole country close to the kingdom of heaven.' Martin pointed out that the coronation was an Anglican service, and only a few of those who enjoyed it were actually members of the Church of England; none but the erudite could be expected to gather spiritual benefit from its 'obscure excursions into the legendary past'. Yet the ceremony was widely appreciated, despite the lack of close religious identification, and despite some critical opinions. What Kingsley Martin showed, in effect, was that 'master symbols' of the type Mills described are rarely simple. They are complex combinations of many elements, each with a different emotional and intellectual charge, appealing in different ways to different kinds of people, and often imperfectly. Hence 'their use to justify or oppose the arrangement of power in a society' as Mills puts it, cannot be necessarily taken as a uniform process, predictable in mass terms. The coronation was part of the supporting mechanism of the monarchy; it employed a range of traditional symbols, both political and religious, to enhance the significance of the 'master symbol', the monarchy itself, personified in the Sovereign. The manipulation of this master symbol by the power hierarchy, including the Archbishop of Canterbury, undoubtedly had the effect, with many people, of reconciling them with an existing power structure to a greater degree. Yet some people were alienated, by what seemed to them needless waste of resources, or mystic jargon, or pandering to public sensationalism. The symbolic relevance of the ceremony was not exhausted by interpreting it simply in power terms; it had aesthetic and moral interest even for many who rejected the assumptions of power distribution built into it.

The social relevance of symbols may indeed appear to be split on occasion between their power correlates and the more diffuse relationships that they may stimulate through their aesthetic and moral qualities. Charles Morris, writing on what he called the social pathology of signs, pointed out how religious symbols which are no longer adequate to a society may be used by a sub-group to maintain its own privileged status. Not only this, members of the society at large may resist changes in the symbols because of the reassurance these give as to the status and destiny of the society as a whole. This is in line with Wright Mills's general sociological formulations. But as the illustration of the coronation ceremony indicated, even in the somewhat acid reference by Kingsley Martin, while the symbolic behaviour could be interpreted in terms of a power-conservation hypothesis, some of it was undoubtedly maintained in satisfaction of deep aesthetic interests, not only of heraldic and ecclesiastical specialists, but of a great body of people who delighted in the drama and colour of the spectacle. Moreover, it may be argued that the people were not really fooled. They tolerated the symbolism of the ceremony because they enjoyed it and had already accepted the Queen. Much of the symbolism found response in a set of ideas and sentiments of a diffuse moral kind about British social relationships, family life and institutional patterns focused upon and epitomized in the person of the young Queen – such appears to be a fair inference from their behaviour.

This line of argument can be reinforced by considering the different interpretations sociologists put forward. Shils and Young held that the coronation ritual was a demonstration of the way in which the Crown kept British society intact. In their view the Crown symbolizes the authority system of British society by representing generally the hierarchy of values of the society, and specifically the benign aspect of the governing elites (Shils and Young, 1953). This view was strongly contested by Norman Birnbaum, who argued that the very absence of shared values in Britain accounted for much of the attention paid to the coronation. It provided, he thought, a surcease from conflict, and the object of fantasies and identifications akin to the cult of adulation built up around certain film stars. In essence this was a difference of opinion about the acceptance of a 'master symbol' at face value. Both parties agreed that the symbol was accepted in the sense of attracting favourable attention in general. To Shils and Young the coronation was interpreted by the public as a justifying symbol, representing the positively valued aspect of the power structure – 'an act of national communion'. But to Birnbaum it was interpreted as a diversionary symbol, a distraction from the realities of the power struggle. I do not think there is enough evidence to come to a firm conclusion on this issue. But it indicates the difficulty of projecting an idea, even when drawn from a vast array of material of literary and historical kind, as the 'subjective experience' of people in contact with ritual performance and other presentations of symbols. It also indicates the strong possibility that different interpretations of the validity of the ritual have been current in the society, not merely among sociologists, and that some of these may have been very alien to the conceptions of those in authority responsible for organizing the ritual performance. Also, by comparison with the historical accounts of the behaviour of the populace at earlier British coronations, all this suggests the strong possibility of the attitudes of the people to its symbolic value having changed over time.

An indirect comment on this view was given by Thomas Carlyle, who also discussed an English coronation, that of George IV about 150 years ago. This too had attracted criticism. Carlyle commented that the hereditary Champion of England, whose symbolic duty was to defend his Sovereign, and who therefore in theory should be a powerful knight, was so infirm on this occasion that he could scarcely mount his horse without help. Carlyle described him as 'a Symbol well nigh superannuated'. But in more serious vein he also remarked that while Time adds much to the sacredness of symbols he also defaces or desecrates them. Symbols wax old, Carlyle said, though poets can shape new symbols. But 'we account him Legislator and wise who can so much as tell when a Symbol has grown old, and gently remove it' (*Sartor Resartus*). Yet this is still a grimly difficult issue since not only legislators but also the people whom they serve are apt to cling desperately to old symbols even when their original referent has radically altered.

In raising the questions – 'what is a symbol?' and 'what does it mean?' – I have tried to show the complexity of the issues involved. Our concept of what a symbol is depends on our view of the nature of reality. We can take the view that reality, if not an illusion, is at least undiscoverable, and that we are operating therefore only with symbols. Or we can hold that for much of our life we deal with reality, in our relations with people and things, both mental and physical, and that symbolization is a mode of operation which is basic and ubiquitous, but not the sole mode of dealing with reality. Its functions are those of convenience and simplification, of giving scope for imaginative development, of providing disguise for painful impact, of facilitating social interaction and co-operation. This latter view is of the kind which I myself hold. But while I have gained much from other students of symbolism, I find I still need a personal lens through which to examine the phenomena. I find it necessary for instance to challenge the concept that all social interaction is symbolic interaction, because I think this blurs the distinction between direct co-operation and representative co-operation. On the other hand, I have reservations about such labels as 'master symbols' or 'dominant symbols' because they seem to assume too great a uniformity in reaction of the people concerned. I would prefer to speak of 'emphatic symbols' and 'non-emphatic symbols' with reference to their being a focus of attention and an object for manipulation, without assuming that they necessarily exercise control.

The next three chapters review briefly the statements and findings of anthropologists and other writers of allied interest on symbolism, in the light of these issues.

Chapter 3

DEVELOPMENT OF ANTHROPOLOGICAL INTEREST IN SYMBOLS

The title of this chapter emphasizes both continuity and change. There is an impression that the study of symbols is a modern development in anthropology. It is true that explicit anthropological focus on symbolism is recent. But the subject as a whole has a considerable history, going back a century and a half, to a time of intellectual ferment and questioning of traditional modes of expression.

Over a century ago literary and scientific interest in symbols was part of the general intellectual heritage. Thinkers about the human condition tried to distinguish ways in which men might have represented phenomena from the phenomena as they appeared to external observers. There were several components in this. There was a need felt to separate truth from semblance (often called fiction). There was recognition that some underlying realities demanded less stark, more attractive, or more easily comprehended modes of expression. There was also a sense of historical change, a feeling that certain forms of institution had survived the disappearance or alteration of their content. And there was some excitement in puzzle-solving, in seeing present-day forms as clues to the practices of a vanished past. What came to distinguish the anthropological treatment of symbols from that in theology, art or philosophy, especially, was the cool analytical treatment of a wide range of comparative instances specifically sought for their coverage of institutionalized variation, particularly from fields of magic and religion outside ordinary Western knowledge. Then and later, major anthropological interest was in identifying objects or actions as symbolic, not literal, explaining what they meant, and looking for systematic ways in which such symbols were formed or transformed. In interpretation, analogies were important; the meaning of objects or actions in one culture was explained by their associations apparently present in another. But the analytical development was at first shot through with other strong interests.

SPIN-OFF FROM THE ROMANTIC MOVEMENT

Basic notions of symbols and their practical significance were not unknown to the moral philosophers of the eighteenth century. Adam Ferguson, for instance, in discussing the monarchy, pointed out how the Sovereign owed a great part of his authority to the 'sounding titles and the dazzling equipage' which he exhibited in public, and subordinate ranks owed much of their importance to the constant display of 'the ensigns of their birth, or the ornaments of their fortune'. These things marked out to individuals the relation in which they stood to others, served as distinguishing features of the various social ranks, and helped in the preservation of order in a society otherwise disunited by ambition and interest (Ferguson, 1967, 104). However generally this be couched, it would be surprising if an Edinburgh intellectual – and a Highlander – had not been viewing somewhat ironically here the appeal of a Hanoverian ruler to a Scots populace. But Ferguson did not turn his attention directly to the subject of symbols in any general way. The temper of the Enlightenment, that belief in the rational perfectability of mankind, was not much interested in symbolism.

It was as a phase of, or as related to, that complex set of challenges to eighteenth-century rationalism known as the Romantic movement that interest in symbolism began to develop overtly and systematically. The Romantic movement was by no means a mere sentimentalism. It had many diverse aspects. It included: a disbelief in ordered progress and a feeling for change, even of a revolutionary order; an interest in conflict and violence, in nature and in man; a return, as it was seen, from the complexities of man's society, exemplified especially in urban conditions, to the purity and simplicity of nature, especially in the countryside; a refusal to accept the conventions of society, and a renewed exploration of the values of the self; a rejection of statements and solutions made on the basis of pure reason and a recognition of the importance of feeling and emotion; a questioning of the outward-seeming and a search for inner meanings. For such conditions and interests, new symbols were required. They were sought in man's inner invention, as in poetry, in myth and in dream, or in the objects and forces of external nature.* A new interest also developed in language. Novalis, one of the more influential figures in the German Romantic field, expounded a symbolist position about language quite strongly, in terms which call to mind some issues concerning magic formulae. He held that if poesy, fantasy, is capable of creating life it is on the condition of finding again the dynamic and magical power of language, or more exactly, the Word, of which the suggestive power by rhythm, cadence, harmony, will be able to create the symbols of higher reality. Nature as a whole, he said, could be looked upon as a vast symbol; and all, between spirit and matter, is only correspondences. A symbol is only the representation of another order of reality; a symbol provokes a spontaneous activity (Michaud, 1970, 23–4).

Towards the end of the eighteenth century many writers were preoccupied with problems of the self in relation to society and the external world generally. Among internal modes of expression of the self, dreams became one focus of attention. The significance of dreams as premonitory had long been accepted or been a matter for inquiry, but now more positive views of their relation to the self were being developed. The remarks of Lichtenberg, for instance, indicate this, however briefly. Georg Christoph Lichtenberg, physicist, rationalist with a mystical residue – Albert Schneider has said he had 'a sort of nostalgia for belief' – had a keen analytical mind. He was interested in the production of images in dreams, and raised the problem of dream definition. The dream is a part of human life, and dreams lose themselves in our waking life; one cannot say where the waking life of a person begins. 'One can just as well dream without sleeping as sleep without dreaming,' he argued. He held that whatever dreams might reveal about the future, they had a present significance. 'From the dreams of men, if they themselves reported them exactly, perhaps much could be concluded. However, not just

* A 'nature symbol' of minor anthropological interest was the concept of primitive man as 'Noble Savage'. This picturesque idealized figure was not without its critics; but was taken to represent simplicity, sensitivity and allied virtues, fresh, sincere and unsophisticated love, freedom, mystery and passion in poetry. See the exhaustive study by Hoxie Neale Fairchild, 1928. For general treatment see, for example Béguin, 1939, and Sørensen, 1963, as guides in a vast literature.

one, but quite a few would be needed.' 'When people tell their dreams properly, that will allow their character to be divined sooner than from their faces.' 'Dreams can be of use, in that they produce unbiased results about our whole being, without the compulsion of often feigned reflection. This thought deserves to be taken to heart.' 'A dream often alters our resolution, assures our moral foundations better than all teaching, as it goes by a roundabout way into the heart. . . . When in dream I argue with someone, and he refutes me and enlightens me, it is I who enlighten myself; so I reflect. This reflection has come under the form of conversation.' It is clear from such statements that Lichtenberg realized the expressive symbolic function of dreams, and regarded them as having an 'auto-diagnostic' value (Lichtenberg, 1764–70, in Grenzmann (ed.), 1949, 92–3, 102–9; Béguin, 1939, 14). Karl-Philipp Moritz had some analogous views. Grappling with the rationalism of the Berlin school, disturbed by interior conflict, a wanderer across the face of Europe, a novelist and a friend of Goethe, Moritz tried through the study of dreams and other symbolic images to come to terms with his own inner tensions. Dying of tuberculosis in 1793 at the age of 36, Moritz was much concerned with the prophetic quality of dreams, and impressed by his disagreeable memory of them, since they created disorder in his daily thoughts. Afraid of dreams, he nevertheless advocated exploration of them in order to understand better what goes on in ourselves. A character in one his novels – specifically termed 'psychological' – questions reality in a solipsist way by virtue of dreams. Since his dreams were very realistic and vivid, could he be dreaming in the full light of day? Could the people he saw around him be purely creations of his imagination? Such suggestions of the merging of dreaming and waking life, of the confounding of inner sensation with external reality, clearly link with Lichtenberg's views – and could be taken as forerunner to some present day anthropological approaches to experience. More broadly, Moritz's second major novel *Andreas Hartknopf* (1786) with its sequel (both with portrait of a sphinx on the title page) have been claimed as essentially symbolic in quality, in the way in which he used the phenomena of nature to describe aspects of his self-analysis. But Moritz himself described the novel as an allegory, and did not generally use the term symbol (Langen, 1962; Schrimpf, 1968,

20–4). (Allegory and symbol had been contrasted in a wider reference by Goethe and Schelling – Sørensen, 1963, 249.) Much of the early discussion of dreams was not couched in the idiom of symbolism, which did not assume overt importance until the Romantic movement was gaining ground, and which was especially reserved for the treatment of myth.

Towards the end of the eighteenth century and in the early part of the nineteenth century a very lively intellectual interest in the symbolism of myth became manifest. One of its mainsprings was a reinterpretation of Greek mythology, by Clarke, Ernesti, Heyne, Hermann, arguing that the classical gods, and some Homeric heroes too, were symbolic representations of natural forces or abstract principles, in a kind of primitive philosophy. The chaining of a god meant strife between the elements; Apollo and Artemis were sun's rays and moon's rays, signs of fertility, part of the age-old genius of nature; the torch of Ulysses was the light of his wisdom, reflecting in another form the golden lamp of his protecting goddess Athene, the symbol of her clarity of understanding . . . and so on. But there were dissenting voices, or at least alternative treatments. K. P. Moritz published a general account of Greek and Roman myths, mainly for young people, which became a favourite school textbook and ran into many editions. In this, myth was treated as a development of folk belief, as a product of fancy, which should be considered in its own terms, and should not be dissolved into mere allegory, or made the subject of premature historical interpretation. The symbolic themes were muted, and any grossness eliminated.*

Very different was the treatment of Jacques Antoine Dulaure, author of works on phallic cults and fetishism, first published in 1805 and reissued in 1825. Born in 1755, Dulaure had been trained in architecture and engineering, but became involved in the politics of the French Revolution, as a Girondin, anti-aristocrat but not extremist. Forced to flee to Switzerland, after his return to France he was an opponent of Bonaparte, but survived to the age of 80, to

* His *Götterlehre oder Mythologische Dichtungen der Alten*, first published in 1791, had reached a tenth edition by 1861. Already by 1830 there was a translation of the fifth edition – 'with improvements' – into English, published in the United States. This was entitled *Mythological Fictions of the Greeks and Romans*, and was praised in an Advertisement (by S. H. T.) issued with it, for the 'chasteness of its language' and its 'pure and elevated feeling'.

write various historical works.* In his work on symbolism he struck a blow for behavioural studies. He criticized his predecessors for having been much more attached in their interpretations to the mythological fables than to the practices of the cult, to the idol than to its attributes, to the personage of the role than to the actor. And, one of their gravest errors, they considered only as symbol what in its origin had been the divinity itself. In his own treatment Dulaure emphasized the grossness, the materialism, of the classical cults. He stoutly defended his study of phallicism, on the grounds that we should be prepared to accept the facts as they are – we pronounce without shame the names of instruments of death, such as dagger, poison; we should not blush to utter the names of the instruments of life! He argued that the priests of old had allegorized the great operations of nature to render them more venerable to the ordinary worshippers. The classical myths were not the result of wise theories or the discoveries of early natural science; the philosophical commentators had given currency to primitive errors. A proto-anthropologist, Dulaure adduced considerable data from India and America to back up his contention that cults of the type he described were well-nigh universal. His basic assumption, that men in an early state of civilization were incapable of forming elaborate abstract ideas of the forces of nature and of rendering them symbolically, was a hangover from the Enlightenment; it cannot be

* Dulaure's work seems little known. His name does not appear in the usual histories of anthropology, nor (any more than that of G. F. Creuzer) in Slotkin's volume on early anthropological materials. But an elaborate study by Marcellin Boudet, historian of Auvergne, *Les Conventionnels d'Auvergne: Dulaure* (1874), gives much biographical detail. According to this it was Dulaure's History of the Beard (*Pogonologia*, see *infra*, p. 266) which inspired him with a taste for historical studies. Dulaure had a stormy political career, typically espousing the Girondin cause only when it had been defeated. He was a deist, a *Théophiloanthrope*, who rejected revelation and Catholic dogma, though he believed in the existence of God, the immortality of the soul, and moral virtue. According to Boudet, Dulaure's research into primitive religion was pushed forward by his interest in understanding how the Catholic church, which he hated for its alliance with aristocracy, had survived the revolution – he looked to discover a human explanation.

A new edition of *Divinités Génératrices* was published in Paris in 1905, with an editorial explanation that it was issued in order to help put Christianity in its place among the diverse religions which share the world. The book was to be regarded not as anti-Christian, but a work of science though '*fort curieuse aussi*'. It was also stated that it was originally conjoined with Dulaure's other work on cults under the title of *Histoire abregée de differens cultes* in order to deceive the harsh censorship of 1825. A complementary chapter by A. van Gennep to bring Dulaure's work up to date did little more than give information about American and Australian sex customs and interpret them in terms of sympathetic magic, relating to correspondence between man and nature.

supported. But he did put forward an empiricist viewpoint which is still relevant, even if it was largely a protest against symbolization by interpreters.

Moreover, Dulaure had some interesting general ideas about symbolism. He said: symbols are not at all purely natural objects, but are works of art. Let us define what we mean by symbol – it is ordinarily the image of a representable object, which has evident relationship with another object that cannot be represented. An image is a work of art; hence a symbol must be so. More than that: to conceive a symbol, one should presumably have perfect knowledge of the object that one wants to symbolize – without which the symbol cannot be exact. This knowledge presupposes at first the need of a symbol, then following, a certain instruction, the art of combining ideas and of appreciating the relations which exist between objects strange to each other. He argued that this need, this illumination, these operations of the spirit do not belong to people who are still savage. Then comes the point of his contention: when certain writers have said of barbarous peoples that in their adoration of sun, moon, mountains, flowers they considered these things as symbols they have committed an error. What these writers have done, he held, was to have loaned their ideas and their knowledge to men who could not have had them because they were much more practical (1825, I, viii, 24–6). In particular, Dulaure was critical of his contemporary Dupuis's view that the most primitive form of religion was worship of the heavenly bodies (*Sabaism*). Arguing with his usual pragmatism that man worshipped the stars because he needed them for his agriculture, Dulaure held that a cult of fetishes preceded Sabaism, with an interest in the material objects for their own sake. But man was a hunter before he was a cultivator, which meant search for religious origins in Africa and America rather than in Chaldaea. Dulaure was thus an interesting bridge between the empiricism and rationalism of the Enlightenment and the symbolism of the Romantic movement.

But there are still several problems about this period. If, as is often said, symbolism was at the base of the Romantic movement, in what relation to each other did they first emerge? I have not found any clear account of these matters. But it would seem that a number of disparate threads were involved: scholarship in the classics, interest in philology, concern for historical and cultural connections, curiosity about mental functioning, philosophical and aesthetic explorations – all in a setting of a more speculative, more adventurous temper than before.

A very influential contribution specifically on the theme of symbolism now followed, from (Georg) Friedrich Creuzer, Professor of Philology and Ancient History at Heidelberg. In 1806, with his *Idee und Probe alter Symbolik* he began a vast series of studies, which in his own view were not intended to be of a philosophical order, but rather philological and historical. Indeed, Creuzer seems to have been responsible for much of the elucidation of the historical meaning of the word symbol which appears unacknowledged in later writers. Creuzer's treatment was distinctly comparative, including material from India and Persia as well as from Egypt, Greece and Rome. He also specifically entitled one section of his huge *Symbolik und Mythologie der alten Völker* (begun in 1810, with a second edition in two volumes in 1819–22, and a third edition in four volumes, 1837–43) 'ethnographic observations' on the old heathen religions (of Persia etc.). I find it impossible to summarize Creuzer's general treatment of symbolism, but a few of his leading ideas can be indicated. In his earlier work on Greek historiography, which Momigliano has regarded as the first modern history of the subject* Creuzer tried to set empirical history within the framework of the new idealism, and his whole work on symbolism gives the impression of wishing to weld together a concept of the pragmatic significance of symbols as instruments of learning with the idea of their mystical religious expressiveness. Momigliano has described his work as an attempt to give a scientific basis to the Neoplatonic interpretation of Greek mythology, but it seems much more than that; apart from his involvement in the ways of thought of the Romantic movement, Creuzer made a real attempt at comparative generalization, and also put forward some pertinent if provocative conclusions about the analogies of Christian festivals with the course of the seasons in nature, and with Judaic and heathen festivals based upon the annual cycle (Creuzer, IV, 725 ff). The breadth of his treatment is indicated in the title given to the French trans-

* Arnaldo Momigliano, 1946, 152–63. Momigliano holds that Creuzer did most valuable work as an editor of Neoplatonic texts.

lation of his work – *Religions de l'Antiquité considérée principalement dans leurs formes symboliques et mythologiques* (Guigniaut, 1825–41).

In his general analysis Creuzer devoted much attention to the many meanings of symbol and its allied forms found in Greek literature, and he pointed out that writing about symbols specifically could be traced back to Greek times. He cited Proclus to the effect that those who speak of things divine by means of sensible signs intuitively express themselves either in symbols and in myths, or in figures (simple images). But those who announce their thoughts 'without veils' do it either by scientific method or by inspiration from the gods. And he further cited the view that the exposition of divine things by the way of symbols is orphic and proper to the authors of 'theomyths', whereas that which uses figures is pythagorean. Creuzer himself went on to construct a diagram in which he distinguished these various modes of intuitive and discursive exposition, with symbolic, mythic and iconic (mathematic) under the first head, and scientific and inspirational under the second (Creuzer, IV, 497, 502, 503–17). Starting with the notion of *symballein* as meaning basically bringing together that which has been parted, Creuzer tended to emphasize constantly the unitive notion of symbol until it reaches the theological idea of sacrament. He saw the symbolic as the root of all imaginative expression, and traced it through a variety of forms in art and ritual. And while he argued for the scientific significance of symbols as means of clarification, he linked them very firmly with mystical and religious expressions, and with myth. Indeed, he puts as one of the conclusions of his study of religion and philosophy the return and re-insertion of mysticism and symbolism into mythology and their continuing mastery there, at the same time as he speaks of the 'pragmatic art of treating myths' (Creuzer, IV, 665–6, 670). I cannot claim to have mastered all his thought, but I see him as trying to say that while symbols are dark and mystical by nature (537) by their many-sidedness they help to clarify even more obscure aspects of the relation between spirit and matter. In the Reformation the symbolic as 'expression of religion's secrets' tended to disappear (687), he argued.

But Creuzer's handling of symbolism, particularly his attempt to demonstrate the influence of Oriental symbolism upon Christian symbols, soon plunged him into controversy. A Protestant, his defence of symbols got him accused both of Catholicism and of paganism. He was also accused of overestimating the value of Oriental cults and of ancient mysteries – a controversy of which the ripples were still perceptible a century later. In particular, Johann Heinrich Voss, a scholar of an older generation, objected so strongly both to what he regarded as maltreatment of the classical texts generally, and to some of the religious implications of Creuzer's work, that he published an *Antisymbolik*. In this, among much else, he complained of the 'foreign-sounding labels' of myth and symbol which had been attached to the classical tales, and to the transmutation of them into units of philosophical discourse, the 'philosophemes' (a term which seems to have escaped modern itemizers).*

The pursuit of symbolic forms continued. In 1814 Gotthilf Heinrich Schubert, nature philosopher and dramatic writer, published *Die Symbolik des Traumes*. This continued the interests of Lichtenberg and Moritz in dreams but also combined philosophical views of Herder and Saint Martin on the nature of man, and interpretations of myth and poetry by Creuzer and A. W. Schlegel, with Schubert's own somewhat mystical views on the character of unconscious images. Much of the book was not about dreams as such, but about a range of manifestations of the human spirit in poetry and myth. But essentially what Schubert was arguing was that the dream and its allied forms constituted a language of images (*Bildersprache*), unique in that it did not need to be learnt as ordinary language – the prose of the conscious – must be. The dream then is opposed to ordinary speech and with its related myth is the oldest original tongue of man – a view which seems to have some echo in ontogenetic theory in some branches of modern psychology. So this dream symbolism can be a basis for new experiments in poetics. Linked with this was the notion of art, including manifestations such as poetry, as hieroglyphic† – a kind of symbolic mode in which the

* Voss's *Antisymbolik* (two vols, 1824–6) was published soon after Creuzer's second edition appeared. For fairly recent discussion see Ernst Howald, *Der Kampf um Creuzer's Symbolik: Eine Auswahl von Dokumenten*, 1926. A denigrating reference to Creuzer is given by P. Gardner – 'the fancy world of Creuzer, who traced the influence of the mysteries everywhere on Greek vases and Roman reliefs' (*Hastings Encyclopaedia of Religion and Ethics*, New York, Scribner, n.d., article on 'Symbolism').

† There was an interest in hieroglyphs at this period; the mediaeval idea that they were mystic symbols still had currency, but their decipherment by de Sacy and Akerblad had begun, and a few years later Young and, definitively, Champollion published their results.

spirit of man (or in some of Schubert's expressions, the mind of God) declared its inmost quality. So dreams are an abbreviated hieroglyphic form of speech (cf. Freud, 1952, 183, 209, 241), corresponding more closely to the nature of our spirit than ordinary words do; the images often go in much faster succession than do those of speech, often reversing the situation of things as we know them. On the one hand, such images are linked directly with the system of nerve ganglions, Schubert thought; on the other hand, they relate to our moral culture, and serve to awaken the soul to its true character and needs. This book produced by this 'peaceable son of the starry night', as one of his friends called him, was muddled, and at the bottom was a Christian apologia. But as Albert Béguin says (1939, 107), it remains the most original of all the theoretical works consecrated to the Romantic myth of the Dream, because it 'looked into the inner world', its author sought in himself the solution of the 'universal enigma'. The book went through several editions, but it is symptomatic that the anthropologist E. B. Tylor made no reference to it in his discussion of oneiromancy, the symbolic interpretation of things seen in dreams (1873, I, 121).

A little later attention was paid to the concept of the unconscious. Already by the early part of the nineteenth century the contrast between conscious and unconscious mind had been drawn, as by the educationist J. F. Herbart (1824); now it was developed, in particular by Carl-Gustav Carus. Physician, painter and romantic philosopher concerned with the nature of personality, Carus held a view of the world which was a variety of pantheism. He opened his work *Psyche* (1846), on the history of the development of the spirit, with the announcement: 'the key to the understanding of the nature of the conscious life of the spirit lies in the region of the unconscious'. He argued that whereas the conscious is an individual attribute, the unconscious is a subjective expression for a general characteristic, designating what objectively we recognize under the name of Nature. Carus distinguished between a relative unconscious, those aspects of the conscious mind in temporary retreat; and an absolute unconscious, which remains inaccessible to consciousness. As Béguin has indicated (1939, 45, 135, 141), these correspond quite closely to the notions of personal unconscious and collective unconscious put forward by Jung. For Carus, a dream was the activity of the consciousness in the soul returned to the sphere of the unconscious, and enfeebled by sleep. In the interpretation of dreams he postulated an interior equilibrium disturbed, producing a sentiment which evoked an image akin to a poetic symbol and by which the interior betrayed itself (Carus, 1846, 218). But in Carus's view the participation of the unconscious in a kind of pantheistic universal life gave it a relation with near and far, past and future, which allowed the dream to bear a predictive value – a mystical conception which preserved the symbolic significance of prophetic dreams. In his study of the symbolism of the human form (*Symbolik der menschlichen Gestalt*, 1853) Carus was less insightful. He was here concerned with symbolism in the sense of the clues that the variant characters of the human body might give to mental disposition and spiritual life, and much of his treatment seems superficial; he also drew some unwarranted inferences about racial psychology from racial physical characters.* It is in his more direct psychological reflections that his substantial contribution lies.

THE CONTRIBUTION OF BACHOFEN

The early interest in symbols and their meanings had been widespread among intellectuals; but its specific developments had been primarily on the part of classicists, allied with theologians and philosophers. But the field of ideas expressed in myth attracted scholars of many kinds, and took on a more definite comparative aspect. An outstanding example here was J. J. Bachofen, a jurist by training and a pupil of the very influential Savigny. From the ordinary viewpoint of the history of anthropology Bachofen is usually regarded as the author of a highly speculative, generally discredited work on mother-right which nevertheless has the merit of having opened up

* A later work by Carus on 'life-magnetism' and magical operations generally is not of great interest anthropologically (1857). Among his many commentators Johannes Volkelt (1873) places him with Edouard von Hartmann as one of the few philosophers who had given clarity of expression to the notion of the unconscious, and stressed its importance, especially in its biological relationships; Christoph Bernoulli (1925) argued in similar strain. Erwin Wäsche (1933) held that while preoccupation with the unconscious was a mark of nearly all the Romantics, Carus was perhaps the first to be so outspoken about it in non-poetic fashion. Wolf Farbenstein (1953) wrote of Carus as a forerunner of Freud, while Artur Krewald (1939) in a publication for the Wehrmacht Psychology centre, tried to bring out his interest for racial studies.

the whole subject. But Bachofen was also, indeed primarily, concerned with symbolism. He regarded himself basically as an historian of antiquity, dealing with a period before the emergence of written history, and therefore dealing with a different kind of material, namely myth. He saw no breach of continuity between myth and history (a position akin to that which for other reasons, Lévi-Strauss has advanced against Sartre). He stressed the importance of myth as a guide to the truth of past conditions. But, he held, to understand this guidance and grasp the historical meaning, myth had to be analysed in its own terms; the scholar had to comprehend the spirit of the times in which it was created. For Bachofen, the key to the interpretation of the ancient myths was the theme of gynaecocracy, the rule of women. Here lay the significance he attached to the idea of symbol. He had been much impressed when in Italy by the care which the ancients had given to the monuments of their dead, and in 1859 he published his *Versuch uber die Gräbersymbolik der Alten.* In this he interpreted the symbolism of the grave monuments as a most ancient cult of fertility. He thought it presented the image of the creative force residing in the earth, with the phallus, the symbol of fructification, as a common design. He entitled his study of mother-right 'an inquiry into the gynaecocracy of the ancient world, according to its religious and legal nature', and he carried his symbolic interpretations very far in pursuit of these aims. Even anterior to the phallus Bachofen saw the egg (depicted on various monuments) as primal, the beginning of all creation. In religion the egg was the symbol of the material source of all things. The phallic god himself springs from the darkness of the maternal womb; he stands son to feminine matter; the bursting shell of the egg discloses the mystery of phallic masculinity, hitherto hidden within it; the egg is the symbol of matrimonial consecration. Bachofen also identified all bull forms appearing in the classical mythology as symbols of maleness, of the life-awakening side of the power of nature (1897, 39; 1925, 130). He went into detail on the symbolism of the use of hands and fingers, as in counting, and tried to relate symmetry and asymmetry of hand use to indications of femaleness and motherhood (1925, 173–4). In all this, though Bachofen did not apparently draw much directly from Dulaure and Creuzer, he was following a recognized scholarly tradition, but he gave it his own particular flavour.

He seems to have pursued his archaeological inquiries more widely than did his predecessors, and his thesis of the primal significance of mother-right was more sharply conceived and more seminal for anthropology. Moreover, with Bachofen the Romantic tide came to a flood. In his study of symbolism he went beyond the classical conventions of his day in making much more articulate abstract statements about the nature of his subject (1925, 46–8). He argued that human speech is too poor to convey all the thoughts aroused by such basic problems as the alternation of life and death and the sublimity of hope. Only the symbol and the related myth can meet this higher need. The symbol awakes intimations; speech can only explain. The symbol plucks all the strings of the human spirit at once; speech is compelled to take up a single thought at a time. Into the most secret depths of the soul the symbol strikes its roots; language skims over the surface of the understanding like a soft breeze. The symbol aims inward; language aims outward. Only the symbol can combine the most disparate elements into a unitary expression. . . . Together with such almost lyrical statements Bachofen also developed a position about the relation of symbol to myth. 'Myth is the exegesis of the symbol. It unfolds in a series of outwardly connected actions what the symbol embodies in a unity. . . . The quiescent symbol and its mythical unfolding represent speech and writing in the graves; they are the language of the tombs.' Historically, when he writes of 'the simple old symbolic faith, in part created and in part transmitted by Orpheus and the great religious teachers of the earliest times' and sees this 'resurrected in new form in the mythology of the tombs' Bachofen's arguments do not stand the test of modern scholarship. But from a literary point of view they have offered stimulus. He argued that thoughts, sentiments, mute prayers can't be expressed in words; only the symbol, by its calm and immutable silence, is capable of making them come forth. When he speaks of 'the mysterious dignity of the symbol, which so eminently enhances the solemnity of the ancient tombs' or pronounces the dictum: 'Words make the infinite finite, symbols carry the spirit beyond the boundary of the infinite, becoming, into the realm of the infinite being world', one can realize how Bachofen might appeal to some German poets of the 1920s as a kind of ancestral figure in a symbolist movement. By some scholars (for example Alfred Baeumler) Bachofen was termed 'the mythologue of romanticism' and H. G. Schenk (1969, 34, 43) sets him quite simply among the Romantic writers, with a sophisticated nostalgia for the past, and feelings of foreboding for the future. Yet Adrien Turel has defended him from this charge, arguing that it was the Germans who made Bachofen into a 'Romantic', and that the turbulent times in which he lived – born in 1815, in Italy for the revolution of 1848, and surrounded by unrest even in his native Basel – were enough to account for the elements of stress and conflict by which Romanticism was identified in his writings. But I have the clear impression that Bachofen was an enthusiast by temperament. The comparisons sometimes made between him and Nietzsche, stimulated by the latter's Swiss experiences, and even Howald's blunt, unfair characterization of him as 'a half-scientific dilettante' (1926, 28) – Momigliano's 'erratic genius' is kinder – seem to me to have some foundation. His views on symbolism, remarkable for their time, are distinguished for their imagination rather than for their sober scrutiny of evidence in a critical spirit. Hence, perhaps, there is some basis for the opinion that he was a precursor of Carl Jung. It was here that from an anthropological point of view some of his contemporaries and immediate successors were more fruitful.*

PARALLEL INQUIRIES

Quietly proceeding parallel to the theoretical inquiries of Bachofen and less anthropologically-oriented thinkers about symbolism were the empirical studies of symbolic behaviour by the more perceptive ethnographers. A good example of this is given in the work of Lewis H. Morgan, who about the time Bachofen was studying grave monuments in Italy was paying some attention to the symbolism of sacrifice among the Iroquois. He did not call it symbolism, but he was concerned to explain what he termed the 'true principle' involved in a well-known Iroquois rite, the burning of a White Dog at the celebration of the New Year, in mid-winter. A dog was selected, pure white if possible and free from blemish, and ritually

* There is an extensive literature on Bachofen, much of it of little anthropological relevance. I have drawn here mainly upon his two major works: *Versuch über die Gräbersymbolik der Alten* (1859) 1925 edn; and *Das Mutterrecht: Eine Untersuchung über die Gynaikokratie der Alten Welt* (1861) second edn, 1897; and upon the writings of Alfred Baeumler 1965, E. K. Winter, 1928, Adrien Turel, 1938, 1939. See also C. A. Bernoulli, 1924 and Joseph Campbell, 1967.

strangled, care being taken not to break the bones or shed the blood. The dog was then spotted with red paint, ornamented with feathers and white wampum (or in more modern times, vari-coloured ribbons), hung up, and finally burned. Morgan argued that earlier explanations of such sacrifice, in terms of expiation of sin, or transference of guilt to a scapegoat, as among the Hebrews, were erroneous. He explained that the burning of the dog had nothing to do with the sins of the people, since Iroquois had no recognition of atonement or forgiveness of sins – once done, an act was registered beyond the power of change. What the sacrifice represented was a much simpler idea – to send up the spirit of the dog as a messenger to the Great Spirit to convey thanks for the harvest and other benefits of the year. For this a dog was peculiarly appropriate because of his fidelity to man and his companionship in the hunt. White was the emblem of purity and faith. The ornaments placed upon the dog's body were voluntary offerings, each being regarded as a gift for which the spirit would make return. The spirit of the dog was believed to ascend in the flames, and the Iroquois used the dog's spirit 'in precisely the same manner as they did the incense of tobacco, as an instrumentality through which to commune with their Maker' (Morgan (1851) 1962, 210–21).

I find several points of particular interest about this account. One is the succinctness with which various points of theoretical interest, including that of the reciprocity theme of offering, have been incorporated into what is primarily a descriptive account. Another is that the account clearly rests firmly upon empirical data, some at least from personal observation. (Morgan mentions once in February 1846 counting nine different-coloured ribbons on a white dog hung up at Tonawanda by Senecas – though he does not say if this was the only occasion he saw the rite.) Again, Morgan was championing a communion theory of sacrifice, though he did so in concrete not abstract terms, and not involving commensality, as did Robertson Smith more than a generation later. And in a way which foreshadows Radcliffe-Brown's treatment, Morgan adopted a comparative interpretation of symbolic behaviour: he equated the flaming consumption of the dog with that of the smoking of tobacco – using 'the incense of tobacco' – and saw them both as filling the same ritual role as instruments of communication.

In strong contrast to early anthropological studies of symbolism by empirical observation of exotic rites or by pursuing the meaning of images on classical vases and monuments – both of which could be said to be in a Romantic tradition – was the impersonal analytical exploration of the nature of symbolism in the mathematical and philosophical tradition. As yet there seemed to be no *rapprochement* between a general theory of signs and a theory of symbols. The work of C. S. Peirce in particular (Chap. 2) attracted no attention from the scholars interested in more literary approaches – partly perhaps because of different channels of publication, but partly also because of an apparent lack of an adequate social dimension for stimulus in it. In the anthropological field, the social dimension of symbols continued to be developed on a more systematic basis. In opposition, overt or implied, both to the romantically-oriented study of specific symbols as universal types of imagery, and to the neutralist study of symbols as abstractions, was the interest in symbolic behaviour of a more pronounced institutional kind, and with a more specific cultural definition. The difference was not clear-cut at first. Recovery of the early history of the human race continued to be a preoccupation of McLennan and Tylor as well as of Bachofen and his predecessors of the Romantic movement. But the Romantic movement itself had been complex, assuming a variety of national forms. The early Romanticism of the latter part of the eighteenth century had been characterized by increasingly conscious repudiation of ideals of rationalism and urban civilization, and by a growing questioning of established bases of authority. It would be a distortion to hold that the French Revolution was a translation of the idea of the Noble Savage from sentimental literature into politics, but as Fairchild has pointed out (1928, 140, 363) the revolutionary cult of reason and the revolutionary cult of emotion were allied. Yet the developments of the Revolution, leading to some shift of interest from fixation upon nature to fixation upon man as symbol of hope, also produced some disillusion, some preoccupation with interior rather than with exterior states. And towards the mid-nineteenth century, as empirical knowledge of exotic peoples accumulated, and as interest in the time process of life on earth became systematized in a plausible theory of evolution culminating in Darwin's authoritative statement (1859) the Romantic treatment of symbols declined.

So the latter part of the century saw more careful consideration for the immediate ethnographic context of symbols, more interest in what the people who used the symbols might say about them, more concern for a possible range of interpretation of a particular item of symbolism. While curiosity about symbols was not necessarily abated, it was taking a more disciplined form – and it was tending to be satisfied within a broader framework of social studies, in which it assumed a subordinate place. So to Bachofen's successors, mother-right was more important as an institution than as a symbol. This more mundane approach appears in the work of McLennan, and even more so in that of Fustel de Coulanges and Tylor.

EXPLORATION OF INSTITUTIONALIZED SYMBOLS

Like Bachofen, John Ferguson McLennan was a lawyer by training, but of a very different temper. His study of *Primitive Marriage* (1865, reprinted in *Studies in Ancient History*, 1876) was one of the first explorations of the symbolism of a specific social institution from an explicitly comparative point of view. In this study McLennan held that the chief sources of information regarding the early history of 'civil society' were firstly, the study of races in their primitive condition, and secondly, the study of the 'symbols' employed by advanced nations in the constitution or exercise of civil rights. In this he presumably had an eye on Adam Ferguson's work of a century before. For McLennan, a symbol in this sense was essentially a practice which had survived in form though its substance had radically changed – a relic which indicated what the former custom had actually been. As a lawyer he was much impressed by what he termed 'legal symbolism', which he thought owed its origin to reverence for the past. He regarded these legal symbols as 'fictions' in that they did not correspond to the reality of behaviour. 'All fictions, or nearly all, have had their germs in facts; they became fictions or merely symbolical forms afterwards' (1876, 9). McLennan argued, rather like Bachofen, that 'the symbolism of law in the light of a knowledge of primitive life is the best key to unwritten history' (1876, 6); and he found in marriage customs a most spectacular set of materials for his thesis. The archaic Roman practice of coemption, by which apparently there was a mutual fictitious sale of the spouses to each other, he classed as a 'legal symbol' but his interest was attracted especially by the so-called 'marriage by capture'. He said: 'In the whole range of legal symbolism there is no symbol more remarkable than that of capture in marriage ceremonies ... nor is there any the meaning of which has been less studied' (1876, 13). Since McLennan's day it has become clear that the practice of 'capturing' a bride is not in itself a form of marriage; and that its symbolic significance lies not in the representation of a past custom, but especially in presenting a formal expression of relationships between kin categories and social groups involved.*

The influence of Fustel de Coulanges on the development of thought in sociology and anthropology has been much more extensive in the long run than that of McLennan, and possibly more penetrating theoretically than that of Tylor. In the specific field of study of symbols, however, his contribution was on the same general level. A classical historian working with some archaeological materials but mainly with literary sources, he demonstrated with great elegance the significance of religion for the social and political institutions of the Greeks and Romans. In contrast to many of his predecessors – and to many other people with a classical education, even to the present day – he envisaged these ancient societies as essentially exotic, not offering the direct models which people have often tried to derive from them. This 'foreign' character was shown especially in their religion, the basis of which was belief in and worship of dead ancestors, with the sacred fire on an altar as their major symbol. The symbols of this ancient religion became modified in time, as the gods became personified and the sacred fire of the altar,

* E. A. Westermarck, as his great *History of Human Marriage* developed (first edn, 1891) first thought that marriage by capture was due to an aversion to close intermarriage overcome by force. He wrote of it as 'either a reality or as a symbol' (second edn, 1894, 387–8). But later he saw it as a custom expressing the sadness and grief of the bride at being parted from her home and kin; representing – in a sham way – and accentuating antagonism between the different social groups and reinforcing the solidarity of each; and representing also an antagonism between the sexes (fifth edn, 1921, 271–5). Clay Trumbull (1894, see later) was of the opinion from personal observation that the element of 'capture' in Arabian marriage ceremonies was not a 'survival' token of former violence, but a natural response of a groom to overcome the reluctance of a bride who had not been consulted about her choice of a spouse and shrank from the surrender of herself to a stranger. This immediate reaction may well have formed a component in the struggle in some cases, but often the contest seems to have been formal. For further discussion see E. Crawley, 1902, 367–70; R. R. Marett, 1933, 86–9; Raymond Firth, 1936, 530–63 (from an empirical point of view); E. E. Evans-Pritchard, 1965a, 14.

already 'a sort of moral being', was given a divine personality ((1864), 1955, 30–3, 120). Like McLennan, Fustel de Coulanges saw the marriage rite with simulated seizure of the bride as a symbol. But he did not regard it as a token of past hostility, nor a recognition of the modesty of the bride; he saw it as a religious ceremony, arising from the need to transfer the bride from the jurisdiction of her own family sacred fire to that of her husband, where from now on it would be her duty to worship by his side. Fustel de Coulanges's specific interpretation may not be valid, but in this characterization of the symbolic significance of the pretended seizure he had grasped the essential sociological point of the function of formal transfer of the woman between groups.

The role which Fustel de Coulanges ascribed to religion in ancient society has something in common with that given to it more generally by Karl Marx, though as a mirror image. Like Marx, Fustel de Coulanges saw religion as providing a basic order for family, authority, class, and property relationships, giving them pattern and consecration. But he treated this as a positive achievement, not as a means of fixing chains still further on an exploited people. It is true that Fustel de Coulanges regarded the plebeian revolutions as a redress of social justice, but he saw this attained in the acquisition of a religion, not in its overthrow by the deprived masses ((1864), 1955, 305–6). And in the end Christianity was victorious because it occupied itself with the duties of men, not with their interests; law, politics and morals had been freed from the thraldom of the old religion, but religion itself was strengthened by the divorce. In ideals if not in form Fustel de Coulanges was closer to Tylor.

Edward Burnett Tylor is commonly regarded, with justice, as the father of modern cultural anthropology. Considering the significance that is now attached to the study of symbols, it is interesting to see how Tylor treated the subject. In one sense, all Tylor's work can be regarded as a study of symbols. Indeed Paul Bohannan, introducing a new edition of Tylor's first major work *Researches into the Early History of Mankind* (1865) calls it 'a book about the history and processes of symbolization'. Evidently, if culture be defined as in some modern views as a system of symbols, then the two-volume *Primitive Culture* (1871) could be renamed 'Primitive

Symbols'. Yet Tylor is ancestor rather than immediate progenitor of what is now coming to be known rather esoterically as 'symbolic anthropology'. Bohannan himself seems to have realized this, since he says that Tylor's 'mistake' (though later he admits Tylor was not 'wrong') was to tackle a problem such as that of images and names in terms of 'processes of the human mind' instead of in terms of symbolic representation, learning theory and social structure (1964, xi–xii). If one does not try to cram all Tylor's work into a symbolic box, but be selective along the lines of his own treatment, one sees that he used the term symbol in a fairly restricted sense, took the category for granted, and let his treatment of it arise out of his more general studies. While he has some enlightening remarks about symbols, he does not write much specifically about them. In considering why the treatment he gave was so much more measured than that of some of his predecessors, for example Bachofen, one must consider his background. As Radin has pointed out in an introduction to *Primitive Culture*, Tylor not only came from a Quaker family, he also grew up along with the Benthamites and philosophical radicals of mid-nineteenth-century England; he was interested in the same kinds of problems as Darwin and Spencer, Henry Maine and John Stuart Mill. Born in 1832, he was growing into young manhood when the impact of evolutionism struck English intellectual circles, and he wrote as an historian, a humanist, and a rationalist of broad views. He was not in tune with the Romantic movement of the Continent, and so while many primary sources of travellers, missionaries and voyagers are cited among his authorities, as well as classical authors, few general works appear, and he has no mention of the romantic explorations of symbolism by Creuzer, G. H. Schubert or Bachofen. Tylor held that 'the turning of mythology to account as a means of tracing the history of the mind' was a branch of science scarcely discovered till the nineteenth century. When he reviewed the ideas of 'older mythologists' to show through what changes their study had at length reached a condition in which it had scientific value, he did so in very general terms. He criticized Francis Bacon for interpreting the classic myths of Greece as moral allegories. Bacon makes Perseus symbolize war, said Tylor, and when of the three Gorgons he attacks only the mortal one, this means that only practicable wars are to be attempted. Tylor said that this was only making one myth out of another – as any of us might do according to fancy, by remote analogy. If political economy happened to be uppermost in our mind, we might with due gravity expound the story of Perseus as an allegory of trade: Perseus is Labour, and he finds Andromeda, who is Profit, chained and ready to be devoured by the monster Capital; he rescues her, and carries her off in triumph. To know anything of poetry or mysticism is to know this reproductive growth of fancy as an admitted and admired intellectual process; but sober investigation must rest on more stringent canons of evidence, use the body of information now available, be comparative in its survey. 'Scepticism and criticism are the very conditions for the attainment of reasonable belief' (1873, I, 277–8, 280). 'The secret of mythic interpretation', almost lost, was recovered from Aryan language, literature and folk-tale by the brothers Grimm and by Max Müller. With such guides, Tylor saw primitive peoples displaying a myth-making faculty, with belief in the animation of all nature as a foremost factor, rising at highest pitch to personification. Animism looked at from an evolutionary point of view was thus for Tylor the key to an understanding of the symbolism of myth.

As part of his inquiry into the development of religious ideas Tylor dealt extensively with the symbolic connections involved in magical and religious rites. Regarding religious rites as in part practical in intent – 'as directly practical as any chemical or mechanical process' – he also saw them as in part 'expressive and symbolic performances'. As if almost in anticipation of Edmund Leach's view of ritual, Tylor wrote of rites as 'the dramatic utterance of religious thought, the gesture-language of theology . . .' (1873, II, 362). A search for the meaning of apparently obscure, bizarre items of behaviour, which often turned out to be symbolic, infused much of Tylor's inquiry. I think it probably no accident that his first substantial chapters in his prefatory book *Researches into the Early History of Mankind* (1865) were devoted to the interpretation of the near-symbolic gesture-language or the Language of Signs, as he called it.*

* Symbolic or near-symbolic according to definition. The study of visual and aural signs as substitutes for spoken language is not one of my primary concerns in this book. For an interesting contribution, subsequent to Tylor, see for example W. P. Clark (of U.S. Army), *Indian Sign Language* (Philadelphia, L. R. Hamersley, 1885). On the so-called 'Talking

But Tylor was not content merely to study the equation of symbol and referent – to find out that what *a* represented was *b*; he also wanted to know what kind of relation was believed to exist between them. He was much concerned with religious images – 'idols'. He pointed out that *eidulos* – 'the visible' in Greek – has come to be restricted to images of spiritual beings. He argued as others have done before and since,* that such an 'idol' enables the savage to give a definite existence and personality to vague ideas of higher beings, which his mind can hardly grasp without some material aid (1878, 109). As Marett put it much later, primitive thought 'finds it hard to divorce the intelligible from the visible' (1935, 110). But, said Tylor, an idol may tend to be confounded with the idea of which it was the symbol, and thus become 'the parent of the grossest superstition and delusion' (1878, 110, 120). He pointed out that the line between cases in which the connection between object and figure was supposed to be real, and those in which it was known to be imaginary, was very often difficult to draw. He cited the images of saints beaten and abused for not granting the prayers of worshippers; and the symbolical sacrifices of models of men and animals, including the 'economical paper-offerings' of the Chinese, as instances in which symbol tended to be identified with reality (1878, 121, 122). Hanging and burning in effigy, he thought, in civilized countries at least, comes fairly out into pure symbolism. The idea that the burning of a straw or rag body should act upon the body of the original perhaps hardly comes into the mind of anyone who assists at such a performance. But if Tylor had been writing in a modern context, say after a campus demonstration, he would surely have added that burning an effigy is a mode of action in its own right – a kind of relief in the midst of frustration. While not conceived as affecting the

Drums' of Africa much has been written. For an illuminating brief article from a social anthropological viewpoint see Robert G. Armstrong, 'Talking Drums in the Benue-Cross River Region', *Phylon*, xv (1954), 355–63 (Atlanta University, Ga.).

* For example Salomon Reinach (1942, 9) cited G. F. Creuzer's statement that in very remote ages a sacerdotal caste imbued with lofty religious and moral ideas thought to make these more accessible to the multitude by disguising them under symbols, which were then taken literally, as in Greek polytheism and the ancient mysteries. Paul Frankl has quoted A. Wilhelm von Schlegel, lecturing in the University of Berlin in 1801, as stating 'the beautiful is a symbolical representation of the infinite; because then it will be at the same time clear how the infinite can become apparent in the finite . . . The infinite can only be made apparent symbolically, in images and signs' (Frankl, 1960, 452). A. F. Bernhardi wrote to similar effect about that time; the same theme appears in Bachofen, as I have shown already.

body of the person caricatured, it may be hoped to influence his mind, as a form of indirect disapproval by those doing the burning – not so far from beating the images of saints!

In some passages Tylor displayed his simplicist evolutionary limitations and a rather crude rationalism. He writes of superstition in a pejorative sense, and he is scornful of the 'childish symbolism' of Chiromancy – palm-reading. He betrays his value judgement also in his view that man being the highest living creature that can be seen, it is natural that idols should mostly be imitations, more or less rude, of the human form. But as Marett pointed out in due course, we need not treat it as an intellectual achievement of outstanding importance to construct the likeness of a man and attach a symbolic meaning thereto. Moreover, as I myself have shown for the Tikopia, a society with quite developed religious concepts need have no anthropomorphic idols (1970a, 118–21 *et passim*). If a material object is conceptualized as a representative of a spirit being, its shape may be irrelevant; a stone or a house post will do as the spirit's embodiment. Indeed, to cite Marett again, anthropomorphism in imagery may run counter to the spirit of reverence – which is exactly the view taken by orthodox Islam, which explicitly forbids anthropomorphic religious sculpture or painting. The most developed symbolism may be the least naturalistic.

As far as I can see, Tylor did not define the term symbol; he just used it as equivalent to representative (1873, II, 168). But following Tylor, though in more restricted and often more penetrating way, William Robertson Smith, in the *Religion of the Semites*, defined a symbol as the 'permanent visible object, at and through which the worshipper came into direct contact with the god' (1889, 151). This was an action-oriented frame of reference, specifically directed to the explanation of religious phenomena, and not intended as a general categorization. But in his handling of the notion of symbolism Robertson Smith did introduce a social dimension. In his earlier work on *Kinship and Marriage in Early Arabia* he had paid much attention to kinship groups, and in his analysis of institutions such as sacrifice he considered the symbolism in terms of the relationship of groups or sets of people in common behaviour to a given object. In this conceptual frame, a symbol was sometimes a natural object such as a tree or a fountain, sometimes an artificial erection such as a pillar or a pile of stones. Robertson Smith goes to some pains to refute the suggestion – current long before Freudian theory, as Staniland Wake has illustrated – that such a pillar or stone heap symbolizing a god was necessarily a phallic symbol. He thought it was primarily a convenient way of representing the entire god as a whole person (1889, 194).

This notion of what I would call 'the empirical aptness of symbols', a kind of pragmatic appropriateness in the choice of the simple to represent the complex, is reminiscent of though not identical with the notion of 'natural symbols' already discussed (Chap. 2).

SACRIFICE AND COVENANT

Robertson Smith explored a subject of much subsequent anthropological attention – sacrifice. A primary element in such a ritual act is the deliberate initiative of undertaking actual material loss for presumed immaterial gain. Most sacrifices are not purely individual acts but involve sets of people, so questions arise about the basis of their association; what kind of gain is thought to be got; how is it conceived to operate and how is it distributed. Already Fustel de Coulanges had pointed out that in the 'ancient city' the principal ceremony of the domestic worship was a repast, which was called a sacrifice, and which satisfied the need of men to put themselves in communion with the deity, who was invited to the feast and given his share. 'Human association was a religion; its symbol was a meal, of which they [the city members] partook together' (1955, 155–8). He also indicated the expiatory function of sacrifice of animals, by effacing all stain of evil from the city – for which purpose it was necessary to have present all citizens, and only citizens, that no uncleansed member might still contaminate the civic body. Robertson Smith followed much the same line, using ancient Semitic custom as his basic material. He saw sacrifice as a symbol of communion rather than of slaughter, leading to the establishment of a deeper more meaningful relation between man and his gods. Its basic significance lay in commensalism, the 'common table', the eating together by worshippers of a shared meal derived from the flesh of a sacrificial victim identified in totemic fashion with the clan deity. Although ethnographically inaccurate, and largely replaced by a sacramental theory which stressed identity of worshipper with victim,* this type of explanation had its importance in relating symbolic behaviour to structure of society.

Another angle on the communion theory of sacrifice was given by Henry Clay Trumbull, from a comparative theological if rather unsophisticated point of view. His consideration of *The Blood Covenant* (1885), which appeared just prior to publication of the *Religion of the Semites*, was originally delivered as lectures in the summer school of Hebrew at Philadelphia. His main theme was that blood was equivalent to life and the soul, that blood-transfer is soul-transfer, and that blood-sharing secures a union of natures, divine as well as human. Hence in the symbolic sacrifices in the Old Covenant of God with his Chosen People, the Jews, it was the blood which made atonement for the soul. So in the New Covenant ratified by the crucifixion of Jesus, it was by the blood – the life of Christ – not by his death and broken body, the *Fractio*, that atonement and redemption came to man. Although from one point of view it was only another unorthodox contribution in a long tradition of Biblical and Oriental scholarship, and naive by our modern standards, Trumbull's work broke some new ground. Its breadth of comparative instances embraced not only India and China as well as the Near East but also Africa and Central America. This he justified by the view – shared by Robertson Smith – that the Bible as an Oriental book needed consideration in a Semitic context; but to this he added the more original if more debatable assumption that since the Bible is a record of God's revelation to the whole human race its inspired pages can receive illumination from 'all disclosures of the primitive characteristics and customs of that race everywhere'. So anthropology and theology were brought together in a study of symbolism which foreshadowed later more refined scholarly treatment. But Trumbull's citation of primitive rite and myth was less of a contribution, coming after Tylor, than his use of behavioural data. He opened his analysis with a description of an actual blood-exchange rite as witnessed by a native Syrian informant (that is, not cited from a book). This he followed by a linguistic analysis to show that some seemingly very diverse words might conceal a common concept. He

* See Hubert and Mauss, 1899, Evans-Pritchard, 1956, G. Lienhardt, 1961; cf. Raymond Firth, 1963; E. R. Leach, 1972, 266–8.

argued that the Arabic words for friendship, affection, blood, leech or blood-sucker were but variations from a common root – a study of concepts highly commendable in a Doctor of Divinity, even one who had been a missionary! Trumbull pursued this blood symbolism theme further in studies of threshold covenants and covenants with salt, both of which he thought were based upon equivalences with blood and the notion that a sharing of blood meant a sharing of life, with approval from the gods. (He also produced a smug superficial study of 'Friendship, the Master-Passion'.) But his set of lectures on Oriental social life (1894) contained some interesting personal observations from his travels in Arabia, Egypt and Palestine, and some pithy remarks on the sharing of food and drink as symbolic of covenant, and on the symbolism of Oriental weddings and of pilgrimage. An essay on 'the Oriental idea of father' illustrated very well from empirical data the representative role of the head of a non-kin related group of travellers. Trumbull's work serves to illustrate the kind of contribution made to the study of symbolism by an untrained but shrewd observer equipped with knowledge in a related field to anthropology, and fired by a ruling idea of a moral order.

THE SECRET AND THE PROFANE

In their studies of symbolism anthropologists have always tended to be in an ambiguous position, either being invaded by amateurs or themselves trespassing on fields already in occupation by other disciplines. But at times they have also been acquainted with that twilight world of protected knowledge in which secrecy, mysticism, the occult, the forbidden all mingle, and where scientific curiosity easily overlaps with, is even confused with, a search for sensuous experience.

At an early period in proto-anthropological studies of symbolism the notion of symbol as hieroglyph was alluded to, implying that it was a sign of highly condensed meaning, the understanding of which would place one in possession of a range of knowledge of an esoteric kind. So dreams, and art, were hieroglyphic, giving clues to an understanding of the real nature of man ordinarily concealed (cf. Freud, 1952, 181). At the pragmatic level there was a desire to penetrate the secrets of such organizations as those of Freemasonry, not to gain understanding of symbolic processes as such, nor just to know what were the practices hidden from the outside world, but also in 'cracking the code' of the symbols used, to attain control of whatever power they might have as explanatory principles of nature and society. So an elaborate study in three volumes purporting to be a comparative handbook of the symbolism of Freemasonry (Schauberg, 1861–3) excited a lively curiosity and reached at least three editions.* In the latter part of the nineteenth century it was believed by some people that the pyramids of Egypt, in their basic proportions, held the key to significant general relationships of a mathematical order applying to the operations of the world and discovered at an early stage of human history. It was thought that proper scientific investigation would reveal the 'secret' of the pyramids; and part of the conclusion of Flinders Petrie's scholarly studies around 1880 was to disprove such speculations. Such aura of the mystical and occult has accompanied anthropological studies of symbolism at all stages.†

Yet recognizably anthropological studies of symbolism in the secret and the occult have continued to be produced. Apart from inquiries of an avowed administrative nature, into secret associations

* For a modern sociological study of Freemasonry in Sierra Leone see Abner Cohen (1971). Some studies on secret societies begun with political interest have been assimilated to the corpus of anthropological materials, for example Schlegel, 1866, Pickering, 1878–9, Ward and Stirling, 1925–6, and Blythe, 1969, on Chinese secret societies of Malaysia.

† Some recent publications on Polynesian symbolism, while not by anthropologists, have drawn upon anthropological material. For example Leinani Melville, *Children of the Rainbow* (A Quest Book, Theosophical Publishing House, Wheaton, Illinois, 1969) claims to 'decipher the esoteric code of the *tahunas*' (ritual experts). Symbols drawn on the sand by a Hawaiian fisherwoman and seen again twenty years later 'on a rare old tapa cloth from Bishop Museum' were stated to include the Cosmic Egg, the Seven Serpents of Wisdom ...' etc. A recent work in what is described as 'The Penguin Metaphysical Library – Religion/Anthropology' (Joseph Epes Brown, *The Sacred Pipe*, Penguin Books, Harmondsworth, 1971) gives elaborate symbolic explanations of the tobacco pipe, the spotted eagle, the buffalo by the Oglala Sioux priest Black Elk. He is described as a 'man of vision', a 'holy man', upon whom destiny in a time of cultural crisis had placed a heavy burden for the spiritual welfare of his people, and whose account of ritual and beliefs 'could also be an important message for the larger world'. This metaphysical library is stated to have the object of helping man on his struggle for self-knowledge, by offering 'books that can recall in modern man the forgotten knowledge of how to search for himself, knowledge he has lost in his haste to make himself comfortable in the world'. In such views the study of symbolism, with which anthropology is overtly affiliated, becomes a branch of an occult quest. Another very popular text, *The Teachings of Don Juan*, by Carlos Castaneda (1969) is used primarily as material for analysis in cognitive anthropology; but it appears to be treated by some students as a source of more generally utilizable symbolic knowledge.

of a political type, which yielded data on symbolic construction and relationships as a by-product, there have been ethnographic studies of direct scientific intent. I mention only two, for illustration. A somewhat pedestrian examination of symbolic form was Thomas Wilson's study of the *swastika* (1894) presented as a report to the United States National Museum. This dealt with the well-known bent-arm cross (fylfot cross, *croix gammée*) later rendered notorious by the German National Socialists but at that time regarded as a widespread symbol of traditional mystical value. According to Wilson, the *swastika* was one of 385 varieties of cross known to ornament and heraldry, and had been identified variously as the symbol of Zeus, Baal, Agni, Indra, Brahma, Vishnu, Shiva, Thor and Jupiter Tonans. Wilson held too that it was the oldest Aryan symbol, to have symbolized sun, sky, light, forked lightning, water; to have been an emblem of the Great God, Maker and Ruler of the Universe, and to have appeared in the footprint of the Buddha. While throwing little light upon the meaning of the symbol in particular situations, this inquiry did suggest that one should be wary of accepting any single identification of any widely spread symbol. A much more penetrating inquiry of a very different order was that of Michel Leiris into the secret language of the Dogon men's association (1948).* Renowned in enthnographic history for their masked dances and their complex philosophic concepts, the Dogon men have had a special language in which initiates communicate during the dances and funeral rites, and which is incomprehensible to ordinary uninitiated members of the Dogon society. Very restricted, even rudimentary, in its forms, the secret language is yet linked with the use of ritual objects, with myths of origin, and with concepts of an elaborate symbolic order. A gifted literary figure as well as anthropologist, Leiris explained in carefully chosen words the system of symbolic associations involved with this language – the interpretation of red, the symbolic mask colour, as linked with heat, sun, fire, brilliance, ardour, force, danger, anger, power, command; yet the mask linked also with ideas of freshness, humidity, beneficence, peace, fertility. Leiris draws attention to the conjunction of the two

* This work is cited in this chapter because though its publication was post-war, the original texts were collected, with commentary, in 1931 and 1935 and their interpretation should be credited to this pre-war period.

opposed terms, heat and coolness (which seem most appropriate translations in this context of *ardeur-fraicheur*), linked with a male-female dualism, which reappears again in concepts of fecundity. Symbolized also by the mask, and by the terms which represent it in the secret language, are the succession of generations of men, and the concepts of death and reconstitution, all bound together in an interwoven series of ideas, myths and rites responding to the multiple needs of the social life. In this study, the principle of binary opposition in much of the symbolic material is clearly demonstrated.

Anthropological studies of symbolism associated with secret beliefs and practices have also had a vast field for inquiry in the areas of magic and sorcery and especially witchcraft, where things said and things done have commonly borne an evident symbolic significance, and where secrecy was commonly regarded as a necessary adjunct if not an actual symbolic component. Two points are especially relevant here. One is the great success of anthropologists in breaching the wall of secrecy. To judge from the internal evidence of such classic field studies as those of Malinowski in his *Argonauts of the Western Pacific* (1922) and *Coral Gardens and their Magic* (1935) or Evans-Pritchard in his *Witchcraft, Oracles and Magic among the Azande* (1937) or from my own personal experience among Tikopia and Kelantan Malay fishermen, persistent sympathetic inquiry in the vernacular can yield a great deal of understanding of the symbolic system involved. (Penetration of the symbolic apparatus of a specifically secret *association* is another matter; the anthropologist perforce must often remain an external observer who picks up what he can. If he actually becomes a member of the society, this also may have its problems of preservation of the secrets.) The other point is that for the most part anthropological studies of magic and witchcraft until fairly recent years have not been presented in a symbolic idiom. Evans-Pritchard, for instance, wrote of 'notions' of witchcraft, treated the descriptions of witch behaviour as if they were valid in their own terms, and stated that they were less an intellectual symbol than emotional reactions to failure of a person's hopes of achievement.

Mingled in with many practices of secret societies and many concepts of witch behaviour have been elements of sex symbolism. But quite apart from this, ethnographic material about concepts of sex,

sex behaviour in and outside marriage, representations of sex in dramatic and pictorial art, sexual aspects of religious cults, has tended to form part of studies which attempt to give a fairly full systematic account of any culture. Inevitably, some of this material has dealt with beliefs and practices, realistic or symbolic, which have seemed exotic by Western standards, and which have therefore appealed to a section of non-scientific readers looking for sensual gratification. Accordingly, some anthropological studies which were primarily investigations of sex symbolism in ritual or aesthetic cultural setting, or of the relation of sex norms to kinship structures and marital institutions, have tended to rub shoulders in some bookshops with literature of a more 'curious' kind or be relegated to locked presses in libraries. Leaving aside more definitely pornographic work, produced primarily to titillate, there is undoubtedly a continuum of a general kind here, in which classical sex manuals of *Kama Sutra* type, literary and poetic exercises of Burton, Mardrus and Powys Mathers in treatment of the 'Arabian Nights', grimly encyclopaedic studies of woman by Ploss and Bartels, more sensitively directed special inquiries by Albert Moll and Kraft-Ebbing, broad comparative surveys by Edward Westermarck and Havelock Ellis,* and profoundly penetrating clinical expositions of Sigmund Freud, have all shared enough of a common sex theme to have been treated with reserve at some time. The attraction and the danger of sex, especially as presented in the moral codes of the nineteenth and early twentieth century, gave writings about it a quality both secret and profane, until in modern times more liberal views have prevailed. How far anthropological writings have contributed to such liberation it is impossible to say. But the work, for example, of Malinowski (*Sexual Life of Savages*, 1929) and Margaret Mead (*Sex and Temperament in Three Savage Societies*, 1935) probably helped appreciably in the pre-war period.

The stout inquiries of Dulaure and of Bachofen into phallic symbolism have already been mentioned. This line of study continued through the nineteenth century, until it was absorbed into the more broadly-based study of sex as part of the fabric of institutional behaviour and values and concepts looked at as a whole by func-

* A considerable part of Havelock Ellis's massive work was devoted to 'erotic symbolism', a term first used, apparently, by Eulenberg in 1895 in a technical sense.

tional anthropologists. An example is given by two papers read in 1870 before the Anthropological Society of London, one on phallic worship by Hodder M. Westropp, the other on the influence of the phallic idea in the religions of antiquity, by Charles Staniland Wake. Nowadays such material would attract little attention. But then, outside the anthropological sphere it could be subject to vulgar criticism for its 'dubious' quality. So Alexander Wilder, contributor of introduction, notes and appendix to a second edition of the two papers, which had been published together, gave a stern rebuke to possible critics. He pointed out that it was necessary to have respect for the symbols of other religions – a view in line with anthropological attitudes but one which had produced trouble for Creuzer half a century earlier. He defended the investigation of phallic symbols by arguing, much in the spirit of Dulaure, that the ancients 'saw no impurity in the symbolism of parentage to indicate the work of creation. No man born of woman can with decency impugn the operation of that law to which he owes his existence; and he is impious beyond others who regards that law as only sensual' (1875, vii). The main essay in the book was that of Wake, known otherwise mainly for his work on kinship, who devoted particular attention to the symbolism of the serpent. Applying comparative treatment to the Bible story of the Fall of Man, he pointed out that the serpent was at an early date a symbol of wisdom, of healing, of life, and he linked this with its phallic significance. Following Bachofen (and pointing forward to modern views of binary opposition) Wake held that 'the doctrine of reciprocal principles of nature, or nature active and passive, male and female, was recognized in nearly all the primitive religious systems of the old as well as of the new world' (1875, 27 ff.).*

* As an example of later quasi-anthropological studies of sex symbolism Ettie A. Rout's *Maori Symbolism* (London, Routledge, 1927) may be cited. Drawing partly upon literary sources and partly upon some highly-coloured information supplied by an Arawa Maori resident in London, this book attempted to interpret Maori myth, custom and art in symbolic terms, especially of a phallic order. The author had an enlightened approach to sex education, and had done valuable hygienic work with soldiers in the First World War. Assisted by her husband, F. A. Hornibrook, she had developed some interesting ideas on the relation of Maori dancing to bodily health. But she was less fortunate in her approach to anthropology, and too uncritical of the ideas she wished to promote. A preface by Sir Arbuthnot Lane, a surgeon of great skill, with eccentric ideas on disorders of the digestive tract, did nothing for the reputation of the book in anthropological circles. (See review by 'Tangiwai', *New Zealand Herald* (8 January 1927), headed 'Maori Symbolism: A Book of Surprises'.)

STIMULUS AND MYOPIA OF FRAZER

Another development of studies in symbolism with classical association, which can be traced back through Bachofen at least to Creuzer, but which was greatly stimulated by Wilhelm Mannhardt, was the more explicit attention paid to cults of nature. Mannhardt, to whom Sir James Frazer acknowledged his debt, had begun to publish in 1865, soon after Bachofen, but his major work, *Antike Wald- und Feldkulte*, appeared in 1875 and 1877. It was a product of genuine anthropological research, being based on the results of oral inquiry and questionnaires as well as on a scrutiny of literature, and it was an exhaustive exposition of agricultural and allied rituals and beliefs of the peasantry of Northern Europe. Through complex cross-fertilization these schemes of nature symbolism emerged to anthropological attention particularly in the monumental volumes of *The Golden Bough*. This, as Frazer himself summarized its aim, was a prolonged inquiry primarily into the meaning of the concept of the slain god; or as we may put it in more general terms, into the symbolism of generation, change and decay in human beings and nature. Recognition of the significance of this concept Frazer owed to Robertson Smith. Patiently unravelling the symbolic significance of the ancient custom – or purported custom – of killing the priest of Nemi as he began to lose bodily vigour, Frazer constructed his elaborate theory of cults of vegetation. In this, the vivifying force of Nature was represented by an anthropomorphic but divine or semi-divine personality whose birth, death and resurrection were paralleled by and symbolized by the annual progress of the seasons and the cycle of vegetal growth. A theme with an important symbolic content, it has continued to hold the attention of anthropologists, even though their interpretations have tended to depart from Frazer's views. An example of a modern anthropological approach is that of Max Gluckman (1963, 111). He has described how in myths Frazer saw men handling dramatically the dying and resurrection of vegetation with the changing of the seasons, and in ceremonies aiding and reviving the dying hero and with him the vegetation. He held that Frazer undoubtedly over-simplified the problem, but was interested in the intellectual patterns which he believed must lie behind all these customs. Moreover, while a modern anthropologist, basing his analysis on detailed observation in the field, is concerned in greater degree with ceremonial roles of persons, categories of persons and social groups in relation to one another, Frazer could not have pursued these problems for lack of relevant evidence.*

No one can deny the stimulus Frazer gave to the general anthropological investigation of the symbolism of magic and religion. Other scholars influenced directly by him pursued threads of symbolism in classical, oriental, mediaeval and primitive fields. Much of this work ran outside the mainstream of social anthropology. But some, like that of Baldwin Spencer in Australia, resulted in rich ethnographic data; others, like that of Jane Harrison and Malinowski (who were also influenced by Durkheim) contributed theoretical interpretations of importance to students of ritual. But the Frazerian stimulus has been complex. Jessie L. Weston's analysis of the legend of the Holy Grail, *From Ritual to Romance* (originally published in 1920, and classed by its modern publishers as 'anthropology') was pursued in terms specifically suggested by Frazer's work. In its turn it was said by T. S. Eliot to have inspired the basic symbolism of his *Waste Land*. (Eliot also acknowledged his general debt to Frazer.) Frazer himself was of considerable importance in the literary world of his time, and this example is but one instance of a relation between literary and anthropological interest in symbolism which has been manifest sporadically in some periods.†

But the links between literature and anthropology around the turn of the century were less remarkable than the way in which the important literary issue of symbolism almost completely escaped anthropological attention. For some of this ignorance Frazer was responsible. His own literary interests were primarily classical, and stylistic in a broad sense; his anthropological interests were omnivorous, but

* For discussion of Frazer's theme of killing the king see E. E. Evans-Pritchard, 1948, Raymond Firth, 1964, 75–80. For more general analysis of the work of Frazer see I. C. Jarvie, 1967, and Edmund Leach, 1965.

† At the present day, one instance is Victor Turner's citation of Baudelaire's *Correspondances* in preface to his appropriately named *Forest of Symbols* (1967). In the reverse direction Jerome Rothenberg and some other poets have been interested in anthropological work of a symbol character – see *Technicians of the Sacred: A Range of Poetries from Africa, America, Asia and Oceania*, edited with commentaries by Jerome Rothenberg (New York, Doubleday, 1968); and the journal of 'ethno-poetics', *Alcheringa*, edited by Jerome Rothenberg and Dennis Tedlock (New York, 1970, etc. – the name of this journal is taken from Australian aboriginal ritual). In some cases the link has been an integral one, as with Nathaniel Tarn, poet and anthropologist, and Michel Leiris, cited above.

primarily in the collation of facts. 'Theory' he distrusted, and he was not greatly concerned with intricacies of philosophic thought. When his friends pointed out that his ideas about magic preceding religion were remarkably like those of Hegel, he made rather tart amends in his next edition by remarking that he had never studied Hegel 'nor attended to his speculations', and simply reprinting the relevant passages as an appendix. Nor was he concerned with modern changes in ritual and symbolic forms. (As I found out when meeting him for the first time and, being asked about the Maori, I tried to tell him about a modern religious cult service I had attended. His only comment was: 'I am not interested in such things.') Frazer's aim, at least in part, he stated, was to rectify the rationalization in the work of writers on the origin of political institutions who discussed the development of monarchy, and to see that due allowance was made for what he called 'factors of superstition' in the history of sacred kingship. As Malinowski has pointed out, Frazer had a kind of romantic notion of the primitive – not an ignoble, but a magic-ridden savage – whose symbols were capable of interpretation by associational and allied principles. He made a great and original contribution in the study of magic. Yet though his wife was French, and the writings of the Symbolists were probably not unfamiliar to him, Frazer apparently saw no links of any interest in their work, not even in the views of Mallarmé on language. Nor does he seem to have examined the earlier views of Novalis on the power of words (p. 94). What use Frazer might have made of Symbolist writings is mere speculation. But a clearer view of the symbolic operations of magic might have led him to separate off magic from science much more distinctly on theoretical grounds, as Malinowski did later on empirical grounds. But this was not Frazer's temper of mind; he was not concerned with the more abstract issues of symbolism but with concrete practices in magic and religion.

Chapter 4

CRYSTALLIZATION OF PROBLEMS OF SYMBOL THEORY

The nineteenth century saw considerable development in the study of symbols, by anthropologists and writers in other fields. The specific recognition of symbols as a subject of study had begun in the classical historical area but soon broadened out in comparative study in Oriental and other exotic societies, of myth, religious concept and ritual behaviour. Symbols were recognized as constructed objects, human art products, needing instruction to identify and interpret, but subject to rule or principle. There was a notion of symbols as constituting a language, and language as having a symbolic power. Symbols were regarded as corresponding to an 'inner world' of reality not otherwise comprehensible. This inner world was primarily not one of conscious conceptualization; it had intellectual components but a strong base of emotion and feeling. So it was not long before the symbolism of dreams was recognized as reflecting complex facets of the personality.

But there were many aspects of the study of symbols. In the growth of the Romantic movement attention was focused on identification and interpretation of symbols already existing, in nature or referring to nature (for example myth, dream); whereas the Symbolists focused on the invention and construction of symbols out of human experience. They adopted a theoretical, questing mode of approach. So also did the philosophers, for example C. S. Peirce. But with Peirce, as a forerunner in symbolic logic, the prime concern was not the content of the symbols he studied, but the relations – between symbols, and between symbol and content. The content in itself was not important for him; it could be supplied according to the nature of the problem. Now for the Romantics, as for the Symbolists, the question of the content of their symbols was important, even disturbing. Exactly what did their symbols represent – the forces of nature, the inner personality of man, the mind of God? Moreover, they were for the most part looking for a system, a unified set of indices which would represent major facets of experience.

Such interests were not in the forefront of the nineteenth-century anthropological study of symbols. Anthropologists were concerned with understanding the significance of particular symbols, and the nature of symbolic process in an institutional context, largely as a by-product of other studies. Anthropological interest in symbols remained relatively unconcerned with what may be called the final content of symbols studied. Nor did it attempt to construct any thorough-going theory of symbolism, any further than exploring the linkage between different symbols in a given society or between different forms of the same symbol in a range of societies.

ETHNOGRAPHIC DEVELOPMENTS

Around the turn of the century specific anthropological interest in symbols began to crystallize more clearly, as ethnographic studies became more systematic, and representational properties of objects and of behaviour came to be more sharply distinguished from their pragmatic quality. Such identification and interpretation of symbols in specific cultural contexts can be seen in the work of Edward Westermarck. Between 1898 and 1930 he had paid about thirty visits to Morocco, totalling about nine years in the country, and had acquired in vernacular contexts a vast amount of data on a great range of ceremonial and ritual institutions, rich in examples of symbolic usage, noted as such and annotated (1914, 1926, 1930).

But the most obvious field for symbolic study was primitive art, and here the work of Franz Boas is an outstanding example. The results of Boas's thinking about primitive art symbolism did not reach the public for over a quarter of a century (Boas, 1927) but he taught and stimulated research in this field from about 1900. Boas himself stated that Ehrenreich was the first to observe the highly-developed symbolism of the North American Indians, publishing about the Cheyenne in 1899. Based on these results more extended study of the symbolism of American Indian art was undertaken by A. L. Kroeber among the Arapaho, Roland B. Dixon among Californian tribes, Clark Wissler among the Sioux and Blackfeet, and H. H. St Clair among the Shoshone. One of the contributions of such work was to show in detail how abstract ideas such as a battle, or a path to a destination, could be indicated by geometric patterns in colour. Illustrative of some phases of this work was Kroeber's doctoral thesis on decorative symbolism of the Arapaho (1901) in which he put forward a strongly-worded argument against presuming either realistic pictography or symbolic conventionality as the origin of the art themes. With his characteristic caution, Kroeber was against the search for origins and isolated causes; but he was in favour of the study of those general tendencies which he thought to be inherent in the mind of man as a social and cultural being. Problems of the relation of meaning to form were preoccupying many students of primitive art and received evolutionary solution – as A. C. Haddon showed in tracing geometrical shapes in New Guinea art back to realistic forms such as crocodile or frigate-bird. Boas himself was more eclectic. He noted the range of interpretation that could be obtained about the meaning of a particular design, even among the people of one community, and he made suggestions for systematizing such data in field inquiries. He also injected into his treatment of primitive art some remarks on symbols more generally. Referring to the symbolism of national flags, he pointed out that they are not only ornamental but also possess a strong emotional appeal. They call forth feelings of national allegiance and their values cannot be understood on a purely formal basis; they are founded on the association of form with definite fields of our emotional life. Boas also referred to the swastika (cf. p. 120) as a symbol of antisemitism, and to the Star of David as a Jewish symbol in Germany at that time (before the rise of the Nazis to power!). He pointed out that these symbols had a very definite political significance, and were apt to excite most violent passions when used for decorative purposes. Owing to their strong emotional value such symbols, as also military insignia and students' emblems, tended to be restricted to special classes of objects or reserved for privileged classes or individuals (1927, 100–1). Here, though briefly, Boas was making a significant general point about collective symbols of a sacred or quasi-sacred order, akin to the view put forward by Durkheim. I think this is worth noting because in general Boas seems to have discussed problems of this type in an idiom other than that of symbolism. In his introduction of 1910 to the *Handbook of American Indian Languages* (1911) Boas advances towards questions of symbolization but never actually gets there. He mentions linguistic similarity in Chinook mythology – where the Culture Hero discovers a man in a canoe who obtains fish by *dancing* and tells him he must not do so but catch fish with the net, a tale based on the homophonic similarity (Boas calls it identity) of the words for *dancing* and *catching with a net*. Boas was concerned to show how similarities in linguistic form could lead to speculation of a religious or allied kind, and he thought that this might show an important characteristic in the mental development of different branches of mankind. He was inclined to believe, he said, that the 'frequently occurring image' of the *devouring of wealth* had a close relation to the detailed form of the winter ritual among North Pacific Coast Indians, and that the 'poetical simile' in which a chief was called 'support of the sky' had been taken literally in the elaboration of mythical ideas. But Boas did not follow up such leads.

THE DURKHEIMIAN LEGACY

Around the turn of the century two theoretical viewpoints of major significance for the study of symbolism began to be defined, and in due course exercised a profound influence upon anthropological studies in this field. Durkheim and Freud represented very different traditions, both in intellectual discipline and in national background of thought, and they affected anthropology in very different ways. Their views may be contrasted briefly, without qualification and almost without distortion, as complementary opposites. Durkheim was concerned primarily with the symbolism of groups, as an abstract exercise of interpretation; Freud was concerned primarily with the symbolism of individuals, in a clinical setting, as a clue to the solution of pragmatic problems. Durkheim was interested in symbols that were expressive of consonance, of solidarity of the individual with his society; Freud saw symbols as expressive of dissonance, of the individual's lack of harmony with his society as represented especially by his nearest kin. And while for Freud symbols tended to be looked upon as disguises to avoid confrontation with a painful reality, for Durkheim they were means whereby one could more fully embrace a satisfying reality. Both attached great importance to the significance of such symbolic representations, but the difference of their objectives led each to stress a different aspect of the symbolic process. In the anthropological study of symbols it has been the viewpoint of Durkheim that until recently has carried more weight, in line with the effect of his more general social theory. But despite the protestations of some anthropologists about the need to avoid psychology, the views of Freud, supplemented by their transformation in the work of Carl Jung, have affected the anthropological treatment of symbols to a growing degree.

There is no need to dwell on the magnitude of Durkheim's contribution to the understanding of symbolic behaviour. In strong contrast to the nineteenth-century studies of symbols, which tended to treat them as discrete entities, having their meaning hidden within themselves or sharing it with symbols of the same class on a comparative basis, Durkheim advocated the need to relate symbol to social factors. In arguing that not nature, only society, offered sufficient basis for the development of a religious symbolism Durkheim firmly turned his back on the last vestiges of the Romantic movement. His positivism alienated him from interest in symbolism of the poetic kind. He was not concerned with the claims of the Symbolists to attain an inner reality; nor did he attempt too seriously to unravel the genesis of symbols. He looked primarily at symbols as modes of expression, and wished to examine their effect upon other members of a society. For this purpose the study of religious symbols seemed most suitable to him. His study of religious symbols took the rather surprising form of an examination of the 'elementary' class of totemic emblems, in Australia. Pushing much further the idea put forward by Tylor, that it is simpler to consider a concrete object than an abstract idea, Durkheim demonstrated very clearly the relation between symbol, religious sentiment and society. He drove home the idea of society as a system of active forces involved in and conditioned by the symbolizing process. In considering the problem of ritual, defined by things sacred, he concluded that the relation between sacred things and their source was symbolic, not intrinsic. Without symbols, the social sentiments could have only a precarious existence. Enduring symbols were needed to give continuity to memories of social experiences. So, concluded Durkheim, 'social life, in all its aspects and at all the moments of its history, is possible only thanks to a vast symbolism' (1912, 331). In fact, Durkheim wrote ethnographically of emblems rather than of symbols, or occasionally of emblematic symbols, but his message was clear. In the view of Talcott Parsons, who in general was critical of Durkheim's positivism, Durkheim's use of the concept of symbolic relationship opened the door to two great lines of thought. It led to a clearer view of the relation of religious ideas to non-empirical aspects of reality; and it emphasized the significance of active attitudes in this relation. Parsons held that Durkheim, in his explicit discussion of the role of symbolism in ritual, has added a whole new normative category to the structure of action (1949, 466–7). This puts the study of symbolism in direct relation to the metaphysical problem of the nature of reality and what methods can be adopted to apprehend it – a problem which as I have shown was already the concern of Bachofen and others long before. But if stress be laid upon the social dimension then the claim is justified. By comparison with Le Bon, Trotter, McDougall, all of whom contributed to understanding of social process in group behaviour, Durkheim's interpretation, using symbolism as an important instrument, was outstanding (see also Chap. 10, p. 339).

Parsons, a sociologist, is in many ways the most subtle interpreter of Durkheim. But anthropologists have shared the same general view. Even Robert Lowie, who had some scathing remarks about Durkheim in his history of the development of anthropology, did praise him for his excellent treatment of symbolism, in showing convincingly how a symbol may succeed in concentrating upon itself all the fervour that properly belongs only to the ultimate reality it represents (Durkheim, 1912, 219–21; Lowie, 1937, 211). Stanner's critique is more measured and more penetrating (1967, 217–39). He asks the question: To what extent did Durkheim succeed in his main purpose – 'to go beneath the symbol to the reality which it represents and which gives it meaning'? Stanner notes Durkheim's early dependence upon Robertson Smith for an understanding of the role of religion in social life, and the degree to which despite Durkheim's fascination for what seemed the primitivity of the Australian aborigines, he used the material on totemism as an illustration rather than as a proof of his theories. From his great field experience in Australia, Stanner notes certain shortcomings in Durkheim's treatment – his confusions about clan structure; his too rigid distinction between sacred and profane realms; his insistence on giving religious symbols an empirical, concrete reference. In Stanner's view, in line with that of Parsons, there was a basic flaw in Durkheim's analysis of symbolism, namely the failure to appreciate the complex conceptualization processes involved in an act of symbolization. By holding that 'non-empirical symbolic referents *must* be distorted representations of empirical reality' Durkheim failed to realize the multiple incidence of symbols – 'the cognitive aspects of the feelings, values, and aspirations which as well as the conceptualizations go with the symbols'. He consequently assumed, unjustly, that the Australian aborigines were incapable of any very systematic abstract thinking about the basic issues of life and the human experience. So Durkheim's argument that Australian totems symbolized concrete social entities such as the clan is not acceptable; these elements may colour or mediate what is symbolized, but it is broader facets of experience that are represented.

From Stanner's criticism it is clear that Durkheim's assumptions about the aborigines' level of symbolic thinking, and about the concrete collectivity as the prime referent of the symbol must be seriously revised. I would add a few criticisms of my own. Durkheim points out that it is the figurative representations of a plant or animal, the emblems and totemic symbols, which are the source of a 'religiosity' of which the objects represented receive only a pale reflection. The totem is above all a symbol, a material expression of something else – but of what? he asks. Of two things, he replies, the totemic principle, the god; and the social group, the clan. Then Durkheim proceeds to a staggeringly simplicist conclusion. 'If then it is at the same time, the symbol of the god and of the society, is it not that the god and the society make one? How could the emblem of the group become the figure of that quasi-divinity, if the group and the divinity were two distinct realities?' And Durkheim puts the matter quite bluntly: 'the god of the clan, the totemic principle, cannot then be anything else than the clan itself, but hypostatized and represented to the imagination under the sense-perceptible (*sensible*) species of vegetable or animal which serves as the totem'

(1912, 294–5). So in the last resort the symbols are symbols of society, or at least of sectors of society. Here is a wide logical gap. That one symbol may stand for two things indicates that they probably have some element in common, but not necessarily that the two things are the same! The reason for this identification in Durkheim's view is twofold. Society in a general way has all that is needed to awaken the sensation of the divine, because of the control it exercises over its members. And, in particular, society 'maintains in us the sensation of a perpetual dependence', and so becomes an object of true respect. But what Durkheim has given is a magnificent series of assertions. It is essentially an imaginative creation, betrayed as such by the way in which he slips from statements about Australian clans, vegetables and totems into statements about the sensations which society has for *us*. The blandness of such assertions can be seen when one considers the inference he draws from this idea of our dependence upon society: it leads to a sensation of respect, and a concept of the divine. Not for a moment does he consider that in a clash of individual with social interest it might lead for example to a sense of revolt. Little wonder that Malinowski reacted against such propositions on logical as well as on more empirical grounds.

Yet I think a more positive comment may also be made. Durkheim was not writing for anthropologists only, but for the broad spectrum of social studies. What he did for the *anthropological* study of symbolism I do not find easy to describe. But essentially, it seems to me, he focused our attention upon the significance of a symbol for the corporate character of human conceptualization and sentiments. Whether identified in nature or of human design and workmanship, the object chosen as symbol was regarded not as representing some cosmic principle or deity by direct reference, but as having been produced by and as having influenced the conduct of an association of *men*. Since this association, by implication, could be contrasted with other such associations, and that symbol with other symbols, questions of defining characteristics, of boundaries, of structures, were foreshadowed, and stimulated more refined concepts and more precise field research. (Stanner's own remark may be noted here – reflecting 'on some particular questions that arose in my own fieldwork, which was much affected by Durkheim's approach' – 1967, 217). Irritating as Durkheim's misconceptions may be to an Australian specialist, and his dogmatism on points of theory to a general anthropologist, what he did was to provide a novel, daring set of hypotheses with an elaborate arrangement of supporting evidence in carefully and intricately argued form which drove people to seek theoretical and empirical bases for confirmation or rebuttal.

While the work of Durkheim and his colleagues of *L'Année Sociologique* – Hubert, Mauss, Hertz *et al.* – impressed upon anthropologists the vital importance of the social dimension of symbolism, it was to Radcliffe-Brown and Malinowski, borrowing in part from this inspiration, that British social anthropologists looked for development of these ideas in empirical research.

SYMBOLS AND MEANING: RADCLIFFE-BROWN

Radcliffe-Brown's explicit treatment of symbolism was somewhat spasmodic. In 1922, in the *Andaman Islanders*, he specifically discussed questions about processes of symbolic thought. He was concerned to explain Andamanese symbolism so that it should not appear strange to his readers. He pointed out that when Andamanese painted themselves with clay as a protection against becoming what might be translated as 'hot' this term was used symbolically to indicate danger arising from energy produced by power.* Among other 'symbolic representations' of forces affecting the social life he cited fire and red paint. In Andamanese colour symbolism red was pre-eminently the colour of blood and of fire. Blood was associated with the warmth of the body and with life, fire with activity and mental excitement. So, as a symbol of a condition of well-being, red paint was applied to a sick person, to a dancer, and to a homicide (for purification). Radcliffe-Brown suggested that symbolism of redness, blood and fire, which he thought might be universal, could have a psycho-physical basis of a 'dynamogenic' kind (1922, 308–10, 318; cf. Lowie, 1924, 286). Radcliffe-Brown also explained the symbolic significance of Andamanese myths in terms of their expression of interests and relationships of importance to the society. His interpretation of specific symbolic concepts and behaviour in this

* A modern social analogy not available to Radcliffe-Brown then is the concept of a national economy becoming 'overheated' by relaxation of controls on the use of resources. Note that Reo Fortune (1932, 295–6) acknowledges the stimulus of Radcliffe-Brown for his collation and interpretation of analogous ideas about heat in Dobu (cf. Leiris, *infra*).

way was ingenious and convincing. Moreover, though his presentation was very didactic, his method of comparative scrutiny was appealing and his reference to social states suggestive.

The relation between symbol and society was very clear to Radcliffe-Brown in his own formal terms. Of course, it owed much to Durkheim. Generally, he argued, the needs of society require that sentiments regulating the conduct of individual members in accordance with those needs are given collective expression on appropriate occasions by ceremonial customs. Such collective expression constitutes symbols. But he did not examine the concept of symbol very closely. He used the term as a synonym for 'expression'. When in an Andamanese marriage the couple put their arms round each other, and the groom finally sits in the bride's lap, 'the social union is symbolized or expressed by the physical union of the embrace' (1922, 236). Radcliffe-Brown also linked the notion of symbol directly with that of meaning, observing of the Andamanese peace ceremony that the 'meaning' of the dance is easily discovered, the 'symbolism' of the dance being obvious. Yet he suggested that the symbolical was only one kind of meaning by noting that a screen of fibres employed at the dance 'had a peculiar symbolic meaning' (1922, 237). Analytically, such treatment is not very satisfactory; some categories ordinarily separated seem at times to be confused. I would hold that 'symbolizing' and 'expressing' are not necessarily identical: expressing is an observable token of invisible attitudes, whereas symbolizing is a particular form of expression, or has a component of expression. To say of a man that he 'expressed his pleasure' by a smile – implies a direct response to a stimulus; he 'symbolized his pleasure' by some action – such as opening a door he had previously kept locked – implies an indirect representation of his feelings. There are difficulties also about identification of the referent of the Andamanese symbols. Did they express actual sentiments or (as in the essay on taboo) apparent sentiments or the social significance of events or relationships or values? Again, in stating that the Andamanese seemed to associate with the idea of heat all conditions of mental activity or excitement Radcliffe-Brown wrote that there was good ground for thinking that 'all such associations or symbolisms (sensory metaphors)' have a physiological basis (1922, 309). He seems here to have intended to indicate only a particular type of symbolism. Throughout he seemed more concerned with interpretation than with definition of symbolic phenomena. But if symbol did relate to sentiment, was the appropriate sentiment *expressed* by the symbolic ceremonial behaviour, *evoked* by it, or *alluded to* in it – or all of these? The marriage embrace 'by the powerful emotions it evokes' 'vividly impresses' on the young couple what their marriage means. But is this what it really does – or what it ought to do?

It may have been in part because of such obscurities in Radcliffe-Brown's handling of the concept of symbolism that a kind of hiatus developed in his use of the term. In 1926 and again in 1931 he wrote of the rainbow serpent in Australia – as a large mythical reptile found very widely as a concept identified with the rainbow, associated with waterholes and rain-making, and playing a part in initiation rites (cf. Elkin, 1954, 216, 220–1). He characterized it as 'the most important representation of the creative and destructive power of nature' – but he did not call it a symbol, as he did in his Frazer Lecture on taboo later. Again, neither in an article of 1929 on the sociological theory of totemism nor in his classic study of the social structure of Australian tribes (1930) did he mention symbolism specifically; he used the term 'representation' or 'emblem' instead.

In his discussion of taboo (of 1939), however, he was considering the relation of ritual values to the essential constitution of society, and here he introduced the concept of symbolism once again. Ritual acts, he held, differed from technical acts in having some 'expressive or symbolic' element in them. The equation between expression and symbol which he used in his Andamans study re-appears. He also gave a further twist to his argument by stating: 'I am using the words symbol and meaning as coincident. Whatever has meaning is a symbol, and the meaning is whatever is expressed by the symbol' (1952, 143). Such formalistic statement is very shaky. If anything that has meaning is a symbol, and if ritual acts are to be distinguished from technical acts by their symbolic element, then by inference, technical acts, being non-symbolic, have no meaning – which is surely not what Radcliffe-Brown intended. And if symbol and meaning are coincident, then how can one *infer* the meaning of a dance from its symbolism, or speak of 'symbolic meanings', which implies that there are other kinds of meaning which are non-symbolic? Radcliffe-Brown seems in fact in his definitions to be oscillating between a view about all signs (all meanings) and a view about a particular class of signs (with what he regarded as expressive meanings, that is not primarily concerned with change in physical relationships). His discussion of how to determine the meaning of 'rites and other symbols' seems to show that it was really the latter with which he was concerned. He regarded avoidance of personal names (as in the Andamans) as a 'symbolic recognition' of a fact that a person was not at the time occupying a normal position in the social life, but had an abnormal ritual status – hence the name avoidance was an expression of a change in the total personality. The taboos kept by an expectant father when a child was about to be born, Radcliffe-Brown interpreted as a suitable symbolic expression of his concern, in the general ritual idiom of the society. It is felt generally, he argued, that a man in that situation ought to carry out the symbolic or ritual actions or abstentions. (Radcliffe-Brown was at pains to state that he was not trying to explain ritual in terms of human psychology – but here as elsewhere his references to 'feelings of concern' have a personal psychological component.)

Radcliffe-Brown's general view of symbols did not emerge as any very systematic theory, though he did envisage such a theory. In his essay on taboo he put forward the thought that in human society 'social coaptation' depends upon the efficacy of symbols of different kinds, and referred for the broader implications to A. N. Whitehead's observations (1952, 152). Elsewhere he took a more general stand. In his attempt to formulate what he called a 'natural science of society' he drew attention to the existence of common symbols in culture, with common meanings, rendered necessary by the need for communication. He cited words, gestures, works of art, rituals and myths as examples. He defined a symbol, again, rather vaguely, as 'anything that has meaning'. He made certain broad distinctions: between three levels of symbols – universally human, socially specific, and individual. He held that not all symbols, especially personal ones used by 'psychically unbalanced people', necessarily imply communication, and that such non-communicatory ones are not 'culture symbols' or 'social symbols' which communicate a meaning recognized by a group. But his usage was not very precise, especially when he tried to separate words as signs – 'representations of phenomenal reality – from words as symbols, involving communication of meaning or regular association with meaning (1957, 99–103). His attempt to use meaning exclusively as the defining quality of symbol leads to difficulties in his linguistic treatment, since taken literally he seems to be implying that in many circumstances direct, non-meaningful relations could exist between words and the things they indicated. His failure to examine *what kind* of meaning symbols might have – except his rather vague references to expressiveness and communication – was evident in his lack of consideration for the problems of how and in what conditions symbols can change their meaning.

Yet Radcliffe-Brown's statements were important for the development of anthropological studies of symbolic behaviour. What he did in particular was to link theoretical ideas about symbolic process with actual field observation. Durkheim had interpreted in stimulating general terms the symbolism of sacred religious objects, and had done it with the primitive materials with which anthropologists were familiar. Radcliffe-Brown did likewise, but he added a behavioural dimension to the material and a freshness of first-hand observation which carried conviction. So when he suggested that the ceremonial behaviour of the Andamanese was a symbolic expression of basic social sentiments, and that to explain a given instance one had to look around for analogies over a range of social situations with a common theme, this formulation (which L. H. Morgan had sketched in an incidental descriptive illustration) was immediately put to use by other anthropologists confronted by formal procedures in a variety of social institutions.

SYMBOLS AND MEANING: MALINOWSKI

About the same period Bronislaw Malinowski was also concerned with problems of symbolism. Though he shared many of Radcliffe-Brown's basic ideas about the nature of social institutions and the methods to be used in studying them, Malinowski operated in very different territory. Like Radcliffe-Brown, he tended to take symbol as a given term or counter in his arguments. But unlike Radcliffe-Brown, he had great ability as a linguist, was much interested in problems of language at an analytical level, and had already acquired facility in several languages other than his mother-tongue – notably in French, German, English and Trobriand. His treatment of symbols was more deeply rooted in the study of language than that of Radcliffe-Brown, and also developed into a more widely-ranging theoretical construction.

Malinowski's views about symbols were essentially bound up with his theory of meaning. His semantic interests were exemplified by his early contribution to the study by C. K. Ogden and I. A. Richards on *The Meaning of Meaning* (1923 – Malinowski's article was reproduced in a posthumous collection of essays, 1948). On the basis of a diagram produced by Ogden and Richards, Malinowski distinguished three forms of symbol: symbol in active relation to referent (used to handle it); symbol in indirect relation to referent; and symbol in mystically assumed relation to referent. The first was concerned with speech in action; the second with an act of imagery in narrative speech; and the third with the language of ritual magic based on traditional belief. In this essay Malinowski did not define symbol explicitly – he merely contrasted it with referent, the Ogden-Richards term for the object symbolized (1923, 260). Yet he pointed out that since a significant symbol is necessary for man to isolate and grasp an item of reality, there is no definition of a thing without defining a word at the same time (262). He stressed his view that words are symbols – 'the Ethnographic view of language proves the principle of Symbolic Relativity as it might be called, that is that words must be treated only as symbols'. (He was arguing here against the notion still then apparently prevalent, that words could have meaning in themselves.) 'A psychology of symbolic reference must serve as the basis for all science of language' (242). Malinowski argued that 'in the normal use of words, the bond between symbol and referent is more than a mere convention' (258). He stressed the significance of speech as a mode of action rather than as a simple means of communication. He wished to define the meaning of words by what he called the context of situation, which he identified broadly with Ogden and Richards's sign-situation.* In his later linguistic work in the second volume of his study of Trobriand

* This seems reminiscent of the argument of Alexander Bryan Johnson (in a *Treatise on Language*) in the mid-nineteenth century, that words have no inherent signification, but as many meanings as they possess applications to different phenomena. The phenomenon to which a word refers constitutes the significance of the word (see Kretzmann, 1967, 393). For

agriculture Malinowski used the term symbol hardly at all. A cryptic reference to 'sos-symbols' appears in the table of contents, but the word 'symbol' is replaced by 'signal' in the text (1935, Vol. II, 56). But I doubt if his viewpoint had changed;* it was rather that with each new presentation he turned to another angle of vision upon his subject. In *Coral Gardens* he dwelt upon his idea of human belief in the mystic and binding power of words, relating this to the developmental use of language both in the relation of the child to its parents and in that of the member of society to his fellow members. So, in what was like an echo of Novalis, the early German Romantic, the pragmatic effectiveness of speech was to be correlated with the mystical character of the spoken word. But Malinowski took occasion to reaffirm here his debt to Durkheim, saying that the sociological explanation to the belief in the mystical power of words is obviously a reinterpretation of Durkheim's theory that mysticism is but an expression of belief in man's dependence on society. But Malinowski regarded himself as reinterpreting Durkheim in empirical terms while at the same time broadening the Durkheimian analysis. In particular he criticized the emphasis which Durkheim laid on the 'phenomena of material symbolization' – the *churinga*, the national flag, the cross – as generating religious attitudes. Malinowski made a very important contribution here as elsewhere in his publications, in demonstrating the profound organizing functions of the symbolic behaviour of magic, including magical language.

There is no doubt that by modern linguistic standards Malinowski's theory, of meaning of utterance being completely contained within context of situation, is unacceptable. I think that commentators have tended to take his specific formulations too literally and

comment on Malinowski's semantic theory see J. R. Firth, 1957; and for general criticism see T. D. Langendoen, 1968.

* There is some difference of opinion about this. Langendoen has argued that the 'later Malinowski', a much more radical behaviourist, attached overweening importance to the contextual theory of meaning, to the detriment of all other determinants. Moreover, he has stressed what he sees as a shift in Malinowski's position on magical language: in the *Argonauts* Malinowski described magical language as a special kind of language unlike ordinary narrative style, whereas in the Problem of Meaning article he regarded it not as a special kind of language use but an exemplification of the primary use of language, as a mode of action. This opinion is counter to that of Jack Berry, who in his introduction to the Indiana University Press reprint of *Coral Gardens and their Magic* holds that the view of language Malinowski presented in this work was substantially the same as that contained in his earlier works, with little or no development (1965, xi). My impression coincides with this view.

exclusively, and to ignore the value he attached to the 'process of moulding' – 'the effect of traditional cultural norms and modes upon the growing organism' (1935, ii, 236). I am sure that Malinowski would have agreed that by this 'context of presumptions', to use Berry's term, much of the meaning of a word is already determined before its use in any specific situation. He said so in various ways. As I show later, he specifically mentions the significance of the group in transmitting to the individual the elements of symbolism and the understanding of symbols. 'Society and its component groups are the carriers of verbal – that is, symbolic – tradition' (1939, 964). 'By knowledge we mean the whole body of experience and of principle embodied in language and action ...' (1939, 958). By this, as I understand him, he subsumed the significance of all past contexts in the determination of the meaning of utterance, and did not for a moment think that meaning was determined uniquely by present context as represented by the personal experience of the actors. What he would have argued, I think, is that meaning is updated by that experience, given an additive, and so by implication, rendered liable to modification. What I am sure he would not have accepted is a statement of the kind made critically by Berry: that since as part of a 'common sense' view of language we can recognize utterances 'out of context' as meaningful, and can find contexts for them, this seems to suggest that the meaning of an utterance is *not* determined by its context, but rather is 'autonomous'. That an utterance could have an autonomous meaning would have seemed to Malinowski not common sense but nonsense – this is precisely what his 1923 article was arguing against. Malinowski's recognition of the significance of past contexts in determination of meaning – the traditional, transmitted elements – has been noted by Langendoen, who complains however that this broader notion of context as he finds it in J. R. Firth's writings, is unusable – 'nothing can be said about it in any relevant way' (1968, 45). Linguistically, perhaps – but Langendoen makes no reference to Malinowski's article of 1939 where he discusses some related general ideas. What Malinowski made no allowance for, perhaps because he regarded them as too speculative, were determinants of meaning arising from phonological characters and elements in basic patterns of thought. I can see that to linguists his theory of meaning was too specific at one level, too general at another, with his formulations too loosely expressed to serve as a basis for more sophisticated analysis. As Berry points out, Malinowski usually was dealing with speech rather than with language, and in rejecting a distinction between them tended to confuse levels of analysis. Berry calls attention to Malinowski's lack of linguistic training, and in a sense he could be described, I think, as a *parlist* rather than a linguist.

Yet in conceding these linguistic criticisms, I think there is still something to be said about Malinowski's semantic theory. In the first place, some of the critique springs from a basic difference of assumption about the nature of language; in the conflict between behaviourist and mentalistic views some of the arguments over Malinowski have been decided in advance, in what is a kind of cyclical movement. Then, Malinowski's views about meaning in language are in line with his views about history, which have been misrepresented on occasion, as being a denial of the significance of the historical dimension in the interpretation of social facts. Here again comes a question of assumption – as to the relative significance of an event as a unique occurrence or as one of a class of occurrences, the problem which has bedevilled historians and philosophers through the ages. Malinowski, in the light of his reading of anthropology and philology, and of his own personal experience, saw how greatly the interpretation of linguistic material had been impoverished by not considering the verbal framework of utterance (such as the alternation of dialogue), the circumstances which led to the utterance, and the non-verbal behaviour associated with it. It was not that he wanted to deny the significance of historical factors; he wanted to insist that they be given their full value at the moment of exposure. Malinowski viewed each occasion of utterance as involving a creative act, behaviour in which the past was transformed into the present; so merely to describe the past was not enough to interpret the transformation. There is no doubt that despite its weakness in linguistic theory, Malinowski's conception has been of great use to field anthropologists.

As regards symbolism, however, it is rather different. Berry has argued that it is in keeping with Malinowski's ethnographic theory that he should have emphasized the pragmatic functions of language at the expense of the symbolic. But while his theory of meaning was inadequate as regards the *determinants* of the significance of symbols, I doubt if it is enough to argue, as Leach has done, that Malinowski undervalued the significance of symbolic statement and therefore the significance of communication. I think rather that Malinowski gave all verbal communication a symbolic status (all words are symbols), but in strongly emphasizing the expressive value of utterance, failed to make a sufficient difference between the kinds or levels of symbolic statement.

But Malinowski's interest in symbolism was not so much in symbolic forms as such, their classification and their interpretation, as in the process of symbolization in its bearing on the formation and operations of culture. Again he approached this through language, exemplified by his treatment of myth (1926). Following an explicit Trobriand classification (1926, 35) he saw myth as sacred story told with justificatory purpose. He flatly denied that such myths had a symbolic character, because this suggested to him the romantic theories of the nature-mythology German scholars, such as Ehrenreich or Frobenius, who, as he saw it, made primitive man construct 'symbolic personified rhapsodies'. His examination of myths in their social context brought out the way in which themes of importance to the workings of Trobriand society were expressed. He exaggerated the opposing position, and he was unduly suspicious of 'symbolic interpretations' in terms of 'hidden realities' (1926, 79). He was also inconsistent, in denying to the language of myth the term symbol which he had applied to words in general. What he was concerned to emphasize was the overt practical social referent of myths. But he recognized that they could represent at the apparently trivial level of human error and guilt, or of mischance, great elements of fate and destiny – as the Trobriand myths of death and the after-life had a 'deeper metaphysical reference' than the myths of clan origins (1926, 103). He also stressed their coherence as a unit.

Malinowski's relatively late article on the group and the individual in functional analysis contains a more general explicit statement of his theory. He assumed the symbolic character of language: 'since all rules and all tribal tradition are expressions in words – that is, symbols – the understanding of social organization implies an analysis of symbolism and language' (1939, 940). In discussing the routine procedures of eating, involving table, kitchen etc., he began 'the symbolic expressions here used – table, kitchen. . . .' In this Malinowski simply picked up his much earlier analysis of meaning in language. But he went on to give what he called 'the cultural dimensions of symbolism'. This was a very general statement. 'Symbolism is a component of human culture, with language as its prototype. . . . Symbolism must make its appearance with the earliest appearance of human culture. It is in essence that modification of the human organism which allows it to transform the physiological drive into a cultural value' (1939, 955). Malinowski argued that the first discovery and use of an implement already implied the birth of symbolism. Incorporation of the implement into the human sphere of interest and transmission of the idea of its use implied recognition of value; the deferred indirect satisfaction of need involved the mechanism of symbolization. The 'transference of the physiological urge on the secondary reality', as the urges of hunger, sex or security on to objects which could satisfy them, was in its essence symbolic. The social setting is indispensable, because it is the group which maintains and transmits the elements of symbolism, which trains each individual and develops in him the knowledge of technique, the understanding of symbols, and the appreciation of values (1939, 956). But Malinowski went further – he not only traced the symbolic process to the origins of culture, but also gave reasons why symbolism should occupy such a basic position. Early human beings used language and symbolism primarily as a means of co-ordinating action or of standardizing technique and providing rules ('imparting prescriptions') for industrial, social and ritual behaviour (1939, 957). So, symbolism was the means in the very beginning of human civilization, of mastery of implements, production of goods, and incorporation of achievement into a permanent tradition (1939, 964).*

* Just after the war M. M. Lewis, a philosopher of education with a behavioural approach and interested in the social nature of language, stressed the importance of contextual interpretation. Broadly in line with C. K. Ogden and I. A. Richards, Lewis specifically caught up Malinowski's ideas, using his data from the Trobriands and generalizations from *A Scientific Theory of Culture*, with other ethnographic materials, to illustrate an analysis of group communication. Lewis held that 'mind is behaviour mediated by symbols'. He stressed that in group behaviour 'group-remembering, group planning, group feeling and willing – all these are modified by the existence of some form of symbolic communication within the group' (1947, 94). In further consideration of the significance of symbols Lewis pointed out the growth of what he called 'allusive power' in common verbal symbols, through the spread of

Malinowski's outline reconstruction of the role of symbolization as a basic process in culture formation seems to me quite plausible. Moreover, I think that much modern anthropological treatment of notions of basic human thought makes much the same kind of general assumption about 'symbolic function'. But it is a speculative theory, and a mere sketch. Then on the more critical side I think one might challenge Malinowski's statement that 'symbolism from its very inception had to be precise' in the sense that it had to provide a *correct* formula for the permanent incorporation and transmission of the cultural achievement, that it had to be effective in transferring the drive of the physiological need to the given object which could satisfy it (1939, 956). This seems to miss out the possibility of that element of ambiguity characteristic of much symbolization – and in which lies risk of failure as well as function of stimulation. The exposition of Malinowski's theory of symbolization given in his *A Scientific Theory of Culture* (published posthumously) added little to the corpus of his ideas. Again the text argued very strongly that symbolism is an essential ingredient of all organized behaviour, that it is a modification of the original organism which allows the transformation of a physiological drive into a cultural value. It was argued too that a symbol could be physically recorded, described and defined in terms of its 'pragmatic context' (1944, 23–4, 132). The postulate was also stressed that a verbal or other symbolic act only becomes real through the effect it produces. On this point Malinowski has been criticized, with some justification, by Talcott Parsons (1957, 61) for taking altogether too weak a view of the significance of symbolic interaction as a determinant of this context, in the general theory of the social system. Malinowski was relatively uninterested, also, in problems of symbolic forms and their transformations, and of the comparative structure of symbolic systems, which have become increasingly prominent in social anthropology.

In brief, in the recognition of the significance of symbolic behaviour, both verbal and non-verbal, both Radcliffe-Brown and Malinowski made specific anthropological contributions. Both patiently worked out from their field materials an interpretation of

modern communications; and in a chapter on language and social conflict he discussed the position of Blacks in the United States, including the 'condensation', 'displacement' and 'allusion' in verbal symbols for Negro.

symbolic concepts and behaviour – Radcliffe-Brown those of myth and life crises among the Andamanese, Malinowski those of myth, kinship and ritual exchange among the northern Massim. They demonstrated the use of different methods – Radcliffe-Brown that of comparative inference, Malinowski that of collation of speech and behaviour in complex sequences of operations. And more generally, whereas Radcliffe-Brown focused his attention on problems of symbolism in ritual, Malinowski pioneered in more speculative theory of the role of symbolization in language and the formation of culture.

DEPTH PSYCHOLOGY AND ANTHROPOLOGICAL STUDIES OF SYMBOLISM

Side by side with the development of ethnographic study of symbols in ritual, art and social institutions, and with refinement of theoretical insight into the sociological significance of symbols came the emergence of a specifically psychological focus on the subject. This had a long ancestry, to mention only the attention paid to the interpretation of the symbolism of dreams by G. H. Schubert (1814), K. A. Scherner (1861) and J. Volkelt (1875). But in the beginning of the present century it was the approach of Sigmund Freud that began to attract most interest in intellectual circles. Anthropologists for the most part maintained a stout resistance to Freudian ideas about symbolism – Frazer, as Malinowski noted, being one of these. But in Britain and in the United States some began to champion or at least to experiment with such novel ideas.

Freud's contribution to the understanding of symbolism was as startling as it was novel. As an important part of his work in the study of neuroses he wished to interpret – as he said, discover the hidden meanings of – the symbolic forms in which his patients expressed their anxieties. Dreams were very important in this. As he said, dreams are not in themselves social utterances, not a means of giving information, but his aim was to turn them into utterances of value, to treat them as fully valid psychical acts. He pointed out that the use of the symbolism of dreams was not the discovery of psychoanalysis, priority in modern times being due to K. A. Scherner (1861) who particularly stressed the significance of symbolic representations of the whole human form (1937, 221, etc.; 1952, 159, 166).* What Freud did in psychoanalysis was to expose particularly the relation of the dream symbolism to the latent dream-thought and the operations of the unconscious mind. His technique of dream interpretation included a review of the chronological order of dream events, of the 'day's residues', and of markedly striking events in the dream; as well as a patient examination of the 'free associations' of the dreamer. Then if in proceeding to an interpretation of the latent dream-thoughts resistance was met, this was a sign of conflict which had to be investigated. The interpretation as Freud admitted, rested on certain postulates about the meaning of dream symbolism and its associations, but while more cautious than many of his critics allowed, he held that most of these postulates were justified by the analytical evidence. For instance, he held that the number of things represented symbolically in dreams is not great – the body, parents, children, siblings, birth, death, nakedness, sexual organs and processes – and that a large part of the symbolism is an unconscious expression of the sex impulses. But he pointed out that he had never put forward the thesis that all dreams are of a sexual nature. And while he admitted that *why* certain objects have become male sexual symbols is not easy to understand, he maintained that it was unquestionable that hats and cloaks were such – and even argued that this was backed up by some experimental data! Freud also pointed to the widespread nature of symbolic usage, in myth, jokes, poetry, religion, art and language in general. He held that light could be thrown on such phenomena, especially myth, by the interpretation of the symbolism of dreams, but he emphasized that the interpretation is by no means confined to sexual themes.

Freud's specific interpretations of symbolism were clearly culture-bound. Obviously, in the ethnographically 'primitive' fields, umbrellas and revolvers could not be expected as penis symbols, nor apples and peaches as breast symbols; nor is dying likely to be symbolized by travelling on a train. Freud never really faced this anthropological dilemma, as is evidenced by the way he blithely cites a Beduin marriage rite with a cloak as evidence which 'I hope will

* Scherner examined general characteristics of dreams, for example as a 'field for strife', and as reproductive, a source of originality. Dividing dreams into eleven classes, he considered what he regarded as their basic symbolic formations. Schubert and Volkelt are also cited by Freud.

impress you' that in a (Western) woman's dream a cloak stands for a man (1964, 24). But Freud was always less interested in the specific symbol than in the mental process it represented. So, it could be argued, the equivalent pointed, rounded, covering objects could occur in any culture to serve as sex symbols. Moreover, Freud himself emphasized in various contexts the major importance he attached to the study of the 'dream-work' – the process by which the latent dream-thoughts are transformed into the manifest dream. He isolated processes of condensation, displacement and secondary elaboration as especially relevant for understanding of the symbolism. But he looked back continually at the clinical problems so the symbolism was significant for him as a factor in dream-distortion, which in turn gave clues to the nature of neurosis. Indeed he sometimes went so far as to say that the mechanism of the dream-work is a kind of model for the formation of neurotic symptoms, or even that a dream itself is a neurotic symptom, occurring in all healthy people. In the early part of the twentieth century, Freud's views on symbolism were among the most articulate, forceful, systematic and theoretical, so it became difficult for the more thoughtful anthropologist to ignore them, however much he might criticize their sweeping assumptions, lack of cultural sophistication and dogmatic presentation.

One can only indicate, not summarize, the effect of Freud's views upon social anthropologists' concern with symbolism in the early part of this century, and I mention only a few points. Concepts of deep, unconscious motivation existed before Freud, but it was his brutal insistence upon the force and the generality of such motives that led to an almost unwilling recognition of their significance. Concepts of manifest and latent content, resistance, ambivalence and repression exemplified the need to interpret behaviour with an eye to more than its superficial qualities. The frank, overt discussion of sexual elements in dream and neurosis reinforced the rather apologetic examination of phallic cults, premarital intercourse, ritual defloration and other exotic material which anthropologists had felt it necessary to present in order to convey a realistic picture of the cultures they studied. The focus on nuclear family as the core of social action and basic beliefs sent anthropologists back again to a scrutiny of detailed behaviour and ideas over a range of institutions from child-training to the role of the mother's brother.

In the British field the anthropologists first most affected by Freudian views were W. H. R. Rivers and C. G. Seligman. In addition to their early work with Haddon in the Torres Straits, both Rivers and Seligman had done field research independently elsewhere; although they had devoted much attention to rites and ceremonies, their interest in symbolism as such had been slight.* But their interest in Freudian concepts was aroused primarily by their practical concern with neurotic ('shell-shocked') patients in hospital during the First World War. Rivers became convinced of the significance of unconscious elements of the mind in understanding the condition of these soldiers and setting up therapy for them. He carried this interest through into some theoretical examination of dream and other mental process and discussed briefly some aspects of symbolization in Melanesia (for example 1918; cf. 1920, 159–69). Seligman continued this approach, and after the death of Rivers in 1922 he took up the task of advocating psychological and particularly psychoanalytical methods of inquiry in what were considered conventional anthropological fields. He applied his ideas especially to the interpretation of the symbolism of dreams, on a comparative basis, and stimulated other anthropologists in such studies.† From his medical training, Seligman was able to appreciate implications of Freud's work which could escape anthropologists in general. On the other hand he adopted a somewhat uncritical attitude towards psychoanalytical theory, including the central problem which faced anthropologists interested in it, namely the translation from individual to social dimension.

For while psychoanalysis offered a powerful instrument for anthropologists in the study of symbolism, it also raised difficulties.

* For example Seligman discussed in detail the former Vedda custom of a groom giving a lock of hair to his bride, questioned its ornamental value, stressed how the bride prized it, but did not examine the symbolism (1911, 98–100). Rivers likewise described the Toda bow-and-arrow ceremony at a woman's first pregnancy, to establish the social fatherhood of the child, but did not explore the symbolic aspects. His only mention of symbolism I can find among the Todas refers to the swinging of a corpse over a fire, which 'would be symbolic of its destruction by fire', with the 'symbolic burning' having the advantage of not destroying valuable property (1906, 319–22, 363). (Seligman's reference to an arrow symbol is a quotation from an earlier writer.)

† Jackson Steward Lincoln, psychologist and anthropologist, who had also been psychoanalysed, drew considerably upon Seligman's ideas in his *The Dream in Primitive Cultures*, 1935. My own study of dreams in Tikopia was in response to Seligman's interest (Firth, 1967b) but was not along lines directly suggested by him.

First, if all symbolism is unconscious, as orthodox theory seems to require, in order to interpret it, an anthropologist is involved in much more manipulation of spoken evidence and more imputation of motivation, than he ordinarily regards as justified. Then there is the question of sexuality. Few field anthropologists would wish to deny the great importance of sexual factors in the whole field of symbolic behaviour they study, from poetry to magic and myth recital. But as Rivers argued, they tend to identify referents of symbols in social relationships as well as in sexual relationships, and even when in sexual relationships, they see other than genital elements as of prime relevance. Again, in his *Totem and Taboo* (1912) Freud had put forward views that were naive and distorted by most anthropological opinion: not only had he taken up the discarded primal horde hypothesis of J. J. Atkinson, but he also argued that there was analogy between much of the social, especially ritual, behaviour of primitive peoples and the individual behaviour of neurotics. Taken in conjunction with Lévy-Bruhl's parallel assertion of the pre-logicality of the primitive,* there is little wonder that anthropologists reacted vigorously against this last view.

In this turbulent intellectual situation Freud's views on symbols had defenders and interpreters in the anthropological sphere. For instance, working from literary sources, J. S. Lincoln regarded the Freudian theory of symbolism as a most useful and accurate means of approaching latent dream meanings, and interpreted Amerindian data accordingly. A major, if idiosyncratic, figure here was Géza Róheim, by training a psychoanalyst, who also carried out field research of anthropological type in Central Australia and Normanby island (near the Trobriands) and among the Yuma of California. Róheim made a special study of shamans or medicine-men, including their dreams. He was at pains to emphasize that most of these men whom he met were not neurotic; on the contrary they were healthy, capable hunters and leaders, whose symbolism might be conscious as well as unconscious. But their dreams revealed to Róheim's interpretation of their latent content some of the classic analytical elements. When a Ngatatara would-be medicine-man

* Freud used Le Bon's *Psychologie des Foules* (1895) as his source for identification of group mind with primitive, both characterized by lack of conflict in the presence of logical contradiction. He went on to equate this with aspects of unconscious mental life of individuals, including neurotics (Freud, 1965, 15).

begins by eating his totem, a yam, that is 'the oral introjection of the father'. Since the dream that followed was very like the conception dreams of women (in which the latent content was held to be coitus with the father), except that mouth was substituted for womb, 'we may therefore suspect a female attitude with regard to the father as latent in the mental make-up of the medicine man'. Similarly, Róheim saw the 'latent significance' of agriculture, in terms of Trobriand and Normanby island myth and magic, as being symbolic body destruction and restitution fantasies connected with the mother. He acknowledges that anthropologists will probably object very strongly to all this, saying *inter alia* that yams are cultivated because of their usefulness, and these are only the unconscious aspects of an economical, purposeful activity. But he sternly refutes such arguments, holding that all the occupations in the 'seemingly practical core of group-living' are more or less distorted or projected equivalents of the infantile situation (Róheim, 1971, 4–6, 69–76, 93, 127). Róheim's general conclusion, a modification of Freud's view, is that culture is really composed of psychic defence systems against anxiety, and that therefore specific cultures are structurally similar to specific neuroses (1971, 106). But while many anthropologists have not accepted the general propositions resulting from Róheim's filial piety, some have found his specific interpretation of symbols in their manifest field context as very suggestive.

In the inter-war period other anthropologists such as Kroeber, Sapir, Goldenweiser, Prince Peter of Greece and Jules Henry engaged with psychoanalysis, either as a personal experience or as an intellectual problem, to a marked degree, and some of their findings emerged in reflections upon symbolism. Others, such as Linton and Malinowski, were more guarded. In *The Study of Man* (1936), a work which effectively began in anthropology the fruitful study of status and role, Linton pointed to the widespread though not universal development of symbols in society, and mentioned the flag, the cross and the swastika as examples. He stressed the culturally-patterned character of symbols and their frequent lack of intrinsic importance. But he adopted a curiously limited viewpoint in holding that when we find in uncivilized societies symbolic meanings attached to animals, objects or natural phenomena we usually call them totems – ignoring a great range of religious and political symbols to which the totemic label was not attached (1936, 424–6). Linton stated specifically that he had not been impressed by the orthodox Freudian explanations of cultural data he had read in the period between his expeditions to the Marquesas and to Madagascar in the 1920s; he had adopted instead Abraham Kardiner's view of 'basic personality structure' as giving a focal point for social integration (1939, xviii). By implication then, Linton was mainly concerned with other aspects of psychological process than the symbolic.

Malinowski's reaction was of a different order. Intrigued intellectually by the complex arguments about mental process, in so many ways an advance in sophistication on the psychology of Wundt, and even of Shand, with which Malinowski was well acquainted, he was repelled by the naivety and grossness of some of the Freudian interpretation in the cultural field. Malinowski was convinced of the significance of unconscious factors in mental process; he also accepted the view that such factors came to overt expression in symbolic forms such as ritual and myth. But his concern for the empirical evidence, his belief in the importance of cultural conditioning, and his own theses about functional inter-relation of elements of culture made him question the universality of some of the cardinal themes of the Freudian argument. He held that the symbolic form in which the fundamental conflicts of family relationships would emerge must be directly correlated with the particular structure of family, itself an outgrowth of complex historical conditions. In his own previous work on the family among the Australian aborigines he had spent considerable analytical skill in disproving notions of indiscriminate or communal sharing of wives and in bringing out the significance of the forces of co-operation in marital and filial relations. His Trobriand fieldwork had reinforced these ideas. So in the Trobriand matrilineal descent system, with denial (he called it ignorance) of physiological paternity, and overt assumption of authority by mother's brother, he saw the fundamental struggle within the family as between mother's brother and sister's son, not between father and son, and incestuous longing not between son and mother but between brother and sister. He indicated that this came to overt expression in an appropriate type of myth. In *The Father in Primitive Psychology* and more extensively in *Sex and Repression in*

Savage Society (both published in 1927) Malinowski indicated his basic acceptance of the significance of the unconscious in the development of symbolism in myth. But he also argued stoutly for the relevance of social factors in the channelling of the expression of the unconscious. The exponents of psychoanalysis, led by Ernest Jones, rejected these arguments on the ground that the data Malinowski presented could be interpreted more simply as displaced versions of Oedipal material. Despite the authority of the mother's brother, it was the child's father that was sleeping with its mother, and therefore it was upon him that the male child's hostility would be primarily directed. Perhaps orthodox psychoanalysis could not have held otherwise. But it seems to me now, as it did during the controversy, that psychoanalysis lost an opportunity to explore in more subtle detail the relation between sexual (including genital) factors and social factors in a situation where admittedly the structure of family relationships was regarded as being fundamental to the development of the individual psyche, with all its symbolic expressions. But lacking such encouragement Malinowski dropped this particular line of symbolic interpretation which became linked with 'revisionist' argument in psychology.*

Edward Sapir's treatment of symbolism came from another angle. His interest in linguistics combined with his receptivity to Freudian theory and his own great sensitivity gave his views more penetration than those of most of his colleagues. In early papers and in his concise but suggestive review of the field in the *Encyclopedia of Social Sciences* (1934) he put forward views which have served many later anthropologists as a source of ideas. Taking a broad scope for that period Sapir argued that all culture is heavily charged with symbols, as is all personal behaviour. (He did not go so far as to hold that culture is a system of symbols.) Even comparatively simple forms of behaviour are far less directly functional than they seem to be (a protest against Malinowski's influence), but include symbolic elements. Even an elaborate, well-documented scientific theory may be little more than a symbol of the unknown necessities of the ego.

* A thoughtful account of Malinowski's debt to psychoanalysis is given by Meyer Fortes (1957) – though I think he overdoes the argument in maintaining that it was the notion of Oedipus complex that gave Malinowski inspiration for the main features of his kinship theory. See also the stimulating analysis by Anne Parsons, 1969, 3–63.

'Scientists fight for their theories not because they believe them to be true but because they wish them to be so,' he wrote with ironic exaggeration (1949, 566–7). Beginning with a discussion of problems of referential and expressive symbolism in language, he made an attempt to prove that there was an unconscious or intuitive logic which makes phonetic systems constellate. He pointed out that a symbol has two constant characteristics. It is always a substitute for some more closely intermediating type of behaviour, so all symbolism implies meanings which cannot be directly derived from the contexts of experience. It also expresses a condensation of energy, its actual significance being disproportionate to the apparent triviality of meaning suggested by its outward form. So Sapir distinguished two major types of symbols: referential symbols and condensation symbols. In referential symbols, a primary feature was their economy for purposes of reference – such as national flags, or indeed oral speech. Condensation symbols were equally economical, but their main feature was that they were substitute behaviour for direct expression, so allowing easy release of emotional tension in conscious or unconscious form, and diffusing this emotional quality to types of behaviour or situation seemingly far removed from the original meaning of the symbol. The distinction is rather crude, and deals basically with the difference recognized between the need to handle objects of the external world, and the need to handle the problems of the self. But the notion of condensation symbols having an unconscious spread of emotional quality, and of peculiar potency, even danger (with an obvious debt to Freud's theory of dreams) has clearly found continuity in the concept of condensed symbols used by Victor Turner and Mary Douglas.

Psychoanalysts with anthropological training seem to have found little difficulty in adapting Freudian views on symbolism to their needs (for example Bott, 1971). But for anthropologists looking to interpretations of symbols in terms of unconscious elements Freud's treatment has often seemed inadequate. In orthodox Freudian theory symbols are the product of unconscious repressed attitudes of identification, though modification of such views has been put forward (for example by Róheim). But Freud from his clinical standpoint tended to speak of symptoms rather than of symbols, and he was interested primarily in the 'symptom-formation' rather than in the character of the symbol and its object.* In a sense, since symbols were a product of repression, and Freud's aim was to relieve people as far as possible from the suffering of repression by leading them to understand its roots, he wished to free them from the tyranny of their symbols. In the history of depth psychology Carl Jung took up Freud's concepts and made a virtue out of necessity; he embraced symbolism. As Rieff has put it, Jung transposed the forms and figures of earlier systems of symbolism into psychology. So in the very symbols from which Freud wanted to free mankind, Jung saw the principle of man's salvation (Rieff, 1963, 17). Freud himself saw this inversion very clearly – and bitterly. In his *History of the Psychanalytical Movement* he discusses how the 'symbolism in the language of dreams' slowly became clear to him, and how Jung distorted the interpretation of dreams by representing them as means for producing attempted solutions of 'the life-task'. He objected strongly to what he saw as Jung's concept of 'symbolic' as equivalent to 'having no real existence', and to replacement of 'all that is disagreeable in the family complexes' by bland abstract ideas of a 'merely symbolic' order. Freud accused Jung of 'approximation to the demands of the multitude' and of creating a new religious-ethnical system, ignoring the sexual roots of the symbolic forms he studied (Freud, 1963, 53–4, 92–8). But he did not foresee how far in modern times Jung's views on symbolism would 'justly claim to be a liberation for youth' (Freud, 1963, 92). Indeed a considerable vogue for Jung in student circles, including anthropologists, would seem to be linked with a general search for reassurance in personal and social life rather than with a specific intellectual curiosity as such about symbolism and analytical procedures.

Jung's contributions to the study of symbolism have been manifold, stimulating, doctrinaire, sometimes portentous and obscure. His *Psychological Types*, with its notions of introversion and extraversion, was an important and analytically novel work in the 1930s for anthropologists, though there was much disagreement with it. Jung's 'analytical psychology' attempted to reach deep layers of the human mind by focusing less on logical formulation than on sym-

* For example Freud (1921) 1965, 17, 49, 95; cf. also his view of people's apparently purposeless, chance acts as 'symptomatic actions' (1914) 1963, 117.

bol, and by regarding the latter as the product of a range of relatively impersonal factors, not of personal family relations in the Freudian manner. For Jung the symbol was always extremely complex, neither rational nor irrational but with one side that accords with reason and another that is inaccessible to reason; stimulating sensation as well as thought. In the creator of a new symbolism the highest mental achievement is demanded as well as the lowest and most primitive motions of the psyche. Jung was prepared to admit consciously-designed material as symbolic – even a scientific theory – but he focused on the referent of the symbol as being relatively (or at times, he said, essentially) unknown. A symbol for Jung was the best way of expressing a thing, the nature of which is withheld from present knowledge. So for him the Cross as a representation of Divine Love is not a symbol but semiotic (meaningful directly), because Divine Love is an apt description of the fact; whereas that description of the Cross is symbolic which puts it above all imaginable explanations, regarding it as an expression of an unknown and as yet incomprehensible fact of a mystical or transcendent character (1926, 601–10). Important in such a scheme is the well-known notion of the archetype – a symbolic image of great power, part of the psychic content that has not yet undergone conscious treatment, but which can emerge from the unconscious with dynamic force, and be used as part of the redemptive process which the mind fashions for itself when the proper conditions are present. The archetypes are the content of the collective unconscious, and as such are universal, not individual in character. Jung has argued: 'a symbol is not an arbitrary or intentional sign standing for a known and conceivable fact, but an admittedly anthropomorphic – hence limited and only partly valid – expression for something suprahuman and only partly conceivable' (1958, 152). Such a characterization of symbol can appeal to those of a religious or mystical turn of mind, as Freud saw, and it has drawn criticism from those psychologists who feel safer with a personal unconscious than a collective unconscious. As J. A. C. Brown has put it, they regard it as 'certainly unorthodox in science to describe the partly known in terms of the wholly unknown' (1961, 44–5). But Jung's influence has grown nevertheless.

One of the earliest anthropologists to be influenced by Jung was

John Layard, who worked closely with Jung in Zürich. Layard previously had done field research on Atchin and Vao, two small islands of Malekula in the New Hebrides, in 1914–15, under the stimulus of W. H. R. Rivers; he had made an elaborate study of the ritual of the local graded societies, in which he saw evidence of the spread of megalithic culture, probably from Egypt. He interpreted intricate sand drawings as labyrinth designs, and re-birth symbols, from this point of view. But he also made some interesting observations on the symbolism of the rites, pointing out how height was symbol of aspiration, both social and spiritual, and was often associated with light, of sun and stars as male representatives. One of the major symbolic figures in the rites was the hawk, also a symbol of aspiration. Men imitated the fluttering of hawks on critical occasions, hawks' feathers were used as symbols of rank, and giant hawk banners were set up in the form of kites (1942, 732, 734). Layard's opinion that these rites were comparable with the 'mysteries' of classical antiquity, and of the Christian church, links this study with earlier analyses by Jane Harrison and other Cambridge scholars. But Layard's practice as an 'analytical psychologist' led him further in the study of symbolism along Jungian lines. In *The Lady of the Hare: Being a Study in the Healing Power of Dreams* (1944) he examined a series of dreams of a patient, regarding them from a therapeutic point of view as positive achievements. Having discovered in one the critical sacrificial role of the hare, he then engaged in a comparative scrutiny of data on the symbolic (archetypal) role of the hare in China, Africa, etc. With the hare as the major example, Layard's conclusion was that the dream-mind is a storehouse of ancient symbolic wisdom, unsuspected by the most learned scholars of our time, and also quite unknown to the dreamer (1944, 101). This is a generalization directly in keeping with Jung's views, some aspects of which will be raised further in the next chapter.

INTEREST IN SYMBOLIC FUNCTION AND PROCESS

As overt interest in symbolism developed in anthropology more attention began to be devoted to two themes: the nature of the symbolization process, and its relation to non-symbolical thought;

and the functions performed by symbols with particular reference to individual expressiveness and social requirements.

Study of how symbols function in society was tackled in breezy fashion by R. R. Marett, whose contributions seem somewhat undervalued nowadays.* Marett operated with symbolism from a distance, his field observations having been minimal. Enjoying the Oxford anthropological scene between the wars, Marett had a scholarly and ingenious mind, though rather unfocused and over-given to imagery. ('Surf-riding on metaphors' has been my own image for some of his argument.) Marett had become known for his concept of animatism, or pre-animist religion, in which man was concerned with his relation to impersonal forces; this was a supplement or counter to Tylor's definition of religion in minimum terms as belief in spiritual beings. Marett was also well acquainted with the work of Durkheim and others of the school of *L'Année sociologique*, as well as with that of Lévy-Bruhl. But his own interests developed in a more pragmatic way. He concentrated on the view of religion as a kind of simple action-system, and on a major function of symbolism as a means of action for coping with superhuman forces. 'Symbolism, in a word, is in its essential function a spiritual lightning conductor . . . it does some primitive community stricken with smallpox a world of good to carry out an image of the disease-demon and douse it in the nearest stream' (1935, 90). Or again, a symbol allows for substitute action, as against death. 'So long as the ritual of custom is enacted with dramatic thoroughness, the will is taken for the deed, and passion exhausts itself on the symbol' (1935, 188). Sceptical but dynamic; grounded in introspective common sense rather than in concrete observation, his ideas helped to carry forward the concept of the pragmatic value of the symbolic process, though they soon lost momentum through lack of empirical analysis. That symbols may be used with cathartic effect, however, is a notion which emerges in various ways in much subsequent work.

* Another writer often neglected, but whose merits have recently been brought out by Rodney Needham, is A. M. Hocart. But his observations on symbolism were more closely allied to the traditional comparative type of study than to the developing social anthropology. Hocart wrote of the symbolism of settlements, and of 'idols', and of symbolic action in ritual, such as the role of the herald. His observations were pertinent, but obscured for social theory by his commitment to quasi-historical explanations (1970 (1936)).

Other contributions about the same period emphasized the emotional component of symbolic expression. Robert Lowie, in a chapter on association of ideas in his study of primitive religion (1936), discussed how colour may come to acquire a symbolic value, in a manner reminiscent of Radcliffe-Brown's concept of sensory metaphors. (He cited Radcliffe-Brown's remarks about the colour red, in the Andamanese context, but warned against a simplicist interpretation.) Lowie referred to the 'invaluable indivisible emotional experience' which makes a religious symbol intelligible. Yet though he asserted the unanalysable nature of the symbolic experience he dismissed the notion of a pre-logical mentality with which some writers, notably Lévy-Bruhl, had linked it. But Lévy-Bruhl himself, after various works on primitive mentality and the soul of the primitive had established his position, published in 1938 another work directed especially to problems of symbolism. In it he reiterated his assertion of a primitive type of mind – which he withdrew soon after, in his (posthumous) *Carnets* (1949). For the primitive, Lévy-Bruhl argued, the difference between experience and belief, so sharp for us, becomes almost imperceptible. The primitive spirit can seek to apprehend this reality, at once visible and invisible, only through symbols (1938, 170). 'Prefiguration' of the results of desire, and magical formulae, are forms of symbolic action by which the primitive translates and attains his object. Is it surprising that in the eyes of the primitive the symbolic actions have the virtue of making real what they prefigure? (1938, 294–5). This thesis accounted for the intimate link between belief in the validity of mystical experience and confidence in the efficacy of symbolic actions. But the criticism which it drew was widespread, and I add only a few comments. First, in some respects the thesis was a highly literary product; it was very much the view of a European intellectual writing in vivid prose about the ideas of people whom he had never seen – they were essentially his ideas of how the minds of 'primitives' worked. His assertions about their mode of mental functioning had therefore for many field anthropologists an air of unreality – one was reminded of Ezra Pound's reported comment on James Joyce's *Ulysses* – 'the book is all language'. Secondly, the theory was really a statement about a general mode of human thought, not about the minds of a cultural sector of mankind. As Lévy-Bruhl himself came to realize towards the end (and as some anthropologists had tried to tell him all along) what is valid in his thesis can apply to civilized as well as to primitive man. The dividing-line between logical and pre-logical (non-logical in the sense of uncritical) thinking is to be looked for, not between civilized and primitive men, but between different kinds of conditions and wants to which thought is applied. To define these conditions and wants, not an easy task, is part of the anthropological problem. A third point is that the degree of acceptance of Lévy-Bruhl's propositions has seemed to be to some extent a reflection of the particular metaphysical position of the various anthropologists involved – they appear in another guise in formulations of the 'anthropology of experience' which stresses personal involvement in situations being described or analysed. Finally, what I think Lévy-Bruhl helped to do, even if in a somewhat oblique way, was to focus the attention of anthropologists on the significance of symbolic thinking and symbolic behaviour more forcefully than before. Hence, it would seem, the support which Evans-Pritchard has tended to give to Lévy-Bruhl's views in his examination of theories of primitive religion (1965, 78–92).

The period of the 1930s saw publication of the first substantial results from the fieldwork of the generation of social anthropologists who, coming after Malinowski, had gained much from his technique. Though they wrote little in the specific idiom of symbolism they had a lively interest in problems of symbolic behaviour.

Functions of symbolic behaviour in specific social conditions were demonstrated, for instance, with great penetration by two anthropologists working in very different fields and with different backgrounds: Edward Evans-Pritchard, an Oxford historian who had his anthropological training in London under Seligman, and Gregory Bateson, a Cambridge zoologist trained in anthropology under Haddon. Both owed much to Malinowski (Bateson in particular acknowledged this, in his foreword to *Naven*) but each developed an individual approach. In early studies both exemplified the significance of symbols as paradox. Evans-Pritchard's study of witchcraft (1937) showed how the incidence of natural forces impacting upon individuals in Zande society was translated into symbols of personal attack, believed to operate at an invisible level, with a logic intelligible to ordinary human understanding, once the premises were granted. This study has provided a starting-point for many subsequent studies of witchcraft and allied phenomena. Bateson's study of ritualized relations between mother's brother and sister's son among the Iatmül of the Sepik River in New Guinea (1936) was analytically much more complex, and its value took longer to be appreciated. But it embodied a great deal of material on the symbolism of role reversal, with an involved theoretical disquisition on this and cognate subjects. Neither author paid much attention to problems of symbolism in specific terms. Evans-Pritchard assumed a sufficient framework of ideas about the subject for his purpose; Bateson, while taking less for granted, was preoccupied by the explanation of symbolic behaviour in terms of symmetrical or asymmetrical (complementary) pattern of social relationships. Bateson referred in passing to symbols of obvious sexual type – fishtrap and eel as symbols of vulva and penis – and to symbols which he thought could be so interpreted – when a great man dies, a figure is set up to represent him decorated with spears to the number of people he has killed and baskets to the number of wives he has had, these being symbols of his achievement. But Bateson then clearly regarded the 'fascinations of symbol analysis' as a 'pitfall' distracting him from his major aim of constructing a theoretical framework for the explanation of the whole of Iatmül social phenomena. In his epilogue of 1958 he pointed out that *Naven* was written 'almost without benefit of Freud' and that he had ignored some very obvious examples of sexual symbolism in the rites he had been studying (1958, 282–3). But in another field, that of mental disorder, Bateson's later studies of symbolism have been of cardinal importance.

Explicit concern with symbols, in continuity of the Durkheimian tradition in anthropology, was indicated by Fortes and Evans-Pritchard in their basic introduction to the essays on *African Political Systems* (1940), a work which has had a deservedly marked influence on developments in political anthropology. They laid great emphasis on the importance to African society of common interest in symbols. They held that attachment to these symbols, more than anything else, gave to African society its cohesion and persistence. They argued that in the form of myths, fictions, dogmas, ritual sacred places and persons these symbols represented the unity and exclusiveness of the groups which respected them. But, said Fortes and Evans-Pritchard, such things are regarded not as mere symbols but as final values in themselves. To explain them sociologically, such symbols must be translated into terms of social function and the social structure which they serve to maintain. Africans have no 'objective knowledge' of the forces involved – indeed it might well be that if they did understand the 'objective meaning' of the symbols these would lose their power. The power of the symbols lies in their symbolic content and in their association with the nodal institutions of the social structure, such as the kingship (1940, 17–18).

In the light of present views it would be easy to criticize this presentation. There was no definition of what was meant by symbols. So the inclusion of dogmas as well as myths could blur demarcation lines. The reference to 'fictions' – which recalls McLennan and Jeremy Bentham – is also unclear, though presumably it means such items as fabricated genealogies. There seems to be tautology in saying that the power of symbols lies in their 'symbolic content'. And if these myths, dogmas, sacred places and persons are not regarded by Africans as 'mere symbols' but as 'final values', what precisely is their 'objective meaning' which Africans do not understand? What is the evidence that they do not understand that attachment to their symbols serves to support the structure of their society?

But I think a more positive attitude is justified. Fortes and Evans-Pritchard give no bibliographic references for their statements about symbolism, but one does not suppose they invented all these ideas afresh – in fact, debts to Durkheim, Radcliffe-Brown and Malinowski seem clear, and Fortes (1936) had already written on ritual symbolism of political structure. What the authors did was, in a necessarily compressed statement, to affirm a series of general propositions about the character and functions of symbols in a way which specifically enmeshed them very closely with one particular aspect of institutions in society, the political. They offered symbols as a starting-point, particularly in this relatively unexplored field of political structure and organization, for further investigation. But they also re-opened some dilemmas – notably that of ascertaining where the 'objective meaning' of symbols does lie. Can the observer maintain his patronizing claim to more subtle understanding than the symbol-user? Can the symbol-user be fully aware of the sign-function of what he is using and still treat it as a 'final value', or must his awareness of symbolic function destroy his faith and his capacity for action? It is towards such problems of a dynamic kind that some modern trends of anthropological interest have turned.

Over more than a century then, the study of symbols, by pre-, proto- and proper anthropologists had developed greatly: from descriptive to theoretical treatment; from empirical to abstract definition; from elucidation by comparative similarity to that by scrutiny of the social context; from interpretation in terms of individual symbols to that in terms of symbol-system. Basic questions had been raised – about quality of relationship of symbol to referent; about the validity of distinction between sign and symbol; about the relative significance of intellectual and emotional elements in symbol recognition; and of cognitive and expressive features of symbolic activity. The contribution of other disciplines had made itself felt, notably of art, philosophy, psychology and sociology. Even if what had been taken from each by anthropologists had been fragmentary, enough of a framework had been erected to allow of more searching inquiries into symbolism on an institutional basis.

Chapter 5

MODERN ANTHROPOLOGICAL VIEWS OF SYMBOLIC PROCESS

Is modern social anthropology engaged in a retreat from empirical reality? We are concerned with 'deep structure' rather than with content; with models rather than with behaviour; with symbols rather than with customs. Leaving aside the question of how far this is a reaction to fundamental changes in the degree to which men feel they can control their social environment, I think at least three elements can be identified in this anthropological focus. There is a search for abstraction as a heuristic device, to eliminate idiosyncratic variation and perceive general principles more easily. There is the recognition of observer-effect, by which what purports to be a record of fact is admitted to be a record of opinion, or at least to incorporate some quantum of personal interpretation. There is also a challenge to positivism, whereby from a relatively neutral position of criticism or from some specific commitment the autonomy, even priority, of the non-empirical is insisted upon. In all this the language of symbolism, and inquiry into the nature of symbolism, have come to the forefront.

A SYMBOLIC IDIOM

What I call the symbolic idiom is widespread in post-war anthropology. In 1949, as an appropriate tribute to the author of works on primitive symbolism, Maurice Leenhardt wrote of the posthumously published notebooks of Lévy-Bruhl that 'their simple appearance and richness of content might stand as a very modest symbol of the philosopher's personality' (*Carnets*, Preface, v). At the other end of the scale of social complexity, Claude Lévi-Strauss, in his Introduction to the work of Marcel Mauss, gave a clue to much subsequent development in the passage beginning: 'All culture can be considered as an ensemble of symbolic systems in the first rank of which are placed language, matrimonial rules, economic relationships, art, science, religion. . . .' (1950, xix). In the first Malinowski Memorial Lecture, warningly entitled 'Rethinking Anthropology', Edmund Leach propounded the heresy – as he termed it – that the organizational ideas present in a society should be thought of as a set of mathematical patterns; that there is a fundamental opposition ideologically between relations of incorporation and of alliance in kinship and marriage groupings; and that relations of incorporation are distinguished symbolically as those of common substance while those of alliance are viewed as mystical or metaphysical influence (1961a, 9, 10, 21). In an analysis of the nature of kinship in American society David Schneider begins with the hypothesis that sexual intercourse is the symbol in terms of which the family members are defined and differentiated, and grounds this view on the assumption that American kinship as a cultural system is a system of symbols (1968, 1, 31). More summarily – just for illustration – Ronald Berndt, Mary Douglas and Terence Turner have examined aspects of the symbolism of the human body; Nur Yalman has studied the symbolism of food and the symbolic equation of eating and sex in caste relations in Ceylon. Victor Turner has written of the 'forest of symbols' in Ndembu ritual; Hortense Powdermaker looked at symbolic meanings in the Hollywood 'dream factory' of the cinema and in world views of American college youth; Leslie Hiatt has given an analysis of literary symbolism in Nabokov's *Lolita*, which he calls 'a "Freudian" cryptic crossword'.

In all this, symbolic representation has attained an identity and a dignity lacking before. Symbols have become important, not for what they represent, but for what they themselves are thought to express and communicate. They have come to be regarded not as surrogates or evasions of reality, but as a kind of higher form of reality. Some partisan interests have been involved in this trend, but the general mood has been to give symbolism a distinct place in anthropological study.

As a result, certain basic questions have been sharpened. In the range of anthropological materials, where does one look for symbolic forms? How does one recognize symbols, by what criteria of identification? What is the meaning of symbols, in relation to that which they symbolize, and in relation to one another? What is the nature of the symbolizing process as a mode of thinking? And what is the relevance, and the effectiveness, of symbolic behaviour in relation to general behaviour at the individual and the social level? To some extent answers to these questions tend to overlap in the literature, so I begin with some of the earlier statements.

RECOGNITION OF SYMBOLIC FORMS

Modern social anthropology has been characterized by a much more explicit recognition than formerly of the symbolic nature or the symbolic qualities of the phenomena studied. A keynote for a period was struck by Edmund Leach in his crisp expression that in his view ritual action and belief were alike to be understood as forms of symbolic statement about the social order (1954, 14). Ritual in its cultural context is a pattern of symbols, to be matched with another pattern of symbols operated as technical terms by the anthropologist; their common structure refers to the system of socially-approved relations between individuals and groups in the community under study. What ritual performances do is to recall and present in symbol form the underlying order that is supposed to guide the members of the community, in their social activities.

Some of the groundwork for such statements can be found in earlier views. George Homans, in *The Human Group*, a work which used much anthropological material and had considerable influence upon anthropologists of the immediate post-war period, pointed out as Sapir had done, that a great deal of behaviour in the 'internal system' of groups, that is in the expression of the sentiments of group members towards one another, is symbolic. But – for technical brevity, he said – he used the terms symbol and symbolic only for physical objects, spatial relationships and verbal behaviour; he did not apply them to 'ongoing behaviour'. So, in such terms, a gift is a symbol of friendship, but the actual process of making the gift is an expression of the friendship (1950, 137). For most anthropologists, however, an *act* of giving, in its formality, its deprecatory signs, its status consciousness, represents a complex set of social positions in manner which can fairly be called symbolic.

Already Meyer Fortes, in an elaborate structural study which was analytically very productive, had given his conception of social symbols (as exemplified in Tallensi totemism) in terms of material objects set in a complex formation *together* with their associated beliefs, attitudes and conventional actions. To this notion of symbol Fortes attached other criteria: that it had no self-evident utilitarian or logical significance to the observer or even to its users; that it carried a strong emotional charge and had the value of a direct moral imperative; and that its meaning could be inferred from the attitudes and actions of the symbol users (1945, 136). Certain animals were endowed with ritual significance, were symbols of ancestors and so of the moral relations of men in their local connection with the tracts of ground with which the ancestors had been associated. By tying together discrete principles of descent and locality, such ritual symbols also tended to emphasize the functional differentiation of social groups. 'Totemic and other ritual symbols are the ideological landmarks that keep the individual on his course (1945, 69, 142–4).*

My own treatment of the symbolic significance of ritual and belief was of the same general order, though less pointed. From rather casual reference to symbols in pre-war writing (for example Maori heirlooms as material symbols of exchange of goodwill (1929, 346); Tikopia kin terms, even hair circlets, as symbols for behaviour (1936, 184, 271); Tikopia ritual acts as symbols for social rules (1940, 19)) I had given more systematic general consideration to symbols in *Elements of Social Organization* (1951). As well as referring to symbolism in art, money, name change, dreams, funerary practices, millenary movements, I defined ritual as 'primarily symbolic in character'. I designated religion as a symbolic system, exemplifying this by an analysis of a Tikopia communion feast of worship – a kind of primitive Eucharist, a 'willing offering'. In general, I saw symbolism as having two major connotations. In a broad sense, symbols may be said to occur when some components of the mind's experience elicit activity and values ordinarily associated with other components of experience. Not an original viewpoint, this did present a criterion of cardinal importance for the definition, that of mental experience. Almost all language and art is symbolic in this sense. In a narrower sense, symbols are objects or actions that repre-

* Lévi-Strauss (1962, 105–12) gave qualified approval to this interpretation but put Tallensi totemic symbolism, together with that of Tikopia, on a much more general plane. For comment on his view see Fortes, 1966, 9–14, Firth, 1970b, 280–94.

sent other entities in virtue of some arbitrarily-assigned conceptual relation between them (1951a, 176). Note that this definition, unlike that of Homans but like that of Fortes, included 'actions' as possible symbols. Note too that the 'arbitrariness' of assignment of symbolic quality, a feature recognized by many writers on symbolism from at least Peirce onwards, was not claimed as an absolute or random relation, but was seen as arising from a lack of shared experience by the observer or interpreter. The job of an anthropologist studying symbolic behaviour is to attempt to replicate the relevant experience, or indirectly to gain an understanding of it.

One of the most powerful and scholarly thinkers of that period, S. F. Nadel, was more interested in problems of symbolic behaviour. In his study of the Nupe kingdom (1942) he had discussed symbols of class distinction, pointing out how turbans, swords, gestures of greeting, gifts, even language and music, were used to mark position on the social scale. (He noted too how Nupe had 'kept abreast of the times'; a novel symbol of status was an 'alarum clock' in a little wooden case, which body-servants of men of rank carried after their masters! (1942, 128–30).) Nadel's concern for symbols was very largely because of what he regarded as their 'diacritical' role in culture – demonstrating the differential position of individuals in the group and so the range of social tasks consequent upon that position. In his general study *The Foundations of Social Anthropology* (1951) he explored this role quite deeply. His viewpoint, though expressed in abstract terms, was robustly pragmatic. Following primarily John Dewey and Charles Morris and in line with a common distinction, he used 'sign' for a representation having an 'intrinsic', a 'natural' connection with the thing it signified, while the representative capacity of a symbol is 'artificial, valid only under prescribed conditions, and determined by rules of usage' (1951, 67n). He did admit certain symbols as being more 'natural' than others (see above, p. 59) but he saw them all as being employed by individuals in accordance with the cultural canon, their meaning being decided by existing cultural norms. For Nadel then as for other anthropologists, the arbitrariness of what he termed 'artificial' symbols was only relative and temporary; the correspondence of symbol to object lay not in a single reduplication of event or situation but in the systematic arrangement and rules of usage in regard to its position in a set of symbols. Although fully capable of adopting a 'mentalistic' outlook – as the last part of his book, on 'psychological explanations', including 'mental energy', demonstrates – he sturdily argued that the logical consistency of a symbolism does not preclude the intervention also of a purposive and utilitarian nexus (1951, 263). He was concerned with behaviour, and he was concerned with communication. An idea not communicated, he argued, is beyond examination; once it is communicated, by means of some comprehensive sign or symbol, it provokes action. Nadel was not a behaviourist in the technical sense, but he was much impressed by questions of evidence. 'Accepting consciousness behind behaviour is one thing, identifying its operations, another. Here the anthropologist's position is precarious. He is not of the group which he studies; he observes individuals whose motivations, thoughts and feelings may differ widely from those which are to him habitual and self-evident . . . the sentiments, thoughts, and other motives behind behaviour are accessible only within set limits' (1951, 64, 71). He set those limits wide, admitting in his study of incest in the Nuba mountains an approach to consciousness through incest dreams. When therefore Nadel stated that in his view 'uncomprehended symbols' (of an unconscious nature) have no part in social inquiry; if they indicate nothing to the actors they are from an anthropological point of view irrelevant and indeed no longer symbols (1954, 108), he was stressing not the impropriety but the difficulty of their interpretation. I think he made his statement too strong. But in fact he qualified it immediately by distinguishing between 'strict (and comprehended) symbolism' and 'ceremonials' which 'point beyond themselves' in a manner analogous to signs or symbols, expressing implicitly support for principles of social structure or social ideals, or compensatory mechanisms to social control (1954, 110–13), and which it is legitimate for the anthropologist to interpret.* Nadel's exclusion of 'uncomprehended symbols' from the purview of the anthropologist has often been quoted, and criticized. But his qualifications tend to be omitted. Victor Turner argues with strength that a social anthropologist can justify his claim to be able to interpret a society's ritual symbols more deeply and comprehensively than the actors themselves, by being more detached and by having

* A somewhat similar point was made by Evans-Pritchard, 1956, 232–3.

studied the inter-relationships in the society concerned in a structural manner (1967, 26–7). Such a statement, with which I agree, is I think in line with Nadel's attitude towards 'border zones of symbolism in ritual', where the interpretation is established by perception of a relevant parallelism between the form of ritual and the norms governing social relationship (1954, 110).

THE PROBLEM OF IDENTITY

So far I have shown how in recent work in social anthropology symbols have been sought and recognized, especially in the ritual field. But it is clear that even at that stage there were problems of identification. Granted that some kind of representation of an oblique, culturally determined kind was occurring, just where was it to be identified; what kind of isolate could be made? Answers of a rather different kind from those already indicated were given by anthropologists who focused less on the behavioural or action side of the phenomenon and more on the mental, cognitive side. In an exploration of Nuer ideas Evans-Pritchard considered problems of symbols from this angle. In his investigation of what he called 'a relation of Spirit to persons through things' he was much concerned that it should be realized that in many of the Nuer symbolic equations there was an implicit third term. So, in the equation of a cucumber with an ox, or of a twin with a bird, the relation is not conceived of by Nuer as a material one, but is an ideal equivalence, conceived of in relation to God. Broadly, such inferences about Nuer modes of thought, based upon Nuer exegesis, were borne out by observation of Nuer behaviour – though as I have pointed out (Firth, 1966a) this behaviour was not always consistent with their ideal norms. The problem of Nuer religious symbolism was pursued by Evans-Pritchard in terms of a scholastic analysis of the word 'is' in expressions of the order of 'rain is God' and 'a crocodile is Spirit', distinguishing an elliptical statement about manifestation from a symbolic statement about representation.* Evans-Pritchard rejected Lévy-Bruhl's view that a primitive assertion of a symbolic relation-

* The discussion is reminiscent of A. J. Ayer's examination of the problem of ambiguous symbols, also using 'is', involving existence, or class-membership, or identity, or entailment (1946, 62–3).

ship implied a prelogical thinking in terms of mystic participation. His own view was that the problem was one common to all religious thought – that a religious symbol has always an intimate association with what it represents; *that* which brings to the mind with *what* it brings to the mind (1956, 134, 140–2).

An opinion of somewhat the same kind was advanced about the same time quite independently by Dorothy Lee. Evans-Pritchard's formulations may have been clarified philosophically by Dorothy Emmett as he suggests (1956, ix), but Dorothy Lee's inquiries into the behaviour of the self in relation to the cultural codification of experienced reality had other philosophical roots. Yet in her comments on symbolization and value (1959, from 1954) she too emphasizes the notion of what one may call the integrative identity of symbol and thing symbolized. Intellectually, several elements may be combined in this approach, though she might not acknowledge their direct relation: 'field' theory; Lévy-Bruhl's theory of participation; and Whorf's view of the influence of language upon perception. Lee has argued that a symbol is part of a whole, a component of a field which also contains the so-called *thing*, as well as the process of symbolizing, and the apprehending individual. A symbol, she holds, is not a thing but rather a point in a creative process of symbolization, whereby the physical reality is transformed into the *thing*, the experienced reality. The symbol conveys the meaning of the situation in which it participates, and has no existence and no meaning apart from this situation. And language is an important system of symbols through which the individual transforms physical reality into experienced reality. So giving something a name gives it recognition and status in the categories of experienced reality (1959, 79, 80, 83).

In some respects this seems quite plausible. Much general discussion of symbolism has held that the relation between symbol and referent is conceptual – the association between them is a mental one. As Fortes has emphasized, the approach has been an 'actor-centred' (or as I would prefer 'actor-oriented') one, concerned with the meaning of symbols from what can be inferred as to the participant's standpoint. I concur in such a formulation as 'true symbols ... acquire valid existence and value only through participation in meaningful situations' (Lee, 1959, 88). But while Dorothy Lee's more trenchant holistic approach is persuasive, I think it needs some reservations. When I was once talking to some Tikopia about seabirds, and asked about their names for the larger ocean-going petrels, they replied: 'They have names, but we don't know them.' Here surely was the idea of name and object being inseparable, of the name attached to or conjoined with the bird floating out somewhere over the ocean. Yet three conceptual elements were involved: birds; names; we knowing, and these could be separately handled. Even though their specific names were not known (thus, it was implied the birds had such names independent of the knower) the birds could be spoken of and described; moreover, even without specific or general names they could be observed, taken captive if they came ashore, etc. – they had separate recognition and status in the categories of experienced reality. As symbols, bird-names could be conceptually integrated with or conceptually separated from the objects to which they were attributed. The strength of Lee's argument seems to me to lie in the emphasis she puts upon the significance of contextualization, upon the meaning of a symbol not being simply a matter of arbitrary assignment but as arising from its use in concrete situations, in which it has participated and which it has helped to create (1959, 79).

But an idealistic view of symbols must take care not to be disingenuous. Clearly, any statement of the order of '*the* bear' or '*the* crocodile' is a symbol of such-and-such a clan must be referring not just to a material object but to a type or species, that is, to an idea. But it is not *just* an idea that is involved; this has an empirical correlate of some sort. Fortes makes this point in comment on Evans-Pritchard's argument that since a Nuer may rarely if ever see his totem, 'it is no longer a question of a material object symbolizing an idea but of one idea symbolizing another' (1956, 135). As Fortes puts it, without some objective extra-personal reference it would be impossible for such an observance to be held in common by a number of people (1966b, 13).*

MEANING OF SYMBOLS FOR SOCIAL RELATIONS

The recognition of symbolism, and inquiries into the meaning of

* Even unicorns, which Evans-Pritchard cited in proof of his argument, as having never existed, do in fact have an elaborate material base in literature and pictorial art, as well as a putative referent in narwhal and rhinoceros (see T. H. White, 1960, 43–4).

symbols, have been forced upon social anthropologists working in the field (for example, Firth, 1951, 24–6). For the most part they have been content to accept the representative quality of objects and actions, taking as indices the information they acquired about associations with other objects and actions and emotional involvement of the actors, without pursuing questions of symbolic identity very far. In the Australian aboriginal field, for instance, bull-roarer and other sacred objects, clan patterns carved on trees around an initiation ground, stones said to be transformed heroes, Wondjina painted figures on rock walls (for example, Elkin, 1954, 176, 219) could be clearly classed as symbols. At the same time these material things, used in systematic elaborate behavioural sequences, were important means of portraying, implementing and even changing social relationships.

Nadel (1951, 262) indicated three main forms of symbolic behaviour which though not at all exhaustive, can introduce a discussion. The first he cited were emblems, badges and other 'diacritical' signs; whether material objects or gestures or other behaviour, their display indicates group membership or other social relationship and provides expectations for corresponding 'real' behaviour. The second category of symbolic behaviour mentioned was all forms of social nomenclature, including, for example, classificatory kinship terminology; from the use of these too, expectations as to other conforming behaviour are derived. Nadel's third category of symbolic behaviour was the 'dramatizations' pervading primitive cultures, instanced by the initiation rites of Van Gennep's classical analysis. Nadel was concerned with a wider problem – the nature of explanation in anthropology – which is not of immediate relevance to us here. But he made two points of direct significance to the interpretation of symbolic behaviour: that symbolic patterns may vary in consistency, both internally and in their relation to the scheme of social relationships; and that for interpretative purposes the observer is justified in going beyond the actor's conception of the given nexus, provided he can perceive a rational relation between the modes of action (1951, 263–6).

I will expand a little on the last point. In the interpretation of symbolic acts one may have direct contextualization – such linkage with other actions, verbal and non-verbal, that meaning emerges from the set of operations in concert – or parallelism – whereby elements separated in time and space and belonging to different concerted sets may be brought together in the same frame of semantic operations. Take the Tikopia example of anointing the temple post (see Chap. 1, p. 26). The meaning of the symbolic act of rubbing the post with a bunch of aromatic leaves is given partly by the immediate context – the chief as officiant, his fresh clothing and decorations, the formula he recited for welfare, etc. But it is also given in part from comparison with parallel operations elsewhere – washing of sacred stones, bathing of people, use of oil and fragrant leaves in dancing. Some linguistic bridge may be obtainable – the Tikopia term for anointing the post (the same for anointing a canoe) is linked etymologically with that for swimming, and equated also with oiling. But even when there is no linguistic bridge or overt explanation, collateral evidence can be derived from common experience of ritual occasions. Watching the care, even fear, with which people go about their formal procedures, conforming oneself to signs of warning or approval, and seeing other people act predictably in accord with one's expectations, all help to indicate that one is participating in acts of symbolic quality, with meaning for the social group. What meaning? Politically and economically, the rite drew together representatives of the constituent lineages of the clan in orientation towards their chief; it set a positive stamp upon solidarity. But why anoint the central post of the temple? Architectural observation could show that only major clan temples had such a centre-post, so reinforcing the supportive interpretation. In such external behavioural terms, the anthropologist can go a long way in his attribution of meaning. What he could not do without more specific explanation from the people themselves was to understand that rubbing the post with aromatic leaves and oil was not like painting a door – a touch of adornment to a temple to give pleasure to a god – but was believed to be adorning a material representation of the god himself. The post was not an anthropomorphic image – the Tikopia did not believe their god looked like a baulk of timber. Although they called it by a word translatable as 'body', it was the god's symbol, the concrete object to which they could direct physical actions of worship which the god himself could observe in spiritual invisible form from elsewhere. All this was given added meaning when considered in context of a long complex cycle of observed ritual performances, with much explanation from participants and other members of the society, which in itself threw light on social as well as religious matters. From such data I as analyst was able to perceive an order in the pagan Tikopia religious symbolism, and to assign it meaning in the Tikopia system of social relations. But some of this meaning was definitely inferential. I described an initial rite of burning through a stick of firewood in the middle so that it fell in two halves, as 'a symbolic act of parting, of separating the sacred from the profane period'. But I pointed out that I could get no definite Tikopia statement of this general interpretation; I had to infer it from other Tikopia statements and the general context of behaviour, in which the response to the rite was to stop all dancing and cast an aura of sobriety over the whole land (1967a, 49–52).

So, in assigning meaning in social terms to symbolic behaviour an anthropologist is usually not concerned with 'proof' in a definitive sense, but with degrees of plausibility of inference. General categorizations of rites as expressive, communicative, supportive, manipulative, etc., in the symbolization of social relations, are normally inferential to a considerable degree.

SYMBOLISM OF RITUAL

Ritual is a symbolic mode of communication, of 'saying something' in a formal way, not to be said in ordinary language or informal behaviour. This idea of 'not to be said' in an ordinary way means that a special character of ritual is its reserve, its apartness, its 'sacred' quality.* Its 'grammar' is different from that of ordinary language. *What* is said in ritual may refer to individual, personal states and actions, but on the whole tends to refer to social states and interpersonal relations.† This kind of statement may represent several elements in a situation. The symbolic behaviour of ritual may indicate a 'shortfall' in verbal statement – expressions of interest,

* The 'sacred' in my view is not a necessary criterion in the definition of ritual, but rather a quality created as a protective device for rituals which on other grounds are regarded as of prime importance. There can be secular rituals, as there can be secular symbols, rituals varying in the degree of their sacredness. (This is an alternative concept to retention of 'ceremony', which has tended to disappear as a technical term of weight in anthropology.)

† For valuable brief discussion of these issues see Beattie, 1966, 66–8.

respect, anxiety, desire which are put into ritual form because they are thought not to be capable of expression in other form. But ritual may also be regarded as a symbolic understatement of the 'real' situation, going so far as the human officiant can go in terms of his capacity, but recognized as inadequate, a kind of 'token communication'. It may also be seen as a kind of symbolic disguise (see Fortes, 1966a, 409–22), a statement which alludes indirectly to 'reality' not by exposing it but by evading it or representing it as other than it is. Or again, the symbol idiom of ritual may allow statements to be made in terms less brusque, more protracted, more tempered by involvement with other acts, than in ordinary language (cf. Firth, 1967a, 21–5).

Ritual has therefore been one of the great fields for the study of symbolic behaviour, and many modern social anthropologists have contributed to its interpretation. Their primary search for the meaning of symbolism in ritual has focused upon social relations. But it is to be noted that in two of the major areas of theoretical concern – what can be reasonably inferred about unstated aims and functions; and what is the relation of public to private, or social to personal meanings – the treatment and conclusions of different analysts have varied considerably.* I take here for consideration mainly British studies, with which I am more familiar.

An enlivening essay on the symbolism of ritual came from Max Gluckman in 1954 (1963). Using the vivid and impressive account by Hilda Kuper (1947) of the Swazi *Incwala*, often termed a first-fruits ceremony, Gluckman examined the symbolism of political catharsis in the songs and dances of hostility which form part of the complex ritual. Under the title which by now he has made well known, of 'rituals of rebellion', he pointed out that the ritual was organized to exhibit the co-operation and conflict which make up the political system. In the traditional Swazi system the political and social order itself was not questioned, but communal interest, including that

* For contrast may be noted a recent overt preoccupation of some artists with 'ritual', in which they take as subject some common theme that characterizes human behaviour, and in which they believe they can discern a kind of basic human experience of moral or didactic value. So, Romare Bearden has used as theme what he has termed 'The Prevalence of Ritual' to express in painting and collage deep emotion about life's problems, especially in the life style of American Blacks. For illustration and brief discussion of a Museum of Modern Art, New York, exhibition see Carroll Greene, *Romare Bearden: The Prevalence of Ritual* (Museum of Modern Art, New York, 1971).

exemplified in the person of the sacred king, could conflict with individual and segmental group interest, which was thus allowed formal expression in the ritual. So 'ritual rebellion' could be enjoyed as a social blessing, with traditional sanction. Granted the general cogency of Gluckman's argument and the suggestive hypotheses it involved, this example illustrated the difficulties of interpretation the anthropologist faces with such symbolic material. That alternative inferences as to meaning of symbolic behaviour are possible even with highly equipped social analysts is shown by the difference of view of Kuper and Gluckman about a rite in which the king is driven into his sanctuary – whether he is being entreated to migrate with the royal clan or being denounced by them (Kuper, 1947, 216–18; Gluckman, 1963, 124, 258).

But to a non-Africanist like myself there is another more general question: is the title 'rituals of rebellion' not a misnomer? The songs cited do not seem to express the singers' hatred of the king, but *other peoples'* hatred – '*they* hate the king'; 'O King, *they* hate thee'; '*You* hate the child king'.... Several interpretations are possible here. Psychologically, the 'you' and 'they' may be projections, equivalent to 'we'; this seems to be Gluckman's inference, though he does not say so. But taken more literally, they may be accusatory though without specifying anyone; 'they' hate the king, but 'we' are loyal – and the rite thus may be termed supportive, not rebellious in tone. Again, the king himself supplied a clue to a possible further interpretation. 'With sociological insight', as Kuper commented (1947, 224), he explained that the warriors danced and sang at the *Incwala* and so did not fight, although they came from all parts of the country and were proud and jealous. 'When they dance they feel they are one and they can praise each other.' Part of the social mechanism for helping their unity could be to join in asserting that their king is threatened (by persons unknown) both mystically and physically, in 'few, mournful, and tremendously moving' words (1947, 206). My point in traversing these arguments is to show that while inference is often necessary to supply meaning to symbolic behaviour in ritual, caution is advisable in ascribing to it basic themes of either support or conflict in the social system.

The complexity of interpretation of ritual symbolism is well illustrated by the phenomena of sacrifice, which have had a long line of distinguished analysts, from Trumbull, Robertson Smith, Hubert and Mauss, to Evans-Pritchard, Middleton, Goody and Godfrey Lienhardt. To identify the slaughter of an animal as a sacrifice, that is a ritual act of dedication, may pose problems for an anthropologist.* He sees a bull being killed – is this symbolic or is the beast being butchered for meat? The empirical indicators are usually obvious – as when in Kelantan in 1940 I saw a white cloth being held as a canopy over the animal when its throat was cut as it was held down on the ground. I could quickly establish that this was not to shield the Malay actors from the sun, but to indicate that the bull was dedicated to Allah, as a prayer confirmed. There were other religious associations of the act – but there were also economic and social referents. A bull is a costly animal, much more so than a goat or a sheep. But as I was informed, the smaller animal would not do as a sacrifice on this occasion because in the local conceptualization, the donor of the sacrificial animal would have the privilege of riding it before the Lord in the grand parade on the Last Day, the Day of Judgement, and to appear mounted on a sheep or goat would be ridiculous. But few men could afford a whole bull at a time, so elaborate annual purchase of shares in a co-operative venture – in sevenths – enabled a man to accumulate a bull-equivalent in the end. The whole transaction, most carefully calculated, also took into consideration the sharing and consumption of the meat – no nonsense about a burnt-offering for these Malays! Here then determinants at the economic level of poverty then obtaining among those Kelantan Malays affected the form of symbolic conception, which was trimmed to allow a wide range of participation in status behaviour as well as in ritual practice (Firth, 1943, 203). If the symbolism had not allowed of sacrifice on the instalment plan, only the most wealthy would have been able to conform to the religious ideal. (Elsewhere I have pointed out other implications of economic factors for the theory of sacrifice (1963, 12–23). Of course it would have been possible for these Malays to have done as Nuer or LoDagaa have done, and to have used sheep or goat as a substitute for a bull by calling it such. But this does not seem to have occurred to them, perhaps because sacrifice plays no commonly repeated part in their

* See, for example, Goody, 1962, 162–3 for distinction between sacrifice and beast offered as a funeral honour to the deceased.

ritual life and problems of scarcity have therefore different application for them. (For Lugbara attitude also see Middleton, 1960, 88.)

In a caustic comment R. R. Marett (1935, 148) gave a warning against over-interpretation of the meaning of sacrificial practice. When the grosser forms of symbolism survive into the higher religions, as typically in the case of sacrifice, he said: 'a crude affair of shedding blood and appropriate only to those who do their own butchering' – it needs much verbal reinterpretation to allegorize the primitive act. Without accepting this implied criticism, it is fair to note that anthropological interpretations of the symbolism of sacrifice have been affected both by religious commitment and by preoccupation with factors of unconscious mind. There is ample demonstration in the literature of the socially integrative functions of sacrifice: as focus for religious activities of groups; as medium of expiation for individuals to remedy non-fulfilment of obligation or other offence against social rule; as means of social control. There is abundant evidence too that the symbolism of sacrifice embodies complex sets of ideas and emotions, including, it may be, social self-consciousness, tension and release, joy, thanksgiving, apprehension, propitiation – in relation to systems of belief about spirit powers and forces of man and nature. Evans-Pritchard has asserted, very plausibly, that when Nuer give their cattle in sacrifice they are in a very intimate way giving part of themselves, an identification especially easy because what they surrender are living creatures, the most precious of their possessions (1956, 279). But a part of oneself is not the whole of oneself; so it is a further step to argue not only that in sacrifice some part of a man dies with the victim, but also that sacrifice is a self-immolation, the substitution of a life for a life. This complete personal identification of man with victim, which the Nuer themselves do not seem to have clearly acknowledged, and the idea that the life can only be given by its liberation through death, seem to me to be related to Evans-Pritchard's view of the Nuer conception of God, which he treats as a mystery. To say that a sacrifice is a dramatic representation of a spiritual experience is an expression that can probably go unchallenged by most anthropological opinion. To say that its meaning depends finally on an awareness of God and man's dependence upon him – at which point the theologian takes over from the anthropologist – is to give a very personal interpretation (1956, 322). From a very different angle, that of psychoanalysis, interpretations of Nuer sacrifice have taken a new turn. Beidelman has argued (1966, 464) that Evans-Pritchard has ignored the element of sexuality, which he himself suggests is at the very core of Nuer moral ideas. The victim in the sacrifice, an ox, represents by its castration the moral subordination of Nuer male sexuality to social values; the instrument, the spear, 'a socialized penis', represents the aggressive element which subordinates women and through its power of death, initiates the transformations involved in the ideal aspects of agnatic values. So in spearing an ox a Nuer 'expresses a kind of transfiguration, through immolation, of his sexual self and an anticipation of his own transformation, through death, into the agnatic ideal person which his own living, domestic sexual self cannot wholly be and, indeed, cannot wholly accept'. Whether this qualifies as Marett's 'allegorization' or not, it is clear that in such type of analysis many assumptions are being made about mental functioning of Nuer, which are derived from a general body of theory not based – as is psychoanalysis in the West – on a body of clinical evidence. Beidelman does not claim conclusive proof of his argument from Nuer data, but holds that the issues of symbolic interpretation he raises demand attention. Granted the significance of the problem of Nuer sexuality in relation to their identification with cattle, this type of interpretation of ritual symbolism points to a need for much more systematic collection of empirical data about people's mental associations in fields such as sacrifice.

SYMBOLS IN TRANSITION RITES

The interpretation of transition rites has been a stock activity of social anthropologists for more than half a century, especially since the publication of Arnold Van Gennep's *Les Rites de Passage* in 1909. (An English translation with introduction by Solon T. Kimball was issued in 1960, and a series of essays by Gluckman and others in 1962 gave point to modern commentary.)

But in the post-war period probably the most sustained and penetrating analysis of a type of such rites was given by Audrey Richards in *Chisungu* (1956), an examination of a girls' initiation ceremony among the Bemba. Traditionally this consisted of a long elaborate succession of ritual acts including singing, mime, dancing and handling of sacred emblems, lasting more than three weeks, and ending in a wedding ceremony. (Formerly analogous rites were practised in many parts of East, Central and South Africa, but they have all undergone radical change in modern times.) Audrey Richards points out that whereas there are many accounts of male initiation rites in the literature, those of female rites are rare. She sees in such rites a double significance: they celebrate the attainment of sex maturity, hence the possibility of physical parenthood; and they also celebrate social maturity with its responsibilities and privileges. In this twofold aspect Richards sees the possibility of differential stress, and hence of local variation. But with a female there is additional complication: the onset of her menstrual flow is linked with emotionally tinged ideas about the power of blood – negatively associated with danger and mystical damage; and positively with creative fertility. So linked with rites of protection and purification are also those of promotion of child-bearing and domestic efficiency. But within this general framework of assumptions Richards sees many difficult problems of interpretation. Yet it is here that her most distinct contribution lies.

She argues that an anthropologist struggling to interpret a complex ceremony has to use a number of approaches. She distinguishes the expressed or formulated purposes of the rite from what the observer infers, but also separates the short-term specific aims from the long-term more generalized ones. The former are apt to be more clearly conceived and easily expressed – 'we do this to make childbirth easy'; the latter may be vaguer – 'we do this to take anger from men's hearts'. But secondary ends may also be recognized and expressed – to gain prestige from sponsoring a rite, or to bind kin to return an economic service. She therefore makes the point that by the nature of ritual there should be multiple explanations for most of its symbolic behaviour – with the corollary that complete explanations of every item are unlikely to be obtained from any one member of the community. But since rites are necessarily an effort to *do* something, the performers can always give *some* explanation. Yet she holds that what an observer infers (she has written 'deduces') may be an essential part of the interpretation. Indirect evidence as to the meaning of a rite may be: linguistic statements which reveal some common stress or interest; on-the-spot emotional reactions of concern, tension or boredom which show the relative importance of a symbolic act; refusal to omit or shorten a rite, as contrasted with readiness to abandon it, as an index to its critical place in the system. Audrey Richards also cites Radcliffe-Brown's analysis of Andamanese beliefs (cf. p. 135) as support for inferential attribution of symbolic meaning from other rites in which apparently identical or similar acts occur (1956, 115).

Unlike some of her colleagues at that time, Richards was not averse to psychological interpretation of symbols. She noted the prevalence of serpents and other universal-type symbols, and the mimetic representations of journeys through dark and difficult places to reach knowledge and safety. But while linking these with dream presentations and general human experience, she regarded them as primarily a matter of interest to people in allied disciplines, rather than to anthropologists, whose major interest is in the clues which such imagery may give to the emotional expression of elements in a particular social structure (1956, 153–4). A cautionary note, however, is expressed. Rites which seem to cut across the normal institutional modes of a society, especially by display of aggression against established positions, have been interpreted by anthropologists as symbolic outlets for repressed hostility or symbolic compensation for traditionally subordinate roles. Citing analyses by Bateson and Gluckman of women's aggressive behaviour so construed, Richards describes these as unproven conjectures, since evidence was lacking as to whether the people concerned felt the tensions ascribed to them. Rather sardonically, she points out in effect that the existence of the thing signified is really derived from the presence of the symbol; a valid interpretation must depend on independent evidence of the psychological states postulated. This criticism, generalized, has a much wider application.

Richards makes very clear the difficulties faced by an anthropologist in seeking valid interpretations of ritual symbolism, and she frankly admits that she has been unable to resolve some of the incongruities of the *chisungu*. What she does, however, in a constructive way is to relate the ritual symbols to structural situations as well as to emotional attitudes. She shows how in these girls' initiation rites and the marriage rites which follow them it was not the chastity of the girl but the virility of the bridegroom which was emphasized; and she indicates how the symbolism fitted the matrilineal structure of the society. The bride belonged to the matrilineage and the groom was allowed access to her to make her fertile – to produce a further asset for her group. In daily life he was submissive to his in-laws and worked under their orders; in the *chisungu* he appeared symbolically as a roaring lion, a lion-killer, a crocodile, a hunter, a warrior, a chief. So symbolic status as a procreator and impressive figure was a compensation for the pains of everyday life.

The symbolism of these rites expressed themes of significance both for the society and for individual initiates. Richards holds that the rites symbolized the values and beliefs of the group, expressed, reinforced and taught tribal norms, promoted social cohesion – all in a complex way. So mortuary ritual could symbolize the performers' duty to their chief or the values set on economic activities, as well as grief for the dead man. But she makes two important qualifications. The correspondence between the total value system of a group and its symbolic expression in ritual is never exact – some basic values are dramatically represented, others not. And some weighty rites are just as often an occasion of group division as of union – a statement which she refers back to her analysis of social differentiation at Bantu meals long before (1932, 71–2; 1956, 117–18).

As a brief digression I would observe in this connection that the notion of 'group division' in relation to ritual symbolism can refer to several types of situation. One type is that of social differentiation in the sense of Richards's Bantu meal analysis; she points out how from an early age males and females, seniors and juniors eat in separate groups though their food may come from a common household. This is a recognized expression of socially approved norms of structural kind, in direct symbolic form. Another type of symbolic expression of group division is where the rites do not tend to maximize but to minimize the social differentiation. Segmentary groups, each with its own competing interest, are brought together in a community of action which may either have the effect of promoting co-operation and positive sentiments of unity or at least of 'papering over the cracks' of disunity to allow of some broad achievement of common policy. Another type of symbolism concerned with division is the ritual expression of hostility which may be roused because of asymmetric allocation of resources or power, but be inhibited from ordinary overt display because of moral or other values; this is a common anthropological interpretation of much symbolism of the 'conflict' category. Finally, there is the type of group division which arises quite overtly when competing social units struggle for control of the same symbols of unity – as Christian sects do around the 'Church of the Rock' in Jerusalem. Here the shared symbolism of the rite neither marks nor masks social differentiation, but acts as a focus for it.

One of the most interesting aspects of the symbolism of the *chisungu* is the inter-relation shown between the position of the initiates and that of their kin. Most studies of initiation have focused on what the initiates learn, how their status is changed, etc. In my own study of Tikopia initiation (1936, 418–67) I emphasized the significance of the rites in bringing home to the initiates their dependence upon their kin, and the meaning of kinship obligations and categories. But Richards goes further in pointing out how the tests or ordeals which the candidates undergo are also ordeals for their parents and relatives – who are anxious until they see that the young people have proved their competence or at least have been allowed to pass through. Bizarre though some of these tests may seem, passing through them lets the kinsfolk see that their novices have received the recognition of society in their change of status. Richards notes that European accounts of such initiation rites have tended to emphasize either their obscenity or their educational function. She corrects this: there is sex but it is not lewd, and there is education but it is not formal. What Bemba girls gained was not technical but social and symbolic knowledge, and much of that indirectly – a deeper knowledge of the social attitudes and symbols concerned with women's functions in sex, marriage, wifehood and childbirth. They weren't given lectures on marriage guidance, but got a cumulative process of experience, often in apparently disconnected acts, as in jumping over a hurdle, singing obscure old songs and handling odd crude pottery figures of snakes, lions, naked brother-and-sister. The basic point is that these seemingly odd and individually meaningless experiences were pulled together by setting them in a frame of symbolic ideas and values related to the structure of Bemba society.

Finally, Richards insists, as Victor Turner has done, on the manifold associations of such symbols. 'The interpretation of the songs . . . shows that there is in every case at least one double meaning for each symbol. The hoe represents the woman's gardening duties but it also represents the husband who makes his wife fertile' (1956, 164). Some interpretations show how 'as in dream life the symbols of the *chisungu* evoke a variety of linked associations, verbal and other . . . the curious figurines stand for certain emotional associations common to the whole community, but they may also acquire special meanings in the light of that particular ceremony, or even in terms of individual experience.' Other interpretations 'show how the same symbol can at one and the same time represent the thing that must be done, and the thing that must not be done'. 'All symbolic objects make it possible to combine fixity of form with multiple meanings, of which some are standardized and some highly individual' (1956, 165). In these and analogous generalizations the themes of 'ambivalence' and 'multivalence' which appear so markedly in much later anthropological study of symbols, emerge quite clearly.

SEARCH FOR A SYMBOLIC PATTERN

An important aspect of Audrey Richards's treatment of the symbolism of ritual was the breadth and care of its methodological approach, explicitly formulated. The contribution of Monica Wilson has had some analogy with this, though she has been perhaps rather more conservative in her acceptance of the validity of psychological hypotheses and techniques. Her major examination of symbolism was in two works (1957, 1959), the first concerned with the rituals celebrated by kinsmen at death, at a girl's puberty and marriage, at birth and in misfortune; the second concerned with communal rituals celebrated especially in public misfortune such as plague or famine, or at succession of a chief or of younger generation to elder. Using Radcliffe-Brown's principle of similar significance of symbols recurring in different ritual situations, Wilson stresses her view that Nyakyusa rites reveal a symbolic pattern which has an intellectual system of interpretation. She holds that it is foolish to imagine that an individual schooled in one culture can understand the symbolism of another without instruction (1957, 6). Hence she is very careful to cite her vernacular authority for her attribution of symbolic meanings, the more so since like Audrey Richards she regards anthropological literature as being full of symbolic guessing, the ethnographer's interpretation of the ritual of other people. At the same time she points out that not all the Nyakyusa with whom she dealt were conscious of all the interpretations she gave. While a few symbols, such as association of different types of banana with male and female, were known to everyone, knowledge of others was restricted to specialists or was purely individual formulation. But if individual formulations were used 'it was at least a Nyakyusa subconscious, and the interpretation in terms of the culture'. Trenchantly she argued that 'any analysis not based on some translation of the symbols used by people of that culture is open to suspicion' (1957, 6–7). So she reckoned to deal with common, not individual symbols; with sociological, not psychological analysis. It is true that Monica Wilson does define symbol very loosely – 'something which typifies or represents something else' (1957, 9) – which allows her a wide range of descriptive materials to draw upon. Moreover, she does occasionally go beyond her brief and write of the 'implicit' meanings of Nyakyusa symbols; and suggest that 'perhaps' certain rites are symbols of marriage union, etc. She states that while 'the doctor' interpreted water dropping on mourners and nubile girls running in and out of a doorway as a symbol of their receiving spirit-shades back on their bodies, 'we' interpret it, rather more widely, as a symbol of rebirth (1957, 204–5; 1959, 211). But all this is well within the plausible, making use of only a modicum of modern psychological lore. She is very modest in her claims. She admits that interpretations of even the most self-conscious Nyakyusa do not reveal the whole truth about their rituals. She says it is probable that certain Nyakyusa symbols are universal in that they express the same ideas in all societies: spear as penis; house with its doorway as womb (1957, 66, 74, 117; 143, 205). She also postulates that many symbols not always explicitly recognized by Nyakyusa are emotionally intelligible to Westerners when interpreted.

The results of such analysis have been impressive. More than most other anthropologists, Monica Wilson has striven to present the symbolic pattern in the Nyakyusa conception of reality as a total system, with all its range of emphases, its inconsistencies, its blank areas – not just as a few selected illustrations to prove some dramatic theme. The evidence is carefully marshalled. Rite after rite is described, then discussed for overt purpose and symbolism, with anthropologist's questions and answers of informants cited in detail. When eating is labelled a symbol of sexual intercourse it is explained that while everyone knew that a banana stood for a penis, fewer people realized what eating it meant for a bride in her ritual; but some were quite definite – she eats the banana means that she has intercourse with her husband. When it is stated that blacksmithing is felt to be like coition the analogy is given explicitly: 'The man is the smith. . . . The woman is the bellows.' *Question:* 'The woman is a bellows?' 'Yes, because when she is having intercourse she gasps "He, he, he!" . . .' So the recurrent symbolic pattern of the rites is unfolded, and the connections made plain. Wilson argues in all this that contrary to a commonly held theory that ritual is always more constant than interpretation, in Nyakyusa family rituals at least there was variation, whereas the conceptions expressed varied very little. On the other hand in contrast to the symbolism of ritual, common and obligatory, was the symbolism of medicine, individual and free. Nevertheless, the constraints of a common symbolic system operated, and the imagination of the local healers worked within the general symbolism of the people. In medicine as in ritual one type of banana stood for a male and another for a female; a banana sucker represented a kinsman; a sprouting shoot, conception; hair stood for growth and a bald pate a devastated field; pythons, crocodiles, leopards and lions stood for power and majesty; spears and thorns for attack; vomiting and emptiness for innocence; spitting for forgiveness. But in Nyakyusa medicine, associations were much less predictable than in ritual, with much more individual interpretation by specialists. Yet some general principles can be extracted – such as 'Men mime that which they wish to avoid, as well as that which they desire; like things are antagonistic as well as sympathetic' (1959, 153).

Two other features in Wilson's treatment of symbolism stand out: her concern for what is meant by the trite expression 'people of the culture' investigated: and her interest in change in a symbolic system. In all her analysis she distinguishes closely the interpretations of specialists from those of local laymen, headmen from commoners, men from women. She also examines the attitude of Christian

Nyakyusa to the rituals performed by their pagan kinsmen and neighbours – their fulfilment of social obligation but rejection of the religious ideology; the effects of their scepticism or partial belief; the parallel substitution of church rites for the pagan confession, sacrifice and communion with the shades of the dead. To my mind her whole analysis succeeds admirably in bringing out the significance of a symbolic system with respect for it yet without imputing to it any rhetorical mystical quality.

'A FOREST OF SYMBOLS'

Named from an image in a poem of Baudelaire, and dedicated to Monica Wilson, Victor Turner's studies which appeared in *The Forest of Symbols* (1967) commingled an aesthetic and a scientific tradition in a manner quite new in anthropology. His analyses of symbols in Ndembu ritual, first introduced at a meeting of the Association of Social Anthropologists of the Commonwealth in London in 1958, and continued in a massive series of interpretations, have been one of the most vigorous and theoretically suggestive statements on symbolism in modern social anthropology. If at times, like the incense of Baudelaire he seems to 'sing of the transports of the spirit and of the senses' this is done with a sincerity and a power which compel respect. I am concerned mainly here, as with Richards and Wilson, with the general methodological aspects of Turner's analysis, which like theirs is focused very largely upon the understanding of symbolism in ritual.

Turner regards ritual as a patterned process in time, the units of which are symbolic objects and serialized items of symbolic behaviour. Ritual performances are themselves phases in broad social processes, the span and complexity of which are roughly proportional to the size and degree of differentiation of the groups in which they occur. To a high degree ritual helps to correct or anticipate deviations and conflicts in such groups, though its precise goals will vary according to social circumstances. Hence to give an adequate explanation of the meaning of a particular symbol it is necessary to examine the widest 'action-field context' in which the rite is simply a phase; the context of the specific ritual; and the behaviour directed towards the symbol. Turner distinguishes three levels or fields of meaning, essentially by their different contexts. The kind of meaning derived from indigenous interpretation (which with a respect for the vernacular informant he terms *exegetical meaning*) is paralleled by the *operational meaning* derived from observation of the symbol in use, noting the types of personnel involved and the affective quality of their reactions. In turn, these levels of meaning are to be contrasted with the *positional meaning* of the symbol, derived from its relation to other symbols in a patterned totality. Turner also emphasizes as a very important property of symbols their capacity for a single symbol to encapsulate many meanings – to represent many different things, in different contexts or at different levels of understanding in the same general context. This Turner refers to as the property of *polysemy* or *multivocality* – which he seems to equate by a kind of reverse definition, with *condensation*.*

Much of this way of looking at symbols is I think common ground among social anthropologists. But Victor Turner, drawing as we all do on ideas from a variety of sources, has welded them together into an explicit systematic method of approach. He has also introduced some modifications. Audrey Richards drew attention to the positive and negative aspects of a symbol – how at one and the same time it can represent both that which should and that which should not be done. This was a viewpoint with many congeners, for example in the more philosophical statements of Thomas Carlyle or W. M. Urban. She stressed the significance of symbolism to express the accepted and approved as well as the hidden and denied, the rules of society and the occasional revolt against them, the common interests of the whole community and the conflicting interests of different parts of it (1956, 169). She saw the use of symbols in ritual as securing some kind of emotional compromise giving satisfaction to most individuals in a society and supporting its major institutions. Turner also recognizes a polarization in the meaning of symbols. But he stresses the 'ideological pole' and the 'sensory pole' of his 'dominant symbols' – one set of referents being the principles of the moral and social order, and the other being items of desire and feeling, even of 'gross, frank, physiological order' (1967, 28). At the sensory pole

* Turner, 1967, 45–52. Cf. 'By these terms [polysemy or multivocality] I mean that a single symbol may stand for many things' (1967, 50); 'The simplest property is that of *condensation*. Many things and actions are represented in a single formation' (1967, 28). As already noted (p. 81) this use of 'condensation' differs from that of Freud.

come particularly those involvements of symbolism with aspects of the human body which other anthropologists too (for example Mary Douglas) have found so significant.

Another way in which Victor Turner has developed the theory of symbolism is in relating symbols, especially what he has termed 'dominant symbols', more closely to the theme of conflicts in society. As well as showing how the symbolism of ritual helps to mitigate or conceal the more overt elements of hostility, or to give them cathartic expression, he indicates situations of what he has called 'blocked exegesis', occurring where there is sharp conflict between norms, or between norms and wishes. (To some extent he is inclined to identify with this his occasional inability to get an explanation of a piece of symbolic behaviour from the people themselves.) But much more generally, Turner sees the operation of major symbolic forms in society as founded if not in conflict at least in contradiction. He argues that any major ritual that stresses the importance of a single principle of social organization does so only by blocking the expression of other important principles. He also holds that when a dominant symbol is regarded as a unit of the total symbolic system, and not interpreted simply in terms of 'official' explanation, there may be discrepancy and even contradiction in meanings given by informants. This he regards as a 'quintessential property of the great symbolic dominants in all religions' (1967, 40, 43).

On the issue of 'uncomprehended symbols' Victor Turner expresses firm opinion. Taking as illustration the Ndembu 'milk tree' symbolism, he contrasts the overt interpretations of it in girls' puberty ritual as standing for the unity and continuity of Ndembu society, with the unacknowledged discriminatory behaviour shown around it, when women separate from and taunt men as they sing around it, or take part in generation demarcations or matrilineage conflicts. He takes this discrepancy, and the inability or unwillingness of Ndembu informants to acknowledge it, as a standpoint from which to argue that a social anthropologist can justify his claim to interpret a society's ritual symbols more deeply and comprehensively than the actors themselves. Turner is critical of Nadel and Monica Wilson on this debatable issue, though I think that they both might be ready to allow the interpretation of those kinds of non-verbal behaviour which are integrated into a systematic ritual scheme even though no verbalized explanation is given. But in more positive terms, I think Turner makes out a strong case, by demonstration even more than by protestation. In particular, one may underline his argument, for which he provides ample empirical validation, of the possibility and value of analysing symbols 'in a context of observed emotions' when the investigator is well acquainted with the common idiom in which a society expresses such emotions (1967, 39).

In the richness of his treatment there is room for disagreement. I personally find some of the language in which Victor Turner clothes his ideas somewhat ornate. His use of 'orectic' presumably derives not from mediaeval philosophy but from the psychological equivalent to 'affective-conative' suggested by Aveling and some other British psychologists a generation ago (V. Turner, 1967, 54; 1970, 176; M. M. Lewis, 1947, 20n., 195, etc.). But this 'semantic pole' with referents of 'a grossly physiological kind' seems to have much in common with the 'sensory pole' used in other contexts. *Exegesis* for explanation and *hermeneutics* for interpretation sound rather scriptural, while latinisms such as *personae*, *stigmata* and *liminars* (1969, 99, 121, 143), with *communitas*, though possibly more precise than persons, signs, threshold figures and communion, seem rather formidable. But I take it that their purport has been to invest the study of African and other symbolic systems alien to Western readers with the status of data proper to technical study by experts in other fields of symbolism, particularly religious symbolism. They may have emerged, however, in the course of a deeper commitment. Leaving aside questions of religious allegiance, Turner has adopted specifically some of Carl Jung's concepts, with the mode of their phraseology. His critique of Nadel and Monica Wilson uses Jung in support, citing with approval Jung's definition of symbol – 'always the best possible expression of a relatively *unknown* fact, a fact, however, which is none the less recognized or postulated as existing' (V. Turner, 1967, 26). As a definition for working anthropologists this is very unsatisfactory. The notion of 'best possible expression' may conceal a circularity – how is any symbol to be judged as anything but the best, unless some external criteria are given? But if the referent is 'relatively unknown', how precisely is it known that the symbol applies to it and not to some other referent? . . . and so on. (Taken literally, the Jungian formulation would seem to cover, say, the most careful scientific meteorological description of the state of the weather at the North Pole, a relatively unknown fact, but certainly existing on any ordinary plane of conceptualization.) In this connection I think the point of 'symbol' may be, not the element of the unknown in the referent, but the degree to which the meaning of the sign which refers to it is capable of intellectual, aesthetic and emotional development.

But I think that in the Jungian formulation, and in Turner's use of it, we are back to the classical antithesis in another form – the idea of the known as key to comprehension of the unknown, the material as key to the immaterial. It would seem that it has had some of this value for Victor Turner, when he discusses Ndembu symbolism. 'There are religious depths here that cannot be fathomed by the analysis of observational data. The symbols I have discussed have a fathomless lucidity of meaning which men of every grade of cultural complexity can grasp intuitively if they wish' (1962, 172). This is the language of faith. In such statements, as in others about the 'numinous simplicity' of presentation of *sacra* (1967, 108), one is led towards a religious dimension of symbolism. Yet it seems as if Turner does not wish to obtrude this but rather bring down the argument to the level of the difficult and complex relationships between the overt and the submerged, the manifest and latent patterns of meaning, as interpreted in terms of behaviour in social contexts. If we can agree to understand him in such sense, then we can accept his series of vivid formulations about the positive nature of symbols in social situations. With a permissible amount of reification, he points out how symbols, with their complex meanings, unite the organic with the socio-moral order, over and above the conflicts within that order. Powerful drives, associated with human physiology, especially of reproduction, are endowed by the ritual process with a normative quality, and reinforce this, so being made to appear obligatory. So symbols are both resultants and instigators of this process and encapsulate its properties (1969, 52–3). At the same time they have important structural relationships, both as series and as representing elements of harmony, integration, tension or conflict, in the operations of the society.

There is one aspect of Turner's methodology which I think is open to question, not in its results so much as in its claims: I refer to the concept of 'social drama', examined by means of the 'extended case method'. Gluckman is right to contrast this with evidence from 'apt and isolated illustrations', and appropriately credits Clyde Mitchell and Victor Turner with having utilized the extended-case method to great advantage in their Central African social and political studies. But to view social relations 'through a longish period of time', seeing how various parties operate mystical beliefs to serve their own interests, analysing the conflicting pressures of discrepant principles and values as generations change and new persons come to maturity (Gluckman, 1965, 235–8), as in Turner's study of struggles around the succession to headmanship of a Ndembu village, is no such novelty as Gluckman thinks. Granted some difference in scale, though not in conception, Ian Hogbin's analysis 'The Father Chooses His Heir: A Family Dispute over Succession in Wogeo' (1940–41), lays bare the roots of a protracted political issue in dramatic terms, with the richness of perspective and structural appreciation required. The concept of 'social drama' related to this, in its use of sequences of disputes (inter-connected 'eruptions of conflicts' as Turner has called them (1957, 91)) provides a convenient focus for a body of data for analysis of social process. But it has been rather unsophisticated theoretically, in two ways. Generally, it raises the question of what is meant by calling a crisis or conflict a *drama*. This suggests a scheme of role-playing, with possibilities of assumption and abandonment of social positions in response to different types of interest – a plausible but not the only way of looking at social process. More specifically, it calls for comparison with the notion of 'dramatism' in social interaction, a notion propounded especially with great vigour by Kenneth Burke, followed by H. D. Duncan, and applied much more widely than to situations of conflict. Depending upon the double meaning of the term 'act', the dramatistic theory of action (with its 'dramatistic pentad' of act, scene, agent, agency, purpose) purports to be basic to an understanding of the nature of symbolic action, especially in verbal form. Analyses in this frame of reference tend to be somewhat arid by comparison with the vivid sinewy handling of concepts and material by Turner, but the whole notion of social drama seems most effective when used deliberately in a metaphorical sense, not as a methodological tool. The 'processional form' which Turner has identified in his 'social drama' (1957, 91–2): breach; crisis; redressive action; re-integration or recognition of schism – seems not to be intrinsic to the notion of drama, but to be very much in line with Radcliffe-Brown's type of analysis of restoration of equilibrium after commission of an offence.*

A PLETHORA OF INTERPRETATIONS

The image of a 'forest of symbols', with Nature as a temple, and the symbols observing the passer-by with a familiar (? 'old-fashioned') look, is attractive. But Baudelaire was concerned with more than the properties of symbols as factors in social action, as positive forces in an activity field. He was concerned implicitly, in poetic form, with the correspondence by means of symbols between the material world and the spiritual world (cf. Michaud, 1947, 721). I have the impression that something of this attitude is shared by some anthropologists. But this manifestation of the new Symbolism or recrudescence of the Romantic movement, though shared by many people with different kinds of commitment and though reminiscent of the wave of enthusiasm for the study of symbols of a century and a half ago, is really of a new order. The modern attitude is not Romantic in the popular sense of being absorbed by concern for the sentimental or the exotic. It is Romantic in a more technical sense, concerned with stress and conflict in the personality, impressed by ambivalence and ambiguity, emphasizing confusions between appearance and reality, holding that problems of existence are not ultimately soluble – or at least not soluble by human effort. In such a view, symbol, if not mystery, is allied to mystery. In some interpretations, art and religion may be closely intertwined with the scientific pursuit. In some, symbol seems implicitly to be equated with revelation. Symbol conveys truth not otherwise accessible, a truth which intellectual approach is too rational to apprehend.

My own reaction to this is to concur that symbol may embody mystery, and may embody some measure of revelation. But I see that mystery and that revelation as belonging to the realm of human

* For symbolism in what seems more appropriately-termed social drama – for example possession cults – see Leiris, 1958; Firth, 1967d; in theatre proper, see Peacock, 1968 (with reference to Burke).

imagination and human comprehension. Men in their social existence construct and inherit the intellectual and emotional frames in which they set and attribute meaning to the details of the external world. The problem of which is the 'reality'; the world outside or the frame through which we perceive it, is not relevant for our purposes. As anthropologists, we treat the phenomena we study as being in principle capable of elucidation. They may evade our understanding because of their complexity. And there may be a kind of Heisenburgian element in the situation of study, which may prevent us from finally apprehending separately and completely the position both of the observer and of that which he observes. But we make continuing efforts to reduce the area of the unknown. From this point of view, while stress and conflict are not denied, ambiguity is sought for clarification, not for its obscurity. Confusion between appearance and reality are seen as common, but as part of human fallibility and error rather than as part of the nature of things. In all this, anthropologists are aware of the social dimension of symbolic behaviour. Moreover, imagination, intuition, creative capacity, aesthetic sensibility may all be pressed into service in the task of symbol interpretation. And we hope to use the insight we gain from symbol interpretation as we use what we gain from aesthetic appreciation – to deepen our sensitivity of relationships and provide us with fresh ways of conceiving of meaning.

This is one way of looking at a Romantic revival in modern anthropological study of symbols. But other trends in modern 'symbolic anthropology' do not conform to such a pattern. Some are marked by an intense analytical interest in what Victor Turner referred to as 'positional meaning' of symbols and has been more generally characterized as structuralism. Others have displayed a much more pragmatic concern for the place of symbols in systems of action.

In a broad way one can see a series of dichotomies in the application of anthropological effort, partially overlapping but having their separation to a considerable degree in differences of values and philosophical, even aesthetic approach. There is an inclusive view, in line with the thought of G. H. Mead and Talcott Parsons, and represented for example by David Schneider in anthropology, that all relations of people to one another are mediated and defined by systems of culturally structured symbols. On the other hand, without necessarily denying this, many anthropologists have preferred to focus on a study of symbols in more explicit convention, distinguishing them from more pragmatically oriented behaviour. Parallel to this division up to a point is a division on interpretation, between those who, like Lévi-Strauss, are interested primarily in the structural relations and transformations of symbols internally within the system; and those who argue that the validity of such interpretation is very limited and that such meanings make very little sense without consideration of the social uses to which symbols are put. (The situation here is sometimes like that of the religious contrast – in salvation being attained by attention to thought rather than to works, with the claim that the former is both more revealing and also intellectually more rewarding.) There are divisions between those who regard anthropological analysis as concerned primarily, even solely, with the understanding of collective symbols which are socially shared, and those who think that this understanding must remain very incomplete without taking account of individually-developed symbols. There is also a dichotomy of sphere, if not of interest, recognized between the symbol patterns of tightly knit groups, concerned for instance with protection of interests and transmission of codes, and those of looser social aggregates, concerned more with expressive forms of symbolism which allow their members more self-realization. And then, very forcefully, the moral theme offers a dichotomy which some would translate into other terms: should 'symbolic anthropology' be an academic study devoted to elucidation of meanings as a tribute to knowledge, or should it be more bluntly involved in unravelling the knots in social problems and contributing to change in society, or at least to an understanding of change? This last point of view takes several forms. For Mary Douglas, one of the gravest problems of our day is the lack of commitment to common symbols; the whole history of ideas should be reviewed in the light of the power of social structures to generate symbols of their own, deceptive symbols, which purport to separate spirit from matter and lead to alienation; it behoves the anthropologist then to interpret alienation (1970, 1, 151). For Abner Cohen, the challenge to social anthropology today is the analysis of the dynamic involvement of symbolism, or of custom, in the changing relationships of power between individuals and groups (1969, 219).

Here I can illustrate only very briefly a few of these trends, catching up some of the references I have made earlier.

First, a reference to the structuralist approach, led pre-eminently by Lévi-Strauss. Since comment upon his work has now become almost an industry, it is enough here to indicate simply its position in the body of anthropological studies of symbolism. In his discussion of his Nambikwara field material, Lévi-Strauss evidently found little of a symbolic character to interest him; indeed he stated that Nambikwara rites did not seem to be in any way symbolic (1948, 126), being rather pushed to physical extremes and showing sincere spontaneous sentiment. But deeply concerned with the problem of the universality of human nature, holding that the subject matter of social anthropology is the communication of man with man by means of signs and symbols–a kind of semeiology – he has become preoccupied with questions of variation in symbolic form. Led partly by Marx and Freud to believe that if inquiry be pushed deeply and widely enough, variation can be seen to be historically and logically determined, Lévi-Strauss embarked on the gigantic and laborious undertaking of interpreting the vast mass of material of symbolic variation which appears on the one hand in the relations of kinship and marriage, and on the other, in myth. To do this he has had to make certain assumptions of simplification, each open to challenge. The first assumption is that he is dealing primarily with structures, not functions, and can therefore handle the variations and the systems of which they form part, in their own terms. Secondly, the structures are ideal or model versions, not behavioural versions. Thirdly, they are conceived as intellectual structures, both for purposes of analysis and also as representative of human thought process. To be prepared to make such drastic and far-reaching assumptions in the modern climate of social anthropology was in itself a daring, creative act; to follow out their implications so rigorously has demanded an even greater tenacity. The results are well-known. The study of the form and meaning of symbols has been greatly enriched by the method of consideration of them in terms of their structural relations within defined systems, irrespective of their relation to external factors. Even if at times it assumed the shape of an elitist anthropology, structuralism has had pervasive effects, and contributed indubitably a great deal to our understanding of symbolism.

In the most conventional field of anthropological studies of symbolism, that of ritual and associated beliefs, much analysis and argument still proceeds along what have become classical lines. From earlier ideas of witchcraft beliefs, for instance, as symbolic ways of representing explanations of misfortune, anthropological inquiry has delved deep into structural correlates of witchcraft accusations, in terms of kinship and status relations, and economic and political inequalities. Jean La Fontaine has said of the ideology of witchcraft in Bugisu that it is both a symbolic statement of conceptions about society and an active force influencing behaviour (1962, 213). Mary Douglas, in comment on an impressive series of modern essays, says that the symbols of what we recognize across the globe as witchcraft all build on the theme of vulnerable internal goodness attacked by external power – though the symbols vary according to local social structures and local patterns of meaning (ed., 1970, 26). In analogous fashion, the study of spirit medium cults (possession cults) has concentrated in recent years very much on the way in which the actions of the medium or possessed person, and his or her dialogue with the other participants, have symbolized their status relationships, and the tensions arising among members of the community in their daily life. Following on Turner's work on 'cults of affliction' among the Ndembu, Richard Werbner has shown how among the neighbouring Kalanga, illnesses believed to arise from breach of domestic morality are treated by women believed to be possessed by guardian demons. These women symbolically act the part of lions; they assume male, elder symbols (and Werbner here recalls Bateson's Iatmül analysis (1936) where the adoption of male paraphernalia by women serves to symbolize authority in the specific cultural idiom). As lions, the women grapple ritually with selfishness which cheats and dispossesses close kin of what should be theirs; they tell one another home truths through the cult (Werbner, 1971, 312, 322, 324). Moreover, Werbner indicates that such cult performances are used as symbolic means of status competition and manipulation – that they are used for preservation of small group identity and not only as Turner suggested, to give dominant emphasis to unity of the whole society (1971, 321).*

* The symbolic significance of behaviour in spirit medium and possession cults has not yet

A special field of anthropological interest in post-war times has been the 'cargo cults' and other millenarian movements on which now there is a vast literature. Their interest for symbolic study has varied, but among the more sensitive interpreters the problem of their symbolism has always stood high.* With many of these cults the account given of their symbolism, if complex, has been primarily ethnographic. In Weston La Barre's elaborate study of peyotism, 'an essentially aboriginal American religion, operating in terms of fundamental Indian concepts about powers, visions and native modes of doctoring' the symbolic interpretation is very intricate. For example, he points out that the Huichol ritual paraphernalia is 'heavily symbolized'. With his eagle and hawk plumes the singing shaman can see and hear anything anywhere, cure the sick, transform the dead, even call down the sun. The plumes symbolize the antlers of deer, which in turn symbolize peyote and the chair of 'Grandfather Fire', the greatest shaman of them all, whose flames are his plumes. Deer antlers also symbolize arrows, the arrow being *par excellence* the symbol of prayer . . . and so on (1969, 32). Among much else, the development of an elaborate symbolic system of such order means that a social premium is put on knowledge of the symbolic relationships, with obvious status implications. But some anthropologists studying millenarian movements have adopted a standpoint which

received adequate systematic treatment on any scale. Much detail can be obtained, however, from works such as those of Eliade, 1964, Beattie and Middleton, 1969, and I. M. Lewis, 1971, also Marcelle Bouteiller, 1950, and the fascinating study of voodoo by Alfred Métraux, 1959. For emphasis on the importance of symbolic communication in such cults, see Firth 1967d, 1970d.

* For example Kenelm Burridge, 1960, 1969. Cf. John Beattie, 1966, 71. Beattie argues, much as I have done, that what is primarily important in 'cargo cults' is that they are symbolic ways, akin to ritual drama, of doing something about situations otherwise felt to be unendurable. 'They are recourses, in times of stress, to the consolations of rite and drama; in a very fundamental sense to the consolations of make-believe.'

Criticism has been raised against my own use of the term 'fantasy' in reference to some 'cargo cult' behaviour, as by Burridge (1969, 120, 123–4). I think there is misconception here. Some modern anthropologists shy away from any suggestion of 'fantasy' or 'irrationality' as if it was a kind of pollution. Clearly, by themselves 'fantasy' and 'irrationality' are no explanation, nor have I offered 'fantasy' as such. There are also more important things to say about 'cargo cults', as I have indicated. But if the accounts are correct, in some of these cults the people engaged in a simulation of technical procedures which experience must have shown them by comparison were inadequate in themselves to produce the desied result. Their belief that nevertheless they had power to induce aeroplanes to land or ships to call with 'cargo' I term fantasy – an attempt to bridge a felt gap between ends and means by imaginative construction. I see no reason for the anthropologist to abdicate completely his function as external observer of such a situation, in giving such labels. But what is significant is the use made of such fantasy, in socially structured situations.

raises a basic problem in our whole inquiry, significant for the general study of religion: the manner in which the beliefs and practices of the cults can be regarded as symbolic at all. Are these beliefs and practices in fact not 'representations' but direct expressions of a reality which the anthropologist can do no more than accept? There is, in my view, a certain amount of dodging around this issue. Burridge, for instance, in a very thoughtful general review of the theory of millenary activities, is dissatisfied with descriptions of them as 'symbolic means' of dealing with problems – 'true, if it is not wholly a truism', and 'ethnocentric'. He allows that Monsignor Knox's 'authoritative' study of eighteenth-century millenarian movements referred the historic events to 'his own and his subjects' view of the symbolic system' and adopted much the same approach as many anthropologists, particularly Stanner. But Burridge still stresses the inadequacy of 'ethnographic' explanations and in the end plumps for a 'Hegelian' approach which attempts to make use of a total experience to explain itself as well as other kinds of social order, experience or tradition. Such a 'Hegelian' explanation 'admits the operation of a transcendent power'. In recognizing the existence of a force whose nature we do not yet understand, a 'Hegelian' explanation 'is clearly exploratory and therefore potentially fruitful' (1969, 120–37). Such putative suspension of judgement about the symbolic quality of the cult phenomena presumably corresponds to a personal commitment of a broader kind about the nature of reality (cf. I. M. Lewis, 1971, 28).

The study of Australian aboriginal religion by W. E. H. Stanner examined ritual symbolism in an equally penetrating, but more positive, way. Agreeing with Nadel that 'uncomprehended' symbols are not of concern for the anthropologist, Stanner makes the important point that if this means 'unaccompanied by intellectual conceptions' it cannot be simply inferred from wordlessness. Moreover, a methodical search for congruence between ritual facts of different orders may show that an implicit and apparently uncomprehended symbolism of one order is formulated explicitly in another order. But even then, some 'going beyond the facts of observation' is intrinsic to the act of study in every anthropological field, and not even theoretically separable from it. So, in the several levels of awareness of ritual symbolism, a few symbols are clearly recognized as such, but the vast majority of rites are practised without clear recognition of their symbolical character. Yet the symbolisms are constituents of collective acts of mutuality, with a logical structure, a detectable range of meanings, and an aesthetic appeal as well as a 'premial' place in the social development of individuals. Stanner pointed out that the rites involve anything from scores to hundreds of men, in unguided co-ordination, with no master of ceremonies as such; hence the spatial patterns of ritual are of cardinal importance. At the place of congregation, Stanner recognized four systems of symbolism in congruence – spatial configuration, gesture, language, music – and was impressed by the practical, logical and expressive efficacy of the form (1960, 61–4). With a combination of field observation, theoretical rigour and imaginative insight Stanner was able to demonstrate and interpret cogently and systematically the development of symbolic forms in aboriginal ritual. His broad conclusion was that the Murinbata aborigines among whom he worked were in the given rite expressing outwardly a complex sense of their dependence on a source outside themselves – that by an 'inner paradigm' of setting apart, destruction, transformation and return, much of it unverbalized, they were intimating a mystery 'of good-with-suffering, of order with tragedy' (1960, 70, 77). And yet Stanner was prepared to argue that a full understanding of the religious symbolism was to be gained only by a thorough morphemic analysis of the whole language, and while this remains unfulfilled we have not penetrated 'the true inwardness of the stuff of symbolism'.

With this analysis may be compared that of Nancy Munn. In an early study of Walbiri graphic signs she meticulously interpreted aboriginal totemic designs as devices for conveying narrative meaning, and has had a general interest in iconography. In a study of the effectiveness of symbols in Murngin rite and myth (1969) she drew inferences about the way in which collective symbolic forms could transform subjective experience. Though working along very different lines from those of Stanner, with reported, not observed material, she also emphasizes the relation between narrative code and system of ritual action, and in somewhat parallel fashion, sees the myth as conveying body destruction images which the ritual converts into feelings of well-being. But whereas Stanner is much concerned with the symbolic significance of actual spatial forms as vehicles for conception and expression of the meaning of things, events or conditions, Munn uses the concept of what she terms 'symbolic space', referring to the degree to which the individual experience of the ritual performer is identified with the experience of the persons described in the myth. Following a lead from Lévi-Strauss's analysis of shamanism (1949) Nancy Munn argues that the myth-ritual complex acts as a mechanism of social control by providing an external, regulatory system for states of bodily feeling, and indicates diagrammatically a series of postulated cultural codes for this process. Her conclusion is that analyses of symbolic structures should not simply be directed at abstracting underlying conceptual systems, but should be concerned with symbols as mechanisms which regulate the orientations of actors to each other and to common situations.

The symbolism of myth is very often studied side by side with that of ritual, as in the analyses mentioned of Munn and Stanner. But whether influenced by or separate from the structuralist position of Lévi-Strauss, studies of myths alone, in particular of classical myths, have been offered as contributions to the understanding of symbolic forms. I mention here only analyses by Leach (1961b) and by Terence Turner (1969b). In an essay with the intriguing title of 'Lévi-Strauss in the Garden of Eden' Leach points out that the study of myth has always had a central place in anthropological studies, but distinguishes 'symbolists' from 'functionalists' in such sphere. The functionalists are represented by the 'charter' theory of Malinowski; the symbolists by Frazer, with Freud and Cassirer in support. On symbolic lines, myths are interpreted as explaining (away) basic human problems such as the origin of the world or of death by manipulating symbolic representations of these facts. Holding that Lévi-Strauss had reopened what seemed to be an almost closed argument, Leach reviewed his analysis of the Oedipus tale, and went on to examine the creation story as told in Genesis. Without suspending his critical judgement of the structuralist thesis, Leach pointed out that adoption of the view that a myth could be studied as a thing in itself allowed for scrutiny of 'literary myths' for which social context is largely lacking. In a later work (1966a) Leach pursued his structural investigations into the theme of the succession of Solomon, with particular reference to the occurrence of patterned contradiction as a presentation of historical facts. Terence Turner's essay takes up Lévi-Strauss's pioneering analysis of the Oedipus tale and develops it in two ways. On the one hand, he argues that Lévi-Strauss paid insufficient attention to the patterning of the narrative sequence of the myth – that the form of the 'story' is itself significant for an understanding of its symbolic significance. Myth in Terence Turner's view is able to present a diachronic, unique sequence of events as a synchronic model only because of its 'story' development. On the other hand, he argues that myths in their narrative quality provide models which a listener can use to manipulate his tensions about social conflicts, and so help to control them.

In such work one may detect both the strong influence of the structuralist position of Lévi-Strauss, and a moving away from that position towards greater contextualization of the symbolic forms. That with Munn and Terence Turner, for example, this has involved some fairly abstract postulates about the effects of symbolic presentation, and conceptualization upon individual action, is perhaps inevitable.

Finally, in this compressed review I mention two lines of inquiry which both seem to offer prospect of great ethnographic development, even if the theoretical implications are not so clear. One is what I may call an *autologic* study of symbols, which in our Western field means the kind of examination which Mary Douglas has given to our concepts of purity and defilement (1966) or to some social experiences expressed in symbols based on the human body (1970); which Lloyd Warner gave to the meanings and functions of Christian symbolic life in America (1961); or David Schneider has given to the basic symbols of American kinship and their relation to one another (1968). The recent studies of Schneider and of Douglas, offering comprehensive theoretical frameworks for study of symbolism of very different kinds, both take as object lesson the symbolic quality assigned to the biological properties and functions of the human body. On a much lesser scale but more immediately empirically grounded is an analysis by Vieda Skultans (1970) of the symbolic significance of menstruation and the menopause in a Welsh community. She discovered that the concept of the menopause was a cultural rather than a biological one, and was used to reflect ideas of woman's social role as sexual partner, mother and housewife. In particular, in a manner conformable generally to Van Gennep's theory of *rites de passage* the menopause for some women was envisaged as marking the transition from one role to another. (A similar point of view was put by Marion Crawford, *New Society*, 29 October 1970, to the effect that in symbolic terms the menopause is a kind of imposed disengagement from the central role in a woman's life, that of mother.) From some of this autology, this scientific study of ourselves, certain conclusions of practical application may be drawn, for use in social operations concerned with families and with problems of personality.

More broadly, the emphasis given by both Mary Douglas and Victor Turner to the significance of experience carries some didactic force. Turner indicates the importance of experience in dialectical terms (1969, 97, 127), of alternating exposure of individuals to structure and to the communion of fellowship (*communitas*). He holds that *communitas* has an existential quality involving the whole man in relation to other whole men. Mary Douglas too makes the concept of social experience the basis of her programmatic approach to the problem of differences in ritual and symbolic interest, both as regards persons and societies. But at this point they seem to diverge: Turner to look with approval – as I interpret him – at applications of *communitas* or anti-structure, seeing it as a necessary creative phase in the dialectical process of society; and Douglas to regard antiritualism disapprovingly as an ineffective way of humanizing society. In her view, 'it would be more practical to experiment with more flexible institutional forms and to seek to develop their ritual expression (1970, 155).

The second line of inquiry I mention is also autologic to a considerable degree, but starts from a different base: it is concerned with the political function of symbols, and is represented for example by Abner Cohen (1969). Cohen argues that there can be no science of symbolic behaviour in any general sense. Symbolic forms are the product of creative work and their study is partly in the field of the sociology of art. Many men keep their creative symbolization to themselves, while others externalize and try to share it. All social behaviour is couched in symbolic terms. But since nearly all social behaviour has a power dimension, the symbolization of power relations is an exceedingly important feature of social life. Indeed,

Cohen goes so far as to say that in social anthropology we are interested in symbols mainly in so far as they affect and are affected by power relations. I think this is a reductionist argument – that a great range of expressive symbols at life crises, for instance, are not power symbols; and that status symbols, which are equally a concern of the anthropologist, should not be merely equated with power symbols. But power symbols are indeed a critical, under-studied field; and social anthropology can make a basic contribution to their analysis. Such analysis in Cohen's opinion should be of value to political science in the contemporary scene, as well as forming an essential constituent of social anthropology itself.

So in the modern anthropological study of symbols, though there are clear intellectual satisfactions, it is not all simply an intellectual exercise. Some symbol analysts hope to contribute to a further understanding to basic processes of human thought. Others hope to throw light on facets of human experience which can in a general way give guidance and encouragement to people as they face life's problems. Others still hope to expose more directly and more forcefully the operations whereby symbols become social instruments in a struggle for control.

Behind much of this work two major questions still stand. What is meant by saying that symbols or symbol systems have an existence of their own, instigate action, enter social relations as actors; is this more than a metaphorical kind of statement? And what is the nature of collective symbols, in relation to the symbolization of individuals in a society? This latter question will be discussed in an anthropological setting in the next chapter.

Chapter 6

PRIVATE SYMBOLS AND PUBLIC REACTIONS

In the study of symbolism by social scientists there are two fairly clearly recognized domains. In one, the province of sociologist and anthropologist, symbols are taken as being characteristic of sets or groups of people, of institutions or of types of situation. So in anthropology we speak of the symbolism of the Nyakyusa or the Ndembu; the symbolism of sacrifice or of peyote or of witchcraft. Sometimes the word symbol is given such general currency that it is equated with 'custom' (Abner Cohen, 1969, 222); it is the symbolism of collectivity – of myth, of ritual, of social structure – with which anthropologists are mainly occupied. As against this generalizing viewpoint there is the broad psychological domain in which the study is made not exclusively but basically of symbolic forms presented by individuals, often not shared with other people, and corresponding essentially to personal interests, claims, stresses. The symbolism of dream, hallucination, prophetic revelation or drug-induced experience belongs in this domain; and so does much of the initial creativity of poetry and the visual arts. A great deal of this personal symbolism is private in the sense that it is intended to be, or construed to be exclusive to the individual concerned, offering his own particular solution to his problem of adaptation to some aspects of his immediate environment or to his conception of the world. To a person who is dissociated or schizophrenic, the shapes, colours, voices of his vision represent reality in a way which marks him off from ordinary people. This tends to pose special problems to those who wish to be in touch with him or help him. In a notable account of his own psychosis, John Perceval (in a narrative edited by Gregory Bateson, 1961, 271) pointed out how many of his delusions consisted in mistaking a figurative or poetic form of speech for a literal one: when his 'voices' told him to wrestle with his keeper, or to suffocate himself upon his pillow, he tried to do this physically, not realizing, as he later saw, that it was intellectual struggle and stifling of his feelings that were meant, by another part of his personality.

At first sight the relevance of the phenomena, and the problems of interpretation, do seem very different in these two domains. An anthropologist is concerned to find out what a given symbol corresponds to in the general understanding and operations of a body of people. He seeks if not consensus at least the highest common factor in referents. He does this because he is looking at symbols as bases for or expressions of common action; the element of communication of meaning is dependent upon the possibility of shared understanding. A psychologist – using this term widely – may be interested in this too, but he is also interested in the departure of the symbol from consensus, with the clues it offers to individual development, and in the way in which social or physiological stimuli have given rise to specific reactions in the individual personality. Edmund Leach in characteristically brisk manner has characterized the aim of public symbolism as being communication, and of private symbolism as expression; the former he regards as a subject for anthropological study, the latter for psychological study.

As an example of division of spheres take the very rich symbolic field explored by R. M. Berndt in his description and analysis of the Kunapipi cult of north-east Arnhem Land (1951). In this area the name Kunapipi expresses a dual concept: it refers to a Fertility Mother or Mothers, and to the great Rainbow Snake (cf. p. 137). 'This is the symbolism of the Uterus and the Penis, natural instruments of fecundity' (1951, 12). In myth, in ritual and in decorated material objects, this basic symbolism is given form, transmitted to new generations, and validated by ceremonial sexual relations among Kunapipi participants. The elaborate symbolic procedures, accompanied by initiation of novices, co-operation of local groups, intricate kin exchanges, demarcation of roles between men and women, dancing and aesthetic display, are clearly of public concern, and of direct anthropological interest. On the other hand, many men who participated in Kunapipi had dreams which expressed their deep involvement in the ritual, as well as some degree of individual identification with Kunapipi figures – from being ordinary people, in their dreams they become participants in the myth, ancestral or totemic beings. Now dreams, as expressions of the personality, are clearly the province of the psychologist; they are series of private symbols.

The attitude of many British social anthropologists towards psychology has been ambivalent. Twenty years ago, Evans-Pritchard, following Radcliffe-Brown and Durkheim's view (cf. Murphy, 1971, 68) stressed the essential difference as he saw it between social anthropology and psychology, and his argument for independent pursuit of their research has been quoted frequently. Its effect has been seen in part in the attitude complained of by Ioan Lewis – that if there is one thing that unites most British social anthropologists it is their fierce antagonism towards psychology and psychiatry, and their 'complacent contempt' for the psychological aspects of the phenomena they study (1971, 178). Whether this is to be taken literally or not, I have myself argued that British social anthropologists who abjured 'psychology' still made statements about thought and feeling – often on little evidence; that the distinction often made between study of 'the individual' or 'mental systems' and that of 'groups' or 'social systems' was inadequate; and that anthropologists must come to terms with psychology (Firth, 1951b, 487).

Many American anthropologists have done so, with varying results – one of the most impressive, scientifically, being the series of essays produced by Anne Parsons before her death in 1964, combining high theoretical grasp with a range of comparative observational data in open and clinical conditions (1969). In the British field, with varying degrees of acceptance of psychological and psychiatric concepts, many anthropologists have independently illumined their interpretations of symbolism by such means – for example Margaret Field, Elizabeth Bott, T. T. Hayley, Audrey Hayley, J. B. Loudon, Geoffrey Gorer, R. M. Berndt, Victor Turner, Meyer Fortes, Audrey Richards. Problems of integration of findings, of translation of particular results into general propositions, of the kind of assumptions that are most useful to make about mental functioning, still remain. In their bearing upon symbolism, the methodological issues for a social anthropologist can be seen in three main areas: relevance; access; typicality.

Relevance is a matter of implication for interpersonal behaviour.

Thoughts, dreams, emotions of people in the expression and development of their own personality are not an anthropologist's concern but they become so when translated into actions affecting the conduct of other people. To dream of a tiger, to identify one's boss with a tiger in a phase of mental disturbance, are matters not necessarily of anthropological interest – though they may have social components, for example of status resentment. But if in a trance a medium portrays or engages in battle with a tiger spirit as part of diagnosis and therapy of an illness – as can happen in north-east Malaya (Firth, 1967d) – the ideology of this and the reactions of the patient, spectators and religious functionaries are a proper subject of anthropological study. Information about a person's thoughts, emotions and images is relevant for anthropological interpretation if these have social effect, particularly if they affect people's group relationships.

Access is a more difficult matter. To work with verbalized material may offer unfamiliar linguistic problems, and poses basic questions of relation of word to thought and emotion. But the general problems involved are confronted by anthropologists in most of their work. Non-verbalized beliefs, thoughts, feelings are another matter. These may be formulated but unspoken; unformulated but aware to the person's mind; or he may be unaware of them, revealing them only by his actions. The techniques of the anthropologist are slender to cope with such material, and anthropological opinion has differed considerably on whether to admit such material for symbolic study. But in varying combinations of assumption and inference, most anthropologists have committed themselves to some statements about human mental process in general or particular thought and emotional constructs of people, without having been told such by anyone. My own view is a rather cautious concurrence in such methods of inference, provided the empirical basis of the generalizations is made clear.

The question of typicality deserves more attention than it usually gets from anthropologists. The Durkheimian legacy in social anthropology has encouraged neglect of individual variation. In study of local grouping, kin units, and ritual such variation speedily became patent through observation of behaviour. But in statements about concepts, beliefs, emotions it is all too easy to assume typicality from sheer lack of breadth of evidence about degree of variation. Statements about attitudes towards 'master symbols' or 'dominant symbols' often show disregard for this question of typicality, and so may miss important developments in social reaction and symbol formation.

My basic subject of inquiry in this chapter is – granted precautions to be taken in the study of mental functioning, what is the relevance for anthropologists of what can be initially be described as private symbols?

An overlap in content may be of some significance, in that themes familiar to anthropologists in a general, category sense can be seen operating in a personal, private context. So, when John Perceval's 'voices' told him repeatedly that such and such persons were his mother, sisters and brothers, and he later conceived that this was a spiritual idea or that there was some other resemblance (ed. Gregory Bateson, 1961, 274) this is reminiscent of phenomena well known to anthropologists, of men conceiving themselves as kin to others with whom no biological tie can be traced. This implies a basic question as to what is the nature of such concepts, what is their symbolic force.

The problem of significance of private symbols touches the interest of social anthropologists from another angle – that of psychological studies of religion. For psychologists, while focusing on individual behaviour, have often related this to institutional patterns. In his *Varieties of Religious Experience* (1902) William James held that he was examining 'personal religion', which was more fundamental than theology or ritual. Gordon Allport, in *The Individual and His Religion* (1950, 119) cited James to the effect that in religious thinking we make use of such 'poor symbols' as our life affords, though it is unfortunate that they must be the same symbols as do duty for common sense and for scientific discourse. So confusion arises; personalities are infinitely varied; the symbols that appeal to one person may be meaningless and repulsive to another. Yet doubters who cavil at the unclarity or unacceptability of any particular symbol are speaking only for themselves; a re-forming of religious symbols to give greater designative fidelity for one person would merely throw others into a state of doubt. Allport agrees that various religious sects are defined by having approximately common sets of symbols for their members. But he argues that the cosmic conditions pointed to in religious language (the referents of the symbols) are not demonstrable, not knowable in their entirety, and therefore not accurately signifiable. So individuals are justified in effect in matching their symbolism to their aspirations, self-imposed ideals. Where they concentrate on the constituent images and symbols rather than on the general intent of the whole act of worship, they tend to fall into doubt. This, which may be called a case for a private symbolism in religion, contrasts to some extent with Thouless's view (in the *Psychology of Religion*, 1961, 114, 147). Thouless held that if an image has a fairly uniform meaning for different people it is called a symbol. Unconscious thinking tends to use symbols, and this is why symbolism plays such a large part in religion. Some of the processes of religious thinking, he argues, show an alogical and infantile character, as shown by the dependence upon symbolism. So it is difficult to translate religious ideas into the exact language of directed thinking, which is a voluntary activity, using mostly words and is a function acquired late in evolution.

So, from such psychological angles, private symbolism is regarded as relatively free-floating, even at times a kind of dwarfed or underdeveloped intellectual activity, less significant than a reasoned examination of the personal meanings of religious ideas. But from the other side, sociological and anthropological approaches to religion have tended to subsume private symbolism under public symbolism, and to give public symbolism a significant, respectable place in social action. Even more, public symbols have been regarded as having power to regulate individual behaviour, to express personal sentiments, and to dictate forms in which private symbols present themselves.

CARE IN CLASSIFICATION

As an anthropologist I share this approach. But there is a simple question of field methodology which must be cleared before we can consider the relation of public to private symbols more closely. How is the categorization of a symbolic form as 'public' arrived at? Anthropologists do not deny that the symbolic formulations current in a society about the meaning of ritual objects and actions are expressed in personal terms, often idiosyncratically. The symbolic concepts of a group may have concrete representation in flags or statues, but their meaning is described by individual people; it passes through a personal lens. Yet the process by which the anthropologist takes these personal statements and combines them into a formulation about the public meaning of a particular symbol sometimes remains obscure. I take an example from one of the most sophisticated studies of an African religion, that of the Nupe by S. F. Nadel. He describes a masked dance performed to cleanse a village of evil influences, succeeded about a fortnight later by a sacrifice in public before a pair of bronze figures, of a man and a woman, the rite being accompanied by music of rattles and drums. The officiant priest has the two rattle-players on his right and left. 'The place on the priest's left, opposite the female figure, signifies "birth", the place on his right, opposite the male figure, "health"; which symbolism of right and left is unique in Nupe religious practice.' Later a white cock is killed and some meat offered to the two bronze figures, with a prayer for health for the towns and plenty of children (1954, 93–5). Now there is no particular reason to doubt this interpretation, which makes good sense in the general social and religious context. But in the light of discussion about the relative inferiority and inauspiciousness of the left side in symbolic systems in Africa and elsewhere (for example Hertz, 1960; Needham, 1967a; Beattie, 1968) the question of whether we are concerned with a generally acknowledged Nupe symbolism or only a personal interpretation is significant. The offerings and the prayers for health and children were only partially public rites; some of the performance took place before a meal in which only the elders shared. Now one might postulate that the 'right and left' aspect of the ritual might have been connected with a faintly outlined division of the people into two ritual moieties. But Nadel was sceptical of the opinions he got about the exclusiveness of these moities, particularly since he was told of the rule about one moiety by only one old man, albeit of high rank. He did not see the rules in action and suspected that they were mere 'theory' – 'an attempt to lend neatness and logic to an unconvincing and haphazard division' (1954, 86–7). But now who told Nadel about the 'right and left', 'health and birth' symbolism of the bronze figures? Though it was a 'unique' symbolism, he does not say. Could this interpretation too have been an attempt to 'lend neatness and logic' to ritual positions by a reading backwards from the wishes expressed in the prayers – a case of pragmatic interests giving rise to structural interpretation? And a bit of private symbolism, perhaps by the priest, perhaps by one of the elders, to explain something about which there was no public opinion at all? It could even be that the 'right and left' interpretation was meant to support some private view about status. But this we are unlikely ever to know.

Even with Victor Turner's careful description of his methods of elucidation of the meaning of Ndembu symbols, to get 'reasonably reliable' interpretations (that is, as he puts it, mutually consistent interpretations) the relation of public to private symbolism occasionally remains obscure. What Turner gives is what he calls the 'standardized hermeneutics' of Ndembu culture. In such general interpretations he is not overtly greatly concerned with the 'free associations' or 'eccentric views' of individuals. What he is after is the regularities which can be built up into a general pattern (1969, 9–10). This is normal anthropological procedure, and I single it out here only as an example of the problems that confront us all in symbol interpretation. Turner quotes individual opinions in support of his generalizations. But what is it that makes one individual's opinion standard and another's a free association or eccentric and so to be discarded – when it is discrepant from the general pattern? Much information is given to show how the Ndembu regard the *mudyi*, the 'milk tree' which is central to girls' puberty rites and other rituals. Cognitively the Ndembu give the tree many attributes, associating it with breast development, breast-milk, mother-child relationship, matriliny, the Ndembu tribe as a whole. They 'speak and think' about the milk tree as a unity, almost as a unitary power. Yet while Turner was convinced that his informants genuinely believed that the milk tree represented only the linking and unifying aspects of Ndembu social organization, he was equally convinced that in action situations the tree served as a focus for group opposition. Much of the behaviour observable in connection with it represents a mimesis of conflict within the matrilineal units or relationships (1967, 20–5, 52–5). Could it be that more attention to discrepant, eccentric, private symbolism might have thrown some light on this apparent refusal to match ideology to action? Or could it be that the more abstract aspects of the milk tree symbolism were themselves derived from a few informants only, and that this was really the more private, even eccentric symbolism? For instance, the explanation that the milk tree is not only mother's milk but also the matrilineage, 'brought out most clearly in a text (I) recorded from a male ritual specialist' (1967, 21) occurs also in a text cited from the ritual specialist Muchona. But Turner adds the possibly significant note that this man's accounts and glosses were always fuller and internally more consistent than those of other specialists (1967, 134–5). He had evidently pondered long on the mysteries of his profession, says Turner, collating material given to him in the course of his own instruction, in critical review. Here then it seems pretty clear that public and private symbolism have got fairly well intertwined. I repeat, this is a dilemma which confronts all field anthropologists.

But the serious problem for social anthropologists is not so much to demonstrate how one arrives at a general statement of any piece of public symbolism, as to work out how public and private symbolisms impact upon each other. How far do public symbols really condition the forms of private symbolization? What kind of contribution does private symbolism make to the formation or modification of public symbols? In what way, if at all, does private symbolism have an effect in social action? How far does the existence of clusters of private symbols, if known or suspected, disturb the community when they do not seem capable of public utilization but imply social action with which the community may have to deal? Such questions are relevant, though often hard to answer.

A very pertinent field for the study of the inter-relation of private and public symbolization is art. Creativity in an artist is the display of a personal vision, in which symbolization may play an important, perhaps vital part. The symbols must be personal, individual, unique, stamped with the artist's own imaginative power, if he is to generate positive reaction in other people. (As modern examples Paul Klee or Pablo Picasso clearly qualify.) Yet if the symbolism remains purely private, unrecognized, the stimulus of the creative act is lost to the community. Communication is the keynote. There must somehow be enough communication between artist and public for the initial recognition of something of the artist's vision to be caught, absorbed, generate emotional and intellectual reaction, and stimulate further aesthetic reaction. Private symbolism must be able to be communicated to become public symbolism. A symbolic form which is completely obvious may be banal. But a symbolic form which has meaning which stays completely locked up in the artist's private world is not an object of art in any socially-significant sense.

In primitive society the relation is ostensibly reversed – an artist is concerned to portray symbols already recognized by the community rather than to invent new symbolic forms which the community has to construe. But the reversal is apparent rather than real. For the artist still makes a personal contribution which expresses his own rendering of material from the common symbolic stock, just as in our society the artist in fact draws heavily upon already conventionalized symbolic images. But in primitive society the initial common ground is more openly recognized – the symbols of primitive art are shared from the outset by groups of people; there is not the same initial dichotomy between artist and public (cf. Firth, 1951a, 177).

A most interesting analysis in this field is the study of Abelam phallic symbolism by Anthony Forge (1965). He shows how the main symbolic forms are related: the ridge-pole of the ceremonial house, standing for violence and warfare and associated with the spear; the penis as generative, nutritive organ, in paintings on the house façade and in carvings of clan spirits; the long yams, cultivated by individual growers with great care and skill, and publicly displayed in presentations of rivalry and hostility which confer prestige on grower and community. Here in the pictorial art, public symbols are periodically re-created, by private artists, working with almost a minimum of conscious interpretation. The communication is effected by the work itself, carried out in common in a broad context of common meanings. In our society, however, we have the spectacle of artists often operating a private symbolism and striving for its public recognition, but becoming frustrated and angry at the failure of the community to understand what they are trying to convey. And while it often does occur, the conversion of private symbolism into public symbolism may take a considerable period of time.

INTERPRETATION OF DREAMS

Dream is one of the most obvious areas for investigation of the relation between private and public symbols. A dream is a highly personal thing, and its symbolism is private in the sense that the ultimate clues to its meaning depend in some part upon the peculiar circumstances and mind of the dreamer. Yet to some extent its symbols are public in that many of them are clearly derived from shared social experiences, and are recognizably of common form, in 'type-dreams'. In Edmund Leach's categorization, their aim is expressive for the individual dreamer, as representations of unconscious mental process; but it is also communicative, since many dreams are verbally described to other people and indeed are known primarily by such mechanism. Moreover, their symbols become public in that they are often the source of social action. It is not surprising then that anthropologists even before Tylor paid attention to the subject of dreams and recorded instances which seemed to throw light on mental process, belief and individual and public reaction. As I have shown in Chapter 3 (p. 101) study of the symbolism of dreams by others than anthropologists, with attention to unconscious process, was a serious subject for much of the nineteenth century.

Many questions about dream symbols may be raised in psychological anthropology, which do not concern us here.* But apart from establishing norm and variation in dream content and interpretation in different types of society, social anthropologists have been concerned with three main questions in relating these private symbols to the public sphere. First is the significance of dream material as an index to the degree of social commitment, or social involvement. I have referred already to Ronald Berndt's material on dreams of aboriginal men participating in the Kunapipi cult (p. 208). Berndt collected hundreds of dreams from about thirty men, and found that while they ranged over a wide variety of themes, many were concerned with indigenous religion, and were regarded as very important by the people themselves. Men 'dreamed out' the meanings of their sacred ritual, coming into contact spiritually, they thought, with their Ancestral Beings. In dreams they performed ritual, used sacred emblems in unconventional ways, and dreamed additions to their totem designs and rites. This private symbolism has public effect in that, Berndt points out, many sacred designs are altered because of dreams, and sacred songs too are influenced thereby. In

* For example the relation between manifest content and latent content, see M. J. Field, 1960.

a very different context, I myself have indicated how in Tikopia, dreams have portrayed symbolically social situations of tension such as friction between chiefs, or chiefs' feelings of responsibility for the condition of the people (1967b, 166; 1970a, 49n.). Again, Tikopia incest-dreams have revealed a mechanism for removing some of the guilt of incest-wishes (1936, 328) and given some reflection of commitment to a social norm. And some dreams symbolized dramatically the struggles of Tikopia preoccupied with problems of conversion from paganism to Christianity, and helped to induce them to take overt action (1970a, 325, 327, 391, 394–5). So, granted the possibility of distortion and condensation of meanings, dream symbolism has still seemed to offer evidence about the extent to which individuals have felt themselves committed to ritual or other social situations – with implications for the intensity and continuity of their activities therein, in the public field.

Allied to this is the question of how far the occurrence of certain kinds of symbolic presentations in dream leads to social action, not only by the dreamer but also by others. These others may either share the dreamer's belief in the significance of his dream, thus converting a private symbol into a public symbol, or so respect his belief that even without sharing it they are willing to give effect to what he regards as its implications. Evans-Pritchard has recorded of the Zande that their bad dreams were commonly interpreted in terms of witchcraft – not as symbols of witchcraft but as actual experiences of it. Although they usually did not consult oracles about such dreams, on occasion a man would ask his blood-brother, kinsman or friend to make oracular inquiry on his behalf, and if witchcraft was confirmed, would pursue the matter more publicly. Traditional Iroquois attitudes appear to have been more drastic. Unlike the Zande, they seem to have regarded dreams as predictive, with the evil effects capable of being warded off by evasive or cathartic action. L. H. Morgan noted that dreams were often regarded by the Iroquis as 'divine monitions', that a dreamer would wander about inviting others to guess his dream, and that when interpreted, its injunctions were followed 'to the utmost extremity' (1851, 214–15). He recorded the case of the sachem Cornplanter, whose influence had for some years been on the wane with his people because of his friendly relations with the whites. As the result of interpretation by another man of a dream of Cornplanter's that he should relinquish his chieftainship and abolish his ties with whites, he gave up his office and removed from his house or destroyed all presents he had received from George Washington and other white leaders; the only exception was his tomahawk, which he used in unorthodox fashion to nominate his successor. Similar material has been discussed by Anthony Wallace, who distinguishes two major types of Iroquois dreams, symptomatic dreams and visitation dreams, the former in particular being followed by much public acting-out, often of cathartic type. Iroquois dreams are not to brood over, they are to be told or hinted at, and other people rally round with gifts and ritual. 'The dreamer is fed; he is danced over; he is rubbed with ashes; he is sung to; he is given valuable presents' (1958, 246–7).* Yet despite Morgan's phrase of following out the dream's injunctions 'to the utmost extremity', a prudent response to the symbolization is sometimes evident. Cornplanter used his tomahawk, a gift from whites, to ensure his successor. A man whose dream manifested a wish to kill either stops short of immolating his real-life victim provided, or is satisfied with a coat allegedly taken from a dead enemy. The private symbol is not necessarily or always completely incorporated into the public domain.

The third kind of question relates to the degree to which the symbols of a dream are regarded as not merely pertinent to the fate of the dreamer, but are absorbed by the social body and seen as a basis for their collective action. Private symbol becomes identified as public symbol. Historically, millenarian movements, indigenous churches and analogous attempts of people to forge their own religious instruments for coping with their destiny have tended to use symbols provided by dreams. Individual dreams have been regarded as stimulants and guides to action for the corporate body; symbol of one has meaning for all. In the New Guinea 'cargo cult' field, both Lawrence and Burridge have pointed to the common belief in the validity of information derived from dreams (Lawrence, 1964, 167; Burridge, 1960, 179–82). Burridge in particular has emphasized the notion of imperative contained within a dream, and the use made of this notion by dreamers in trying to persuade others

* Wallace's claim that the Iroquois independently anticipated Freud's theory of dreams seems to me far-fetched; it was a very superficial theory of the unconscious.

to a particular line of action or point of view. So for the Tangu, dreams can inform, direct and prophesy; they are not simple fantasies woven in sleep; they are a normal technique for solving problems. Dreams 'tend to pull a future into current, sensible reality; they give definity to hope, adding faith'. When dreams are so believed to have an authority surpassing that of the person who dreams them, they can easily be accepted as sanction for political action. So cult leaders have employed dreams to give their private symbolism a public referent, to make it appear that the individual incidents of a dream have symbolic meaning for all the people, and should be translated into action.

A similar inter-relationship between private and public symbols in dreams is excellently illustrated by Sundkler's study of Bantu prophets in South Africa (1948, 273–4). In the African Zionist churches dreaming in accordance with pattern is a common and accepted way of demonstrating group loyalty; the members of a church 'dream what their church expects them to dream'. Testimony about dreams is produced in Sunday services, and listened to for hours because people believe that Jehovah has revealed Himself in this way. The stereotyped dream is the true, prophetic dream and has great integrative strength. In Sundkler's view the sect thus exercises control over the individual's 'subconscious mind'. It has been noted by various authorities how frequently in these dreams having to do with the position of a person in a church, symbolic figures of authority clad in shining light garments appear. The concept of stereotyped or standardized dreams has been adapted, as Sundkler explains, from Malinowski, who distinguished between ordinary spontaneous dreams arising in Trobriand life from everyday experience, and dreams prescribed and defined by custom, and expected and hoped for. Malinowski explicitly stated (1932, 327) that the distinction between free and standardized dreams was not formulated or recognized by the Trobrianders. But it does lay stress on the obligatory nature of the social component entering into the make-up of many dreams, depending upon the cultural patterns, and it is significant that such standardized dreams are normally followed by socially recognized action. So a Trobriand gardening or fishing magician, in dreams inspired by ancestral spirits, learns of impending drought or rain, or of a coming shoal of fish, and will give advice and orders accordingly. In this way susceptible individuals are used as channels of communication and crystallizers of opinion for the social body, be it an African church or a Trobriand village; their dream symbols are both dictated and received by the social body, which can draw strength from the process.

But while the stereotype dream may be the true and prophetic dream, the social body may not always be able to mould the individual into its own image. The symbolism of some people's dreams may not fit the accepted pattern. One young woman belonging to a Bantu mission church had a hysterical illness which doctors and herbalists tried in vain to cure. In a dream she saw a group of people in white garments, with white veils on their heads, each carrying a long stick in his hand. She had not heard of Zionists before, but after this dream she joined one of their groups, who indeed did wear white clothing for ritual performances. But after a while she discovered that the sticks carried by this group of Zionists did not correspond to the sticks she had seen in her dream. So she left them and was fortunate enough to find another Zionist church that used the right kind of stick. Here the private sign served as guide in the dissatisfied search for health, a kind of symbolic fulcrum for change of group allegiance. Her private symbolism took public shape in a recruitment decision. Here the social effect was minimal. But where it is not follower but leader who has the aberrant dream the results may be disintegrating. The prophet of one Zion church had no children. He told his congregation he had seen in a dream two beds on one of which he himself was lying and on the other a young girl from the congregation; the Spirit, he said, obviously wanted him to take this girl as a second wife. The congregation were in a dilemma. They all believed that dreams were the channel of revelation from Jehovah, but some thought the prophet was mistaken in his interpretation. After a stormy church meeting the prophet was told that his dream would be accepted as true and prophetic only if his first wife corroborated it by an identical dream. Demand for this pragmatic test split the church. The prophet himself carried on with a small group who accepted polygyny, basing their authority on the Biblical examples of Abraham and Solomon. So, the private symbolism of the leader became a public stumbling-block.

This raises an important problem, namely, by what public

criteria is the acceptability of a symbolic experience judged? What constitutes a standard interpretation? What kinds of personal symbolism can be treated as creative orthodoxy, and what must be regarded as heresy? What symbols are meaningful to the public at large, and what are irrelevant?

Sometimes a fairly automatic standard is applied – as when if a dream conforms to Biblical pattern it is inspired by God's angels, but if it is in contradiction to the Bible it has been inspired by the angels of Satan. But even here argument can arise about what is 'contradiction'. Very broadly, I would argue that the criteria for judgement tend to be taken on the whole not from within the immediate framework of symbolic concepts, but from outside it, from the power structure and other institutional make-up of the society. Personal symbolism is accepted as socially relevant and valid when though novel, it does not appear to threaten vested interests of those called upon to judge. When it may appear so to threaten those interests, the interpretation of the symbols or the consequent action following their interpretation, may be tailored to the prevailing norms. So, as I noted with the Iroquois examples, the dreams symbolizing repressed aggression were translated in practice into action dealing with surrogates for human victims. Judgement on the public validity of initially private symbols may of course change as external circumstances alter. Peter Lawrence cites a case of a New Guinea cult leader, a young woman who claimed that an angel had warned her in a dream of the imminence of a Second Flood to destroy the 'wicked' and herald the coming of 'cargo' for the 'elect'. She built a house on tall posts and advised other people to leave their homes and join her. Some destroyed their pigs and other property 'to shame God and the ancestors with their poverty' and did so. When it began to rain the prophetess announced this as a sign of the Flood, and ordered people to sit outside in it to be washed as if in baptism. But as the weeks passed without further events the people grew tired and disbanded, 'the immigrants going back somewhat sheepishly to their homes' (Lawrence, 1964, 162).

Anthropological interest in the interpretation of dreams is directed primarily to their public significance. A dream is initially a private matter, a communication of one part of the self to another, an expression of deep-seated, unconscious or only part conscious feelings. Like myth, a dream commonly has a sequential structure, even a logic of its own. But apart from difficulties of recall, a dream is often so fragmented that interpretation of elements in terms of their internal relations within the dream may not be possible. The anthropologist ordinarily has neither the time nor the training to undertake a systematic analysis of the dream associations which might reveal the underlying significance of the dream in terms of the personality of the dreamer. Nevertheless, as I have shown, the anthropologist can point to the social components which appear in the dream account, and the social issues it reflects; he can also indicate the ways in which the private experiences of the dream can assume symbolic quality for the society and provide a basis for social action.

SYMBOLISM OF PERSONALITY DISORDERS

Over the variety of cultures studied by anthropologists it is common to find that dream experiences are attributed to experiences with spirits. The characteristic mode of expression here is for the dreamer to believe that he has encountered a spirit while he was asleep. But other forms of encounter with spirits are also commonly recognized, of what we would term visionary or hallucinatory character. In many of these, the symbolic forms of the encounter portray the recognition of some social norm which has been breached. In a highly technical study of 'ethno-psychiatry' in rural Ghana, with the suggestive title of *Search for Security*, M. J. Field, an anthropologist with medical training, has examined nearly 150 cases of people with mental illness who were treated by confession at local shrines. Field demonstrates how the range of private symbolizations generated in situations of personal stress conformed in general to the publicly held concepts of the society, including the supernatural determination of mental illness. Interpreting the symbols in such terms, the shrine priests were able to give relief in many cases. An example (1960, 232–3) is that of a man who had hallucinations of being attacked by people sent by a deity to kill him; some tried to make him eat lethal food, others came after him with clubs and cutlasses, and he was in a state of extreme terror. Treated by the shrine priest and making confession he was able to explain that when sweeping the shrine yard he had picked up a small gold trinket and kept it instead of handing it in; so he had incurred the god's anger. After a ritual purification he was discharged, free of disturbance.

There is a view which has received some popular support that madness is created by society, in that society determines the criteria by which certain types of behaviour of individuals are categorized as madness, and treated accordingly. In a formal sense this is correct. But I doubt if many anthropologists would agree with the formulation in a substantial sense. They see a high degree of individual reaction to social circumstances and social norms, varying with complex combinations of personality elements. They see behaviour disorder for the most part proceeding from the initiative of the person concerned, not enforced upon him by society. To the sufferer from mental illness the traps to personality set by the social order no doubt appear unavoidable, just as 'odd' behaviour seems a natural reaction to them. But to other members of the society the symbolic presentations of the mentally ill person are only one of a number of alternative avenues out of a circumscribing social situation. This is the basis of the treatment – to find out where the social pressures are and what alternatives exist, so that the patient can make another behavioural choice. In the case just cited, the patient had the initial choice of handing in the found object. In other cases, often of domestic difficulty, the choices may not be so simple, but some resolution is often open for suggestion. Even with the fantasies described by schizophrenics, which may have no apparent basis in objective reality, their private symbolic expressions can often be interpreted in terms of more general social theses.

What is suggested by some of the literature, and what I would support from personal field experience, is that so-called primitive and non-industrial societies are often more tolerant of the private symbolism of mental illness than are our own societies, more willing to try and enter a dialogue with the patient in comparable symbolic terms, and more successful in alleviating a condition of mental strain.

Another type of behaviour, which may be classed as an alternative order of personality rather than a personality disorder, is that of trance, usually identified in psychological terms as dissociated personality. The complexities of this phenomenon are considerable, likewise the anthropological literature upon it is great.* But interpreted by the societies concerned as spirit possession and spirit mediumship, it has proved a very convenient mechanism for translating private symbolism into a guide to public action. As Field has expressed it: 'dissociation is a mental mechanism, a technique, a vehicle for conveying both the convictions of the prophet and the tenets of contemporary thought and ethics' (1960, 86).

There are two highly significant but related points about such dissociation in many cultures. The first is that the *alter ego* of the dissociated personality is regarded as either having a special spiritual quality – as with Old Testament Hebrew prophets – or as being the actual expression of a different, new spirit personality descended upon the human body of the medium. The spirit encounter is conceived as not just meeting with spirits, as it might be in a vision, but as being physically controlled by a spirit, even to the extent of one's body being inhabited by an autonomous alien spirit. Hence the second point – that the communications of the medium are not simply those of the ordinary man; they have an extra-human authority. So the significance of spirit mediumship is not just that society gets a personal view on its problems from a specially-endowed individual; it is that with this individual as channel, usually vocal channel, society gets an opinion which is credited with authority precisely because it is not regarded as the individual's own.

It is in this sense generally that the term 'symbolic' is appropriate here. What the medium says, unprompted or in reply to questions, is often of a very pedestrian order. As those with experience of trance performances will confirm, few mediums utter lofty thoughts or grand prophecies, and their language is not necessarily highly figurative. But why it can be regarded as symbolic is because the individual's behaviour stands for more than itself; to it are assigned meanings of a complex kind of which the individual himself is by all evidence unconscious or only partly conscious.† In the original Greek meaning he is *prophetes*, a speaker for another, the conception

* Cf. I. M. Lewis, 1971, for a valuable synoptic account. An interesting analysis from a medical as well as anthropological point of view is given by Margaret Field, 1960, 55–86.

† The restriction of the term 'symbolic', as a description of the behaviour of prophets, to conscious, rational gesture –'mimed parables consciously invented and acted out by the prophets in order to enhance the effect upon their auditors of the message they delivered' (G. Rosen, 1968, 44) is a misapplication of the term.

of the 'other' being of an entity whose full mind and powers are unknown. And what gives the symbolism much of its importance is that to some degree it is 'private'; there is an element of unpredictability in it precisely because it stems from an individual, with his own personal background. If what a medium or prophet said was automatic, with no element of uncertainty, much of its value would disappear. But if it was purely personal, it would be meaningless. In the institutions of spirit mediumship and allied phenomena it is the combination of public and private symbolisms that gives them force.

SYMBOLISM OF THE BODY

Use of the human body as basic symbolic material has been discussed by anthropologists and analysts in allied disciplines, from Birdwhistell and Gombrich to Mary Douglas and Mircea Eliade. From this and much other treatment one can perceive at least four kinds of body symbolism in vogue.

As a symbolic instrument, a person may use his own body as a means of communication, to indicate by bodily action or reference some more abstract idea. When a person kneels in prayer he is symbolizing his humility before what he conceives as a higher personality, a god; when he says to someone else 'I bow to your opinion', he symbolizes his deference to authority. These are simple instances, but there are many more subtle ways of using one's body to express a social relationship. As Mauss put it: 'The body is the first and most natural instrument of man' (1950, 372). In Chapter 8 I show how people put their bodies to symbolic as well as pragmatic use in situations of greeting and parting.

A more general kind of body symbolism refers not to any concrete entity but to a set of abstract constituents. A man is the head of a family; the backbone of his team. A social unit is conceived as analogous to a human body, in some of its major parts. Bodily parts in themselves can represent the whole man, or his abstract qualities. He can be weak-headed or swollen-headed, indicating not physical condition but character defects; he can have no backbone or plenty of backbone, indicating similarly degree of resolution. Size of bodily parts can convey other qualities: big-hearted for generosity; big-mouthed for volubility; broad-shouldered for responsibility and endurance. (There is an equivalent symbolism, apparently just as fictional, about male virility.) Translation of bodily parts into other inanimate material can also be used to describe human qualities. If a man is generous he has a heart of gold; if very strong he has arms of steel; if eloquent he is silver-tongued; if loud-voiced he has a throat of brass; if discovered to have grave defects after having been admired he has feet of clay. The symbolism is selective – a stupid man has a wooden head, but traditionally a brave constant man had a heart of oak. Functional associations also vary in their descriptive validity: a heart bleeds in sympathy, and a mouth waters in desire or envy; salivation does empirically relate to desire for food, but the heart's blood has no relation in modern physiology to emotional flow. Some of these usages might be described as simply metaphorical; others have the complex allusiveness of symbolic quality.

Another kind of symbolic usage treats associations of people – 'corporate' social units – as a more literal type of body, not necessarily human, but with human embellishments. So we speak of the body politic, its head and its members; of the Christian church, especially if we are Catholic, as the Body of Christ, its members being in mystical union with Him. As the All Saints' Day Collect in the Book of Common Prayer has it, the elect are knit together 'in one communion and fellowship, in the mystical body of thy Son Christ our Lord'.

This particular example of body symbolism is of interest from the subtle distinctions drawn between the physical body of Christ, which was animate on earth and ascended into heaven; the eucharistic body of Christ which is received in Holy Communion; and the mystical body of Christ which is the inner life of the church. In the Catholic church the concept of 'mystical body' has been examined and elaborated by many authorities, including Pope Pius XII. In this symbolic concept, derived by analogy from St Paul, the church is likened to a body with constituent members each of which functions only through relation to the others in integral form. But as it is explained (for example Brantl, 1967, 106–16) what distinguishes the Catholic notion of 'mystical body' from legal, philosophical or sociological notions is not that the mystical body is conceived as having both an invisible and a visible aspect – such can be true of almost any philanthropic or political association – but that the invisible aspect is constituted essentially by a 'life of grace'. The head of the body is Jesus Christ as God-Man; the members of the body are all the baptized except those who have cut themselves off by schism, apostasy or heresy; the vital principle of the body is the Holy Spirit, Third Person of the Trinity, who informs the body through grace. As the life-principle of the mystical body, grace, the gift of God to the soul, is equivalent to participation in the life of God himself. The church distinguishes between transient or 'actual' grace, given to strengthen a person in his acts, and habitual or 'sanctifying' grace, a supernatural quality inherent in the soul, meaning that the soul partakes of the divine nature and life. So, by virtue of habitual grace the Catholic church, it is asserted, is a mystical body in that it is believed to be united essentially through the supernatural endowment of a special quality by God himself. Hence the 'mystical body of Christ' can claim freedom from human control. So the concept of the human body assumed for Christ has received a double extension: of his physical substance, in form of bread and wine transmuted into his body and blood; and of his metaphorical substance, in form of all members of the church allegedly founded by him. In this case the symbolism is seen as not contingent on human perception, but as intrinsic, absolute, sacred in the sense of not permitting contact with worldly explanations. Indeed, it is argued, not symbol but reality.

In a further kind of body symbolism the object of interest is not the actor's own body, or a postulated metaphorical body, but what is believed to be an actual part of the body of another person. Simple instances are the lock of hair which in Victorian times a person might cherish as a reminder of a beloved; or a tooth of a parent which a Tikopia traditionally might wear on a string round his neck as a token of filial sentiment (Firth, 1957, pl. 7; 1963, 256). Such objects are symbols because they are not just reminders of the existence of the person to whom they belonged, but stand for a complex set of emotional and intellectual dispositions. These tend to be private symbols, with a very restricted range of meaning, much of it not accessible to ordinary external observation. But some actual or putative physical residues of people become symbols of a public order. In this category may be ranked objects such as a presumed tooth of the Buddha preserved in Ceylon, a presumed hair of the Prophet Mohammed preserved in Pakistan, and the undoubted body of Lenin, preserved in Russia. All of these are cult symbols, the object of elaborate public rituals of respect, each representing in its own way the values and history of the religious or political system within which it has been singled out for attention.

Symbols of this public kind tend to have special qualities associated with them. One is the quality of sacredness, having a virtue of a non-empirical kind which demands special precautions of a formal order in any operations connected with the symbol. In theory this sacredness has been derived from the person of whose body the symbol once formed a part; in practice the attribution of sacredness to the symbol has often been a later cult development. In the West, the most common example of sacred bodily symbols are the relics of saints, persons whose lives have been dedicated to God to an exceptional degree and whose bodily remains have therefore an exceptional value as reminders and stimulants for the religious congregations. But another quality apt to be associated with these public symbols is power of a supernormal kind. Muslim saints can be wonder-working while alive (see Gellner, 1969) but Christian saints, thanks to a bureaucratic process of canonization, must wait usually for miracles until they are dead. But in Catholic Christian belief the power of body symbols and associated relics of saints is often regarded as great indeed.

The early mediaeval Christian church had a vast history of dealing with relics of saints, motivated in part by magical belief that by securing a part of a saint's body his protective powers were secured for the local altar and congregation.* But the folk-beliefs of Catholicism still preserve many examples, demonstrating a marked difference in the level of symbol appreciation between ordinary congregations and the more scholarly faithful. The symbolic value of the blood of St Januarius is a case in point. Nothing is known for certain of the life of this saint, traditionally a martyr bishop of the early fourth century, though a legendary account of his death, referred to by Bede, was translated into Greek in the tenth or eleventh century. After some transfers of his remains a portion of his blood said to have been collected after his martyrdom was given in a reliquary to the Bishop of Naples, and is preserved as a dark mass that half

* For data on transfer of relics and beliefs in their powers see Hirn, 1912, 39–47; Haskins, 1958, 233–6.

fills a hermetically sealed small glass container. The special property of the blood is that it liquefies eighteen times during the year, on formal occasions calendrically specified, when the reliquary is held by the priest close to the altar, on which is located what is believed to be the martyr's head. While the people pray, 'often tumultuously', the priest turns the reliquary up and down in the full sight of the congregation until the blood liquefies. Thereupon he announces 'the miracle has happened' and the Te Deum is chanted by clergy and people. Various thermal experiments and spectroscopic analysis have been applied to the contents of the reliquary, but it is held by the authorities that the phenomenon still eludes natural explanation. The blood with its periodic liquefaction is a symbol of the miracle-working powers of the saint.* But the authorities display some reserve on the matter. They point out that while the happening has been recorded for the past 500 years there is no record of it before A.D. 1389, over 1000 years after the presumed death of St Januarius. Moreover, similar miraculous claims are made for the blood of other holy personages, nearly all in reliquaries in the neighbourhood of Naples, and some of the relics, notably the blood of St John the Baptist, are stated to be 'manifestly spurious' (Attwater, 1965, 184). The implication is then that some degree of cult imitation has taken place, a borrowing of symbolic thinking. The essence of this type of body symbolism however is the focus on the overcoming of natural process. Blood dries, and it is against nature that it should again liquefy without human aid. Analogous phenomena have occurred with the preservation of the bodies of saints in lifelike conditions after death, with sweet savour, apparently antithetical to the processes of natural decay. The human body, or portions of it, are used to symbolize the power of supernatural forces to overcome natural law.

SYMBOLISM OF THE SACRED HEART

Mary Douglas is one of the most recent of those who have suggested that the human body is a symbolic medium which is used to express particular patterns of social relationships (1970, xiii). She has en-

* For discussion on a comparable miracle, that of the bleeding Host of Bolsena, see Malinowski, 1936, 48, with some general remarks on relation between physical event and supernatural force.

couraged the examination of Christian ritual and symbolism from this point of view, in line with similar interests of Edwin Smith, E. O. James or Bronislaw Malinowski. I want to pursue this theme briefly, not in regard to bodily style, boundaries and apertures, as Douglas has done, but in regard to one organ, the heart, which gives some significant illustration of relations between private and public symbolism.

For many centuries in the Western world the heart was regarded as the seat of the emotions (elsewhere stomach or liver were often so identified). Long ago, Trumbull pointed out that in more than 900 instances in our common English Bible the Hebrew or Greek word for 'heart' is applied to man's personality, as if it were in a sense synonymous with his life, his self, his soul, his nature. A person can be hard-hearted, tender-hearted, heartless; his heart can be warm, cold; it can be in the right place, in his mouth, at rest. . . . In every phase of man's character, needs, experiences, says Trumbull, 'heart' is employed by us as significant of a man's innermost realest self.

So it was natural that the church at an early period included reference to the heart of Jesus (and that of Mary his mother) as objects of special attention. Christ's Sacred Heart especially was taken as the fountain that dispensed the Spirit from the Saviour's wounded side. There was a gradual transition in patristic theology from the idea of the wound in Jesus's side as a source of grace to the preaching of the Sacred Heart itself as the express object of a more personal devotion. Various religious authorities, including Jesuits, became advocates of this form of devotion, and in the seventeenth century one in particular, St John Eudes, a priest of the French Oratory, though concerned also with the veneration of the Immaculate Heart of Mary, was prominent in bringing devotion to the heart of Jesus into public worship in the church. In such worship the heart of Jesus was specifically the symbol of his love.

But the cult of the Sacred Heart was focused and energized by the visions of a nun, Marguerite Marie Alacoque (1647–90) in the Visitation convent at Paray-le-Monial. What the *Catholic Encylopaedia* describes as 'the private revelations made to her by our Lord' consisted of her visions of reposing on Christ's bosom for a long time, where He discovered to her 'the marvels of His love, and the inexplicable secrets of His Sacred Heart' which could no longer contain within itself the flames of its ardent charity. Jesus said He needed the help of Marie to introduce to the faithful the 'precious treasures' of the physical organ. Christ then demanded her heart, put it in His own, where it was set on fire, and then returned it glowing to her bosom. Later Christ appeared again to her, with His five wounds 'radiant like suns' and complained of the ingratitude of men; He ordered His devotee to communicate on the First Friday of each month, and to prostrate herself for an hour late at night, begging intercession for sinners. Some of this enthusiasm may have been difficult for her fellows to bear. A later commentator has described her ecstasy rather unkindly as a sexual urge disguised as piety. But without accepting such a psychological explanation, even such a relatively favourable authority as Attwater has termed her 'exemplary but perhaps somewhat humourless'. Certainly her willingness to expiate the shortcomings of her companions must have been rather trying. But while not the source of the official cult, her experiences gave a great impetus to publicizing the devotion to the Sacred Heart and shaping its practices.

There was opposition within the church. Theological controversy arose – stimulated by the role of Jesuits in the cult – over the precise object of the officially approved devotion. Was the 'heart' to be understood as physical, metaphorical or symbolic? But by official statement it is now generally admitted, following Pope Pius XII, that the physical heart is included in the object of the cult, and that without the physical heart the public devotion authoritatively approved and prescribed for all Catholics by the Church is not realized. In the upshot Marguerite Alacoque was beatified by Pope Pius IX in 1864 and canonized in 1920.

The official devotion to the symbol has emerged in various concrete forms. Ritually, a feast is celebrated on the Friday following the second Sunday after Pentecost. Holy Hour, votive Mass and Communion of Reparation are observed on the first Friday of the month. Consecration of families, nocturnal adoration (on the model of St Marguerite) and enthronement of the Sacred Heart may occur in the home. The Enthronement is a recently developed rite which, begun in 1907 in the Chapel of Apparitions at Paray-le-Monial, the seat of the original visions, has become an officially recognized public crusade. The cult, begun by Father Mateo Crawley-Boevy, S.S.C.C., and preached by him in many parts of the world, consists essentially in a solemn installation of the Sacred Heart in a prominent place in the home, and consecration of it, though it can be carried out in any institution. What it means is a dedication to a way of life in which love is fostered by the sharing of family interests with Christ and Mary by frequent renewal of the consecration to the Sacred Heart in union with the Immaculate Heart of Mary, and by a fuller liturgical life at home and in church. In 1917 Pope Benedict XV gave formal approval to the Enthronement in a private letter to Father Mateo, and this was renewed in 1948 by Pius XII, who also issued an encyclical on the subject. It has been estimated that since 1915 over 2 million families in the United States of America alone have enthroned the Sacred Heart. It is the official view that through Enthronement and Night Adoration in the home the Congregation of the Sacred Hearts has contributed to family life in the United States.

On the organizational side, many sets of people have devoted themselves to promotion of the idea of the Sacred Heart or have enrolled under its symbolic label. These include: the Society of the Sacred Heart; the Sacred Heart Brothers; the Sacred Heart Mission; various Sacred Heart Colleges; the Sacred Heart University (founded in 1963 at Bridgeport, Connecticut, with completely Catholic personnel). Before the war at least, copra bags in New Guinea might be seen bearing the mission trading label 'Sacred Heart of Jesus, Ltd.' The basilica of the Sacré Coeur in Montmartre, begun in 1875 and approved as a work of public utility stands, as Salomon Reinach has put it, as 'a monument of Jesuit theology, and of the illimitable credulity of the human mind' (1942, 419). Books, a 16 mm. film and a phono-record of the Enthronement have helped the cult. (For general data on the cult see *New Catholic Encyclopaedia*; and A. D. Howell-Smith, 1950, 540–5.)

Iconographically, there have been innumerable representations of the Sacred Heart, with varying degrees of realism. According to Mrs James (1900, xxiv) the Flaming Heart is 'the rather vulgar and commonplace emblem of Divine Love', not to be met with in any of the very early pictures except that of St Augustine. The heart crowned with thorns is given to St Francis de Sales; impressed with

IHS it is given to the 'Jesuit saints' and some others. The popular form, depicting a heart with a wound, encircled with a crown of thorns and a small cross above, the whole radiating light, did not appear till the end of the seventeenth century. Since then, says the *Catholic Encyclopaedia* fastidiously, 'statues and paintings of disputable taste, often of vulgar sentiment repulsive to educated sensibilities' proliferated from the beginning of the nineteenth century.

Now for some general points, on this recognition of a bodily organ as a representative of human and divine love, in terms of public and of private symbolism.

The first point is that the object of devotion (let us call it worship) is conceived as something quite material in origin. 'In the devotion to the Sacred Heart the special object is Jesus's physical heart of flesh as the true natural symbol of his threefold love...' says the *Catholic Encyclopaedia*. Now assuming that there was an historical Jesus, and so a fleshly heart, it is obvious that unlike many of the relics of the saints, there is certainly now no concrete object of adoration; the physical, fleshly heart is only a conceptual object, which has been re-translated into material form by the iconographers. It would seem a reasonable suggestion that it needed the ecstatic private experience of the nun to provide that dimension of concreteness, that illusion of physicality desirable to win acceptance of the heart of Jesus as vehicle of a public symbolic message. Again, the symbolism is conceived to have begun in terms of physical communication. Marie Alacoque saw her heart being received into that of Jesus, illumined there by the flames of its charity, and after these celestial pyrotechnics, returned again to her breast – experience clearly generative of acute physical sensation.*

Secondly, the heart of Jesus is very much of a condensation symbol, in Victor Turner's use of the term. The material object, of red cloth or paint on canvas or what not, is a symbol of a symbol – it stands for an abstract, conceptual heart, which in turn represents a

* An interesting analogy was provided by the principal leader of the Ghost Dance among the Caddo, a man known as John Wilson, about 1890. When Mooney met him he explained that an amulet on his breast, consisting of a polished end of a buffalo horn, surrounded by a circlet of downy red feathers within another circle of badger and owl claws, was the source of his prophetic and clairvoyant inspiration. The buffalo horn was 'God's heart', the red feathers contained his own heart, and the circle of claws represented the world. When he prayed for help, his heart communed with 'God's heart' and he learned what he wished to know (Mooney, 1965, 162).

wide spectrum of meanings, of human and divine love, of family solidarity. And we may note that the meanings are intensified by action – as the institutionalization of the Enthronement provides avenues for emotional expression and development of ideas about family relations.

Thirdly, the meaning of the symbol in a general and public sense is not identical with the message associated with it by its private promoter. It is clear that Marie Alacoque had convictions about the inadequacy of the worship accorded to Jesus: He complained to her about the ingratitude of men; He ordered her to beg for intercession for sinners – among whom were numbered apparently some of her own convent. The manifestation of the five radiant wounds – devotion to which was much practised in mediaeval times – and of the Sacred Heart, was not simply to request increased attention but to protest against neglect. It was a message of accusation as well as of invitation, and Marie was the self-designed bearer of it. Hence the initial view of some of her fellows, not lacking in self-interest, that she was suffering from delusions.

Now it is relevant to this personal interpretation and manipulation of the symbol by its promoter that somewhat analogous conditions appear to have developed in connection with the apparition of Our Lady to children near Fatima between May and October 1917. As narrated in works on the subject, the children were told by the introductory angel: 'The Holy Hearts of Jesus and Mary will be attentive to your prayers and have great designs of mercy on you'. And when the Virgin Mary appeared to them she announced as part of her message that Jesus wanted to 'establish the Devotion to my Immaculate Heart in the world. I promise salvation to those who practise it . . .' One of the children told how they saw a heart pierced by thorns before the palm of Our Lady's right hand, which they took to indicate the Immaculate Heart of Mary so offended by the sins of mankind. A commentator noted the 'amazing significance' of the words: 'the Mother of God tells a child of ten years, who is totally illiterate, that God Himself wants her to work for the purpose of getting the world to know better and love better the Immaculate Heart of Mary.' The emphasis in most of the visions of the children was on the conversion of sinners, for which the children were invited to undergo sacrifice and suffering; and much later in 1929 Our Lady appeared to the survivor asking for the consecration of Russia, which was full of error, to Her Immaculate Heart. In this case the physical image was not so prominent, but the message of conversion and devotion was associated with the concept of a physical seat of the emotions, an immaculate or sacred heart, as in the case of Marie Alacoque.

But conversion of symbol from private to public use needs a process of organization. As so often in such cases, the initial visionary acts as a trigger for the cult – one might almost say a catalyst since though changed by the experience personally, he or she often does not participate in the cult developments, but retires from the scene. The system of organized ritual practices which is erected on the basis of the vision is controlled by other hands. In the case of Marie Alacoque, the developmental role was played by her Jesuit confessor (who in some quarters was credited, apparently wrongly, with having invented or suggested the mode of devotion). And two centuries later the formulation of the Enthronement procedure by Father Mateo reinforced the cult. Students of symbolism, even anthropologists, sometimes write as if the significance and importance of symbols are somehow self-evident to those who believe in and act upon them, or at least as if 'society' somehow dictates their recognition. I maintain to the contrary that there is a process of selection of symbols in which personal, private preferences may be of critical importance. There may be competition between forms of symbolic representation in which the interests of promoters come to expression. In one and the same 'society' there may be conflict of opinion as to the appropriateness of a symbol to the conditions specified, or indeed as to whether the object selected can be properly regarded as a symbol at all. The accusations of 'cardiolatry' levelled from within the church itself in the eighteenth century at the promoters of the Sacred Heart devotion testify to lack of enthusiasm initially for what the highest authority later declared to be the duty of every Catholic to acknowledge. Moreover, there may be symbolic development on a considerable time-scale. In this case it took several centuries for the public and private symbolism to coincide.

A further area of possible divergence between public and private symbolization lies in the processes of material reproduction of the symbol. In this example, the conception is of an original fleshly heart of Jesus, long since disappeared and hence retained only as an ideal form. Material images have been made of this – of plaster, of cloth, of wax, of stone, of metal, of paint on canvas, in many variants. Now aesthetically some of these variants have been unpleasing to some followers of the cult, especially to those of 'educated sensibilities'. Yet by what criterion are these judged? Aesthetically, there are canons of taste in representation, debated though they may be. Also, it has been maintained that the difference between allegory and symbol is that while allegory is moral, symbol is aesthetic. But as representations of an organ which is itself representative, conventionally if inaccurately, of human and divine love, what is the basis of evaluating one picture or object as better or worse than another, if each provokes the appropriate behaviour of devotion? *De facto*, aesthetic and intellectual criteria are introduced in judgement on a religious symbol. Clearly, the Sacred Heart of Jesus, or the Immaculate Heart of Mary, are public symbols of devotion in the sense of general rather than abstract concepts, the content of which can vary greatly in the people who share it. The public symbol is a general idea; the private symbol is its working out.

THE VALIDATION PROBLEM

Material given in this chapter on dream, dissociation, vision has illustrated the intricacy of the relationship between private and public symbolism. In the interpretation of dreams by the uncovering of unconscious wishes, a technique in which Freud above all showed his mastery, success is based on an assumption that there is a certain set of experiences, rooted in family life, which have been common to all men and women, and which find their reflection in times of stress in recognizably similar patterns of dreaming. The nature and ubiquity of those experiences has been disputed, as also the techniques by which they can be recovered from individual evidence. Lévi-Strauss, who acknowledges his debt to Freud for the pursuit of phenomena involving the most fundamental structure of the human mind, emphasizes that the family experiences may have been symbolic, not historic. He even goes so far as to accuse the analytic method of dealing with patients as the invention of myth to explain the facts – the analyst conniving with the patient instead of diagnosing or interpreting him (1949, 610–11; 1969, 490–2). Yet in his own essay analysing the efficacy of a Cuna shaman's treatment of a sick woman he argues 'that the mythology of the shaman does not correspond to an objective reality does not matter. The sick woman believes in the myth and belongs to a society which believes in it' (1958, 217 1963, 197). I am not concerned with the question of the efficacy of myth; I merely wish to make the point again that the private experiences of dream, sick person's fantasies, shaman's trance, each with symbolic components, all embody recognizably socially-engendered material, upon which their interpretation mainly depends.

But the problem of interpretation of the symbolism may have a double significance. The symbols may be regarded as means whereby the individuals simply express their own experiences or feelings and attempt to communicate these by comprehensible images to other people. Any question about the validity of the symbols then relates to the degree to which they are thought to reflect accurately the experiences and feelings signified. The meaning of the symbols is the clue they give to the state of mind of the person who expresses them. Quite another significance of the private symbols may be thought to lie in the degree to which they express experiences or feelings of what may be called the audience. The dream, trance presentation or other symbolic form is regarded as relevant not only to the individual's situation but also to that of those to whom it is communicated. It is thought to correspond to their feelings, be explanatory of their circumstances, even be predictive of future events. Other types of semi-private symbolic formation, engendered in discussion and controversy, such as a new scientific theory or a new theological statement, may also be regarded from a similar standpoint.

A central problem here is what secures public acceptance of the validity of private experience conveyed symbolically? To some extent, conformity with fresh increments of experience – as with many scientific theories, up to a point, and with many dream and vision symbolisms. We may recall the case of the New Guinea prophetess cited by Peter Lawrence (p. 222) whose supporters trickled home again after the dream-symbolized flood did not occur. But other kinds of symbolic statement either cannot be subjected to such empirical test, or the test is rejected as unsuitable. This is true of many statements of mystical experience, of many theological statements and indeed even of many scientific theories of the more abstract kind: they are symbolic constructs, often alternatives to others in their field, deriving their acceptance from their capacity to include a wide range of phenomena in their explanatory scope, but not directly testable by external observers. For public acceptance of symbols privately created, a consistency in the symbolic arrangement, a degree of logical fit, seems necessary. But also, I would hold, there is a prime element of aesthetic concern, a positive interest in patterning which is not simply reducible to logical principles. If one looks at some of the modern theological statements, say of protagonists in the so-called 'Death of God' movement, the level of personal symbolic content is high, as also is that of logical argument. But in the last resort the appeal of concepts such as the kenotic or self-emptying process of self-annihilation of God, the divine self-transformation from transcendent to immanent, from Spirit to flesh, is an aesthetic (or aesthetic-moral) appeal. The radical theologian's concept of God as dialectical process rather than as individual being has been joined with Nietzsche's poetic phrase that God is dead, and Blake's symbolic view of God's self-annihilation. But contemporary preoccupations also help in acceptance – as the conjunction of the dialectic with the idea that Christ is (and presumably ought to be) in the world – clearly reflects the deep commitment of the 'Death of God' protagonists to the problems of modern society. A final word on the more personal side. Some private symbol formations seem to receive public acceptance because of the special gifts of the person who communicates them. From this point of view one may define charisma as the ability to get private symbols publicly accepted.

There is a further problem in the translation of a personal symbolism into a public symbolism. With a truly private symbolism the social problem is one of action only in the sense of whether the private symbols inhibit or enhance the operation of the personality in its external contacts. If so, then questions of communication, identification of the symbols, interpretation of their significance arise in relations with the person concerned. But with some other types of personal symbolism the problem is more forcefully posed. It is characteristic of many mystics that they have felt a need – almost a compulsive need – to communicate their experience and to assert its validity. Not only again do they claim their symbolic presentations as true; they claim this truth as having more than a personal application. So, commonly the personal symbolic experience of a mystic has resulted in a call for a commitment by others, for a recognition of the social validity of his symbolic order. And this in turn has often meant a need for judgement by the established forms of authority in the society. (The personal symbolism of a poet is usually easier to handle; except perhaps in a dictatorship, his market is apt to be uncluttered by power considerations.) Any attempt to get private symbolism translated into public symbolism may involve the social body in strain; it may mean organization, mobilization of resources, reactions upon existing social and political structures. There may be always a danger that the innovative activity of a mystic and his followers may threaten the established order. Hence in established religious bodies a careful watch is apt to be kept by the authorities over personal statements of a symbolic kind related to doctrine by their members. Divergent symbolic attributions have often been a form of expression for cleavages of a more substantial organizational kind, concerned with struggles for power. Historically in Christianity, as in Judaism and Islam, the mystic is apt to operate on a knife-edge – his imaginative symbolic creations lift the expression of his religious body to a new height; but they may also claim an authority which the established religious body is not willing to concede. For a personal symbolism in the religious field to be both creative and successful it would seem to have to reflect some unsatisfied demand in the power structure.

II

Chapter 7

FOOD SYMBOLISM IN A PRE-INDUSTRIAL SOCIETY

If every society or culture has its own set of symbols, as anthropologists have demonstrated, one may expect the symbols of a pre-industrial society to differ very markedly from those of a society of industrial kind. The case for some symbolic universals has been made – or at least for some symbolic general ideas – as in the status significance of up-and-down or right-and-left; the sexual significance of water or hair, or pointed and cleft objects; the emotional significance in the contrast of light and dark colours and the stimulus of red. Examples of all of this can be found in nearly any pre-industrial society that has been reasonably well studied. But a pre-industrial society tends to have a smaller range of man-made objects to get symbolic about. In the relative absence of machinery its members tend to be less concerned with symbolic problems of alienation of man from the products of his labour. With one major product then, food, should we expect to find it embedded to a high or to a low degree in the symbolic system of the society?

Claude Lévi-Strauss has already shown in great detail and with consummate skill how in apparently crude empirical categories connected with food, such as raw and cooked, fresh and decayed, boiled and roasted, there can be identified an intricate set of abstract ideas, of a kind that may be called symbolic, and that constitute in one of his expressions 'a logic of sensible qualities' (1964, 9). This logic has been exposed, by exercise of great analytical power, over more than 800 myths, many of which contain only incidental references to the subject of food, but which bear in one way or another on the basic structural principles being examined. In his analysis Lévi-Strauss is concerned only with the internal structure of the system, conceived in terms of intellectual process, for reasons which he stoutly defends: 'Authentic structuralism seeks to seize above all the intrinsic properties of certain types of order'; and 'it is these (intellectual) operations alone that we can claim to explain, because they participate in the same intellectual nature as the activity which attempts to understand them' (1971, 561, 596; cf. 1964, 172 ff.).

In this brief chapter I cannot attempt an adequate analysis of the internal structure of any substantial part of the system of symbolic relationships to be discerned in a pre-industrial society. In this respect I can do no more than indicate a few features of what Victor Turner has termed the 'positional analysis' of some symbolic items related to food, together with an examination of statements and behaviour in regard to them. The society I take for consideration is that of Tikopia in the Western Pacific, which when I first knew it more than forty years ago had almost no literacy, was ignorant of the use of money, had very rare contact with the outside world, and maintained a highly traditional social system almost untouched by modern political forces.

A small isolated island in a vast ocean space, with no food imports and few imports of any other kind, traditional Tikopia was preoccupied, one might almost say obsessed, with problems of its own food supply. Drought, hurricane, population increase, famine were recurrent fears, and much thought was given by responsible leaders to coping with these problems.* Planning for the availability of some types of food took place months, even years ahead – in the planting of long-term crops, the fallowing of land, and the construction of fishing canoes. A major daily concern of all adults and most children was getting food. No one who has lived only in a society where food can be bought in shops, can be stored in refrigerators or in tins, comes pre-packed, prepared, almost predigested, can conceive fully of a life where all food has got to be obtained raw, direct from nature, uncleaned; where storage facilities are very few and cannot be applied to many kinds of foods; where people must go out to seek nearly every meal afresh. In an industrial society getting a meal is an interval or a conclusion to the day's work; in a society such as Tikopia, getting a meal *is* the day's work. Some people go inland, digging up taro or yams, plucking bread-

* For data on these problems, and on the place of food in Tikopia life generally, see my various monographs, especially Firth, 1936, 94–116, 451–3, 546; 1939 *passim*; 1940, *passim*; 1959, Chaps 3 and 4; 1970a, 227–30, 248–50. For an analysis of social and political symbolism of food in a Massim society see Young, 1971.

fruit or coconuts, or culling forest products; others go out on the reef, sweeping it for fish; others (only men) take canoes out to sea for long-lining by day or flying-fish netting by night. With the insignificant exception of a few occasional birds, traditional Tikopia knew no animal meat. Their cookery also was limited since they had no pottery or metal vessels that could take fire; mostly they baked food with hot stones in an earth oven. Apart from a little roasting of fish in leaves over an open fire, and occasional boiling by sliding hot stones into liquid in a wooden bowl, their cooking patterns were determined by the oven technology – which also gave indicators externally for social and ritual purposes (see p. 65). But despite its limitations their food technology was shrewdly adaptive and diversified, they commanded a fair range of food ancillaries, and had some quite imaginative food recipes (1936, 103–10).

For individual Tikopia, getting a main meal, usually between about noon and mid-afternoon, was one of the most important features of the day's business. But it was not just an individual search for and preparation of the day's food; it was a highly organized, planned co-operative activity in which not only division of labour but also transfer of food played a significant part, particularly among households of close kin, if only to fill gaps in immediate supplies.

From all this it should be obvious that much of the relationship of people to food in Tikopia is strongly pragmatic, empirical. They want to eat it, they are anxious about the supply of it, they organize a great deal of their activity around getting it and making it ready for eating. They also are very interested in the idea of food, intellectually and emotionally. They talk a lot about food; they enjoy their own foods cooked in their own way; they are very hospitable in pressing food upon visitors; and very pleased when visitors enjoy it too. With all this the Tikopia have quite an elaborate set of symbolic concepts in which food figures – either being symbolized by other things or itself symbolizing activities and relationships.

I want here to make an important point: strictly speaking there are no symbolic objects – there are only symbolic relationships. To speak of food in Tikopia as a symbolic object is often a convenient short-hand term, but it is the conceptualization of the object in a given relationship that is significant. This bears on the notion of 'master symbols' or 'dominant symbols' which have been regarded as key features in ritual (cf. p. 86). Victor Turner has argued that Ndembu dominant symbols refer to values that are regarded as ends in themselves, axiomatic values. He also has pointed out that there may be discrepancy, even contradiction between many of the meanings given by informants to a dominant symbol when it is regarded as a unit of the total symbolic system; and that such discrepancy is a quintessential property of the great symbolic dominants in all religions (1967, 20, 43). Now food in general has certainly an axiomatic value to all Tikopia, and was a prime symbolic element in the traditional religion. But I do not think there was any basic 'quintessential' discrepancy between the views of Tikopia informants as to its basic significance in the symbolic system. I suspect that there may be variation in this as between different kinds of symbols, if not among different kinds of ritual or symbolic systems. But for Tikopia I think this problem does not emerge if one looks upon the issue of dominance in a somewhat different light, as referring to relationships, not objects. I doubt if it would be adequate to speak of food as being a dominant symbol in Tikopia, though as I shall show it enters into every ritual situation; I think it preferable to speak of the symbolization of food as a dominant – or at least prominent – theme. At the same time the symbolic relationships of food in Tikopia society can function side by side with non-symbolic, quite pragmatic relationships. Food is not wasted in Tikopia, as one may imagine from the care taken to conserve it; so food which serves a symbolic purpose also serves the purpose of a meal. The symbolic and the non-symbolic relationships are intertwined.

LANGUAGE OF FOOD IN TIKOPIA

Tikopia has a rich series of linguistic expressions to describe food in general, in specific forms, and in social relationships. The basic Tikopia term is *kai*, which according to preceding particle can mean food in general, foods in plural, a particular food, etc.; also the act of eating, in its various verbal modifications. In contrast to the concept of 'the land' as a whole, meaning the whole population, the expression *te kai* can mean the total food resources of the island. Within this general category there is a great variety of names for many kinds of food. (It can be noted that quite a number of the staple vegetable foods have simple two-syllable names: *niu* for coconut; *ufi*, yam; *taro* (like potato); *mei*, breadfruit; *futi*, banana.) There are also series of linguistic categories of the order of: raw, cooked; unripe, ripe; fresh, rotten; tender, tough – with connotations outside the food field. But I want to focus on certain discriminations of a more striking character, which lead more directly into the field of symbolic relationships.

The Tikopia term for food, *kai*, is often contrasted much as in Western society, with the word for water, *vai*. Not only are generally food and water bracketed together as requirements for life; they are specifically linked in complementary fashion in a Tikopia meal. Eating in traditional Tikopia style a person first takes food from the leaf platter set before him, then is handed a water bottle (traditionally made from a coconut – nowadays a cup serves instead) and drinks. So *kai* and *vai*, solid food and liquid, are the twin components of a meal. *Vai* is ordinarily water – as *vai tai*, sea water; *vai marie*, fresh water. But *vai* is also liquid more generally and can refer to liquid food, as to soup-like foods made by sliding hot stones into wooden bowls of watery mixtures. The reference here is to the consistency of the food, and the adjective *vaivai* in usual reduplicative form means watery. But there is an anomaly: when mourners are confined to the house in which a dead person has been ritualized, they are fed for three nights by kinsfolk and neighbours who have been free to collect food from the cultivations, and who enter brusquely when the sun has set, wail with the mourners and then insist on their partaking of the food they (the visitors) have brought. Traditionally they bring with them waterbottles to assuage the thirst of the mourners, who have been fasting all day, and the drink is offered as soon as the wailing ends. But not only the drink but also the solid food is termed *vai*, and to urge the mourner to eat the expression used is '*Inu se vai mou*', 'Drink (a) water for yourself'. The Tikopia are quite aware of the inconsistency of calling solid food liquid, and explain it first by pointing to the association of the food basket with the water bottle. But when pushed further they say that the gift is called *vai* and not *kai* because to speak of it as *kai* would imply that one was boasting about it (1939, 374). It is for this reason that periodic gifts of food from commoners to men of rank, especially chiefs, are described as *vai*. Such gifts to men of rank are reciprocated (*tongoi*, the appropriate category term for a food-to-food transaction) later on in no particularly prescribed style. But mourners' *vai* are reciprocated on the last night of the feeding by non-food goods (*koroa*, in the category *fakapenu*) and the obligation of the transaction is carried on until in due course another funeral offers an opportunity of repayment. The reason for this double transaction would seem to be that the mourner's *vai* is not just a gift of food to someone who can go out and get his own food; it is the service of a meal to someone who has been fasting and inhibited from going abroad to sustain himself. Now what underlies this nomenclature of calling solids 'liquid' is the symbolic concept that in status situations where food is an instrument of social policy liquid rates lower than solid. But it is also more complex. The recipients know they are getting solid food – and incidental to my argument here, though not to Tikopia, the solid food should be of high quality, containing pudding and ideally fish. With people of acknowledged rank, such as chiefs, the power recognition is evident – commoners are afraid of seeming to boast lest they suffer for it. But with mourners the situation is in reverse – they are the disadvantaged ones, and the bringers of food do not wish to seem to boast lest the mourners be shamed. The motivational part of my interpretation follows Tikopia explanations, but the rating of solid over liquid is an inference which the Tikopia did not overtly cite.

In the symbolic field where food is made to serve social relationships, then, the concept of *kai* as solid food opposed to *vai* as liquid food can be intellectually manipulated and emotionally supported in a distortion.

An even more startling distortion occurs in the field of edible and non-edible. *Kai* is the word for 'edible' in all general contexts. One asks of fish, fruit and many other things *e kai?* and one is told *e kai!* or *sise e kai*, edible or inedible accordingly. There are several categories of inedible objects recognized by the Tikopia. There are objects or substances which are not edible by their physical nature, because they cannot be masticated or cannot be digested or their flavour is antipathetic: earth, wood, grubs, some marine fauna, etc. Then there are others which are inedible because of their social nature – certain fine fish and other good foods which a person in mourning 'cannot' eat because of restrictions conventionally imposed or voluntarily assumed. (This is the condition in which a person is known as *pali* to such foods – Firth, 1966b.) Finally, there are other objects which are inedible because of their spiritual nature – most birds and certain fish, in particular eels, which traditionally have been regarded as material representations or emblems of spirits. Such objects, some of which in other circumstances might be considered as food, are *tapu*, taboo. Linked with this last category are other things ordinarily very definitely in the food category, such as coconuts, which are *tapu* and therefore theoretically inedible, because they have been temporarily reserved for consumption by a chief or other man of rank. ('Theoretically' inedible because such *tapu* was not infrequently broken in time of food shortage.)

Now high in the inedible category of the first order, physically antipathetic, is human excrement. It is regarded as disgusting, and though excretion on the beaches is common, or in the sea, this is treated by the Tikopia as a sanitary measure not calling for remark but not lessening their distaste. Some of the most filthy – and most frequent – Tikopia curses invoke the father or other kinsman of the cursed to eat excrement, to eat the inedible. Excrement is *tae*, and favoured epithets begin *kai tae*. . . . In metaphorical terms the cursed one is invited to bring together the incompatible ideas of eating and non-edible, a conjunction supposed to imply frustration, shame and degradation.

What then is one to make of the many Tikopia ritual invocations to gods and spirits which begin with an announcement by the priest: 'I eat your excrement' or more fully 'I eat ten times your excrement'. In an address to the gods above all, on a most formal occasion, when people sit around in strained attention in a temple heavy with sacredness, why should the priest bring together eating and the non-edible in such a clashing, putatively disgusting way? The first thing to remark is that whereas a curse by ordering to eat excrement is taken laughingly or regarded as offensive, this formal statement in a prayer was simply accepted, without comment, as part of the ritual procedure. I have sat through many temple rites and seen the congregation pay no more attention to it than does say a Christian congregation to the opening words of the Lord's Prayer. When asked to explain, both officiants and congregation members made little of it;

they said it was deprecatory speech, supplicating speech, pleasing to the spirits in emphasizing the lowly character of their worshippers. One of my most thoughtful informants, pushed hard, said that the origin of this kind of speech was not certain; it was ritual speech, known effectively only to the chiefs. But to the chiefs themselves it was clearly only traditional ritual phraseology; they could explain its meaning but not its genesis. But the meaning of such excremental speech was reinforced by two analogies. On the one hand, it was part of a general set of deprecatory phrases, in which the priest described himself and his people in terms of poverty, said they were orphans (in need of food and protection), thieves (because they lacked food of their own). As it was explained, the whole object of such prayers was to turn the mind of the spirits favourably towards the priest and his people, to grant rain, crops, fish and health, which were believed to be dependent upon spiritual power. The second reinforcement of the 'eating excrement' meaning came from chants of thanks ceremonially shouted to a chief who had just given a great feast to the people – an official chanter might incorporate phrases of eating excrement, addressed to the host, as 'Excrete hither for me to eat, for me to drink....' This also was a status affirmation, placing the beneficiaries from the feast in a very lowly position before their chiefly host. It was also a message of thanks, acknowledging the bounty given by the feast.

But there is still a further element in the interpretation of this phraseology. 'Eating excrement' in this context is not like eating dirt; it is a metaphorical way of expressing the eating of *food*, in the nutritional sense and not just the sense of something consumed by the mouth. In the Tikopia ideology the notions of human abasement and god-bounty were combined in the idea that god's excrement was human food in the full, rich sense of the term. The shoals of fish in the sea, the breadfruit, taro, coconut and other products of cultivation were conceived at this level of expression as being the excretions of the gods. So in some prayers gods were asked to produce excrement for their orphaned land, or to excrete into the sea to make shoals of fish. So in such solemn religious context the inedible becomes edible, the disgusting becomes pleasurable, the voided is once more absorbable – one of the type of reversal-transformations with which Lévi-Strauss has made us familiar.

So far the interpretation of such symbolic language about food has followed Tikopia explanation fairly closely.* But there are further implications which Tikopia did not overtly draw, but which are latent in their usage. I have shown that in different contexts solid food can be equated linguistically with water and with excrement. But the context is very relevant. In behavioural terms, it is specified, transactional, physical food that is equated with water; and unspecified, non-transactional, conceptual food that is equated with excrement. Using the colloquial English terms of today, when a mourner is presented with a funeral meal he is told: 'Drink the water I've brought for you' – not 'Eat the shit I've brought'! But the priest said to his god 'I eat your shit', not 'I drink your water', when reciting his prayer. Yet when he made the actual food offerings to the gods he called it neither 'shit' nor 'water' but just 'food'. Here the status and transactional elements are of prime relevance. Superior to grossly inferior (god to priest) is alleged to give 'shit'. Situationally superior to social superior or relative equal (commoner to chief, funerary provider to mourner) is alleged to give (and in part does give) 'water'. Grossly inferior to superior (priest to god) gives 'food'. It is from this point of view that an apparent exception to the rule that only conceptual food is 'shit' fits in. When the official chanter gives thanks to a chief host by 'eating shit' in the form of his bounty, this is physical food. But in Tikopia ideology, a chief is in quite a different category from a commoner – he has mystical qualities. Since commoner is to chief as chief is to god, it is linguistically and symbolically quite appropriate that the food from the chief's feast should be described as 'shit'. But it would be unthinkable for a commoner to label the food which he presented to a chief as 'shit'; it is 'water'.†

I think it will be clear from what I have said that expressions of the

* For details see Firth, 1970a, 151, 225–6, 256–8.

† A comparative point may also be made, again in colloquial terms. Tikopia curse by commanding to eat the inedible. In some societies people curse by commanding to 'fuck the unfuckable' – to copulate with mother or sister, for instance. But note that the 'unfuckable' is only ideologically so; physically mother or sister can be copulated with satisfactorily, and there may be suppressed desire to do so; whereas coprophagy is a rare condition. Tikopia do not command people in ordinary curses either to eat eels, or to copulate with their sisters; that is, they avoid swearing by the physically quite feasible though ideologically incompatible. Only at white heat are incestuous curses hurled, and fighting results (see Firth, 1936, 314–21). (In some Tikopia contexts eating and the sex act are equated linguistically, as when the organ of one partner is said to 'eat' that of the other in intercourse.)

order of 'I eat your excrement' are symbolic statements of a highly elliptical kind, the ultimate referents being food and status. Set out in ordinary language, the statement is equivalent to: 'I acknowledge my gross inferiority and believe in your power to provide food if appealed to in humility.' It will also be clear that the Tikopia equation of excrement with food has much in common with Freudian notions. This is reinforced by Tikopia dream interpretation, in which a dream of coming into contact with ordure is regarded as a sign that the dreamer will catch fish (Firth, 1967b, 168–9). What I hope to have shown is that such symbolic expressions are part of a relatively systematic set, operating on principles which are intelligible, a logic to which the non-rational is subject, once the initial assumptions are understood.

For this purpose I have taken primarily linguistic expressions about food in general. But there is also Tikopia linguistic symbolism about particular foods, also conforming to principles of logical arrangement. For instance, in a 'totemic' system which allocates one of each of four major vegetable foodstuffs to each of the four clans which compose the society, each foodstuff is identified with the major clan god. Coconut and breadfruit are each the 'head' of a god, and taro and yam are each the 'body' of a god. The symbolism is based upon a rough physical analogy: the first two are round and sizable; the latter have thin brown skin. But a feature which is not so apparent is that the symbolism is part of a symmetrical arrangement linked with the relative status of the clans. The symbolism, which reaches out into economic and ritual procedures, is part of the process of expressing responsibility and control over foodstuffs in a segmented fashion at both human and spiritual level (see Firth, 1966a, 11; 1967b, 228–32). On the other hand, reference to a particular type of food can serve as a symbolic expression for a type of emotion. There are no highly formalized incest prohibitions in Tikopia, except for parents and children or siblings; but unions between other close kin tend to be the object of scornful remark if not actually opposed. The dislike of such a union, putative rather than actual, was expressed in the phrase of 'eating *soi*', a bitter fruit (actually an aerial yam) which takes a great deal of steeping in water to render palatable (Firth, 1936, 549). Or again, names for some kinds of food can have a symbolic value which has significance according to context. An areca nut much used as masticant has several names, one of which is very suggestive of the word for testicles. Accordingly, when relatives by marriage are together, people between whom only 'proper' speech should pass, the sexually suggestive name for the nut is avoided.

TRANSACTIONAL SYMBOLISM OF FOOD

In linguistic expressions relating to food, sometimes 'food' and its congeners such as 'eat' are symbolized by other terms, and sometimes they themselves are used as symbols. But in the transactional sphere, food is normally the symbolizer, not the symbolized. One of the few exceptions was in a special ritual offering known as *Manava-o-te-Kere* (Firth and Spillius, 1963, 21–2; Firth, 1970a, 253). The name which may be translated 'Belly of the Land' was applied to a small food basket in which offerings to two principal gods of Tikopia were placed at the outset of each great seasonal cycle of ritual performances for fertility and welfare. Ordinarily, the basket held food. But when famine struck the land a stone was put in as well. The symbolism of this offering the gods 'not bread but a stone' was not that of insult or lack of sympathy; it was an indirect way of advising them that the land was grievously short of food and asking for their help. The stone was both a surrogate for food and a symbolic request for food, a vividly mute appeal. An analogous symbolic statement, with a slightly different rationale, was to put a small package of stones in with a small basket of food when formal gifts were exchanged between chiefs in famine periods. Here also the stones symbolized lack of food, and were intended to inform the gods and stimulate crop fertility. But they also were a tacit statement about the desirability of co-operation between chiefs – even if there is no food to give, *something* must be sent to acknowledge the relationship. A tacit statement of another kind about poverty was made in some rites by making the offerings to the gods quite small, in the hope that this would be taken by the gods as a hint to increase the food supply from which offerings were drawn.

The Tikopia use food as a symbolic instrument to express ideas of social co-operation and social status, by many subtle variations in amount, composition and style of presentation. Every type of formal social occasion tends to have its own type of food transaction, often with a special name. I have described many types of such transaction in my various publications on Tikopia, and select only a few here to demonstrate some main points about food symbolism.

But first a general theme running through all these transactions – that food is the major mechanism whereby the kinship ties which are basic to the structure of Tikopia society are given concrete expression. Since food is so important pragmatically to Tikopia one of the best ways in which kinship can be shown to be meaningful is to help with food – to assist in providing the raw materials, to help with labour in preparing it, to give supplies of food ready to eat. One of the most stringent and well-kept rules of the Tikopia social system is that which requires men who have married women of a lineage to attend any formal ceremony of the lineage as cooks. They are known collectively as 'firewood' or 'oven stones', and their job is apt to be hard, hot and dirty. Each man comes with his bundle of firewood and bunch of coconuts, while his wife carries their raw food contribution, a backload of taro, bananas, etc. This raw food is the *fiuri*, a term applied to any contribution of green food brought or sent to a formal oven. Its normal reciprocity is a share of the proceeds, some eaten as a meal on the spot and some borne off in a basket to be consumed at home. *Fiuri* and its normal reciprocal, *taumafa* – raw contribution and cooked share – symbolize the network of kin relations of Tikopia society.

A special relationship, political and formerly ritual as well, is that with the chiefs of the clans, who receive acknowledgement whenever any man of rank performs an important ceremony, and at all major life crises such as initiation or marriage. Such a present of food to a chief, known as *fakaariki* in reference to the chief's title (*ariki*), is much larger than the share of an ordinary commoner, and usually has a supplement of coconuts, both dry and sprouting, and perhaps some bundles of raw taro as well. That the gift symbolizes a social and political relationship and is not just a package of food supplies is shown by the fact that commonly a man from another clan than that of the chief is selected to bear the food to him, so tacitly stating the importance of breadth in co-operation (Firth, 1936, 453). Formerly other special food gifts of large size went from each lineage to their clan chief on the occasion of re-consecration of their clan temple and their sacred canoe. That these symbolized political and religious ties of major import was illustrated by the manner in which the baskets from the canoes were topped by bark-cloth ritual vestments dedicated to the gods concerned; and the baskets of both types of gift were ritually offered by the chief to the gods when he received them.* Formal food exchanges between chiefs also symbolized their political unity, and a special relationship believed to have been created by an ancestral marriage about eight generations before was annually celebrated by an enormous food exchange, with bearers staggering along a path between two temples in conditions of high ritual tension (1967a, 131–8, 249).

The general symbolic function of raw food contributions has been mentioned, as representing social co-operation. But special types of raw food served also as ritual symbols. Freshly plucked green coconuts were associated with canoe and fishing rites, in one of which a coconut was smashed by the chief and thrown out to sea in a symbolic dismissal of the sea deities to their work (1967a, 85–7). In another rather touching piece of ritual symbolism, raw food from the cultivations of a dead man was stood on his grave, as a last farewell to him – 'it is announced to the man who is dead; it is his severance from the middle of the orchard; that is the parting of his hand from the woods'. This was not just a piece of sentimentalism. It was believed that if no such symbolic gesture was made, the spirit of the dead man would take umbrage and afflict the cultivations with pests (1970a, 249).

In the Tikopia scheme of presentation of food after it has been cooked, great attention is paid to the manner in which it is packaged, and also to the term by which this package is called. The usual method is to wrap the food in banana or giant taro leaves – the equivalent of paper in industrial society – and then put the parcels in a basket. These baskets, made from strong leaf strips, vary in size, fineness of workmanship and durability, and normally serve different purposes. *Tanga*, small fine bags, hold betel materials and

* I have observed an apparent contradiction on a small point in my various accounts of this. In one general passage I state that these gifts were reciprocated by the chief by a basket of cooked food (1939, 374); in more specific passages I state they were not (1967a, 109, 224, 249). The latter is technically correct. But as I point out in the same context, there tends to be indirect reciprocation by redistribution of food by the chief, so substantially there is some basis for the first statement.

other objects, not usually food. *Longi* are medium-sized very open baskets to hold household food; *raurau* are of the same type but of finer quality. *Kete* are rectangular baskets to hold raw fish and other things when people are at work. *Popora* are rough open-work baskets meant to hold already packaged food or coarse food only, and to last only for a few days. All ordinary gifts of food are taken in *popora*, and given a name associated with their particular institutional function or just called 'food'. But some gifts, though carried in *popora*, are named *tanga*, *longi*, or *kete* – it is as if bread and meat carried in sacks were to be labelled 'a handbag', 'a briefcase', etc. In traditional Tikopia social life there were not many of these substitute labellings, and I cannot suggest in all cases why they should have been given. But some seem to refer to rather critical phases of ritual. The general meaning of the special labels was deprecatory, like calling 'food' 'water'; in each case a large mass of food was spoken of as a small mass. The idea of calling a large gift a small one is of course well known in many societies, and is linked with ideas of acknowledgement of status. But it is significant that this is really an acknowledgement of the symbolic value of language. No one actually believes that the gift is small – the large containers are there for all to see; but the polite forms are observed. Clearly it is in the selectivity of such appelations that their value lies. If *all* large gifts were termed small, the reduction process would have to be reconsidered. It is the particular social context that gives the categorization its meaning.

I give a couple of examples, one from marriage and the other from initiation (Firth, 1936, 558, 452). In the series of reciprocal presentations between bride's kin and groom's kin on a Tikopia marriage, a very large basket of cooked food, prepared by the groom's kin, is carried by the bride in particular to her kin. The package is so heavy that it may tax her strength to take it. Early the next day its reciprocal, also a large mass of cooked food, is sent over to the bridegroom's kin, some of it being carried by the bride too. Normally a transaction is ended by the return gift. But on this occasion when the bride returns again to her husband she takes with her what is termed a *tanga*, literally a little bag, of food. Actually it is quite a big basket, and it is intended to provide a meal for the immediate household of the newly-married pair. I was at first unable to explain why such a derogatory name should be given to a substantial gift, and Tikopia were no help on this specific point. On further consideration I think two structural elements are involved. By ordinary social rules the transaction is finished before the *tanga* is given, so this is *hors de la série* – it can be described appropriately then as 'just a little something' about the size of a betel bag, and so not start up another round of exchanges. The second element is that by intending the food for the household of the newly-weds, the groom's kin are being a bit more restrictive than usual in such presentations. This is quite in order since masses of food have gone to a wide range of other kin. But in calling this gift in effect 'just a little bag', of the kind to contain betel materials or tobacco, they emphasize its domestic quality, diminish its social significance and so fend off possible difficulty in exchange. These are my inferences, but they fit general Tikopia attitudes.

My second example refers to the *longi* from which boys are fed on the morning after their circumcision-type operation. *Longi* are essentially household food containers, semi-personalized, used normally for carriage and storage of meals within the domestic sphere. Now the food on this occasion, though called *longi*, consists of large packages in a *popora*. Significantly, it is brought from the adjacent oven-house to the more secular 'profane' inland side of the dwelling-house where normally formal food displays do not go. The reason for this is that the food is designed not just as a meal for the initiated boys but also as a gift for their mother's sisters and mother's brothers' wives, who have spent the night sleeping as a kind of guard of honour at their feet. The women eat too, but then carry off the remainder of the food to their own dwellings, while the men at the ceremonial site are catered for separately. The food of the *longi* is brought in to the more secular side of the house because that is associated with women, and since the formal context is female, the domestic food basket is an appropriate symbolic title for the food presentation. Again, this my inference, but it accords closely with other Tikopia explanations.

As in any Western society, differences in the quality of Tikopia food can be indices to recognition of social status or attribution of putative status as a matter of etiquette. There is a vast difference between offering someone a few green bananas or yams roasted over a fire, and an elaborately prepared pudding made with sago flour and coconut cream. In traditional Tikopia society formal rules prescribed very closely what types of food should be served on different kinds of occasions and to whom. And a variety of symbolic statements could be made with fish!

In concluding this empirical analysis I refer to two types of symbolic use of food in which though quality of the food is important, the mode of its handling is critical.

The first type is the practice of bringing a parcel of cooked food as a household meal to a communal affair such as a formal dance festival taking place during the daytime. Ordinary Tikopia informal dancing, primarily a recreation for young people, takes place at night, and daytime dancing is apt to be a formally organized event. People go in family and lineage groups, taking their lunch. But this is not a casual meal. They sit according to social divisions, these depending somewhat upon how the affair has been conceived by its initiators; and the food has been carefully prepared, with a proper balance of delicate components. Moreover, units do not consume what they have themselves brought; a system of exchange of contributions ensures that everyone consumes someone else's food. The lines of exchange are partly traditional, partly organized on the spot, but essentially the consumption of the food by the communal gathering *after* the exchange is a symbolic statement of social unity. In the traditional Tikopia religious rites this principle of exchange of food contributions at a dance was developed to a high degree. Both women and men were involved, in separate series of exchanges at different stages, those of the women being expressly the more important. Huge amounts of food were prepared, requiring the labour of many more people than the nominal principals, and though termed *longi* in typical Tikopia deprecatory style the baskets were no domestic food-holders but great *popora* containers. The exchange was conducted with formal procedures, the baskets of the chiefs being assigned a special precedence. There was also a special role signalized by an especially large food contribution, for novices. The whole intricate system, focused upon food, was a symbolic mode of emphasizing some basic principles of the social structure: clan and lineage groups; the chieftainship; the complementary roles of men and women; the social significance of first experience in an institution; the meaning of kinship ties. And yet, in addition to all the necessary technology and economic organization, an occasional optional pragmatic note crept in. If a very efficient household got its food cooked by early afternoon, it might fill its basket and send the contribution along to its exchange partner without waiting for all the formality of public allocation. It was described then as having been 'sent in by the back way' – 'that it may arrive for their hunger'! (1967a, 316–19, 361–4).

In a second type of Tikopia symbolic use of food the emphasis is not upon exchange of contributions, but upon the meal itself. This is the *kai fakamavae*, the farewell meal. Tikopia are prone to formalize and sentimentalize partings – as for instance the pagan Tikopia chiefs performed a religious rite of farewell to their traditional gods before they officially converted to Christianity (Firth, 1970a, 391). As part of the ceremonies for marriage, a set of young bachelors and unmarried girls who have been friends of the married pair gather near the young couple at the stage when they are about to have their first formal meal together, and then all eat from the same basket of food. This is the 'food of parting from the unmarried state'. It is a symbolic farewell, reminiscent of their carefree days and nights of work and dance and song and sexual adventure together. Eating in common, from the same food container, is the last intimacy they will share before the married pair take up the new responsibilities and new stereotypes for action which will put them in a different category of social beings. This type of meal is a symbolic farewell, since all participants still continue to be members of the same society and may meet daily. But nowadays the Tikopia have adapted the concept to meet the frequent case of people going overseas to work or to school. (I was given such a farewell meal when I last left Tikopia, an affecting occasion at which speeches were made in the best banquet tradition.) Here the act of eating together symbolizes the last association before a physical parting as well as a social parting, and tends to carry a considerable affective load.

GENERAL CONSIDERATIONS

For an illustration of an anthropological analysis of symbolism I have taken the theme of food. In contrast to the more common anthropological studies of symbolism in myth or ritual I have deliberately chosen as material and pragmatic a field as one can get. Granted that meaning is ultimately 'in the head', in this case as Tikopia would probably agree, head and stomach are closely allied. Reality may lie in the world of ideas but illusion demands that the body be fed. Yet food and eating have a distinct symbolic quality for the Tikopia. Concrete object and act represent abstract complex ideas of events and processes relating to basic social and personal elements. The pragmatic and the symbolic are closely intertwined – as Leach pointed out about totemism, things which are good to think with may also be good for eating.

Tikopia food symbolism has a recognizably specific mode of expression, conformable to the particular vegetables and fish in the diet* and to the structural demands of the society. Some principles of general application can be seen: that for symbolic purposes rough, hard foods are inferior to smooth, soft foods; hot, dirty labour around the oven is degrading – it is forbidden to chiefs even though they come in the affinal category of 'cooks'. But for the most part, though the interpretation of the food symbolism can be made intelligible to an outside inquirer, it needs an apparatus of knowledge of the social context to seem meaningful in any very precise terms. Moreover, the symbolic spheres are often quite limited. Anthropologists sometimes have a tendency to write as if once a symbolic equivalence has been arrived at in one context then it is available for application in all other social contexts. I do not believe this to be the case. As I have shown, because food can be equated with excrement in some Tikopia ritual contexts, it cannot be so equated in other contexts, where such equation if attempted would be offensive. One is not entitled to say that the Tikopia word *tae* is used purely equivocally when applied to ordure on a beach and to the bounty of a god in a prayer. Both have an excremental connotation. But the symbolic equation, excrement = food, is of restricted range; it serves certain purposes in prayer, and can be otherwise discarded. I suppose that one might describe Tikopia food symbolism from this point of view as a series of limited analogies, but such a scholastic description would not seem to add anything to its meaning.

What I think is clear from my analysis is that there is a structure

* Cf. the symbolic 'decipherment' of a Western meal by Mary Douglas, 1972.

of meaning in the field of Tikopia food symbolism, but that it is not a completely systematic structure. Not only do symbolic categories sometimes contradict pragmatic categories – food is excrement; big baskets are termed small. Symbolic categories sometimes contradict one another or at least cannot be fitted into the same scheme at the same time. I have shown how food can be equated both with excrement and with water, with a rationale for both; but both symbolic statements cannot be made in the same context. One of the reasons for this limitation of symbolic spheres is that symbols have work to do. They are not just static expressions of social relationships or ideas about the meaning of the world; they are instruments in an on-going process of social action. They are linked with ideas of labour and resources, status and power, and are focused accordingly. Hence over the symbolic landscape the various features show differences of clarity, intensity, diversity.

Finally, in lighter vein, one may compare food in its symbolic significance with another highly important symbol of social relationships which Lévi-Strauss has done so much to elucidate – women. In contrast to words, which have wholly become signs, woman, states Lévi-Strauss (1969, 496) has remained both a sign and a value. The same may be said of food. Women as signs to be communicated have the advantage of durability, and of auto-mobility – they last, and they can be sent to bear their own message; food soon perishes, and it must be carried. Women are also instruments of production in the way that most food is not – though Tikopia occasionally present seedling foods which can be grown, as a social message. On the other hand women are, objectively considered, of less variety than food for symbolic transfer, though in more personal terms they are capable of almost infinite symbolic transformation. At times also they are capable of disconcerting initiative, such as running away and spoiling the message, as against the inert quality of food. But perhaps the quality which is of most importance in the symbolic values of food, is its divisibility. Women can be shared but they cannot be divided, whereas food can be almost infinitely portioned out without loss of quality. Ultimately too, there is no threat of a food liberation movement which may destroy its symbolic values and seek to make man rather than woman the bearer of the social communication.

Chapter 8

HAIR AS PRIVATE ASSET AND PUBLIC SYMBOL

A few years ago an anthropologist addressing a group of people on a social studies course confessed that before meeting them he nearly went and had his hair cut – that he did not was due to the length of the queue (line) at the barber's. He used this as an illustration of how bodily characters, such as length of hair, are used as symbols, create expectations about conduct and provoke social reactions (Harré, 1968). Put this together with Hallpike's recent generalization (1969) that among men, wearing long hair is equivalent to being outside society while short hair is equivalent to social control – and that in an attenuated form the same principle can be extended to the hair of women. Add to it the Elizabethan John Heywood's proverb 'long hair, short wit', or the French '*longues cheveux, courte cervelle*'. We can then ask what is there about hair, especially in its length, that makes it of such social, even symbolic interest?*

A person's hair is a biological accessory, a very personal, private thing, growing and changing with his bodily condition, and capable of only very limited voluntary regulation by him. Hair is a horny product of the epithelial or skin tissue, and is a character peculiar to mammals. Man is remarkable for the general scantiness of his hair, except on the scalp, where though inferior in hairiness to gibbon and gorilla, he has about twice as many hairs per sq. cm (312) as the orang-utan and nearly three times as many as the chimpanzee. Among mammals man is unique not for his general lack of hair – whale, elephant and hippopotamus are more naked, area for area – but for his complete absence of tactile hairs, such as a cat's whiskers, which are organs of great delicacy. Despite metaphors of his hair

* A general study, *Hair*, by Wendy Cooper (London, Aldus Books, 1971), appeared after this chapter had been prepared.

'standing on end' with shock or terror, man's hair is relatively inert. According to physical anthropologists, hair is apparently a true racial character in man, hereditary and unaffected by environment. Racial variables include length of head hair; hairiness of body exclusive of scalp hair; form, texture and colour of hair. In evolutionary terms, an important function of hair has been for protection, especially in serving as an insulator to retain heat, but for human beings this has long ceased to be of much significance (Hooton, 1946, 41, 192–9, 469–75, 483–8; Howells, 1947, 33, 214; Turney-High, 1949, 22). Hair is not only perishable, a wasting asset; it can be lost completely with only social, not physiological disability, or at least minimal physical discomfort.

It is striking to note how out of this sluggish, physiologically almost functionless appurtenance of his body, man has imaginatively created a feature of such socially differentiating and symbolic power. But in contrast to other bodily appurtenances hair has a number of qualities which recommend it as an instrument for social action. Though personal in origin, it is multiple, any single hair of a person tending to be like any other. It is detachable, renewable, manipulable in many contexts, so to some degree can be treated as an independent object. Yet there is some variation in texture and colour, so it offers scope for social differentiation. And it is associative, tending to call up important social ideas, especially concerning sex.

Consider first the general association of hair with ideas of multitude and fineness. Before modern technology had developed processes of counting and measuring to present refinement, hair represented in Western thought an exemplar of extreme number and extreme delicacy. The Biblical statement that 'the very hairs of your head are all numbered' (Matt. x: 30), whether metaphor or not, was intended to emphasize the interest of the Omniscient in humanity by his having a knowledge that it was regarded as absurd for any human being to attempt. (According to the *Jewish Encyclopaedia* the number was supposed to be one billion seven hundred thousand, though actually, authorities report that the human head has about 120,000 hairs). Terms such as hairs-breadth, hair-spring, hair-trigger, hair-splitting, all indicate extreme fineness and delicacy, whether in mechanics or in the dialectic of argument. When Samuel Butler wrote of his Presbyterian Knight:

He was in *Logick* a great Critick
Profoundly skill'd in Analytick
He could distinguish and divide
A Hair 'twixt *South* and *South-West* side
(*Hudibras*, I, Canto 1)

he meant to indicate, if ironically, the making of minutest distinction. Now with computer and electron microscope, use of hair as a measure (only 1/150 to 1/1500 inch in thickness) has become outdated, even ludicrous in its grossness. But metaphorically, hair has been able to hold its place, presumably because of its close relationship to human personality.

In some contradistinction to the notion of hair as indicating fineness is the idea of its wild quality. Man has often been differentiated from other animals by his lack of hair ('the naked ape'), so people with an unusual amount of hair may be given feral qualities. Traditional notions of man living in a state of nature have represented him as shaggy, in a manner shown by early histories of mankind – and by old English inn-signs (cf. Hallpike, 1969, 261–3 for other data). Wildness or lack of refinement are specified in the contrast between the Biblical Esau as a rough hairy man and Jacob as a smooth-skinned as well as a smooth-tongued man. 'Hairy' as a colloquial expression for rough, miserable, uncomfortable (*Webster's Dictionary* gives it as a slang equivalent for 'rugged', 'trying') is probably related to this notion of wildness. 'Hair-shirt' as a synonym for penitential suffering has a direct material referent in roughness of texture. 'Hairy-heeled' as a synonym for coarse would seem to refer to the difference between the rough hocks of a cart-horse and the finer ones of hack or hunter, and so by implication to a difference in social quality between them. But when an English society girl reported that when living in Paris she ended up in 'a hairy place on the sixth floor with no lights on the stairs', this was clearly a metaphor, probably involving a social as well as a physical judgement.

An extended use of this meaning of 'hairy' links it with danger, a development apparently associated with flying aeroplanes. In the American 'parlance of the pilots' ready rooms' the kind of encounter between them and aircraft of other armed forces engaged in reconnaissance can be 'pretty hairy' if they get close (for example *New*

York Post, 19 May 1964; *New York Times Magazine*, 22 November 1970). In a clearly related usage, a new model automobile was launched some years ago as 'the hairiest looking sporty car in America, even at the risk of scaring some people off', with an instrument panel 'that may make you feel more like a pilot than a driver'!

HAIR AS MALE AND AS FEMALE SYMBOL

But in a further related association hairiness in a man has been treated as a sign of his virility. Differential distribution of hair on the body as between the sexes, particularly in facial and thoracic hair, has given a basis for the link between hairiness and roughness to be focused on the male, and to have some association with sexual aggressiveness. 'A hairy body and arms stiff with bristles, give promise of a manly soul' (Juvenal, *Satires*, ii, 11); and in de Sade's *Justine*, Roland, one of his symbols of exaggerated male sexuality, was described as 'covered in hair like a bear'. In Western countries, growth of hair on the face, physiologically a sign of maturation, has often been put into a social framework and linked with courage and experience. In the late eighteenth century Démeunier noted that when women have seen only men who are bearded, they feel aversion and repugnance at the first sight of a shaven chin (1776, iii, 186). 'He that hath a beard is more than a youth, and he that hath no beard is less than a man', said Beatrice (*Much Ado About Nothing*, Act II, Sc. 1). Again, Shakespeare differentiated military from civil usage in *As You Like It* (Act II, Sc. 7) in the soldier – bearded like the pard; and the justice – with beard of formal cut.

Yet this is a sphere where cultural differences may be very marked. Starting from the purely physical basis of racial differences in male facial hair – less common among Mongoloid peoples than among Caucasoid or Australoid (cf. the 'Hairy Ainu' and the Japanese) – some societies such as the Chinese have traditionally attached more importance than others to beard development. But with similar beard potential some societies have categorized beards positively or negatively in terms of cultural demarcation. Jews are said to have worn beards proudly through the days of traditional Egyptian bondage while the Egyptians were shaven. While Greeks and

Romans mostly went shaven they stigmatized beard-wearing 'barbarous', people as outside the pale of polite society. Historically in the West beards have been sometimes an index of social class, or a badge of a profession; sometimes an object of sumptuary laws – as when Peter the Great taxed them. Sometimes worn by soldiers, they were often prohibited to the military, ostensibly to preserve uniformity and discipline. And the transitional state may be socially disapproved – for an ordinarily clean-shaven man to appear obviously unshaven is apt to be regarded as a mark of disorder, even an affront, or at the mildest, as an indulgence permitted on holidays.* In short, hairiness on the faces of men has often been in an ambiguous position between manliness and savagery – perhaps because conventions of manliness may entail some conception of physical brutality.

This is exemplified in the West by a curious facet of literary history – a series of works on the wearing of beards, semi-informative, semi-facetious, from the sixteenth century onwards, by Johan Valerian, Antoine Hotman (with Hervet, Calmet, Oudin also), and culminating in J. A. Dulaure's *Pogonologia* of the end of the eighteenth century. Translated from the French with the subtitle 'A Philosophical and Historical Essay on Beards' this last work had an elaborate discussion of fashions in bearded chins, false beards, golden beards, whiskers, beards of priests, etc., citing ethnographic evidence, and bringing out the social significance of the practice. 'In ripe age, the beard is a sign of physical powers; in old age the symbol of veneration.' There was a joking apology for long beards, and the work appears to have been composed in half-serious, half-joking mood for the author's circle of friends (Boudet, 1874, 40–1; see also above, Chap. 3, p. 97). It is in such sense presumably that one should take his theme – that to suppress the work of nature is an outrage on nature of which depraved societies alone are capable; that people who shave are those where woman has rule! But what Dulaure does bring out are two other themes of sociological significance: the great variation in estimation of the beard in the same society at different periods; and the very strong affective reaction associated with such estimation. He remarked that the beard was worn and highly respected at some periods and despised at others –

* That such a view may still obtain in a modern family see Katherine Whitehorn, *Observer*, 7 May 1972.

that by the Roman church, for instance it was successively considered as an odious heterodoxy or the symbol of wisdom and Christian humility. 'Like objects of great worth, the beard never excited petty quarrels; both its enemies and its partisans were violent....' And he asked, now that it was a whole century since his society men wore beards, had they gained by the change? (1786, iv, 51, 64).

In the West, until modern times, the ambiguity of the male beard was not matched by any parallel oscillation in women's hair growth. Facial hair was apt to be reckoned as a disadvantage to a woman, but in general presented no serious problem. While there was great variation in head-hair style, long hair was the convention for women. So in a kind of polarization, beard intermittently and long hair regularly have come to epitomize man and woman. Darwin's theory that by process of selection the male with the longest beard and the female with the longest hair would acquire choice of mates by mutual recognition of superior sexual attraction, has not received much modern anthropological support – at least by Ernest Hooton (1946, 197). But traditionally in the West a woman's long hair has been an ultimate token of femininity, as hackneyed references to 'woman's crowning glory' or to Milton's phrase from Lycidas – 'sporting with the tangles of Neaera's hair' indicate. Yet there are paradoxes in this. So far has poetic licence gone in the West that in metaphor, by the strength of feminine attraction, one hair alone is enough to hold a man captive. Both Dryden and Pope used this theme:

> She knows her man, and when you rant and swear
> Can draw you to her with a single hair
>
> (*Persius*, satire v, 246)

> Fair tresses man's imperial race insnare,
> and beauty draws us with a single hair
>
> (*Rape of the Lock*, can. ii, 27)

But I prefer the earlier Howell

> One hair of a woman can draw more than a hundred pair of oxen
>
> (*Letters*, book ii, iv–1621)

So female hair, head hair in particular, is made to be the symbol of contrast in character, and reversal of qualities: physical weakness of a woman and strength of her femininity; frailty of a single hair and yet its power to move male desire and love.

But this poetic imagery and the symbolism it represents are essentially contingent upon social conditions. While they have had considerable historical continuity, fashion, class relationships, moral ideas, have tended to affect the mode of expression. In an essay on *Womankind* in the latter part of last century Charlotte M. Yonge was all in favour of sobriety and refinement. Hair is the woman's glory, but she ought to reduce it to 'well-ordered obedience' – 'not wasting time in needless elaboration, but obtaining the fresh sensation of a head thoroughly brushed, and securely and neatly arranged. Tumble-down hair, falling dishevelled on the shoulders, sounds grand in fiction, but it is disgusting in real life. . . . The associations of the loose unkempt locks of Sir Peter Lely's portraits are not those of pure and dignified maidens or matrons.' Simplicity was to be the watchword, so 'refinement, as well as truth, will forbid her eking out her own tresses with other people's, or changing the colour. This is finery – that very different thing; though it is one of the great difficulties to draw the line between the two, especially when dealing with classes below us . . .' (1889, 112). Moreover, while a woman's long hair is a symbol of her femininity in general, the mode of wearing it may be an index to the quality ascribed to that femininity. By nineteenth-century convention a girl wore her hair long over her shoulders until late adolescence, and then 'put it up' in a roll on the top of her head; this was a sign of maturity and specifically in a young woman, a sign of marriageability. After this transition, to allow the hair once more to float freely over the shoulders took place only in intimate personal circumstances – as in a bedroom.* The simple technology of putting up the hair daily was delegated to maids by upper-class women. Hence the advice of Charlotte Yonge – to middle-class girls of small income – 'when the melancholy moment of "turning up the hair" has come, no girl whose life is to be spent without a maid should be content till she has learned to make her edifice firm, and as graceful as nature will permit'.

* Note that the stress is upon informality, not on the bedroom – in Singapore it was customary for Chinese prostitutes to let down their hair as a sign that for the time being they were *unable* to receive their clients (Ward and Stirling, 1925, I, 26n.).

All such conventions have become much confused and overlaid by modern developments. Apart from the multiplicity of rapidly changing women's hair styles in which length becomes subordinate to fashion, the traditional imagery in which the femininity of a woman's hair was expressed has lost much of its point through the rivalry of the advertising profession. If one compares 'a cascade of lustrous curls' with 'the loose train of your amber-dropping hair', Milton (*Comus*, 859) is only marginally ahead of Madison Avenue.

But in the sphere of sex differentiation, hair symbolism is focused primarily on hair of the head, and nearly all literary statements (until recent years at least) have concerned this. Hair on other parts of the body, though also allowing some degree of differential development, has in the West been treated with much more reserve. Hair on the chest, normally an attribute of men, may be held to connote strength and sexual vigour, but also tends to have an association of lack of refinement. Men who devote time and money to careful dressing of hair on scalp and face may make no attempt to barber their hair on the chest – though I have been told by a colleague that 'chest toupees' have appeared on the Costa Brava! Axillary hair, common to both sexes, is commonly regarded as neutral on a man, but unfashionable on a woman, as also with hair on legs. Both can be in the category of 'superfluous hair' recognized by purveyors of depilatories. This 'superfluous' is a complex social category. It can include hair of legs and armpits, conventionally unaesthetic, to be concealed or removed. But what about pubic hair? In the West and fairly generally elsewhere this should be concealed from public view – except in vulgar nudity shows, of which it is a high point, or in some modern ballet or other stage presentations in which the aesthetic focus is on the nude body as a whole and not specifically on the sex organs. But the pubic hair is not normally removed by either sex, presumably because of its private erotic interest – leaving aside the fullsome descriptions of pornographic literature. But this concealment, yet preservation, of pubic hair is a Western custom. Other societies vary, from taking nakedness and open display of pubic hair completely for granted, to complete depilation of the genital area. So, in Western society, hair on the upper part of the body, especially the face for men and the scalp for women, has been traditionally an object of admiration and solicitous care, whereas hair on other parts has been a matter of private interest, indifference or embarrassment, according to the particular social context.

Historically in Western society there seems always to have been a considerable range of variation in the treatment of women's head-hair, particularly in upper-class 'polite' society. What is remarkable in modern conditions is the variety of such treatment, and its extension through all grades of society. Hair conditioners of many kinds claim to keep the hair soft, silky and manageable, shining clean, with beautiful sheen, glowing and alive. . . . Diversity of style allows matching of features, temperament, occasion. The names of the styles themselves invite semantic inquiry – to take a few haphazardly: Pony Tail; French Knot; Veil; Bangs; Helmet; Puff; Bird; Cornrow; Poodle. A vast flourishing industry of hairdressers, with training schools, advanced academies, magazines, guilds, festivals and world championships – and a comically serious belief in its own importance – helps to support the technological, social, almost mystical values involved.

The development of new modes and the change of standards of evaluation is shown in hair colour. Physically, variation in hair colour depends on amount and quality of pigment, brown-black or red-gold, to be found in the hair, and on the extent of unpigmented spaces in it that reflect light. The result is a range of variation in two distinct series, from black through brown to blond; and from intense red to golden red; with a mixed red-brown series as well. In addition there is the greying or white appearance of hair in the ageing, due to growth of hair lacking in pigment. Traditionally, social values have been given to different pigmentation variants. Broadly, the extremes have received the clearest value-ratings – as when red hair is looked upon as fearsome in an unsophisticated black-haired population. In Western society it may no longer be true that 'gentlemen prefer blondes', but very light hair colour has long seemed to have attracted favourable attention. Use of precious metal terms 'golden' and 'silver' for yellow and white hair show this.* But jet-black hair has been found seductive, and red hair equated with a fiery temperament. In poetic treatment some odd shades have been identified. So Milton

* Salomon Reinach (1930, 154–5) cites Procopius, Ovid and Virgil for instances of life-principle being believed to be contained in golden hair. Cf. George Peele 'his golden locks hath time to silver turned' (*Polyhymnia*); Alfred Tennyson 'sweet girl-graduates in their golden hair' (*Princess*, Prologue, 141).

described Adam with 'hyacynthine locks', a hue which some dictionaries define as 'light violet to moderate purple' (*Paradise Lost*, iv, 300),* and which clearly is meant as a term of approval. But in the modern world of hair bleaches, dyes and rinses such evaluations of hair colour have largely lost their meaning. Dyeing the hair to conceal effects of ageing, or to offer specific sexual attraction, has long been known but the advances of modern chemistry have allowed a freedom of treatment not possible before. As a consequence, the line between nature and culture has been blurred for the observer's judgement, the aesthetic range has been widened, and discrimination on moral grounds of the kind suggested by Charlotte Yonge is rendered much more difficult.

As a broad impression then it could be said that in addition to physiological differences in the hair of men and of women, social differences tend to be created and maintained, with symbolic value. But a question arises as to how far in modern conditions these social differences and their symbolism tend to be lost in the almost bewildering variety of forms of hair treatment available and utilized.

NORMS AND STATEMENTS WITH HAIR

In all cultures, it appears, hair has social as well as personal significance. There is material from all over the world to demonstrate how styles of wearing the hair of the head are used as indicators of social difference, varying according to age, sex, marital and other status and crisis situations. What is particularly important is that these styles are often not just aesthetic modulations or a matter of individual preference; they are strongly conventionalized, given moral approval and used as instruments of social expression and social control. They are not just signs, they may be symbols too. For example, it has been common among Amerindian tribes for a woman's mode of wearing her hair to indicate whether she was a maiden or married, but often the hair style represented also a complex set of ideas and beliefs about

* The expression has equivalent in Homer's *Odyssey* – 'locks like the hyacynthine flower'; and before Milton was used by Blount (*Glossograph*, 1656) – Hyacynthine, of Violet or Purple colour. Pope also has it in his version of the *Odyssey* – 'His hyacynthine locks descend in wavy curls'; and it occurs as late as 1874 with Lowell, who describes Agassiz as 'shaking with burly mirth his hyacynthine hair'. But in such modern usage it seems equivalent to reddish-brown or tawny.

the particular condition of her female powers. So, recently Terence Turner has reported (1969a) of the Tchrikin, one of the least known peoples of the central Brazilian wilderness, that recognition of a woman's reproductive powers is symbolized by her being allowed to wear her hair long only upon the birth of her first child.

Yet even in the less developed, remote societies, hair styles can change rapidly when new stimuli are presented. More than forty years ago, when I first visited Tikopia, their hair styles were the exact reverse of what then obtained in Western culture – women wore their hair cropped short, and men wore theirs long, down their backs. Women also wore their hair plain whereas men, especially young men, often bleached their hair with lime to a golden colour, giving them a most spectacular appearance. There were customary variations – young boys grew a tuft of hair on each side of the head; marriageable girls had a fringe at neck and brow, cut off at their wedding. But the contrast to Western custom was clear. Nowadays this is no longer so. For as Western young men have grown their hair long (to be like the Tikopia?) Tikopia young men have cut theirs short, to be like the West. And Tikopia young women, formerly with shaven scalps, now sport crops of curly or wavy locks, bleached or parti-bleached in modish fashion. Only in one respect have Tikopia men tended to be conservative: they still cut their hair at mourning for a close relative. (And some women still wear head-rings made up from the shorn hair of their menfolk, as a token of sentiment and propriety – as a Western woman used to wear a hat when she went out publicly.) On the other hand, an exception to the shearing process was the chiefs, whose hair was taboo and was not sacrificed at the death of a relative; until quite recent times they did not cut their hair with the rest of the men.*

In the wearing of the hair one may recognize custom, or standard modes of behaviour, and fashion, or an oscillation of focus on particular styles. But in addition to these norms, the manner of wearing the hair has sometimes been used to make a more personal statement. This has been so even in Tikopia, where the traditional conventions were strong. Among the generation of women who were staid mothers of families when I first visited Tikopia, were a few who as girls, unmarried, had scorned convention and grown their hair long.

* Firth, 1936, 503–9, and Plates VI, VII, IX; 1967b, Pl. 1, 96.

This had been regarded, probably correctly, by the young men as something of a challenge to their privilege; and it fitted in with the spirit of sexual display and antagonism which tended to characterize relations between young people. It was remembered especially because the girls' long hair had been a subject for the jeering dance songs through which each sex both taunted and invited the other (Firth, 1936, 507–9). Another kind of personal statement by hair used to be made by young American college girls. Upwards of twenty years ago a teen-ager 'going steady' with a young man could let this be known by various signs – such as a single ear-ring 'for one man'. One such sign was the wearing of the hair in a single braid, in contrast to two braids or none at all if she was free. A more recent kind of statement, indicating not a personal relationship so much as a personal commitment, has been the wearing of 'Afro' hair styles by black American women. Appearing in the mid-1960s as a manifestation of black pride, with its suggestion of African, not American origins and independence, the 'Afro' became a symbol of ethnic identity and as such a political statement. So it could be noticed that a young woman student arriving from the south at a northern university might soon abandon her straightened, wavy hair style for the frizzled, heightened style which affirmed her solidarity with other blacks on the campus. Now that black identity has been made much more clear and some political advance made, it seems, the 'dramatic spherical cloud' of the Afro is less commonly worn. The reasons also include the pressures to change any fashion, and the fact that the Afro demanded special treatment in combing and conditioning which could not only be more costly than some other styles but also could affect the quality of the hair. Yet it has been pointed out that the Afro has been important in helping to free black women from the problems of dealing with kinky hair in a straight-haired society, and stimulate them to adopt a wider variety of bold hair styles. In this context it is revealing to read what E. A. Hoebel wrote at an earlier period: 'A definitely New World symbolism has arisen among American Coloreds in the matter of hair form. The passion for hair-straightening and kink-removing compounds among American Coloreds reflects an identification of non-kinky hair with social status of whites' (1966, 283; cf. *Time Magazine*, 25 November 1971). How faded and distorted does this opinion now seem, however accurate it may then have looked! More generally, just as some Tikopia young women asserted their individuality and a challenge to men by growing their hair long, so in the West some women have done likewise by cutting theirs short. For a woman to wear her hair short in Europe or America has often been interpreted as a sign of masculinity, and may well have sometimes been an accompaniment of her homosexuality. But in many cases it has surely been a statement of egalitarianism with men. Women who rightly believe that they should be given equal opportunities with men occupationally, may tend to emphasize their attitude by adoption of a hair style associated with greater freedom of action, and by rejecting the conventional image of the long-tressed feminine weaker role.

Hair is a very personal thing, in two ways. It is very much attached to the body, associated with personal growth and maturity. But it is also a personal asset, detachable in large part from the body, transferable to other persons, even on a commercial basis (see later). With the manner of treating it personal statements can be made, either of fairly simple sign order (as when an adolescent college girl wears a braid to show she is emotionally engaged and so theoretically not socially available) or as more complex symbols (in expression of sex challenge or of ethnic identity). Such personal statements may be more or less group-promoted, but what is especially interesting is the keenness with which they are group-judged, and the strength of the expressions of approval or disapproval which they evoke.

In recent years this has emerged particularly in regard to the wearing of long hair by men.

MODERN SIGNIFICANCE OF MEN'S LONG HAIR

In the West until recently, norms of hair style were based on the convention that while curls or ringlets might be permissible to children of both sexes, in adolescence and maturity the hair of females was worn long and that of males was short. Style might indicate social progression, as when a girl symbolized her maturity by 'putting up' her hair into a roll or 'bun' on the nape of the neck or top of the head, equated with 'growing up'; or in parallel, a boy began to shave. For men, short scalp hair had been the custom for more than a century. With men's facial hair more variation was allowable, and fashion saw changing styles, from clean-shaven to combinations of beard, whiskers and moustache. But less than twenty years ago the view could be expressed that shaving of the beard continued in all ranks of life in England, though the moustache, in vogue for many years, had become less common (*Pears Cyclopaedia*, 1958–9). As for scalp hair, Hoebel in the third edition of his *Anthropology* (1966, 282) could remark that 'in America, the culture pattern with its attendant symbolic quality is still so strong that short-haired women are considered mannish and long-haired men effeminate', though he added cautiously – 'at least by most individuals over 30'.

But such opinions have been overtaken by events. In recent years, much more tolerance has been extended to male facial hair. What in England we thought were the occupational beards of submariners during the war turned out to be merely the advance guard of an army. Beards are now so common among men of all ages as to attract little attention, and indeed have become almost standardized pattern in some circles.* Many men well over the age of 30 can be seen with long-haired coiffure, from shaggy strands to duckstail or other neck fringe. Seasonal factors may enter – as a Prime Minister known socially as rather a trend-setter was reported to be having his hair shortened for the summer after having it long during the winter. Essentially, many men have been using their hair for aesthetic experiment with their personalities.

But as well as personal aesthetic and conformity to fashion, it seems clear that deliberate statements are often being made by such practices. Quite generally, in line with modern values of self-expression, the wearing of long hair by men, from hippy to university student, can express an attitude of *laissez-faire* – avoidance of the trouble and expense of hair-cut, letting nature take its course, and so on. There may be also an attitude of sexual awareness, though in a contrary direction to that put forward by Darwin in his theory of the value of hair in sexual selection. When I once asked a graduate student why he wore his hair long, he replied, laughing, because his wife considered it more sexy;† she, listening, only

* There is some point to a *New Yorker* cartoon (23 May 1970) of two clean-shaven business men standing on a commuter platform filled with an array of wearers of beards and whiskers; one saying to the other: 'I feel like a damn fool'.

† For an elaborate examination of the sexual significance of head hair see E. R. Leach, 1958.

smiled. Complex elements of identification may also operate between a young man and young woman who are socially and sexually associated, and both of whom wear their hair long – though each may adopt a different mode. Again, there may be a definite rejection of the hair patterns of an older generation, which in their demands for cleanliness, 'tidiness', etc. represent the authority of the 'establishment' which must be defied.

In a more general sense, the wearing of long hair by young men came to take on the character of a quasi-political symbol. Mingled with anti-establishment views were other values, including those of some degree of political commitment to the idea of a different type of society with institutions of another order than those current in the West. Whatever be the particular form of commitment, long hair came to become a recognition signal among young people, of some sharing of common values and differentiation from the rest of society. But this situation became blurred with the passage of time, as the fashion of men wearing their hair long spread. Long-haired people often turned out to be 'fad-followers' in the eyes of those whose convictions they did not share. As one student commentator on this subject expressed it to me: 'You used to be able to trust long-haired people, but not any more. Now some of the people you can trust are short-haired; there are "freaks" among short-haired people too.'

Now modern Western society has become more permissive about many kinds of social identification – a striking instance being the toleration now extended in Britain to private behaviour of homosexuals, and to public representations of homosexual attitudes in the theatre. While some of this permissiveness has extended to modes of the wearing of hair, much resentment is still visible on the part of the public to the long hair of young men. Symbolically, the former individual idiosyncratic behaviour has become stereotyped: while in fact there is great variety of style in which modern young men wear their hair long, in the eyes of the public it is all 'long hair', and to many people equally obnoxious.

What is noteworthy is the widespread reaction of criticism, from ridicule to high indignation and even physical violence, which this male wearing of long hair has aroused. If its effects were not often so serious, the popular response of outrage would be comic to an external observer. To many middle-aged people in Europe and in America, a canon of absolute value has come to be attached to short male head-hair, associated with cleanliness, efficiency and masculinity. Ignorant of the widespread practices of wearing male hair long, accepted and esteemed, in other cultures; and in seventeenth- and eighteenth-century society among men of the highest status and fashion, modern outbursts against male long hair illustrate not only the changeability of fashion but also the relativity of the moral judgements so expressed. Reasons for public expressions of outrage seem various. Long hair of young men in its more extreme forms is equated with wildness, calling up suggestions of a feral animal nature, and rationalized by allusions to untidiness and dirt. It is seen as a confusion of symbolic categories, not only suggesting a potent feminine symbol, but also blurring actually at times a casual identification of man from woman. It is also a breach of the code of uniformity, indicating – since hair length is a matter of personal control – that the wearer does not wish to be subject to the ordinary norms of social style. But what seems to exacerbate public reaction almost to a frenzy is a realization that long male hair may be a symbol for a deliberate protest against society, or those sections of society which represent authority. And what is unfortunate is that public reactions do not always distinguish between long hair as a statement of personality in aesthetic choice – a personal symbol of primarily individual reference – and as an act of recoil from the style of the establishment – a communication of meaning to the wider society.

One type of public reaction has been the use of information about male long hair for its incongruity, as news items, often with a touch of ridicule. So, a society wedding is noted in which the spouse with the flowing, shoulder-length locks was the groom, while the bride had her short hair done up in ringlets. News articles on hairstyling either note the decline of barbers – 'an endangered species in New York State' – or the development of salons for men which provide services similar to those which women have been having for years – to have their hair 'stripped, bleached, dyed, streaked, "relaxed" (straightened), curled, and teased'. Such salons, which cater not only for homosexuals, report that men are more fussy about their hair-styling than women, and some are beginning to have their hair 'done' for special occasions, just as women have done. Such items draw attention to sex in an indirect way by emphasizing the approach of men to feminine patterns (for example *Chicago Tribune*, 7 November 1970; *Chicago Daily News*, 22 April 1971; *New York Times*, 13 January 1972).

Another type of reaction has been of an official kind, on the basis of long hair as an offence against public morals. Until recently, male travellers passing through Yugoslavia were scrutinized at the border and if their hair was thought to be unduly long, they were made to cut it before being allowed to enter the country. Similar action was taken at various times by the governments of South Vietnam, Panama and Singapore. In Malacca a magistrate warned that he would not hear evidence from long-haired male witnesses, as it was unbefitting the dignity of the court (*Province*, B.C., 25 May 1970; *Chicago Daily News*, 7 November 1970; *New York Times*, 2 December 1971; *The Times*, 1 March 1972). An interesting analogy is given by the treatment of transvestites who play female roles in Javanese popular plays, and who formerly let their hair grow long. In the name of modern progress an attempt has been made to clean up the transvestites' sexual image, to discourage their homosexuality offstage, and to develop the idea that their role is adopted simply as a means of serving the national cause through the political propaganda of the plays. Hence most transvestite players have responded to pressure and have cut their hair (Peacock, 1968, 206–7).

In this connection, in his study of social and symbolic aspects of Indonesian proletarian drama, James Peacock has raised an interesting theoretical point. He holds that for these transvestites the haircut seems to have been a particularly traumatic part of the Revolution, and adds that perhaps long hair had an especially potent meaning for transvestites since it is the only gross male body-part that can be made more womanly by the natural process of letting it grow. Other womanly qualities were artificial – powder, padding, rouge, – but hair could not be removed; it is peculiarly between body and culture, having attributes of both. Thus long hair may have signified a more sustained commitment to the womanly role than did interest in the more external feminine trappings. This suggestion ignores the possible parallel of long finger-nails, also a symbol of femininity intermediate between body and culture. But it is very plausible, if it be remembered that it can be valid only in a culture in which long hair is a recognized female symbol.

Linked with the reaction of moral indignation at male long hair is the view that it is prejudicial to discipline, for instance in schools and colleges, or on athletic teams. It was reported recently from Croydon, London, that 100 fourth-formers walked out and held a protest meeting after their headmaster had banned boys from having long hair. The banning of a boy from a Sunderland school until he got his hair cut provoked a public controversy in which artists' representations of Christ with shoulder-length hair were countered by a quotation from St Paul to the effect that if a man have long hair, it is a shame unto him (*The Times*, 10–17 February 1971; 19 January 1972). Various American university football and swimming coaches established dress codes which specified that the hair of male athletes must not touch the collar, and threatened offenders with suspension, against protests from student leaders and campus newspapers (for example *Chicago Sun Times*, 25 September 1970; *Chicago Daily News*, 31 October 1970; 1 November 1970; *Chicago Today*, 22 November 1970). With a motto of 'discipline, dedication, duty' the coach of the professional football team, the Kansas City Chiefs, imposed a fine of $500 on any of his men who let their side whiskers grow longer than his, and forbade moustaches and beards (*New York Times*, 22 November 1970). But it is significant to note that such reactions were by no means universal, and that in some cases suspensions were challenged as being an interference with personal freedom, and taken to the courts. The father of a high school student who was suspended for defying the school dress code brought suit in the district court for his son to be reinstated and damages paid, on the ground that his son had the right to wear his hair as he wished. But the legal, like the moral issues, seem by no means clear. A United States Court of Appeal, faced by cases from Colorado, Utah and New Mexico opposing hair-length regulations for public school boys, gave the opinion that the Constitution and statutes did not impose on federal courts the duty and responsibility of supervising the length of a student's hair. The Court, despite claims of freedom made, did not recognize the existence of any federally protected right as to the wearing of hair (*New York Times*, 29 November 1971; *Time Magazine*, 1 November 1971). And in a recent London case of a schoolboy barred from school till he had his hair cut, an Education Department spokesman said there was a school rule which stated that hair must be of 'reasonable' length – which obviously leaves room for a great deal of interpretation (*Evening Standard*, 12 May 1972).

The complications of the male long-hair issue emerge still more when questions of employment arise. The managing owner of a Chicago taxicab company posted a notice warning his drivers that those who did not soon get their hair cut would not be allowed to drive. He argued that passengers had complained about their long hair, and unless he conformed he would lose business and money. 'We gave them [the drivers] a choice,' he said, 'either get haircuts or don't drive. It's their choice.' The retort of the drivers was to collect signed statements from passengers who had no objection to long hair. Another manager, in Honolulu, defended his long-haired drivers against criticism on the grounds that if he did not hire such men they would be standing in the compensation lines for unemployment benefit (*New York Times*, 29 December 1970; *Chicago Tribune*, 17 November 1970). But the benefit issue itself was not clear, since if prospective employers were known not to be interested in long-haired men, these might be thought to be unwilling to take work if they refused to cut their hair. So on several occasions in California unemployment benefit has been refused on this score. The manager of the state unemployment office for the Monterey peninsula was reported in May 1970 to have said that men whose hair, beards or sideburns were long and scraggly could not collect unemployment insurance on the peninsula. He said that after a survey of 900 employers it was clear that the overwhelming majority of them would not accept long hair on male employees – hence 'we feel that those who persist in wearing it are voluntarily restricting their availability'. Such men had only to shave or trim their hair and they would receive insurance payments. At the beginning of 1972 the California Unemployment Insurance Appeals Board ruled that jobless men with long hair were not eligible for unemployment compensation benefits in towns where most of the employers rejected long-haired applicants (*The Province*, B.C., 29 May 1970; *New York Times*, 9 January 1972). Note that in this type of case, as with the taxi-drivers, the operative factor was public opinion, real or alleged. In some employment fields orders to employees to cut their hair have been successfully challenged. The policy of the New York City Housing Authority for some time had been against the wearing of beards by their patrolmen, and a patrolman who insisted on wearing a beard had been discharged for insubordination. But presumably it was later thought that public sentiment did not provide sufficient sanction for such action, and the Authority rescinded its 'no-beard' rule, on the ground that 'where it is not clear that the rule has anything to do with the proper performance of duty' it was 'unwise' and 'an unwarranted infringement on personal freedom' to enforce it (*New York Times*, 23 April 1970; 16 May 1970). It may be that legal sanctions also were not thought strong enough. For instance, a volunteer fireman of Long Island was suspended for a year for not conforming to the rules about hair; he brought a case against the Board of Fire Commissioners of his district, and the state Supreme Court upheld the constitutional right of a public employee to determine the length of his hair, sideburns, moustache and beard. When the fireman promised to obey the department rules, the judge said, he did so not in waiver or violation of his constitutional rights (*New York Times*, 3 December 1971).

But with more direct organized sanctions, the reaction against long hair has tended to be firmer. On various occasions the United States Army and Navy have issued directives about grooming of hair and beards, and made it plain that they do not condone long unkempt hair. In December 1969 it was reported that a black airman was convicted of refusing to obey an order to trim his Afro-style haircut, and was sentenced by special court-martial to three months' confinement, demotion, and $60 a month fine for three months. The offence was not wearing his hair long but refusing to obey a military order, but the issue was clear (*Life*, 8 May 1970; cf. *Newsweek*, 23 November 1970; 29 May 1971; *Chicago Daily News*, 3 December 1970; *New York Times*, 28 November 1971).

The most extreme forms of reaction against male long hair in the name of discipline have occurred in prisons, where haircuts have been imposed by force. Two kinds of rationalization have been invoked in such cases – that the shearing has been for 'sanitary reasons', or to destroy a possible hiding-place for forbidden goods. Both the United States and Britain have had recent instances of this, with offenders who have been involved with the law primarily on moral or political grounds, and in some cases local public support was shown for the authorities. In February 1970, members of the 'Chicago Seven' had their long hair cut in Cook County jail, and the sheriff was reported to have shown pictures of them to an amused Republican gathering as an earnest of energetic action. In May of the same year a local branch of the Barbers Union awarded an honorary barber's degree to a Michigan sheriff who had ordered the hair of a group of students cut while they were being held in the local jail for bond to be posted. The sheriff was congratulated by the barbers for 'following our own barber book which says long hair is not good' (in this case the sheriff had a suit for $200,000 filed against him, arguing that he had violated the constitutional rights of the students) (*New York Times*, 25 February 1970; 2 May 1970). In July 1971 the three editors of the underground London magazine *Oz*, awaiting sentence on obscenity charges, had their shoulder-length hair cut in Wandsworth jail, it was said at the request of prison staff. In subsequent public discussion it was pointed out, with some truth, that this act would be interpreted by many young people as a desire to humiliate the defendants for being unconventional and disrespectful to society (*The Times*, 31 July 1971; 1 August 1971).

To sum up the material in this field – it appears that modern Western reactions to the wearing of long hair by men are diverse, but that there is in conservative circles a widespread if sporadic type of censorious judgement. It tends to be emotional, and on occasion to take aggressive form, and it offers various rationalizations, principally those connected with order and discipline and with femininity. The sanctions involved are not always clear, but a basic issue tends to be the degree to which an individual has the right, against what are interpreted as the interests of society, to determine his own physical appearance.

But there are ambiguities in the situation. In the name of order, long growth of both facial and scalp hair may be stigmatized. But there is an opposition involved here: both beards and long head-hair may be wild; but beards are manly, while long hair is feminine. So rules which would make men both shave and cut their hair are to some extent at cross purposes. Moreover, long hair in itself is not disordered; if bound up on the top of the head it is not so, and in fact it seems to be loose flowing men's hair to which major objection is taken. But the interpretation of constraint or freedom in the treatment of men's hair is largely a cultural matter. With traditional Tikopia, in everyday affairs in house or village a man normally wore his hair floating freely. But in work, for convenience, he usually tied it at the nape of his neck or in a roll on his head. This was an individual choice. But if he was appearing formally before his chief, or was taking a critical ritual role, he had to loosen his hair and allow it to hang free. So there was equation between physical constraint on the hair and freedom of movement in work, and physical freedom of the hair and constraint in ritual observance. This conceptualization, tacit only, as far as I know, seems to have been that lack of constraint of hair indicated an openness to direction and control, a submission to authority – of chief or patron god – as opposed to a man's own exercise of control in binding his hair. To loosen one's hair for a formal occasion was a symbolic gesture of submission* – almost the exact reverse of a conservative modern Western view that loose, long hair is a 'symbol of lawlessness and subversion'.

LONG HAIR AND BEARDS IN RELIGION

When the symbolism of scalp and facial hair is not simply part of a diffuse set of social norms, but is integrated with an organized set of religious norms, the issues take a different form.

Many religious communities have incorporated regulations about hair into their body of rules for the faithful, involving both cutting or shaving of hair and growth of hair, according to circumstance. Judaism, which tends to equate male hair with strength and vitality, has rules for Nazarite-vows, focusing upon a man's growing his hair for thirty-day periods (or multiples thereof), ritual cutting and burning of it, and presentation of animal offerings in celebration. Detailed specification of such vows includes a distinction between one kind of lifelong Nazarite, who may lighten his hair with a razor if it becomes too heavy; and another kind 'the like of Samson', who may not so lighten his hair (*Mishnah*, Nazir – Danby, 1933, 281). In orthodox Hinduism a shaving of a child's head leaves only a tuft of hair, a topknot, 'universally' recognized as the distinctive mark of a

* But note that in other cultures the symbolism may take a contrary form. Before a Toda man entered the dairy, a sacred place, for ritual performance, he *tied up* the straggling hair at the back of his head (Rivers, 1906, 92, 221).

Hindu. Rationalizations are that it is a hygienic measure, or meant to keep the head cool, or more esoterically, that it removes impurities contracted in the womb before the child had any conscious existence. Some modern sophisticated Bengalis cut off the topknot, while others wear a small lock which they keep inconspicuous generally but display in orthodox company. The special status of ascetics is indicated by their lack of adherence to rule: some have their heads clean-shaven, others have their hair braided and coiled up on the head, often with artificial braids added, and others have long dishevelled locks. As religious devotees, they are above conformity (O'Malley, 1935, 116, 207–8). In these two major religious systems, then, a man's long hair is not an object of suspicion and disapproval, but is used as a defining characteristic, either generally or in relation to some specific commitment. Moreover, the greater the religious intensity of commitment, the more freedom allowed to the individual to determine his own hair length.

But conflict can take place when the dictates of religion are not in keeping with the norms of society. This has occurred in Britain in recent years with Sikhs, whose custom of men wearing long hair and beard has clashed with job requirements or with public opinion. Some of these people have shaved and cut their hair accordingly. But the majority have not, and a running controversy has taken place in one city, with Sikh bus conductors protesting against the Corporation employer's decision that they should abandon their turbans when on duty, cut their hair and wear regulation caps.* The direction of popular prejudice (even if mingled with personal animosity) was indicated by the case of a Sikh in England who brought an action at law against people who, he claimed, had invited him into a house and there cut off his beard and moustache. A leading Sikh commented: 'Cutting off a Sikh's beard is worse than killing him. It is a symbol of his religious identity' (*Times*, 21 August 1970). But the police, though sympathetic, seemed uncertain about how to classify the offence. The point about some of these cases is that while the right of

* An analogous issue was involved in the decision of the New York Stock Exchange to recognize a Jewish employee's right to wear a religious skull cap (*yarmulke*) during working hours – a practice it had refused to countenance until threatened by a complaint of religious discrimination with the City Commission on Human Rights. The claim was made on grounds of Jewish orthodoxy and granted by the Exchange on grounds of 'established religious requirement'.

individuals to freedom in the disposal of their personal hair is at stake, and is not seen publicly as an unambiguous right, some concession is made to religious symbolism. There is a tendency to see long hair or beard not as just personal idiosyncrasy or protest, but as conformity to a recognizable set of sanctions which can be treated seriously even if they are not accepted fully.

In some religious contexts, however, there have been internal controversies. In Eastern Christianity beards have traditionally been held appropriate for priests, but this has not been the view of the Western church, where there has been considerable divergence of opinion. The long-standing controversies in this field are illustrated by a work on clerical beards by Johan Piers Valerian, published in Latin in Paris in 1533, and in London in the same year, in translation: *A Treatise Written by John Valerian a greatte clerke of Italie, which is intitled in latin Pro Sacerdotum barbis translated into Englysshe.* Valerian, a Roman, addressed his essay to Cardinal Ippolito Medici, whose cultured aesthetic interests and dislike for the ecclesiastical life might have predisposed him to sympathy for the argument in defence of priests' beards. Valerian argued that – presumably as part of the re-ordering process of the Counter-Reformation – pressure was being put upon the Pope to bring forward a law about beards, previously common, and clergy were therefore being advised to shave. He held that this was against Roman tradition, that the ancient Roman gods had beards, that only children, women and gelded men went beardless, and that both Hebrews and Christ and his disciples wore beards. 'The Beard is a garment for manly chekes given of nature for comfort and health. . . .' Half a century later Antonius Hotoman produced a treatise entitled *Pogonias* [in Greek] *sive De Barba*, republished in several editions in the early seventeenth century. In argument similar to Valerian he held that without a beard, men get confused with women; a beard is a sign of maturity; it was sacrosanct in ancient France . . . etc. A major point in such controversy, from which the work of Dulaure on beards mentioned earlier (p. 266) was a development, is the significance of the beard as a symbolic demarcator. The problem involved implicitly was what should be the categories of prime concern: the distinction of men from children and women, tacitly less mature and less responsible; the distinction of priests from other men, of less ritual aura; and possibly the distinction of Western priests from Eastern priests, who could be thought to be of less fine grain, since they not only wore beards but in the lower ranks could take wives?

The sociological significance of long hair as group demarcator in a religious sectarian context has been brought out in J. A. Hostetler's examination of Amish symbols (1964). From the sixteenth century the Anabaptists passed a resolution forbidding the trimming of the beard and hair 'according to worldly fashions', though the moustache came to be opposed because of its military associations. For Amish men beards are expected to appear by baptism, and though during courtship young men manage to keep their beards very short, after marriage they no longer dare to trim them. The hair of Amish men is worn bobbed, cut below the ear or slightly above the ear lobes, depending on their local community. Hair-length is an index to the conservatism of the community, and an Amish man makes himself subject to the sanctions of his church by wearing his hair too short. The hair of Amish women also must be long and uncut, parted in the middle only, and combed down the sides. From infancy, girls' hair is braided and with adolescence is put up at the back.

In a religious context, long hair has sometimes been assigned a specific symbolic character, not as group demarcator but as indicative of moral quality. So in Christianity, as in Judaism, long hair worn by men may sometimes symbolize strength, in allusion to the story of Samson.* It is held too that since in ancient times unmarried women wore their hair loose and long, virgin saints are frequently portrayed in art with long, flowing hair. J. J. Bachofen, linking hair with sex themes, argued that the sacrifice of a woman's long hair was a symbolic offering of her chastity (1925, 326 ff.). And early Rabbis held that a woman's long hair was such a powerful augmentation of beauty that a married woman was recommended to hide it; and the cutting of it was taken as a sign of mourning or of degradation (*Jewish Encyclopedia*, Hair). Yet in Renaissance art loose, flowing hair was also a symbol of penitence, in allusion to the woman who washed the feet of Jesus with her tears and wiped them with her hair. This Biblical story, it is alleged, led to the custom of hermits and

* Cf. 'the virility of horses is extinguished when their manes are cut' according to a Bestiary (T. H. White, 1960, 86).

others doing penance, letting their hair grow long (George Ferguson, 1961, 47, 135, 137). Interpretation varied according to context.

LOSS OF HAIR

Considering the positive values attached to hair, one can understand that loss of hair can also be invested with social significance. Natural hair loss, leading perhaps to baldness, whether temporary or permanent, is usually deplored – hence the many remedies against 'falling hair', which are a tribute to hope rather than to scientific insight. The negative value attached to baldness is illustrated by many classical observations, from the story of Elisha and the jeering children to Ovid's reference to a head without hair as a field without grass.

Unlike almost all other parts of the body, hair is detachable with relative ease while growing, and several strongly contrasted attitudes tend to be associated with hair purposely detached, as contrasted with hair shed involuntarily. Hair shed involuntarily tends to be treated like other human exuviae and regarded as unpleasing. That which was tolerated, even admired, while it was an integral part of the human personality now becomes an object of disgust. To find a scalp hair in one's food or a pubic hair in one's bath may cause acute revulsion. She may, as the poets say, be able to draw you to her with a single hair, but not if the hair is in the soup! Such reaction does not seem to be merely a matter of incongruity, the 'dirt as matter in the wrong place' argument which Mary Douglas has used effectively in her study of pollution. Nor do I think it is because of specific sex associations, as psychoanalysts might argue (see below). It seems to have the double suggestion of intrusion of another personality into one's own intimate operations of eating and cleansing; and also of some association with the other person's eliminations, that is the rejected part of his personality. In my view it is this status-laden symbolic confrontation, this giving for incorporation into one's own personality something which another person has discarded, which lies at the root of the strongly emotional rejection of hair exuviae. It is not surprising then that the use of such hair takes on a more elaborately symbolic form in ideas and practices of sorcery (see later). On the other hand, hair intentionally severed from the head has often been prized and used as a symbol for manipulation, especially for memorial purposes. In the eighteenth and nineteenth centuries aristocratic and middle-class circles in Europe and America made great play with lock, tuft, curl, tress or ringlet of hair – as reminiscence of her child's babyhood for a mother, token of affection for a lover, or sign of mourning in a close relative. An exotic example of this kind of interest is the recent sale of a lock of George Washington's reddish-brown hair, which his wife Martha had given to a New York society belle, for $550 (*Chicago Tribune*, 2 November 1970; *Chicago Daily News*, 22 November 1970). Analogous customs have existed in many other cultures – as my example from Tikopia has indicated (p. 272).

In many societies, however, it is the act of severing a person's hair rather than the fate of the hair which attracts prime attention. In ordinary modern Western conditions the focus is upon the skill of the operator and the result, for which he is highly rewarded, but in some other cultures the relationship between the parties may be the main object of concern. A striking instance of how cutting a person's hair may imply a special relationship is given in traditional Dobu society. Care of hair is a reciprocal service between husband and wife, and is interpreted as associated with sexual intercourse. So an adulterer will openly cut the hair of a woman with whom he has committed adultery if he wishes to make the matter public and defy the woman's husband (Fortune, 1932, 50).

In other conditions it is the shorn state of the person that is the most significant element. Simulated baldness, as by shaving the pate, has been used to give relief from heat or to cope with scalp infection or – formerly – as part of treatment in some fevers. Socially, head shaving has been used for dramatic effect, as by the 'soul' singer Isaac Hayes (*Ebony*, 1970, 86; *New York Times*, 18 April 1971); or as a demarcation sign, by British 'skinheads', teenagers opposed to long-haired 'hippies' and bearded 'Pakistanis' (*New York Times*, 29 March 1970).

But on the whole, deliberate shaving of the head, or close cutting of the hair, has taken on a ritual quality, intended to mark a transition from one social state to another, and in particular to imply a modification in the status or social condition of the person whose hair is so treated. At many periods women have cut their hair short to demonstrate if not an equality with men at least a repudiation of the woman's traditional sex role.* But cutting the hair close or shaving the head often denoted mourning. In a soliloquy on hair in *Gryll Grange* Thomas Love Peacock, quoting Aristotle, wrote: 'In mourning, sympathizing with the dead, we deform ourselves by cutting off our hair,' and he added the reflection that: 'A woman's head shaved is a step towards a death's head'. A recent exemplification of this was the act of four young women associated with the notorious principal in a murder trial; they appeared outside the courtroom with their heads shaven and vowing self-immolation if the man was sentenced to death (*Chicago Daily News*, 29 March 1971). Again, where the initiative does not lie with the person primarily concerned, an enforced cutting or shaving of hair may convey contempt and degradation, an extreme reduction in status. In some countries which had been occupied by the Germans during the war, after the liberation there was some shaving of heads of women accused of collaboration with the invaders, especially in sexual favours. Recently, in the tragic events in Northern Ireland, this practice has been revived by Catholic 'patriots' against girls wishing to marry British soldiers or thought to have given information (*New York Times*, 11–14 November 1971). It is in circumstances such as these especially that the statement of Antonius Hotoman applies – that the cutting of hair is a sign of *tristitia* – sadness!

The symbolism of shaving the head becomes more complex when it is used as one of the marks of participation in a religious ritual, or entry to a religious order. An example of the former, occurring as part of a great ancestral festival of the Dogon of West Sudan, was the shaving of the heads of participants so that symbolically they resembled new-born infants, and had their dependence upon their ancestors forcefully demonstrated by a reduction of status. A well-known example of shaving the head as a ceremony of initiation required for reception into a religious order is the tonsure of the Catholic church. The tonsure, described by the *New Catholic Encyclopaedia* as a sacred rite, is said to be the outgrowth of an

* A fourth-century Christian mystic condemned marriage and encouraged the celibate life for both sexes, inducing many women to leave their husbands, cut their hair, adopt male attire and enter monasteries. This form of asceticism was condemned by the Council of Gangra, in A.D. 340 (Margaret Smith, 1931, 43).

Eastern custom of cutting the hair of slaves (essentially a mark of reduction of status); and to have been adopted first by the monastic orders and then by the secular clergy for its symbolic value in manifesting the dedication of the cleric to the service of God. By general law all Catholic clergy are bound to wear the tonsure, the most usual being the Gallican mode of shaving only a small circle at the top of the head.

I have pointed out that in most general terms shaving the head is a sign of *tristitia*, as Hotoman put it, of diminution of the self, whether in terms of status or of relation to the world and human affairs.* The hair of the head is an intimate element of the personality, and to remove it by intention is in effect a reduction or at least a change in the personality. Yet there is a kind of dialectical relationship here. For reduction of the personality in one direction may allow of its growth in another. This is illustrated particularly by the values attached to hair and to shaving in Indian myth and religion. The classical description of Shiva shows him with tresses long and matted, partly streaming, partly stacked in a kind of pyramid – the hair of the model *yogi* of the gods. Supra-normal life energy, amounting to the power of magic, resides in such a wilderness of hair untouched by scissors. Shiva does not shave or shear his hair, which loosens out as a halo around him when he performs his cosmic dance. But then there is the contrast. To enter upon the spiritual path of absolute asceticism one must be shaved. When the Buddha set out on his path of Enlightenment he severed his topknot. Ascetic hostility to the hair of the human organism is such that Jains tolerate no hair at all on the person of an ordained holy man. Part of the ritual of ordination consists in a thorough weeding out of every hair growing on the head and body. So in this symbol-system, long, unshorn hair, and completely shorn, no-hair, are both conditions of power (see Heinrich Zimmer, 1946, 157 ff.). In such a complex subtle ideology and symbolism, as I interpret it, long hair symbolizes the cosmic power of growth; no hair symbolizes the power of subjugation of the self to social rule. (In this context, Hallpike's thesis,

* A seventeenth-century voyager to Batavia observed of the Chinese there that their hair, in which they were very neat, they valued at the highest rate, since it is the last thing they would stake at play, gambling away their wives and children first. But when a man had lost his hair by gambling, he lost with it all his credit and reputation, and was looked upon as a slave, to work for others (Fryke, 1929, 29).

referred to later, has a limited validity.) So, broadly, loss of hair symbolizes destruction of personality – either in the course of nature, by ageing; or artificially, by act of man – or alteration of personality. It generally implies a lowering of status, though the lowering of status may be only temporary, a reduction of the individual to order in the name of a collectivity or an extra-human being with which association gives the individual a special new status.

WIGS AND PERSONALITY

Since loss of hair is commonly regarded as lowering to the personality, it is not surprising that in many cultures efforts have been made to remedy the deficiency, by wigs. According to the dictionaries, 'wig' is an abbreviation of periwig, which in turn is an adaptation of the French *perruque*, from which the German *Perücke* is also derived; this illustrates the cultural range of the wearing of wigs in European polite society from about the sixteenth century. But with modern technology and mass fashion the wearing of wigs has become much more widespread and the class association has tended to disappear. In modern times too male wigs have tended to conceal baldness while female wigs have primarily been additions to a normal head of hair to meet the changing dictates of fashion. Current usage gives wigs, wiglets; toupees for men and 'falls' for women; and more elaborate descriptions speak of 'quality hairpieces' or 'hairpieces of distinction'. Not so long ago a 'switch' was not only a tuft of long hairs at the end of a cow's tail but also a heavy strand of hair added in some coiffures to a person's own hair.

The nature of the mass appeal is indicated by newspaper advertisements: 'For every woman who says "I can't do a thing with my hair" we have a wig that says you can.' Wigs are described as exclusive, coming in all colours, having a wonderfully natural look, adjustable to any head size, soft to the hand – and the cheek – romantically realistic, washable, stretchable, sensuous, lightweight, comfortable. . . . Not only are they worn professionally by fashion models – they are even made for female children. 'It was bound to happen: wigs for little girls. Practically every fashion idea these days filters down, crosses over age and sex lines.' Wigs for children started apparently as playthings, but became more serious fashion items, as for parties (illustrated in *Chicago Daily News*, 21 October 1970).

A special development has occurred in modern wigs for men. Apart from concealing loss of hair, wigs for judges, barristers and actors have long been in vogue, for defining their roles. But a striking use of auxiliary hair has occurred recently in some United States military circles, of getting a long-haired wig to cover up the normal short-haired military style when a soldier is off-duty among his friends. Reports indicate that social pressures about their short hair brought young men into wig shops on such pretexts as that they ran a music shop or played in a band and needed long hair as an occupational badge – whereas what was really worrying them was the opinion of their girl-friends. So in March 1970 a wig-shop near a well-known military establishment was selling thirty male wigs a week, at a price of $25 for human hair and $20 for artificial hair – which was not so popular. But a reverse quirk was the wearing of short-hair wigs by army reservists when they had to go into training, covering their long civilian hair. Realizing that the prejudices of army sergeants and commanding officers might order them to the barber, some ingenious men hoped to pass muster with short wigs for the training period and keep their normal long-haired image in civilian life (*New York Times*, 4 March 1970; *Newsweek*, 29 November 1971).*

In the religious field, similar problems can arise as with the shaving of hair or the growth of beard, in the wearing of wigs. In the history of the Catholic church there has been argument about the propriety of wigs for clerics, illustrated by the *Histoire des Perruques* by Jean-Baptiste Thiers, a work printed at his own expense in Paris in 1609. Thiers, a cleric and doctor of theology, argued that many ecclesiastics of his day wore wigs, thinking that such was not interdicted by the church – but they were in error! Whereas wigs then were common in France, formerly only kings had a right to long hair (but cf. Wallace-Hadrill, 1962) – until the mid-twelfth century. Wigs of ecclesiastics were condemned by the doctrine of St Paul, who held that the heads of men should be uncovered while praying;

* An alternative to a wig for men has been a hair transplant of scalp grafts from sides to top of the head (*Chicago Daily News*, 20 April 1970). Analogous to wigs as enhancement of personality have been false beards for men and false eyelashes for women.

and the Fathers condemned disguises, but wigs disguised the clerics who wore them.... Thiers proposed various measures, including a papal bull, to stop such abuse. That his arguments had some effect is seen by the publication of his work in Italian nearly a century later, with episcopal authority from Benevento.

An interesting question about the concept of personality is raised by the wearing of wigs. Ordinarily, contact with another person's discarded hair is apt to be repulsive, if there is no positive affective tie, as with a lock of hair from a relative or lover. Yet human hair in a wig is acceptable, even preferred to artificial hair. How can this be so? It is clear that many external elements from living or dead things can be associated with the human personality without strain – leather, wool and meat from animal tissue for shoes, clothing and food. Even elements from another person's body may be incorporated nowadays by blood transfusion, corneal grafts and organ transplants. But it is a delicate issue. Apart from susceptibilities about food taboos on pork, or beef, or meat generally, there may be religious objections to some surgical transfers, as in Muslim debates about the propriety of eye grafts.

What is interesting about wigs made from human hair is that they seem to arouse no serious objection. A few people seem relieved to know they are wearing man-made plastic, but most seem happy to sport 'real first-grade human hair'. This is so even when ethnic boundaries are crossed – for much hair made up into Western wigs comes from Oriental heads. Two conditions here are relevant. The first is that people incorporate other people's hair into their own personality on their own responsibility – they are not just confronted with it at random; it is under their own control. The second condition is that it is de-personalized. Once on the commercial market, human hair is treated and sold just as if it were a fibre of animal or vegetable origin. This point can be emphasized in another way, by contrast of custom. I mentioned that Tikopia women with close-cropped heads have customarily worn, not a wig, but a ring of their menfolk's hair as a kind of everyday obligatory ornament. In the West, however, whether women cut their hair or not, men until recently have done so. Yet I have never heard of a woman's tresses being made into a wig for her father or brother, or a man's locks for his sister or wife; this would probably be regarded as eccentric if not disgusting. One may wear or treasure a lock of the beloved's hair, but not have the locks made up into a wig. Yet to wear some other man's or woman's hair on one's head is quite proper, so long as it has come through the market process, and by definition the previous owner has not been known. So in the West personal association but not incorporation is appropriate for the residues of someone with whom one has identified social contact; for incorporation one needs anonymity. Fusion of physical personalities is frowned upon if the personalities are related; one must dehumanize or depersonalize the body tissues in order to absorb them. (A main exception to this is kidney grafts, presumably from the gravity of the case.) In strong contrast is the use made of wigs by men of the Mount Hagen area, New Guinea; they combine their own hair, hair collected from other men, their own wives and other women – whom they pay for the service – to make elaborately decorated wigs, with symbolic meaning (Andrew and Marilyn Strathern, 1971, 22, 65, 84–94).

MAGICAL SYMBOLISM OF HAIR

The intimate relation of the hair of the head with its owner's bodily appearance and movement, and his personality, makes it an obvious object of emotional association and stimulus, so that it may be said to have force or power as a symbol for the personality, as in poetry or sentimental conservation. But ethnographic literature gives a wide range of examples where the power of hair is regarded as not simply emotional but magical. The hair is believed to have in itself some quality of affecting either the person from whom it has been obtained, or the person with whom it is newly put in contact. It is not uncommon in traditional sorcery for hair of an intended victim to be secured as an object for spells, a vehicle to convey the mystical power. On the other hand, hair is sometimes used as if it had therapeutic or prophylactic qualities, such as a cure for snakebite, an aid to recovery after circumcision, or a reinforcement of a warrior's virtue.*

In cases of negative magic or sorcery using hair of a projected victim, what seems to be dangerous to the owner is not the involun-

* For data of classical type see for example Seligman (Veddas), 1911, 197; Rivers (Todas) 1906, 257, 267; Tylor, 1878, 127–30; Crawley, 1902, 107–8, 202. For ideas of sacredness of organic tissues see Durkheim, 1926, 137–8.

tary detachment of the hair – loss of 'soul-stuff' in the older anthropological terminology – but loss of control over it. Hair detached but under owner's control cannot be used against him. So until recently old Maori men who might go to a barber to have their hair cut often made a contract with him to have all the hair ends gathered up; the owner would then go and hide them away to avoid the possibility of having them used for sorcery against him. Conversely, a controlled hair of one's own could be launched against someone else. There is a story of a Maori in quite recent times who had begun to drink a glass of beer in a public house when he noticed a hair in the liquid. He reacted swiftly, not aesthetically in disgust but ritually in fear. Supposedly plucked from a sorcerer's head, the hair was a sign of evil power against him; he vomited, ejected the hair and so, he thought, escaped death. What such a sorcery interpretation does is to translate a kind of careless aggression on the physical plane – leaving one's hair lying around – into intentional aggression on the conceptual (putatively spiritual) plane.

But as Leach has pointed out in his subtle analysis of 'magical hair' (1958) such symbolic conceptions are not simply an outgrowth of individual theories about personality; they are highly patterned social responses, elaborately integrated into a system of beliefs about protection and pollution, sacred and profane. As he indicates, too, there are many types of situation where it is not just individually identified and associated hair that is the object of magical interest, but any hair as an object in its own right, infused with attributes of a mystical kind. I can illustrate this from a Malay example.

At the end of 1939 a woman in the village where my wife and I were living fell ill, in her delirium trying to distribute the rice from her household and making sexual advances to men. One of our neighbours, who had been an object of such advances, said that earlier she had learned magic and had a tiny familiar spirit (*pelesit*) which attacked people. Now it had turned on her. She was given relief by spirit medium performances. Subsequently I found out that one of the most respected and feared spirit medium performers (who had not on this occasion been called in to the woman) had a lock of female hair attached to his *rebab*, the fiddle of Arab type which is a prime instrument of the master of spirits. He said the fiddle was 'a bit potent' because the lock of hair was the repository of a *pelesit*, and that in fact he had obtained it from the woman in question. I gathered that she herself had given it to him some years before, after the death of her first husband, who was thought to have been attacked by the familiar spirit. She was alleged to have bought the hair in the first place and used it for black magic. The spirit master said he had been offered $15 for it but had refused; his intention was to throw it away at sea some time. In the meantime his idea in attaching it to his fiddle was apparently to nullify its evil properties while at the same time making use of its power to increase the potency of his fiddle in therapeutic action. This was a clear case of 'anonymous' hair being regarded as having special properties other than those of simple pollution. I was also told that people would sometimes steal hair, presumably for magical purpose, since when caught with it they would not explain why; it was cut from the head of a sleeper, or from a corpse when the watchers were asleep. But empirically, there is a kind of fusion here between an interpretation of private fetishism in terms of a public conception of magical intention, and actual intent to practise sorcery along lines suggested by the public image of it.

The problem of why hair as such occupies an important place in the magical scheme, as well as being involved in ritual transfers among kin, and ritual sacrifice at life crises such as funerals, has been answered in psychological terms by its unconscious sexual associations. This issue has been very adequately dealt with by Leach, who points out that while sexual themes are very common in ethnographic data on use of hair, the symbolism is often quite overt. Moreover, the significance of hair often seems to lie not in its narrowly sexual reference but, as earlier anthropologists indicated, in its usefulness as a manipulable representation of the entire person. So, when used as a ritual instrument, its symbolism was to be interpreted as referring to relations between persons, or categories or groups of persons, who were defined socially, specified, demarcated or united by such symbolic mechanism.

HAIR SYMBOLISM AND SOCIETY

Most anthropological discussions of hair have been ethnographical, concerned mainly with stylistic differences and ritual use, and their symbolization of social status and social progress. A more theoretical treatment, following Leach's pioneering essay, is that of Hallpike (1969). Hallpike argues that the ritual uses of hair are of such widely varying types that no theory of hair in ritual can reduce them all to sexual symbolism. But he puts forward a generalization regarding the contrast between long hair and short hair, with particular reference to the reduction of one to the other. Briefly, he holds that long hair is associated with being 'outside society' either wholly or in part, and the cutting of hair symbolizes re-entering society or living under a particular disciplinary regime in society. 'Cutting the hair equals social control' (1969, 260–1).

Now this thesis has some plausibility, especially if one confines it to Western and Oriental society. For instance, the shearing of recruits to the army or prisoners in a jail, or the tonsuring of candidates for admission to a religious order are symbolic of submission to social control, just as the long hair of modern 'freaks' is an affirmation of a wish to be free from control. But the phenomenon is not uniform if a wider range of ethnographic evidence is taken. Different forms of social control may demand different forms of hair treatment, even in the same society. Hallpike argues that in Western society the long hair of intellectuals, rebels and women is an indication of their being in some respects less subject to social control than the 'average man'. But what about Tikopia, where as I pointed out earlier (p. 272) men traditionally wore their hair long and women wore theirs short: can one really suggest that men there were less subject to social control than women? If it is contended that woman exercised less power in political and ritual fields – were the takers, not the makers of the rules – then cannot the same be said of our Western society, still largely male-dominated in these fields? But Tikopia men cut their hair off in mourning for a dead relative – subject to social control – whereas women having much less to lose made only little reduction; yet both sexes wailed equally, in response to the same controls. And since a Tikopia man appearing before his chief or performing a key ritual role had to let his long hair flow loose instead of tying it back or up on his head, different types of hair mode corresponded to different types of social control. Much other ethnographic data could be cited to show that in many societies the wearing of long hair, by adults of either sex, is fully consonant with social responsibility and amenability; hair cutting does not mean re-entry to social control, but immediate transfer from one form of social control to another or emphasis on the controls of a particular type of situation. Indeed, when modern Western women cut their hair it is very often not to 're-enter society' as a symbol of submission to its controls, but rather to demonstrate their wish to be free of many of the restrictions thought to attach to the image of the long-haired mother-wife-drudge, who is only too acutely controlled by 'society'. Moreover, the long hair of members of sub-groups or categories, from Amish to 'hippies', is not an index of being outside 'society' in any very subtle sense; their long hair is a response to very definite social canons within a particular sector of society. The jurisdiction within which the norm operates is a very important element in the interpretation.

As anthropologists have amply demonstrated, the essence of interpretation of such symbols, hair or other, lies not in attributing empirical significance to the symbolism of each item in itself, but in recognizing the symbolism of the conjoined likenesses and contrasts, in systematic arrangement. Man is an ingenious creature, making much social capital of small physical resources. So, if women have long hair, men may have it short; if women wear theirs short, men may grow theirs long. And if both sexes wear their hair at much the same length then they differentiate by style of dressing it. Refinements within the system can mark out also stage of social progression and social status. The cutting of hair can be made a formal process, and a symbolic process – but not simply of sexual loss, as Berg would have it, or entry into social control, as Hallpike would have it. It may signify social loss – of a display feature of the personality, an abasement of the personality, a sacrifice. When one shears one's head for a person who has died, or on entry to a religious order, sentiments both of loss and of submission may be thought to be involved. But anthropologically, attention is directed to the marks of personal status that are sacrificed with the locks of hair, or more simply to the social definition of a change in relationship. Such hair symbolism means that men and women in specific kinds of society at specific periods are using their own physical raw material in terms of the social norms to provide indices to their personality and make statements about their conception of their role, their social position and changes in these.

Chapter 9

BODILY SYMBOLS OF GREETING AND PARTING

Greeting is the recognition of an encounter with another person as socially acceptable. Parting, in social sense, is the recognition that the encounter has been acceptable. Both concepts involve a postulate of a positive social quality in the relationship. Encounter of a physical kind may take place without such social relationship – as by two persons rubbing shoulders in a bus. They recognize the physical presence of each other, but the encounter is not socially acceptable; they do not speak; the existence of each is not incorporated into the social universe of the other. It needs some exchange of signs, as by a word or a nod, to create a social relationship. Forms of greeting and parting are symbolic devices – or signs if they are just specifically descriptive – of incorporation or continuance of persons in a social scheme. A greeting or parting sign is often represented as conveying information or expressing emotion – an announcement that one has come or is about to go, a statement of pleasure at someone's arrival or sadness at his departure. Granting that this may often be so, the informational or emotional content of the sign may be highly variable, even minimal. What is of prime relevance is the establishment or perpetuation of a social relationship, the recognition of the other person as a social entity, a personal element in a common social situation. This is indicated by reverse behaviour, what used to be called 'cutting' a person who is already known but found objectionable – the refusal of a greeting to him on passing him in the street or meeting him in society. This refusal is a tacit denial of him as a social entity in what would normally be a shared situation. So too, when two people are 'not on speaking terms' they do not greet each other and so reduce the area of their common social relationship to as small a compass as possible. As with all social relationships, reciprocity is important; an expectation in greeting is that it will elicit social recognition in return.

GENERAL NATURE AND FUNCTIONS

Great variety of custom in greeting and parting behaviour has been observed across the world. But this variety occurs through the range of a relatively few, simple sets of words and non-verbal actions, involving usually speech organs, head, hands and body. Limited as these components are, with few cultural accessories, their expressive power is considerable and their social implications of great sensitivity. Greeting and parting signs, though highly conventionalized, are not merely formal empty recognition procedures. Perception of them can be instrumental in modifying the behaviour of the person to whom they are directed. There is usually no suggestion that the procedures in themselves have any independent effect, though historically some accompaniments of greeting or parting behaviour have stated or implied a peculiar virtue of their own, as in the giving of a blessing.

Study of greeting and parting procedures has behind it some considerable fields of inquiry. One is the study of personal encounters developed particularly by Erving Goffman, and itself using results obtained from work on language, on small groups and on psychotherapeutic relationships. Another is the study of body movement and the use of the body as an instrument of communication, associated especially with the work of E. T. Hall and of Ray Birdwhistell. Linked also, in contrast as well as in similarity, are the studies in animal behaviour conducted by ethologists under the general head of ritualization (for example Julian Huxley *et al.*, 1966).

While each of these types of inquiry can supply fruitful suggestion about the significance of bodily behaviour, they cannot be transferred completely to the problems of greeting and parting as studied by a social anthropologist. These demand knowledge of a broader social context, an institutional matrix, often lacking in the more individually focused human studies. In the ethological field, the lack of a developed language in animals means not necessarily a less sensitive interpretation of signals among participants, but the absence of a medium for diversification and amplification of communication which is so fundamental to human society that it can be regarded as constituting a different dimension of behaviour. If one is considering only non-verbal human behaviour of greeting and parting, however, the formalized use of body and limbs often strongly suggests analogies in animal behaviour of a routine communicative kind, with display elements, signalling relevant information on, for example, sexual accessibility or territorial interest. But such animal ritualization is normally characteristic of all members of a given species in the given situation, and is regarded by ethologists as being adaptive, with positive implications for survival. Seemingly corresponding behaviour in man has a much greater range of variation, not only within the species but also within a society, and its adaptive possibilities are often obscure.

Leaving aside possible analogies with ritualization in animals, human formal behaviour at greeting and parting is often termed ritual. If by ritual is meant symbolic action in relation to sacred objects, the term is often inappropriate for the actions when people meet or part. But in a broader sense it is relevant since the actions are commonly formal, institutionalized, and credited with moral, sometimes almost mystical value. They are communicative, but the information they convey refers to the control or regularization of a social situation rather than to some descriptive fact. For instance, an explorer greeted by indigenous people may be given signs about food and water, but more commonly is welcomed by expressions of friendship, which may be termed symbolic of social relationship. In general, greeting and parting conventions may be regarded as a mild variety of Van Gennep's *rites de passage* – what Elsie Clews Parsons characterized as *crisis ceremonialism*, 'ceremonial to signalize or allow of the passing from one stage of life to another' (1916, 41). Following her lead, one might coin the term *teletic rites*, from the Greek concept of *telesis*, putting off the old and putting on the new. One can apply this term to greeting and parting behaviour, where the major stimulation is provided by the arrival or departure of a person from the social scene.

In the human field, forms of greeting and parting vary not only according to differences of culture, which might be regarded as subspecific areas, but also within individual cultures, according to relative status of persons involved and type of social situation:

individual or group confrontation; formality or informality of the occasion; prior acquaintance or unfamiliarity of the parties; conventional emotional quality ascribed to the occasion; face-to-face or at-a-distance communication. Even between people well known to one another, the relative formality of the occasion may affect the style of greeting or parting. At a public reception the structure of the words and acts of hosts and guests tends to be rigid and highly prescribed, in contrast with the easy exchanges of welcome or farewell at a week-end party or any other ordinary social gathering. Even if an occasion is not classed as a formal one by the nature of the invitation, the presence of merely casual acquaintances among one's friends may have an inhibiting effect on greeting or parting behaviour. American or British people who might exchange a kiss in private greeting may refrain from such intimacy in public. But this is a highly cultural matter – a Frenchman in office may bestow a kiss on another on a formal public occasion when he would not do so at an informal private meeting.

In ordinary social intercourse formality may be enhanced when the person to be signalized in greeting is previously unknown to the signalizer. I myself have observed a simple form of this in travel in the United States. When two men previously unknown to each other are seated side by side in an aeroplane on a long trip, informal social relationships of an elementary order may be established in getting to and from seats, remarks about the weather, etc. But after casual exchanges may come formal identification. 'I'm James Brown,' says one man, extending his hand, whereupon the other normally follows suit with his own name and handclasp. Search may be made for further points of contact – home town, business, common acquaintance. But presumably gratifying, this is not of primary relevance. What is of main significance is the act of identification, which has been sealed by the clasp of hands. Indeed, once the name has been uttered the hand gesture is almost automatic; as an experiment, one may disconcert such a casual acquaintance by uttering one's name but withholding the hand movement! Yet in materialist terms the act is almost meaningless – the men are seated side by side, have already talked and could continue to talk; they will probably never meet again; neither wants anything of the other except his temporary companionship, which is already available. The name given may even have been false. But what matters is that *some* name has been given, and *some* personal manual contact made. The accidental travel neighbour has been socially pin-pointed, and the handshake is the formal symbol of a social relationship established, of the reduction of an unknown to a (putatively) known social position. The handshake has been interpreted as equivalent to a disclaimer of aggression, as a residual pledge against resort to force of arms. But in such modern conditions the risk of physical assault is minimal (these words were first drafted before air hijacking had been invented). If a threat is conceived it is of interference with the personality, not with the person, and the handshake has a much more subtle function of serving to reduce social uncertainty.

In such a situation the social identification has been provided by the two parties immediately concerned. The relationship is casual, the identification nominal. But it is not automatic; if neither party takes the initiative no formal greeting takes place. Moreover, it is status-regulated. Handshake in such travel conditions is primarily behaviour between male equals or those making a show of equality. My guess is that it occurs much less frequently between men and women; and between women no handshake at all may be exchanged – though other identificatory signs may be. Between adults and children the handshake of casual acquaintance is nearly always lacking. When children shake hands, it is commonly a concession to adult, usually parental, direction, and is primarily a symbol of relations between the adults involved – the child is a kind of instrumental extension of adult greeting.

Modern anthropological idiom stresses both the communicative and the expressive functions of ritual. In rituals of greeting and parting the inter-relation of these elements is quite complex. There is conveying of information – of social recognition and acceptance, of status and general quality of the relationship. But there is also an implication, in popular estimation in Western society, of emotional involvement, if even low-keyed. Greeting behaviour is expected to express approval of the encounter, even pleasure; parting behaviour is expected to express the opposite, or at least a recognition that the severance of the encounter is necessary. Yet it is a matter of common knowledge that the reverse may be the case, or that the parties may be indifferent. Popular jokes make play of the incongruity between outward behaviour and inward feeling on such occasions. But while such incongruity is openly admitted out of the immediate context, there is general demand that the forms of emotional interest be preserved, and to omit them gives offence. Politeness consists in not allowing incongruity to be overtly perceptible, though it is possible to so shade wording, tone of voice, mode of gesture and even posture in greeting or parting behaviour as to allow indifference or even negative attitudes to be inferred. In reflective comment, then, forms of greeting and parting can be regarded as 'empty', as 'meaningless'. But while their expressive function may not correspond to their superficial form, greeting and parting behaviour is still significant as a communicative device. 'Pleased to meet you ...' on introduction, 'How good of you to have come ...' at parting, as overt expressions of satisfaction may be directly contradicted by more private behaviour. But what they express by implication and communicate explicitly is a willingness to enter into, or to continue a social relationship. Their simulation of emotional involvement or moral approval may be only part of the conventional 'small change' of social intercourse, but it has an emollient quality. It is a 'softener' of the social relationship because by convention it sets the relationship in a status frame, implying respect by the speaker to the personality of the recipient.

The significance of such communicative function is brought out by forms of greeting or parting in societies which use no expressive modes implying affect, but confine themselves primarily to descriptive phrases of acknowledgement or invitation. 'You have come'; 'Enter (the house)'; 'You are going' are typical expressions of greeting or parting in many societies. It emerges clearly from such evidence that the primary factor of importance is not *what* is said but that *something* is said. The action of verbal utterance signifies recognition of the situation in social terms; potentially threatening silence in which intention is uncertain is broken; the physical movement of coming or going is put into a social frame, and the parties are in communication.

In greeting and parting rituals verbal and non-verbal behaviour is in close relation. Utterance and bodily action are often simultaneous or juxtaposed – as saying 'good morning' with a smile and handshake, or calling 'hi' or 'hullo' with a wave of the arm. Much of this is reinforcement behaviour, intensification of what is expressed and communicated; but sometimes it may be alternative, as when one waves a greeting to a person too far off to hear any words. In greeting, an interesting combination of verbal and non-verbal behaviour occurs in what is known conventionally in English as 'an introduction'. Traditionally, in sophisticated European circles, greeting between two persons not previously acquainted should be prefaced by an introduction by a third party previously known to both; without having been 'introduced' the two people should not address each other in a formal social situation. This rule was especially severe when a man and a woman were concerned. Though the rule has now been relaxed except in the most formal circumstances, an intermediary may be still employed. 'Will you introduce me to . . .' can still be an intelligible and appropriate request in some social situations. The role of the third party here is twofold: he (or she) is a social bridge, a mediator who facilitates the social contact of the other two people; he may be also an ostensible guarantor of their social identity, and up to a point, of their reputation. In such introduction the words 'May I introduce/present . . .' are commonly accompanied by changes in orientation of the head, movements of the hands, inclination of the body, which relate by metaphorical links the two persons who are being introduced, and give signals to them to begin their own greeting patterns. But the concept of introduction is not simply a relating of persons socially; it embodies the notion of one party being displayed, led forward, 'presented' to the other; it is a sequential operation. Hence the element of relative status tends to emerge – it becomes important to indicate who is presented to whom. By convention the latter, who is the recipient of the introduction, is deemed to be of higher status than the former who as the person being introduced is in a dependent position. (In ordinary social introductions both parties are assumed to be of equal status, and the traditional rule has been for the introducer to repeat the names of the parties, in reverse order, so that each in turn has the status of recipient.) Rules of formal introduction follow general rules of social precedence: a younger man is introduced to an elder man; a man to a woman (a 'gentleman' to a 'lady'); an unmarried woman to a married woman; a commoner to a member of a Royal Family. But this rule may be overridden, according to context, when immediate role may be more significant than general status, or than rank. So, an elderly clerk may be introduced to a younger man who is manager of his firm, a member of a Royal Family to the head of a college where she is becoming enrolled as a student. But as already noted, such cases are usually narrowly defined by the immediate role situation. So, in a formal university degree-conferring ceremony, an officiating dean may introduce an honorary graduand to the Chancellor, with mutual acknowledgement of tipping of hats in salute, while in private life all three may know one another very well and be on first-name terms.

A general point of theoretical significance is the parallelism which obtains between much greeting and parting behaviour. Some societies, for instance the Japanese, have an identical term to cover both meeting and parting salutations. Formerly, in Western European social circles, a gentleman raised his hat upon taking leave after an open-air encounter just as he did when the encounter took place. In Tikopia an expression of what sounds like dismay (*aue*) is uttered in greeting a friend not seen for a long time, just as when he departs; and pressing of noses takes place on either occasion. In such cases the parallelism of greeting and parting ritual can be regarded as an expression of formal recognition of change in the social situation. In the marked behaviour of the Tikopia example, there is communication of affect, but what is being expressed overtly is not goodwill primarily, but emotional disturbance and modification of social relations. The arrival is represented as a moving event, analogous in this sense to a departure. Emphasis is placed not on the contrast between the joy of greeting and the sorrow of parting, but on their similarity. Both arrival and departure of a friend alter social routine, and are disruptive of ordinary emotional routine; regret for past severance and regret for future severance are aligned in behaviour (cf. Radcliffe-Brown, 1922, 239–42). This parallelism in greeting and parting ritual brings out the symbolic quality of the behaviour – it is not just an immediate reaction to the arrival or departure of a social acquaintance – a kind of register of fresh presence or impending absence. It embodies elements of less obvious significance, relating to the social implications of the movement of persons, in which implicit reference to the time dimension may be involved, and to values associated with presence and absence.

In the remainder of this analysis I am concerned primarily with non-verbal aspects of greeting and parting behaviour.

SYMBOLIC USE OF THE WHOLE BODY IN GREETING AND PARTING

Metaphorical use of concepts associated with the physical human body to refer to some types or aggregates of social relations is a common ethnographic phenomenon, and Mary Douglas (1970) has made an interesting study of some aspects of this. Among other themes she has emphasized the argument of Marcel Mauss, that the 'social body' constrains the way the physical body is perceived. Granting the general relevance of this, there is a great variety of circumstances in which the physical structure and powers of the human body are perceived in direct relation to performance, irrespective of the character of the social body. Simple mechanical actions such as lifting a pot or paddling a canoe are interpreted cross-culturally in similar terms, with recognizable common evaluation of achievement. Perception of arm and body in movement, and conception of their function, would seem to involve minimal social determination. But the context of associated ideas soon becomes important. When in northern Nigeria I saw men raise their arms by the roadside and shake clenched fists at me I soon realized that this was not a threat but a greeting; the form of the body movement and its interpretation were constrained by conceptions of a social pattern (Firth, 1951a, 23). Here I consider briefly not the social relevance of general concepts of body, but the social interpretation, in contexts of greeting and parting, of use of body movement.*

The human body is far more of a social instrument than is often suspected, in the greeting–parting syndrome. Such instrumentality is mainly symbolic, the element of physical performance being

* Underlying much of the modern anthropological approach to these problems is a rejection of the Cartesian dualism of mind and body. An important set of essays on the difficult metaphysical issues involved has been assembled by Stuart F. Spicker under the title of *The Philosophy of the Body* (1970). In his studies of body motion communication Ray L. Birdwhistell, a pioneer in the 'kinesics' field, points to the misconceptions in vogue about so-called 'natural' gestures, stating that after fifteen years' research he and his associates have found no body motion or gesture which has the same social meaning in all societies (1970, 81). For other relevant analyses see Macdonald Critchley (1939), D. Efron (1941), E. T. Hall (1961, 1968). A popular treatment of 'body language' by Julius Fast (1970) attempts some practical inferences about meaning of communication by bodily posture and movement.

usually small. A greeting movement may occasionally be of primarily physical import, as when a host opens a door or unlatches a gate for a guest, but even here the physical act of admission may also involve a symbolic act of welcome, a throwing wide of defences in a way which has other obvious analogies. The body as a whole can be a greeting or parting symbolic instrument in three main respects: by maintaining a distance gap between the parties; by adopting an overall posture; and by movement in meeting or dismissing the other party.

Degree of spatial distance kept between the parties is apt to be broadly an index to degree of social distance between them. In Western societies this operates unsystematically as a rule (military regulations offer contrary instances). But in societies with a developed caste system, especially where notions of pollution by contact occur, bodily relationships may be strictly regulated by distance, even to a measurable index, and meeting and greeting behaviour structured accordingly. A. Aiyappan has recorded (1944, 38–9, 46) that in traditional Malabar society a member of the Irava caste (the highest of the 'castes that pollute from a distance') polluted a Namputiri (Brahman) from a distance of thirty-two feet, and had no access to the houses, temples and wells of the higher castes, and no freedom to use roads or footpaths in the presence of members of these castes. To obtain communication with a member of a higher caste an Irava might then have to use an intermediary while himself remaining at bodily distance.

Bodily posture is important in many greeting conventions. One mode of showing respect is by sinking to the ground, conveying a depreciation of the self and symbolizing humility and recognition of superior status. Hence in ordinary social intercourse a mutuality of esteem is expressed by mutual body lowering. S. F. Nadel has noted (1942, 129) how Nupe men of equal rank greet each other by sinking low (his word is 'cowering' which seems hardly apt) for half a minute or longer while exchanging salutations. If they are well acquainted, they stretch out their hands several times in succession and lightly touch each other's fingers. A man of lower rank when meeting his social superior will bow very low or kneel down, and only if difference of rank is slight or obviated by personal intimacy will he venture to offer his hand. If he is on horseback he will dismount, if he is wearing sandals he will take them off, though it may be on the road, and put them beside him. The man of higher rank will stand or sit still, make a short perfunctory gesture of bowing, and hardly move his arm to meet the other man's hand. Eugène Mangin has given an equally-detailed description of the traditional form of greeting known as the 'Mossi salute' (1921, 18–19). In order to give such a greeting a Mossi would put down his load, hat and sword, remove his shoes, sit on the ground, fold his legs slightly and lean the upper part of his body forward. The elbows rested on the ground, as far apart as possible; the forearms, folded in front of the chest with the hands half-closed and the thumbs raised, struck the ground together three or four times. In such humble posture, the man concerned did not look the person being greeted in the face. Father Mangin noted that though complicated, the Mossi traditional salute was rendered easily and gracefully, not in the clumsy awkward manner in which Mossi attempted to imitate the European military salute. Such a form of greeting appears to have been used in all the Black empires of the Sudan, especially Ghana, Mali and Gao. In such type of greeting, the lower the status of the person initiating the action, the more the disturbance to which he subjects himself – a principle which is of very general application. To greet by a disturbance of the whole body to such a degree that one sinks to the ground is alien to Western notions of everyday behaviour – though not to some notions of ceremonial behaviour – and Westerners have often reacted with strong ethnocentrism at the sight of it. Mangin observed how foreigners on first entering Mossi country were shocked to see men thus lower themselves before others. A generation later, in Nigeria, I myself heard the labels of 'undemocratic' and 'degrading' applied to an analogous Hausa greeting convention in which men mutually sank to the ground in a flowing movement and lightly touched hands. In early relations with Far Eastern societies, examples of body-lowering in greeting, such as the Chinese 'kow-tow', provoked shocked, contemptuous interpretation from Westerners, who ignored the occasional practices of kneeling, crouching and even prostration in some Western institutionalized contexts. (Some study of these is given in my consideration of postures and gestures of respect (1970c), in some ways a companion piece to this chapter.)*

* For early discussion of this subject see Tylor, 1878, 46–8. As recent additional examples

Even where status differences are not highly marked in ordinary social intercourse (as in the West in modern times) and etiquette demands equalization of posture in greeting between social equals, some modulations are still observable. Commonly, a man sitting in a room rises to his feet to greet another man who has come to see him. But in social conventions which still have some currency, it is 'proper' for a lady to remain seated while greeting a man who has entered the room and who stands before her. Yet a man who is manager of a firm may not rise in saying good morning to his woman secretary ('lady' and 'woman' here being status indices). Such differences in greeting posture correspond to recognized if minor status differentials. Yet ambiguity can occur, especially if the categories are mixed. However, modern practice allows considerable personal discretion, so a range of variation is found. A manager may rise to greet his woman secretary when she first comes in, in the morning, in recognition of the general sex rule that a gentleman should not remain seated when a lady is standing; or he may stay in his chair in accordance with his interpretation of the professional situation. Or he may be guided by some rule-of-thumb – remain seated if the secretary is a young girl or rise if she is a mature woman, in response to a cross-cutting age rule; or he may rise when she first comes in as a general acknowledgement of the sex rule, and remain seated thereafter in conformity with the professional rank rule. What is of special significance here is how, in what is characterized as an ordinary practical business situation, other codes are still allowed to intrude. But the point of most general interest is how in such situations of 'manners', which are supposedly matters of delicacy, we use our bodies in a lump, as it were, in crude mass, as expressions of social relationship.

may be cited: a woman kneeling to be ordained as deacon by a Bishop of New York Diocese; the Duchess of Windsor curtseying to Queen Elizabeth who was taking leave after a visit; 200 candidates for the priesthood in the Philippines lying prostrate in front of the altar as part of their ordination ritual by the Pope (*New York Times*, 14 November 1971; 4 January 1972; *The Times*, 19 May 1972). An elaboration of a greeting gesture took place when Queen Elizabeth visited France. Having been told that the Queen liked horses the French introduced a white horse which had been trained to kneel, and which at the appropriate moment went down on its knees 'in a dutiful manner' on a pile of sand provided for the purpose. In contrast to such proceedings was the attitude of Mrs Martha Mitchell, wife of a high United States official, who remained upright when presented to Queen Elizabeth at a garden party. 'I feel that an American citizen should not bow to foreign monarchs', Mrs Mitchell wrote in explanation – curtseying apparently being optional for guests who are not British subjects (*Time Magazine*, 29 November 1971).

Moreover, we tend to do this as a matter of course, as if manipulation of the body mass is the recognized equivalent of an agreed articulate language. A further point is that in a very rough way, the amount of bodily displacement engaged in by each party is in inverse proportion to his status – the lower the status the more the bodily movement. The material act of expenditure of energy is translated into a symbolic act of status acknowledgement.

What I have just considered is mainly vertical body movement. But a similar broad symbolic interpretation is given to horizontal body movement in greeting and parting. In Western society only in diplomatic protocol and analogous ceremonious exercises, such as those of a university graduation, a Royal Court or a religious initiation, is much formal expression given to the significance of body progression in greeting or parting. But tacitly it is fairly well understood in higher business or professional circles. To be conducted into a businessman's office by a secretary is usual, but gradations of being farewelled – at your host's desk, at the door of his inner sanctum, in the outer office, at the door of the lift (elevator), down at the front entrance of the building – are recognized status indicators. As with the Nupe and many other peoples, the degree of disarrangement of the one party indicates the relative status of the other. In traditional Chinese officialdom such gradations were expressed with much greater finesse, and had much more specific status significance.

SYMBOLIC GESTURES IN GREETING AND PARTING

Gestures are commonly regarded as movements of the hands and face in particular, accompanying speech for purposes of emphasis – a kind of italicized speech, as Macdonald Critchley has put it (1939, 11). But some gestures may serve as substitutes for speech, especially when they act as a general means of communication or expression for which no simple speech equivalent can be found, or when speech would be inappropriate, as during a solemn church service. In the translation of movement of parts of the body into symbolic gestures of greeting or parting the range is wide. If one includes what may be called the 'receptor-parts', which are involved as platforms or bases against which the action is performed – for example breast to which another person is clasped – very many major external features of the body have been called into service in different cultures. Western societies confine their greeting and parting gestures very much to the upper parts of the body.* But in areas of highland New Guinea, as I myself have seen, a greeting embrace between men is accompanied by mutual patting of each other's buttocks – a kind of 'pat on the back' which has slipped down. Even the feet, which one is inclined to associate primarily with gestures of rejection or contempt (spurning with one's foot; stamping in disapproval), may serve as receptor, as in the Oriental gesture, simulated or actual, of 'kissing the feet'. But I confine myself here to consideration of the symbolic use of head and hands, and features of these.

As a prime sensory centre the head may perhaps be expected to serve as a major medium for gestures of greeting and parting, which involve recognition of another person, usually by visual means. In fact, some movement of the head, linked with eye movement, is a characteristic recognition and greeting signal in many societies, either with or without verbal utterance. But cultural nuances occur. Commonly in Western societies an upward nod is a recognition or greeting signal, whereas a downward nod is a signal of assent in reply to a question. By convention in some circles an upward lift of both eyebrows is a recognition signal to someone in a crowd whereas a raised single eyebrow is a quizzical comment not articulated. (The wink, a lowering of one eyelid, is a wordless gesture directed at a person to indicate a familiar relationship of complicity. It may be used in greeting, especially where a more formal action might disturb a gathering.)† But among Melanesians of the Solomon Islands an upward lift of both eyebrows is a common sign of assent. Generally, the greeting or parting function of the eye is expressed by the *look*, which would seem to be produced primarily by subtle local muscle movements around the eye and not by the eye itself.

* But cf. a fictional incident in the Battle of Britain, in Elleston Trevor's novel *Squadron Airborne* (1962): a male corporal pinched one of the Women's Auxiliary Airforce on her bottom; she protested but walked away amicably 'mincing her hips in an aircraftwoman's farewell'.

† Charles Darwin studied nodding and face movement in terms of signs of affirmation or negation, and concluded that despite some cultural variation the forms were too general to be regarded 'as altogether conventional or artificial'. But he was looking for innate responses (1872, 274–7).

(Modern psychological studies have thrown much light on the significance of eye movement, though in somewhat restricted social contexts.) Values attached to changes in modes of treating the hair, as symbols of greeting or parting, have been discussed already in Chapter 8.

In Polynesian societies the nose was the organ traditionally used in greeting, and is so even nowadays, though 'nose rubbing' has been supplemented by handclasp (for details see Firth, 1970c, 196, 199–201). The tongue seems an unlikely greeting medium in its own right, since use of it outside the mouth inhibits speech. But putting out the tongue symbolically as a greeting gesture has been well authenticated for Tibetans (where it apparently has no overt aggressive significance) and for Maori (where it forms part of their superficially aggressive welcoming dances for visitors). Although the cheek is a relatively immobile part of the face it plays quite an important role as the site for delivery of a large proportion of kisses, and as a lip-substitute in cheek-to-cheek greeting gestures of familiarity which are not so intimate as to require use of mouth. Only the ears, as far as I can judge, seem not to be involved symbolically in any greeting or parting gesture. Though not less mobile than the nose, and in modern civilized life far more involved in the recognition of objects, their position at the sides of the head away from the eyes has seemed to disqualify human ears from any significant cultural use as greeting signals. (The ears of most animals seem to fill such a function much more directly.)

Apart from the importance of the mouth as a focus of interest for verbal greeting, its use in greeting gesture is twofold. In many human societies the curious gesture of drawing back the lips and baring the teeth – the smile – is one of the major signs of welcome. The significance of this in non-human primates has been extensively studied, and also in children. But as far as I know no systematic study has yet been undertaken of smiling by adults, in different cultural settings of greeting and parting situations. Ray Birdwhistell, who probably has come nearest to such a position, has some very pertinent observations on the differences in the frequency of smiling among the inhabitants of different areas of the United States, on smiling as a learned response, and on the complexity of behaviour involved in smiling and of the concept given this name (1970,

29–39). At a crude level of differentiation it seems clear that the baring of the teeth when they are tightly clenched is a sign of anger or of other strain, not of pleasure, and an inference sometimes drawn is that smiling as a greeting sign may be related developmentally to baring of the teeth in defence. But this is hypothetical. It would seem that any subtle interpretation of the meaning of a smile demands attention to other muscular behaviour of the face – around the eyes, at the corners of the mouth – as well as to type of lip position and movement, and degree to which the teeth are displayed. Subtle differences of this kind account largely in Western society for our reading of mouth gestures as: the fixed smile, indicating stress or underlying unease; the secret smile, indicating private thought; the dubious smile, indicating only partial acceptance of what has been said; the sneering smile, indicating contempt; as well as the welcoming smile. Anthropologists familiar with particular alien cultures will probably agree that granted a reasonable margin of error, they can interpret the behavioural clues of smiling in those cultures. The evidence for this view would probably be the conformity of what happened later to their expectations from the smile. Though the published evidence is slim, and systematic research on the subject largely lacking, superficial experience does suggest that the smile is one of the most characteristic mouth-greeting signs in very many societies. But how far the smile is a formalized sign of acceptance of a greeting situation rather than a spontaneous response to the advent of a visitor is a more difficult problem.

KISS OF GREETING

Certainly not all mouth gestures are universal. A type of gesture which is thoroughly built into the conventions of Western society is the kiss. Primarily a lip gesture, the kiss is susceptible of a great many modifications. Linked with the sensitivity of lips is their function in erotic contact, which introduces a possible ambiguity into their use in gestures which are intended to signalize social but non-erotic greeting. It is presumably for this reason that many non-Western societies ignore the kiss as a conventional mode of greeting and confine themselves to its analogue in the lip-play of mother on babe, or of lovers. Some societies, as for instance India, even regard the kiss with distaste and are apt to treat it as immoral. It appears that Indian films do not involve kissing scenes so popular in Western films, and censors have been required to cut out kissing scenes from foreign films before passing them for local distribution. This is not a revulsion from the symbolic presentation of sex themes, but rather from the public display of non-symbolic sex contact. By contrast, in many overt Indian ritual contexts the phallic symbols of *linga* and *yoni* appear with no disapproval shown, and historic sculptures to which symbolic meaning is given have much erotic content. By contrast with the tender associations of the kiss in Western eyes, reinforced by many literary references, one can cite specific counter-views from other cultures, especially in Africa. Henri Junod reported from the Thonga that kissing was formerly unknown to them, and laughing at Europeans Thonga would say: 'Look at those people! They suck each other! They eat each other's saliva and dirt!' (1927, i, 352; for analogous Chinese ridicule see Doolittle, 1876, ii, 375).

Even when established as a greeting, the kiss is subject to many variations. In England over the last century the normal convention has been that women may kiss women, but men do not kiss men, except in intimate family circumstances such as greeting or parting between father and son – and even then it is optional. In circumstances of some familiarity, such as close kinship, men and women may greet one another by kissing. Both men and women may kiss young children of either sex, possibly with no prior tie at all (for example the classic 'kissing of babies' by a parliamentary candidate). In the past the rules have been fairly clear, and at the periphery could be invoked to justify familiarity, as when a man might claim a kiss from a girl on the ground that she was a cousin. But in modern times these rules have been considerably relaxed. In circles that I know, kissing between men and women friends has become much more common, in line with general relaxation of social norms in favour of more individual freedom, and less perturbation about possible erotic implications. In Britain the idea still seems to hold that except in special circumstances such as those of family life, kissing between men is a sign of effeminacy. But it is well recognized also that in some other Western countries, for instance France and Russia, kissing between men is a definite part of social conventions of greeting, especially on public occasions. But an accompaniment to kissing in many social circumstances is the embrace by the arms, and it is this arm-breast contact rather than the lip-lip or lip-cheek contact that appears to be of prime significance. Certainly the greeting-hug is as much a public demonstration of amity as the greeting-kiss.*

The kiss itself presents several forms, graded roughly according to type of social relationship. Lovers (commonly) and spouses (often) greet each other with a lip-to-lip kiss of varying duration and intensity. Parents and children may greet lip-to-lip, but other kinsmen and close friends usually greet lip-to-cheek – normally on one cheek but sometimes on both if moved by affection or continental experience. But while in members of the immediate family and among close kin or friends the erotic implications of a kiss are expected to be absent or subliminal, they may have more overt interpretations between people of more distant relationship. (I have noted a recent letter to an American newspaper columnist in which a young woman asked for guidance – she had greeted her husband's father with a kiss on the cheek but he had insisted upon a kiss on the lips, which shocked her.) So, in some circles there is a custom of what may be called cheek-to-cheek kissing – a facial contact without use of mouth at all. This delicate gesture of greeting may have an emotional charge, but it is removed from the more erogenous zones. (Such a cheek-to-cheek greeting is treated as a completely appropriate gesture by Westerners, whereas a nose-to-nose gesture is treated as odd – 'nose-rubbing'!) In some sections of European continental society another delicate if more socially distant usage is that of man taking a lady's hand and bringing it up before his lips as he bends over it. 'Kissing the hand' need not involve any actual contact of lip with hand; though the simulated gesture of brushing the lip over the lady's fingers can be made to serve a variety of purposes from respectful to erotic messages. A further simulacrum, in which the respect motif

* As a demonstration of cultural difference, compare English football players who have just won the much-coveted Cup hugging each other in delight (but not kissing), with the Russian greeting of returning cosmonauts when Leonid Brezhnev gave each 'a bear-hug and a kiss'. Recently Brezhnev was described as sometimes going 'the traditional Soviet bear-hug one better by kissing men and women alike smack on the mouth' (*Newsweek*, 1 November 1971).

of greeting is uppermost, is to substitute for the actual kissing motion a verbal statement of the 'I kiss your hand, Madame' type.

When greeting takes place outside the domestic circle or circle of friends, the implications of a kiss may include quite complex political considerations. In general, the familiarity of the kiss, ordinarily reserved for intimate acquaintance, signifies a compliment, implying that the recipient is worthy of a more intimate social relationship, of positive sentimental content. In Hawaii, the custom of greeting visitors with a *lei* and a kiss has been turned to account in public receptions as a symbol of amity between the parties. On a recent visit of Queen Elizabeth to France the President greeted her with a warm handshake, whereas his predecessor 'the avuncular President Coty' had earlier greeted her 'with a decisive kiss on both cheeks'. A political explanation that after monarchical governance by de Gaulle had ended, the institution of monarchy may have lost some of its allure, may be far-fetched; but it would not be surprising if political as well as personal undertones could be found in the difference of greeting (see *Observer*, 21 May 1972).

The significance of the lips as erogenous zones has given kissing a kind of danger-quality as a greeting. It is regarded in Western society as a form of greeting for which above all permission may have to be asked. To kiss someone is apt to be held as an intrusion on the personality more intimate than that of any other form of greeting. To ask 'May I shake your hand?' apparently sometimes occurs, as a frank signal of respect, though my impression is that it has rather a formal literary quality. But no one asks 'May I clap you on the shoulder?' – this would seem ridiculous. So, kissing on special occasions such as birthday or wedding, or in congratulation for some honour gained, takes on a special quality of exchange of personalities, in which the sub-erotic qualities of lip-contact may be a significant component. (Hence, one can imagine the press interest in such incidents.) So too, granted that in Western society kissing is an acceptable form of greeting between given categories of persons, a number of associated patterns have been developed to mitigate its side-effects and to reduce to a minimum any suggestion of erotic elements in the exchange. What is of particular interest is the way in which Western societies are prepared to skate upon thin ice in juxtaposing so closely an erotic and a merely social gesture, while most other societies have avoided this problem.

In some circumstances a kiss is overtly a respect signal rather than a greeting signal. Such instances as kissing a bishop's ring, kissing the toe of St Peter's statue and certain other effigies of saints in Rome, 'kissing hands' of the Sovereign before taking up an overseas diplomatic appointment, exemplify this. But the gesture also conveys a sense of greater intimacy than others – some element of self-involvement of an emotional kind in the relationship. A point here is that the involvement is one-way: in such contexts the gesture is not reciprocated, hence the emphasis is on acknowledgement of superiority, on respect for status, rather than on greeting as such. It is from this point of view that the most notorious kiss in history – or mythology – that of Judas Iscariot, carries its shock effect. The gesture of respect shown in the kiss, and shown intimately, was incompatible with the repudiation of respect and of intimacy shown in the betrayal. This example also shows a significant function of the kiss in some circumstances – as a marker of social position. A critical social indicator may be provided by who is greeted and who greets in a group, by kissing.

HAND AND ARM IN GREETING AND PARTING SYMBOLISM

Comparable in mobility with the mouth as a greeting instrument is the hand with the arm. Here too great variety of gesture is shown, both cross-culturally and within any single society. Broadly, greeting and parting gestures may be conveyed by salutation with one hand, by joining one's hands, or by joining hands with the other party. Avoidance of physical contact between the parties in the one case and seeking it in the other may be symptomatic of deeper cultural attitudes about the nature of personality and the degree to which it can be compromised or reinforced by intrusion of another personality upon it. One-handed greeting may be made with open or closed fist. In the West we have been accustomed to regard the clenched fist as primarily a sign of aggression and defiance, and it has been conventionalized on such a basis into a political communist greeting and display. But as I mentioned earlier (p. 307) the shaking of clenched fist in northern Nigerian pagan society may be an ordinary greeting, a token of amity. Open-handed salutation may vary from the casual wave of greeting to a passing acquaintance or the more regular flapping of the hand on an uplifted wrist in farewell, to the precise military salute, formalized and designed expressly to indicate and support differences in rank.

Traditionally, in the East, a person has joined his own hands in greeting, either clasped in front of him in Chinese style, or set palm to palm in front of the face, as in India and many parts of South-East Asia. In some of these societies the height at which the hands are held or to which they are raised is a measure of the social status of the person greeted. As with posture (Firth, 1970c) this is one of the simple physical indices which can be made of great symbolic importance by setting them within a social framework. In the West the tradition has been for each person to proffer a hand to the other, and the greeting has consisted of a handclasp or handshake. An Oriental variant of this is 'hand-joining', with both parties using two hands. One, normally the junior, places his hands palm to palm within the similarly-held hands of the other. In Malaya, for instance, such hand-joining has had rules governing who by sex, age and difference of rank may properly join hands with whom. Only elderly women, not young women, should by tradition join hands with men; this should be in respect and motherly or sisterly affection, and by custom a clean layer of cloth should be placed between the pairs of hands (Zainal-'Abidin, 1950, 47). Another form of two-handed salutation, clapping, is significant partly because it is commonly non-reciprocal – though in some countries it is customary to join in applause given to oneself as a gesture of appreciation of the compliment paid. But it is also significant because as a form of percussion, it is one of the simplest accessories to bodily display in a field which uses a variety of noise-making instruments of salutation (cf. Needham, 1967b).

Some other societies than those of the West have used the single handclasp in greeting. Rattray has observed that handshaking as a salutation appears to have been an Ashanti custom before the advent of Europeans (Rattray, 1916, 43; 1929, 103. Cf. Speke, 1912, 168, 169). In such case hand had to lock in hand – 'five must lie within five' was the Ashanti way of expressing the full grasp. To give the tips of the fingers only was discourteous – as in England it has also tended to be, except in special circumstances of formal reception by a person of high rank. Where the handclasp has been in vogue as a greeting, it has often been customary to use only the right hand; the left hand, especially in Oriental countries, has often been associated with the toilet and is unclean. But the reversion of this rule may mark a special type of social relationship, as with the Boy Scouts of Britain, or the Ogboni society of the Yoruba. According to Ajisafe (1924, 91) the latter use the left hand 'in a peculiar way known only to members of the cult'. Such a focus on the right hand in ordinary greeting is clearly part of the much more general polarity of right and left examined by Robert Hertz (1909, trans. 1960) and attributed to mystical religious categorization. Hertz did not discuss the predominance of right-handedness in greeting, but it is important to note that this applies to the handclasp rather than to waving – in other words, the mystical value of right-handedness is relevant primarily in personal physical contact. This illustrates the complexity of symbolic values in salutation – relatively superficial indication of amity in the handclasp as such, and deeper less aware aesthetic and moral significance of use of the right hand.

Since the handshake has been the traditional greeting of Western countries, with the spread of Western technology and consumer habits the practice of handshaking has become much more common. Many societies where it was formerly unknown have now adopted it, as an ancillary to or substitute for their own traditional greeting. So, in modern Polynesia, a clasping of hands may be accompanied by a leaning forward and pressing of noses. But the introduction of the handclasp has sometimes been cautious, because of other possible ritual values involved. Junod has recorded how among the Thonga it was formerly taboo to shake hands with a chief, owing to the belief that contact with the body of such a person of ritual quality was dangerous. However, even more than forty years ago Junod observed that the ruler Muhlaba, on the adoption of Christianity, was somewhat reluctantly accepting the hands held out to him by the most modest of his subjects, even by children, on Christmas Day (1927, i, 383) – the new faith presumably being regarded as protecting from or nullifying the ancient powers.

Like other forms of salutation the handclasp can be used as a status differentiator. It has been reported of the Bambara that traditionally a man saluted his superior by extending his palm upwards, whereupon the superior put his own hand palm downwards over it. Inversely, when a man greeted an inferior he extended his hand with palm down; but for an equal his palm was held perpendicular to the ground (again, notions of upwards and downwards physically involved with ideas of status). But a most significant status indicator has been the demarcation of categories of people with whom one does *not* clasp or shake hands. Among the Bambara, according to Paques (1954, 118) a woman should never shake the hand of a man in order to greet him. In Western society of the 'polite' order it was formerly proper to greet servants verbally, but never to shake them by the hand, which would have been an admission of equality. There are still occasions of a very formal kind in which it is appropriate to bow before Royalty or other people of high status but not to offer to shake hands. Towards the end of President de Gaulle's official life it was recorded that at presidential receptions at the Elysée a blue triangular mark at the top left-hand corner of an invitation card indicated guests who would not be introduced to the President and guests of honour. 'Restricting the number of handshakes at Elysée functions is a relatively new practice which a French newsmagazine has seen as an indication that the 76-year-old general now tries to conserve his energy' (*Atlantic Monthly*, May 1967, 116). Clearly the presence or absence of handshake entitlement was a status indicator of considerable note.

ACCESSORIES IN GREETING AND PARTING SALUTATION

In enhancement of bodily movement and posture in greeting and parting rituals, any one of three main types of accessory may be involved: use of items of dress such as hat or gloves; use of elements attracting attention, by sight or sound, such as waving flags or firing guns; presentation of gifts such as greeting cards or scarves. I deal here briefly only with types of accessory most nearly related to bodily movement.

In greeting and parting behaviour items of bodily covering which are easily removable, especially from extremities, are often treated as ritual elements. Their removal is conceptualized as a symbol of respect to the person greeted, in accordance with the implicit principle that lower status is equated with disarrangement of the person. (This is in line with the custom of showing respect to sacred places, as by removal of hats by men going into church, or of shoes on going into a mosque. Conversely, that which is bare should be covered, as the heads or arms of women in church.) The removal of sandals or shoes in greeting has already been described for Nupe and Mossi. Westerners do not remove their shoes in greeting, but in the period when hats and gloves were worn outdoors by gentry, gentlemen greeted ladies at a distance by taking off their hats or at least raising them briefly from the head; and when shaking hands, they removed the right glove. A lady, of putatively higher status, was expected to keep on her hat and gloves in greeting. For more formal occasions in polite society, variations of glove-wearing and glove length were associated with differences of greeting.

Visual signals to celebrate greeting or departure are manifold. As extensions of the arm, flags, green branches, garments have commonly been waved, sometimes with specific messages as well as general salutation meaning. The use of some other accessories may combine visual display with presentation of gifts according to a complex code. On formal occasions in Fijian society the presentation of a whale's tooth is still a most important element in the rituals of greeting, in an elaborate context of prescribed bodily movement and speech. (In 1970 I myself took part in such greeting ritual in Beqa, under the guidance of the late Dr Rusiate Nayacakalou.) In Central Asia traditionally a similar function was performed by the silk scarf. Owen Lattimore has described how in Inner Mongolia a scarf is exchanged in greeting between friends, sent with messages and used in all kinds of ceremonies. Its symbolism is specified closely. It is folded three times lengthwise; it should be held on the palms of the outstretched hands, with thumbs hooked over the top; the open fold or 'mouth' must be towards the front, towards the receiver – if reversed towards the giver it is discourteous and unlucky, since the virtue of the gift will 'spill out' (Lattimore, 1941, 38–9). Tibetan exchange of scarves in greeting used to observe gradations of rank scrupulously. Sir Charles Bell has noted that if the recipient was of much higher rank than the giver, he remained seated while the other person laid the scarf at his feet. If the recipient was only a little superior the presentation scarf was placed on a table in front of him; where both were equal in rank, they stood and laid their scarves over each other's wrists. Should the giver of the scarf be of higher position he laid the scarf over the neck of the recipient, who bowed to receive it (Bell, 1928, 100, 253). Another extension of bodily greeting procedures is the practice of drinking 'toasts' to guests, involving arm and head movement, focus of attention upon a glass held up, and appropriate words. Where reciprocal toasting on a personal basis is part of a formal dinner, status considerations may enter; it is a mark of respect to invite another person to drink a mutual toast, but it is the role of the senior to take the initiative.

GENERAL OBSERVATIONS

Greeting and parting behaviour is often treated as if it were a simple acknowledgement of arrival or departure, or a spontaneous emotional reaction to the coming together or separation of people. The social message carried is regarded as overt. But sociological observation, in line with findings of kinesics and ethology, suggests that such behaviour is highly conventionalized, and culture-specific, not universal. In a broad sense greeting and parting behaviour may be termed ritual since it follows patterned routines, it is a system of signs which convey other than overt messages and so may be categorized as symbols, and it is sanctioned by strong expressions of moral approval.

But though human societies show a wide range of variation in greeting and parting behaviour, everywhere they tend to use a comparatively small set of basic materials for the purpose, primarily involving the human body. Ancillary cultural instruments are often utilized – hats, gloves, scarves, guns, flags – but for the most part these are extensions of an individual's physical apparatus, his body and limbs. They serve to supplement his waving and shouting, the alteration of his features and movements of his limbs, his getting up and sitting down. This instrumental use of the human body, with its attachments, for social purposes, is a marked feature of greeting and parting behaviour, which so far has not been given the systematic study it deserves. Functionally it involves the participants directly in the operations, and promotes the establishment and working of social relationships. It helps to insinuate new individuals into social situations, and to fill the gap when known individuals depart; at the same time small differences in procedure are standardized and made to serve as carriers of significant social features.

In greeting and parting behaviour involving use of the body as an instrument I see several major social themes, each connected with the concept of personality. The first theme is that of attention-producing. A primary object of much greeting or parting activity is to attract the attention of the other party – by directed glance or out-thrust hand if close by or by oscillation of the hand (waving) if at a distance. By focusing attention on the personality of each participant a sign is given that further communication is desired. A second theme is that of identification. The people concerned are differentiated as persons entering or continuing individually the social relationship. One function of much greeting and parting behaviour is in providing a framework within which individuals can identify one another as preliminary to further action. A third theme is that of reduction of uncertainty or anxiety in social contact, particularly between persons who are not previously known to one another. Confrontation without communication is threatening. Even the most casual greeting gesture tends to remove an element of uncertainty from the encounter. To nod or say a brief word to a stranger is more than a token of friendliness; it puts him in a social context, within which further communicative action can follow. Salutation at parting serves in parallel fashion to put a definite point to the departure, to establish the severance as a social and not merely a physical fact – not leaving the relationship hanging in the air, so to speak, as an unresolved issue.

An important element in much greeting and parting behaviour is status demonstration. Relative posture and gesture, especially in degree of elevation, are used in very many cultures symbolically to indicate the relative status of the parties engaged. In this a kind of rough logic is displayed, whereby bodily elevation is correlated with social elevation. I would argue that a common, even basic function of greeting and parting rituals is in creating occasion for establishment of relative status positions, against the possibility of future social action. Another basic function is in providing a code (a 'vocabulary') in which status relations can be simply and concretely expressed. Such rituals may also provide conditions for exploration or assertion of changes in status, as Junod's Thonga example of Christian handshaking indicates.

Of special interest in all this is the way in which some simple physical actions involving the body as a whole are given symbolic significance. Forms of greeting or parting in which a person lowers himself, sets himself at a distance, or removes articles of clothing indicate inferior status to other persons who do not behave in this way, or do so only to a modified degree. The visible lowering, distancing, stripping of the body – all acts which metaphorically if not physically leave the individual relatively unprotected – emphasize by contrast the other person who is protected by height, distance and covering. So social inferiority is expressed symbolically by a simulacrum of physical defencelessness.

Analogies with animal behaviour here are clear. With animals social identification is linked directly with personal security. The kind of contact that is made, often in exploratory way, has a function of establishing the freedom of the individual animal from immediate danger, and in some cases of promotion of sexual co-operation. By visual, aural, tactile and olfactory means animals establish identity and social relationship. Human beings do not use the physical range of the senses so widely or so acutely – smell is rarely used in greeting behaviour, though sometimes it is discriminatory. But the bodily means of establishing relationship by touching – with hands, lips, noses – in such context is most marked, and would seem directly relatable to animal behaviour.

But the analogies between man and other animals cannot be pushed very far. Ethologists assume that ritualization in animals is adaptive for the species, and broadly of the same general order for each species. Greeting and parting rituals in human societies are of very wide variety, and their adaptive function is discernible only in broadest outline. Known aspects of human conceptualization of time period give a quality or dimension to greeting and parting behaviour which animals seem largely to lack. Anticipation of greeting as distinct from generalized precautions against meeting seems absent from animal behaviour. Ability of an animal to differentiate length of time during which another will be absent seems fairly limited, whereas human parting conceptualizes a future to which a time scale can be assigned and by which ritual at parting can be modified accordingly. (For instance, it would seem ridiculous to farewell with the same intensity a member of the family who is going round the corner to shop, as one who is going abroad for several years.) Then, whereas for animals greeting rituals are vital on personal security grounds, and in relation to territory and mating, their parting rituals seem empirically scant and theoretically less significant. Human greeting and parting rituals have developed elaborations: use of intermediaries to provide introduction – animal mothers do this only to limited extent; separation of formal from informal roles, so that a person can be greeted in two very different ways, even on the same overall occasion; adoption of representative status, so that a person may be greeted or farewelled not simply for his own sake but as a symbol of a group of others not present. Much of this is completely alien to animal society. Then overwhelmingly, the flexibility which human speech allows in greeting and parting, and the associated development of concepts gives a completely different dimension to the whole set of operations. As part of this flexibility the specification of personal identity by use of personal names is a marked characteristic of human greeting and parting rituals, allowing a high degree of manipulation of the situation.

Finally, a feature which marks off human greeting and parting rituals from those of animals is the relative ease with which they may change. Apart from modifications associated with changes of fashion in dress – men who do not wear hats cannot raise them, and must bow or wave a hand instead – what appear to be deeply-rooted modes of behaviour seem able to be changed quite rapidly. The comparatively recent spread of the Western handshake is a case in point. There is a paradox here. At any one period in any one society conventional forms of greeting and parting tend to be fairly limited, and to be regarded as of aesthetic and moral significance. Failure to give the 'correct' signals tends to be criticized, even in children, as insulting to the party affected. Lucy Mair has reported from her experience among the Ganda thirty years or so ago that children began to be taught phrases of greeting and farewell almost before they could speak, and were drilled in the correct gestures – to kneel and put their hands between those of the stranger. 'Refusal to do this is one of the few reasons for which I have seen a child beaten' (1934, 65).

Yet despite the moral sanctions in vogue for carrying out the 'correct' behaviour it is remarkable how easily such patterns have altered. The more elaborate formal procedures of many African and Asian societies – including the Ganda – have tended to be abandoned in modern times as familiarity with Western patterns has spread and as Western economic, educational and religious institutions have affected traditional status alignments. I would put status considerations at the core of the symbolism of greeting and parting rituals.

Chapter 10

SYMBOLISM OF FLAGS

Like the symbolism in the manner of wearing the hair, and in behaviour at greeting and parting, the symbolism of flags lies primarily in their display. But whereas hair is basically a personal symbol, a flag is basically a social symbol. Not an attached, growing, shearable part of a human personality, it is a manufactured object, often made to a formula, detachable from maker or user and meant to show to others rather than to be an ornament to oneself. And yet a flag may be an object of strong sentiment, its symbolism may be deeply felt, and as such it may serve as a symbol for the unity of a large body of people. Now when it is said in Durkheimian fashion that a flag is a symbol to which sentiments spontaneously attach themselves, and that this intensifies social solidarity, what is meant by such statements?

I begin with a piece of personal observation. A couple of years ago, from my room overlooking the quadrangle of an eastern university in the United States, I heard one day the sound of a kettledrum in even taps, at the same time as I saw the statue of one of the founding fathers of the university, a seated bronze figure, being draped in a plastic robe. Then a procession came into view, headed by a single male figure with head-band and long hair, slowly carrying an uplifted American flag on a pole. He was followed by about twenty young men, some carrying a large chair. To the sound of the drum the procession advanced to the plinth of the statue, the chair was set down, and a black student was seated temporarily in it. Then the student was 'rescued' and the chair was set on fire. A speech was given, inaudible to me and apparently to other people at a distance – some lying on the grass reading, some talking with backs turned. From later report the speech gave some explanation of these events.

The interpretation was briefly that it was a ritual parody, concerned with the agitation for freeing a member of the Black Panther group who was then being held by the United States authorities for trial. The parody was an illustration of the thesis that, as alleged in various posters, the Fascists of the government had decided that this particular man must die in the electric chair. The seated bronze figure in robes was therefore meant to represent the judge in court; the black student represented the prisoner who ought to have been rescued; the chair which was burned represented the punishment seat which ought to be destroyed. The whole event was designed to dramatize the Black Panther trials, to decry the justice of the United States courts, and to mobilize support for protest movements against them. What now was the place of the United States flag in this performance? It was clearly a symbol, intended to serve as a hallmark of the proceedings, a leading feature, representing the court of the people of the United States. But the use of this flag in parody raises some general issues about the symbolism of flags which are worth discussing analytically from a more theoretical sociological standpoint.

ETHNOGRAPHY OF FLAGS

There is some comparative ethnographic data about the nature and use of flags, particularly in display, but little precise examination of their functions.

Simple forms of flag have existed in many cultures. In the Pacific region, for instance, among pagan Tikopia forty years ago a streamer of white bark-cloth was used as a flag to celebrate the completion of yam-planting in a sacred cultivation during the great seasonal ritual cycle (Firth, 1967a, 185). According to Tikopia tradition the early occupation of the neighbouring island of Anuta by a Tikopia chief was signalized by his setting up a pennant of bark-cloth; when Tongans later came there they took his pennant down and substituted their own (Firth, 1954, 121). In the first of these cases the bark-cloth streamer, compared by Tikopia to European flags which they had seen on vessels, was said to stimulate the growth of yams, and to warn people to keep clear of the taboo area. In the second case it was intended as a token of ownership. In northern Luzon a flag of another kind, presumably combining both ritual and status components, was the piece of bark-cloth dipped in the blood of a newly-taken head and hung up in a house after a successful head-hunt (DeRaedt, 1964, 315). But for flags to be fully developed a more efficient textile in the form of woven cloth has been historically necessary, and many ethnographical references concern calico or similar material. Nearly a century ago Colonel Richard Dodge was exploring among Sioux Indians when, crossing a fresh trail, he saw on a hill a pole to the top of which was fastened a streamer of white cloth. Under a small cairn of stones at the foot of the pole was a bundle of sticks and a cotton cloth with totemic hieroglyphs, and a pouch containing tobacco and corn. These things were a message telling the number of men in the party, who they were and where they were going and that they intended to eat and smoke in peaceful company. The white streamer was to call attention to the message and invite their friends to follow them (Dodge, 1883, 411–12). But in small-scale societies with much face-to-face contact, the need for flags as signals would be small.

While preceded in the West historically by insignia of various kinds, such as the eagle standard of the Roman legions, carried especially in war,* flags of cloth in modern form seem to have been an Oriental invention, transmitted to Europe probably by the Saracens. The function of flags in display is illustrated by countless instances in descriptions of Oriental culture of their use in horse or bull racing, in the travel of princes or high officials. Such flags often had two important functions in addition to general ostentation and attraction of attention: they might embody ritual values in their colour – as in the yellow royal standard of an Emperor; and they might have inscribed on them identificatory devices such as the 'cognomen' of a lord. Such specific marking of the individuality of the person whose banners were carried bore a more direct relation to social group structure than the inscriptions of the 'welcome' or 'happiness' character which were also very frequent. The Western use of flags as heraldic devices is well known. An interesting parallel was the use of the Mongol 'banners' which gave rise to a technical term in English. As a flag the Mongol banner was a cloth bearing the

* The Latin *vexillum*, a military standard, from which allied English words have been derived, is related to *vehere*, to carry.

emblem of a prince, and by English commentators the term 'Banner' has been used to indicate the social group related to this – the tribal following of the prince. By a further complication, as Lattimore points out, the Manchus took over the Mongol concept, but developed their Banner as a regimental formation, applying to military but not to general political units (Lattimore, 1934, 146–52).

Apart from decoration and display, expression of social unit solidarity, or specific individual identification, flags have often served to mark out personal life crises in a more dynamic, even dramatic way. By followers of the Sapilada religion among the Igorot of Luzon a white flag was formerly characteristic. When a young couple got married such a flag was tied to a long pole set up in front of their house. It was taken down on the third day of the wedding ceremonies, then put up again after another three days. When the cult was revived during the last war red flags were used as well as white, possibly in imitation of Japanese troops (Eggan and Pacyaya, 1962, 95–113). In Japan, so much was the use of flags associated with holidays that as Embree records, national holidays were indicated in the calendar by little symbols of crossed flags. But flags also served sterner purposes. In Suye Mura flags were not only set up for holidays, boys' ceremonies and completion of house framework – they also marked funerals and memorial services for the dead. They also indicated the drafting of young men into the army. Before the war, when a youth was selected to serve as a soldier, a tall bamboo was cut and stripped to a topknot of leaves. Below this leaf cluster a national flag was fastened and the flagpole was erected in the house yard. The flag was left in position while the son of the house was away in the army, and those houses which had soldiers in training or overseas could be told by the location of the flags (Embree, 1946, 94, 147, 149, 199, etc.). Differentiation of symbolic function was indicated by the fact that while marking the absence of the soldier was presumably a form of mourning, the use of the national flag and not just any coloured banner, showed respect for the nation whose cause he was serving.

The symbolism of status combined with an implicit comment on marital relations is illustrated by M. G. Smith's description of a Carriacou wedding. In this Caribbean ceremony, there is a fight between flag bearers representing groom and bride, until the groom's flag defeats the bride's flag and is crossed over it. Then the two flags are hoisted above the house, the groom's again on top. The symbolism here is obvious in one sense, but whether it represents male dominance in actuality or only in wish-fulfilment is not clear. The flags bear various devices, such as the Union Jack, and embroidered mottoes such as 'Long Life', 'Prosperity' or (a rather depressing comment on the future of marriage) 'In God We Trust' (Smith, 1962, 127–8).

FLAGS AS SIGNALS

Whatever be the theoretical argument about use of the terms sign, symbol and signal, it is convenient operationally to separate the use of flags as signals from their use as symbols. In the one case they are intended primarily to convey information, in the other they are meant to express ideas or emotions, often of quite complex order.

A simple instance of a flag signal is when at a country cottage a flag is put on a pole in the hedge at the roadway to attract the attention of travelling milkman or newspaperman. The message is – milk or newspapers are wanted; it is imprecise, has minimal content and almost no emotional loading. Moreover, the flag is non-specific. Shape, colour and design are immaterial, or nearly so – the flag should not be red. For an analogous signal in such a country lane, a red flag means by convention that men are at work on the road ahead, perhaps out of sight round a bend. Here too the signal is imprecise, with little emotional loading beyond a mild anxiety until the reason for the signal is made clear. But while the response to both signals is left voluntary, that for milk or newspapers is a request, and that for caution against men ahead is virtually a command. The sanctions for disregard of each are of very different order, those of the latter being definitely punitive. Within limits the size, shape and exact position of the red flag of warning are irrelevant, but its colour is not. The red fabric has been deliberately chosen because whatever may be its physiological stimulus, by social convention red in such contexts of road travel and in social movement generally is recognized as a signal of danger (cf. the red flag flown by a vessel carrying explosives, or hoisted on an artillery range when firing is in progress).

The complex use of flags as signals has been developed to a high degree as a means of communication between vessels at sea, especially since the eighteenth century. These maritime signals have used combinations of the cardinal elements of shape, colour, pattern and position to achieve a very elaborate code, which has attained the status of an international convention. In a general way, simple coloured flags have been used at sea as on land to convey stock types of message. A yellow flag is a sign of quarantine, or of infectious disease aboard; or more broadly, of a health condition needing clarification and permission to proceed. A white flag in time of war indicates a wish for a truce, or a surrender, or at least absence of hostile intent.* But the international signalling code, dating from 1857, is much more specific. The yellow health flag is the letter Q in the international code, whereas a yellow flag with a black ball in the centre is the letter I; a flag with alternate yellow and blue stripes is the letter G, one with blue cross on white field is the letter X – and so on with different colours and designs for all the alphabet. Nearly all these signal flags are rectangular, but a series of number pennants are distinguished in part by their tapering shape. So messages may be spelled out in detail over any visual distance by hoisting series of such flags. Yet an alphabetical message is cumbrous to send and read, so for economy small groups of flags have been given more elaborate if still specific significance. So while yellow with black ball in centre, and blue cross on white field mean independently flag letters I and X, the two-letter group IX in combination, flown from the halyards, means 'I have received serious damage in collision'. So on for a large set of combinations – said to be 78,000 in all.

Here the meaning of the signal is to be obtained from the flag in its structural context: the particular pattern, shape and colour combination cannot be construed in isolation, but only in association with other flags, according to their order and precise position on the display field of the vessel. The significance of this structural dimension is seen by the manner in which the colour pattern flag signals of this maritime international code can be translated into the equivalent codes of semaphore signalling, and of morse. Semaphore

* In the troubles in Belfast in mid-1970 a man with a white flag emerged from a housing block engaged in exchange of fire with the police, asking for medical attention for injured people. After guarantees of mutual safety, this was arranged (*Daily Telegraph*, 26 June 1972. Cf. Hulme, n.d., 25; also on use of black and of blood-red flags).

is essentially a visual mode of signalling; while flags have commonly been used, their relative position, not their colour, is the critical index. (Blue and white is the convention, but is not obligatory.) Hence wooden or other arms can substitute for flags, as does a central post for the human body which is the elementary reference point and source of mobility in the original semaphore system. (If flags are lacking a semaphore signaller can use his own arms alone.) In this system it is the position of the arms and/or flags in angle to the body, individually or in combination that gives the key to the interpretation. So colour in context is translated into angle in context. With morse the transformation is made from position to sequence; the meaning is given by the differential flow of a series of short and long pulses. These can be given by flags, waved rapidly in a short arc or slowly in a long arc; but vision can be replaced by sound or by inaudible electrical impulse. This possibility of transformation underlines the contextual, structural nature of the code significance of flags as signals.

Conventions of more widespread order allow the use of almost any flag as a signal of limited kind by variance of its normal position. By dipping a flag, that is lowering it slowly and raising it smartly, a salute can be given in respect. A flag set at half-mast is taken internationally as a sign of mourning. A flag lowered and not flown again can be a sign of abdication of control – as in the ceremonial ending of British rule when a colony becomes independent. A flag flown upside down may be a sign of distress, and is commonly so interpreted at sea. But the meaning of the signal must be read according to circumstances. The British union flag (commonly called Union Jack, though it is rarely flown from the jack staff of a vessel) is often flown by ordinary citizens for special celebrations of a national order, and sometimes in error appears upside down, with a narrow instead of a broad stripe uppermost near the staff. This is not interpreted as a sign of distress, even by those who realize the inversion. (For special interpretations of inverted national flags see later, p. 361.)

FLAGS AS SYMBOLS

Many flags in ordinary use must be regarded not primarily as signals conveying information, but as symbols representing ideas or objects of value, often in a very general and emotional manner. In maritime history the white flag of surrender often seems to have meant much more in value terms than a simple message of intention to stop fighting and hand over the ship to the enemy. The black flag popularly, if apocryphally, attributed to Spanish Main pirates stood for a whole attitude of mind towards property and sovereignty, and was not just a signal of aggression. The modern red flag of revolution also represents a complex set of ideologies and behaviour.

In addition to their flag signals, the military establishments of most countries have tended to use a considerable amount of flag symbolism. 'Colours' carried on formal occasions by regiments of many nations, and displaying their battle honours, stand for the reputation and solidarity of the unit. In Britain, such symbolism is illustrated specifically when the Sovereign or other dignitary presents new colours to a regiment. The use of ensigns by ships also has symbolic function. In the Royal Navy the flag of an admiral is a white square bearing a cross of St George in red. When flown by a vice-admiral the flag bears one red ball in the upper canton next to the staff, and when flown by a rear-admiral it has two red balls in the upper and lower cantons next to the staff. As signals, such ensigns denote the presence of an officer 'of flag rank' aboard, but they are also status symbols with elaborate rights, privileges, duties and rules behind them. The degree to which display of such flags goes beyond mere signalling is shown by the ceremonial manner in which they are hoisted and lowered, on occasion with appropriate bugle calls, or other formal recognition.

Broadly we can distinguish symbols of situation, such as a white flag of surrender, from symbols of status, such as an admiral's flag, though they often tend to merge. But a more relevant distinction is between symbols of office status and symbols of personal status. So, an admiral in the Royal Navy is entitled to his status symbol of the flag of St George while he remains in that office, but he must relinquish it when he retires to private life. But if he is of armigerous family, he remains entitled to his personal heraldic symbols as long as he lives. But even official and personal status may merge in the use of symbols such as flags. Historically, a great number of symbols of personal status have been supplied by flags of heraldry – banners, bannerets, banderoles, standards, oriflammes – which displayed the particular devices of the nobles and knights on occasions of collective assembly, especially at court or in war. As signals they indicated the position of their owners and served as markers or rallying points, but as symbols of personal status they represented or evoked a complex set of sentiments relating to prowess in battle, wealth in land, strength of followers. Yet many of these flags also symbolized the official position of the bearer's lord, as head of an important and powerful social unit. As such, a flag of this kind represented a collectivity, not just a person.

NATIONAL FLAGS: THEIR COMPOSITION

The symbolic character of national flags illustrates most clearly the sociological significance of the status theme. Consider first the major features of their composition.

National flags vary greatly in ancestry, some being of very old design, others being quite contemporary as a function of admission to the United Nations. But all have been constructed very much in terms of differentiating signs, not autonomously conceived, but having much of their meaning from the contrast that each presents to others of the same general class.*

All national flags except one so far (Nepal) are rectangular in shape (in contrast to pennants for signalling and other uses). Colour is a distinctive attribute of them all, and most are multi-coloured. Historically, presumably due in part to the Muslim aversion to depiction of the creatures of Allah, Islamic flags tended to be of single colour without device, but many modern flags of Muslim countries now bear coloured devices or are multi-coloured.†

* Detailed systematic information on national flags is given in many publications, for example E. M. C. Barraclough, *Flags of the World*, 1959; British Admiralty, *Flags of All Nations*, 1965. A valuable content analysis of colour combinations and devices, with some examination of their symbolic meanings, has been made by a sociologist, Sasha R. Weitman (1971) quite independently of my own inquiry for this chapter. Weitman also has discovered the existence, for sociologists, of the Flag Research Centre which conducts studies of 'vexillology' with great energy, from Lexington, Massachusetts.

† Black (alleged to be the colour of vengeance) is supposed to have been the colour of Mohammed's banner; it was adopted by the 'Abbasid Caliphs in the eighth century, and is still used by Shi'ites, as in Iraq. By contrast, Omayyad Caliphs took white, and the Khawarij took red (such a plain red flag has been kept to modern times by the Sultanate of Muscat and Oman). But green, the colour adopted by the Fatimid dynasty, eventually became the most

Many national flags are distinguishable only by their specific colour variations, their design of cross, vertical or horizontal stripes being identical. So, the green, white and orange of Eire parallels the green, white and red of Italy. The flag of Poland has a white horizontal section above a red one, while that of Indonesia has the reverse. Denmark has a white cross on red, Sweden a yellow cross on blue; Switzerland has a white cross inset in a red field, while, though not a national flag, the International Red Cross has adopted the reverse style. Western Germany has black, red, yellow in horizontal bars, as against Ethiopia's green, yellow, red. Some national flags have the colours identical, but in different arrangement: Belgium shares the black, red, yellow with Western Germany, but in vertical as against horizontal bars. The defining character of each flag is provided by the uniqueness of the combination as part of a group of related colour masses. What this means, *inter alia*, in these days of modern mass media, is that only those flags with a distinctive device – such as a pattern of stars, or a hammer and sickle – are capable of being reproduced easily in black and white form, as in newspaper cartoons. But while the colour range of national flags is considerable, it does not cover the entire spectrum equally. Orange, indigo and violet are much more rare than red and blue. Of the mixed colours, green is popular, but brown seems to appear only on flags of Bhutan and a few other small countries, and almost no use is made of special shades of the 'kingfisher blue' or 'shocking pink' type. White and black, on the other hand, are commonly used as if they were colours. In all this selection, historical factors are important, but so also is clarity of perception.

The problem of a natural basis for colour selection has provoked much argument. Forty years ago Radcliffe-Brown wrote of the 'stimulating dynamogenic power of sensations of redness' in explaining the use of red paint by Andamanese (1922, 318), an idea to which Lowie gave only guarded approval. Recently Lévi-Strauss and Charbonnier discussed the matter briefly in another context. Like Radcliffe-Brown, Charbonnier pointed out that red is a source of

commonly recognized colour of Islam. (That a green flag in other contexts can have secular meaning is shown by the custom of 'topping-out' in the building trade when the frame of a building is finished. On completion of the new London Stock Exchange building, it was reported that 'in accordance with tradition' a green flag was hoisted, with a sprig of evergreen; for this ceremony the chairman of the Stock Exchange presided (*Times*, 16 July 1969).)

physical and physiological excitement, and inferred that it is paradoxical to choose red for 'Stop' signs, as in traffic lights. Lévi-Strauss commented that red might be a sign of heat and communicability, just as green might be a chilling and rather venomous symbol. But he argued that this underlying meaning was extremely weak – not completely arbitrary but so to a large extent (Charbonnier, 1969, 116). In the symbolic context of national flags this 'dynamogenic' significance of red can be broadly seen, but it is by no means universal (see later).

Sometimes the pattern of a national flag is intended to symbolize linkage as well as differentiation. Flags of Australia and New Zealand, for instance, bear the 'Union Jack' in an upper corner to indicate the continuing connection with Britain and the Commonwealth, while adopting individual arrangements of the stars of the Southern Cross constellation to mark their autonomy. But the linkage may not necessarily mean any acknowledgement of former political authority. I was intrigued to see when I lived in Hawaii that the state flag bears the 'Union Jack' in one corner – not that the British ever owned Hawaii, but before it was annexed by the United States, when it was an independent Polynesian kingdom, it had a friendly relation with Britain, and marked this symbolically in the flag.* So also the crescent and star on flags of Egypt, Libya, Malaysia, Pakistan indicates Muslim relationship, though historically not all of them acknowledged the suzerainty of the Ottoman Turks who originated this symbol on a national scale. (Cf. also the Red Crescent substituted for Red Cross by some Muslim nations, on the grounds that the latter is a Christian symbol.)

GENERAL SYMBOLIC VALUE OF NATIONAL FLAGS

'Explaining' the symbolism of a national flag in terms of its history is a common school exercise in some countries. But it is not so much the individual histories that are of sociological interest as the question of what values are attached to these pieces of coloured cloth, and what social acts are related to these.

* In 1776 the new Continental Army of the American colonies had a flag of red and white stripes with the British union flag in the canton – the Grand Union Flag, before independence was sought. Not till 1777, a year after the Declaration of Independence, did Congress decide on the Stars and Stripes, and no official flag of this pattern seems to have actually appeared till 1783.

A key problem was referred to by Thomas Carlyle, when he noted the small intrinsic value of such flags. 'Have I not myself known 500 living soldiers sabred into crows' meat, for a piece of glazed cotton which they called their *Flag*, which, had you sold it at any market-cross, would not have brought above three *groschen*', he wrote in *Sartor Resartus*, on 'Symbols'. But in sociological terms it was Durkheim who made the classic statement which I quoted at the beginning of this book. In connection with his analogy that the Australian totem was the 'flag of the clan' he put forward a series of propositions. It is a well-known law, he held, that sentiments aroused in us by something spontaneously attach themselves (or are communicated) to the symbol which represents them. The idea of a thing and the idea of its symbol are closely united in our minds. The soldier who dies for his flag dies for his country, but as a matter of fact, in his own consciousness, it is the flag that has first place. It sometimes happens that this even directly determines action. Whether one isolated standard remains in the hands of the enemy or not does not determine the fate of the country, yet the soldier allows himself to be killed to regain it. He loses sight of the fact that the flag is only a sign, and that it has no value in itself, but only brings to mind the reality that it represents; it is treated as if it were this reality itself (1926, 219–20).

This statement, classic though it be, needs some comment. As my quotation from Carlyle has shown, the idea of the discrepancy between the market or 'intrinsic' value of the flag and its symbolic value was no novelty, though Durkheim's statement was more neutral in tone. Durkheim's statement has its defects. Note the superb arrogance of the remark that with the soldier who dies for his flag it is *as a matter of fact* the flag that has first place in his consciousness (or 'value recognition', depending on which meaning is given to *conscience*). This is either a tautology or an unwarranted assertion. Assuming there is historical basis for such an imaginary illustration, the soldier may have been prepared to die 'for his flag' deliberately as an act of leadership to induce others to follow and capture the position, with all that may have implied; the flag may have been quite secondary in his judgement of the military issues involved. But Durkheim's statement calls attention to certain basic elements in the symbolic use of flags. First, the flag, a specific material object, is taken as the representative of a very general object, a country, of abstract as well as of material character. Secondly, the material symbol becomes in itself an object of sentiment, which is transferred from the object represented. Whether such transference is 'spontaneous' as Durkheim argued, or has been a much more complex process, including elements of indoctrination, can be a matter for argument. In some countries quite overt conscious efforts have been made to impress such transference upon children. But such transference of sentiment, or development of sentiment for symbol as well as for original object, raises the question of incongruity to which Carlyle and others have drawn attention. Thirdly, attitudes to the symbol are not merely intellectual and emotional; they also tend to take shape in action. Whether attitude to the symbol and attitude to that which it signifies can ever be completely separated may be an academic question; but certainly with national flags the symbol is a common and highly important behavioural focus, often treated as an object of value in its own right. And lastly, national flags tend to be placed in a special category. Even more than regimental colours, school banners and other unit symbols, national flags tend to be assigned a quality of special reserve, removing them from the more sordid aspects of common handling. They represent 'society' much more, in its broadest political aspect. Use of the term 'desecration' for behaviour not regarded as appropriate to handling of a national flag indicates how the notion of reserve is related to the Durkheimian concept of the sacred. A representative in the United States Congress has recalled how reassuring it was to him as a child when the teachers opened the day with a pledge of allegiance to the Flag and a prayer to the Supreme Deity (*Newsweek*, 22 November 1971).

The discrepancy between attitudes which might be expected towards simple objects taken alone and the same objects taken as symbols seems to have been a continual matter of remark, even among sophisticated sociological analysts, when they came to the example of flags. Edward Sapir shared this view. He wrote: 'By gradual extensions of meaning the terms symbol and symbolism have come to include not merely such trivial objects and marks as black balls, to indicate a negative attitude in voting, and stars and daggers, to remind the reader that supplementary information is to be found at the bottom of the page, but also more elaborate objects and devices, such as the flags and signal lights, which are not ordinarily regarded as important in themselves but which point to ideas and actions of great consequence to societies. . . . In the case of a national flag or a beautiful poem, a symbolic expression which is apparently one of mere reference is associated with repressed emotional material of great importance to the ego' (1934). The interest of this statement does not lie so much in the hint of latent wonder that such mediocre objects should arouse such strong sentiments – which one would expect to be a lay reaction rather than a professional one in such a sensitive sociologist. It lies rather in the notion of the symbol evoking emotional responses of a *repressed* kind. It is not clear just what Sapir thought this repressed material to be in the case of flags. But the statement is an echo of Sapir's psychoanalytical interests, and a pointer to some later anthropological ideas about symbolism.

The Durkheimian sociological viewpoint about flags has been repeated by many writers, including Boas, Linton and Lévi-Strauss. It is epitomized in the kind of statement made by J. J. Honigman about the rituals of the United States Memorial Day – that the emotions canalized towards flags, images or dead heroes intensify solidarity (1959, 515).

QUALITIES OF FLAGS USED AS SYMBOLS

But what I have not found in sociological writings about the use of flags as symbols is any systematic examination of why *flags* should have attained such prominence. It is true that other national symbols have been of great importance, especially national anthems and national emblems. Indeed the government of India has been so aware of this that a few years ago they issued a series of brochures explaining the origin, meaning and use of these symbols of the Indian nation. 'The National Flag, the National Anthem and the National Emblem are the three symbols through which an independent country proclaims its identity and sovereignty and, as such, they command instantaneous respect and loyalty. In themselves, they reflect the entire background, thought and culture of a nation.' This might be called an exercise in practical Durkheimianism.

Postage stamps, seals, coins also serve as national symbols of importance.

But the special qualities of flags which make them prime choice for symbolic use are availability and variability. Flags can be made of any fabric. Bunting, a particular kind of woollen cloth, has become conventional for many official flags because of its durability, but cotton, silk, satin and man-made fibres have also been used; primitive flags such as Tikopia pennants have been made from simple bark-cloth. A flag is often cheap and can be hastily constructed. The history of national flags has many examples of flags having been put together from materials at hand by hard-pressed warriors or their inventive ladies. When such tales pass into legend, as that of Betsy Ross in the United States, this is another way of associating the national symbol with the ordinary people. Flags are also capable of being greatly varied in shape and design, by use of different patterns, colour combinations and specific motifs. The adaptability of flags in display means that their symbolic value can appear over a great range of ritual occasions. Again, their basic characteristics can be recognized at a distance, and they are as effective among illiterate as among literate populations. Finally, simple actions with a flag can implicate complex themes. Because a flag is cheap to make or buy, easy to manipulate, observable by numbers of people at once, it is a prime vehicle for conveying attitudes towards a social unit of which one is a member, or expressing other sentiments. Hence there is opportunity for personal identification with the symbol which can give added force to its use.

So, on occasions of national rejoicing, individual citizens fly flags, wave flags, in ways which express their direct involvement with the occasion and their social group.

TRADITIONAL SENTIMENTS TOWARDS NATIONAL FLAGS AS IDEAS

Before examining behaviour towards concrete examples of national flags, I consider briefly some attitudes traditionally expressed about the idea of a flag in the abstract. Among the best indicators here are nineteenth-century poets, among whom national enthusiasm rode high.

It is a fair assumption that poets have expressed both their own personal sentiments and those of a wider public in those verses which have passed into the literary and educational heritage of the countries whose national flags have been celebrated. In the English-speaking world a parallelism can be clearly seen in British and American writers, who have lauded their respective national symbols in what have by now become hackneyed quotations. (The examples which follow have been taken from common anthologies.) Take a couple from Thomas Campbell, in the early nineteenth century:

Ye mariners of England
That guard our native seas
Whose flag has braved a thousand years
The battle and the breeze . . .
(*Ye Mariners of England*)

This is a touching sentiment – if one ignores the fact that the flag commemorated has not been the same flag for the whole period. But one cannot ignore the passage of history so easily when reading

With Freedom's lion-banner
Britannia rules the waves . . .
(*Ode to the Germans*)

Nor is the claim advanced by Rudyard Kipling to be conceded without a pang nowadays:

Never was isle so little, never was sea so lone,
But over the scud and the palm-trees an English Flag was flown.
(*The English Flag*)

American sentiments have been analogous, while tailored to the circumstances of the development of the United States. There is the invocation of the flag in Whittier's *Barbara Frietchie* and in Emerson's hymn sung at the completion of Concord Monument (with the classic phrase of the 'shot heard round the world'). There is Fitz-Greene Halleck's poem named *The American Flag*:

Forever float that standard sheet!
Where breathes the foe but falls before us
With Freedom's soil beneath our feet,
And Freedom's banner streaming o'er us.

There is Francis Scott Key's *Star-Spangled Banner* (of 1814):

> Praise the Power that hath made and preserved us a nation!
> Then conquer we must when our cause it is just,
> And this be our motto, 'In God is our trust!'
> And the star-spangled banner in triumph shall wave
> O'er the land of the free and the home of the brave.

To these patriotic sentiments, which seemed very justifiable in the nineteenth century, may be added the more sardonic contemporary comment of James Russell Lowell:

> We've a war and a debt, an' a flag; an' ef this
> Ain't to be inderpendent, why, whut on airth is?
> (*Biglow Papers*, 2nd series, no. 4)

Strong sentiment has often been expressed in the United States on the use of the flag in schools, to promote 'sane Americanism'. Evidence given to a 1937 Senate hearing was in favour of furnishing a national flag by the government to the funeral of each man and woman who was formerly in the armed services, and giving the flag afterwards to the kin. It was argued that 'it is a patriotic thing to provide that the symbol of the unity of our country, the national flag, should be placed upon the casket of every deceased man who has served.... The expense involved would be an investment in patriotism which will bring back huge dividends to our beloved Nation in the future.' It was pointed out in comment that a flag of the specified size and materials would cost $5.47, and that the numbers of people entitled would be considerable – so the 'dividend' was judged to be too low (S. 947, *Hearings of Committee on Military Affairs of U.S. Senate*, Government Printing Office, Washington, 1937). In the regional field, some massive publications dealing with local regimental flags of the United States reinforce the attitudes towards the national flag by describing how the flags were a 'beacon star', consecrated by the blood of the state's noblest sons, carried amid toilsome marches, bloody strife, heroic achievements ... and so on. (At the same time the records often speak of the difficulty of preserving such flags, though money had been set aside for the purpose, with the implication that people's interest in the symbols had tended to wane when once the crisis period had passed.)

Though the British literature is less voluminous, analogous views emerge. I cite here simply an instance, like some American ones, of manufacture of a national flag during siege. At the siege of Chitral of 1895, a British union flag was made of red and white cotton and a blue turban, from the design found on a Navy-Cut tobacco tin. This design was in fact incorrect – it showed white stripes of equal width, whereas the union flag has unequal white stripes. Nevertheless, while technically 'wrong' the symbol performed its function. The leader of the force, Sir George Robertson, reported that the flag was an inspiration to all in the fort – 'it helped us greatly. It cheered our hearts and stiffened our backs' (M'Millan, n.d., 215–16).

The more patriotic of these American and British effusions now have a pathetic quality, with the shrinking and change of status of the British Empire to Commonwealth, and the loss of much of Britain's international political role; and the fading of the American dream of linking the ideals of liberty, democracy and equality with the brute facts of economic and political power and material prosperity. Yet, tattered like historic flags, the ideals still remain, and with them their symbols. Both in Britain and the United States the national flag remains a symbol of high importance for a great majority of the citizens. Moreover, it remains also a symbol for citizens of other countries – who can be moved to action against it or treat it with respect, according to circumstances. Indeed, the expression 'showing the flag' is still used metaphorically for a demonstration of the power, influence and reputation of a country abroad – the expression deriving from the practice of naval vessels entering foreign waters on visits of courtesy or aggressive warning, flying their country's ensign. Most standard literature about flags contains some rather sententious statements of positive sentiment about those of major political significance. The *Encyclopaedia Americana*, for instance, asserts straightforwardly: 'A national flag is the symbol of the nation. . . . A nation's flag is reverenced by its citizens and respected by the citizens of friendly nations. An insult to the flag is considered as an insult to the nation' (1968, 308).

Analogous treatment can be found in a range of literature dealing with other national flags. For example, the centenary of the attainment of Italian unity was celebrated by a survey of the history of the Italian flag – 'il simbolo più significativo della Nazione: la Bandiera Italiana'. Allusion to the colours which have become incorporated in the Italian tricolour was traced back to Dante's *Purgatorio* (the whole analysis denying by implication the thesis sometimes advanced that the Italian tricolour is merely a Napoleonic adaptation of the French tricolour). Linked with the spirit of independence historically demonstrated, the flag is 'the living symbol of the country' (Colangeli, 1965). The history of the national flag of the West German Republic (Friedl, 1968, 23 etc.) shows poignant association of the colours of the flag with ideas of democracy. An analytical treatment of this whole matter begins with the blunt statement 'symbols are realities', and considers Paul Tillich's distinction between 'discursive' and 'representative' symbols. Adopting this latter idea, of the symbol as indicating what is not immediately grasped in historical consciousness, Friedl traces the history of the German flag in terms of its meaning for German nationhood. He cites a declaration of Scharnhorst of 1808 – 'The war must be pursued for the freeing of Germany by Germans. This must be expressed in the banners of the local militia.' Friedl points out that after the capitulation of Germany in May 1945 there was no more German flag. German ships had to fly an international flag (the code flag for C, blue-white-red-white-blue – colours which were not politically significant for the German people). Four years later the flag of the former Weimar Republic was decided upon by the Federal Republic as West Germany's new flag. The colours were laid down by law, and the spokesman said: 'The tradition of black-red-gold is Unity and Freedom; or perhaps I may say better – Unity in Freedom. This flag shall serve us as a symbol, so that the idea of freedom, the idea of personal freedom shall be one of the bases of our future State. . . .'

As this latter example demonstrates, it is not just a particular form of flag which has symbolic value: it may be primarily the colour combination, if it be sufficiently distinctive. So, the black-red-gold of Germany, the blue-white-red tricolour of France, tend to stand for national interests. So also with certain distinctive designs. In black and white drawing, the Union 'Jack' of Great Britain, the Stars and Stripes of the United States, the Soviet hammer and sickle, are easily recognizable and can have symbolic force.

CREATION OF NEW NATIONAL FLAGS

It is a mark of the power of flag symbols that the process of their creation still continues. A new national flag is a potent symbol, a highly condensed focus of sentiment which emphasizes the independence of the newly created political unit. One need not subscribe to the cynical view that along with a flag and an anthem the symbols of nationhood all too often include a prestigeful but money-losing national airline. But it is significant that the entry of the many new states to the United Nations has always been accompanied by a cheaper symbolization – the display of their new flags. Even a change in type of government may be symbolized by abandonment of the old flag and creation of a different one. This happened at the French Revolution and at the Russian Revolution. A recent instance is the making of a new Cambodian flag. When towards the end of 1970 Cambodia became a republic under the government of Lieutenant-General Lon Nol, the republican flag was created from red, white and blue cloth. On a blue ground a red rectangle was sewn in the upper left-hand corner. A white cut-out image of the main temple of Angkor was placed on the red, and three white stars on the blue. The Western press identified the red, white and blue in terms of the French tricolour or the American flag. The temple image represented the most famous national monument. The three stars seemed more difficult to place: according to report the principal of the school where the prototype flag was made said they represented the north, centre and south of Cambodia; but no one else had a clear idea – except some people who assumed they stood for the three stars on General Lon Nol's uniform collar. What did catch the imagination of the press reporters was the alleged requirement that according to Cambodian tradition a new flag must be made by 'vestal virgins' – who seemed to be most appropriately represented by the pupils of a girls' high school. Nine students accordingly sewed the flag, sitting in a circle on the floor, under the supervision of their principal, and following the instructions of the Cambodian parliament. While the sewing proceeded a Buddhist altar was set up, silver bowls of fruit were placed at its foot, and tall candles lit. The flag was furled and unfurled by a bevy of young girls specially dressed, while monks chanted, and showered jasmine blossoms over the girls, who had also knelt with lotus flowers. The rite was said to have been improvised for the occasion (so much for the 'tradition'!). But clearly it involved Buddhist elements of chant, lotus symbolism and offering, with concepts of purity and more general symbolic behaviour of kneeling and other signs of respect. It was both a dedication of the new national flag to public state uses, and also a respectful recognition of its importance as a sacred symbol (*New York Times*, 9 October 1970).

The creation of a national flag is so much part of modern political symbolism of nation-making that a people may even proceed to the recognition of a flag before they attain nationhood. So in the movement of East Pakistan towards autonomy as Bangladesh, the Bengal Nation, when militant students and workers began to demand complete independence, the green, red and gold flag of Bangladesh was unveiled in anticipation (*New York Times*, 29 March 1971). Many Blacks in the United States have adopted their own liberation flag – black, with three horizontal bars of red, black and green. (These were colours popularized by the late Marcus Garvey.) According to the chairman of the Pan-African Congress, U.S.A., the red bar stands for the blood shed by black people to achieve the Black Nation. The black bar represents the 'black race' which, though fallen on evil days, will rise again to take its rightful place in the world. The green bar is symbolic of land and nationhood, for land is the basis of power and freedom. The creation of this flag is regarded as based on the black American's 'passionate belief that the true meanings of the nation's patriotic symbols and ceremonies have never been extended to include him'. The broad truth of this statement can hardly be questioned. But one may surmise that the creation of this flag, and the recognition of a 'black national anthem' as well, are perhaps symbols of compensation, substitutes for more tangible independence in terms of political and economic power (L. F. Palmer, Jr, 1970).*

An interesting light is thrown on the relation between symbolic

* This black-green-red flag of 'Negro nationalism' was raised over the coffin of one of the convicts killed in retaking the Attica prison in September, 1971. It was also waved in an African-American Parade in Harlem in the same month. In Vietnam a 'Black Power flag' displayed 'Black Unity' in black letters at the top, and a black fist in the middle, on a red ground. In August 1971, the Black-owned and Black-operated *Amsterdam News* of New York adopted a combination of red and green ink with its black print. As the editor stated: 'This was our symbolic way of expressing typographically and in our format our commitment to

creation and considerations of expediency by the history of the wheel symbol in the national flag of India. It has been said that the *chakra-dhvaja* or the Wheel Flag of India is the symbol of her civilization as evolved through the ages. When the national leaders of India were fired with the spirit of asserting the country's independence they naturally felt the need of a national flag. Various designs were used from 1906 onwards, commonly with red, yellow and green. The Home Rule movement of 1917 devised a flag which incorporated the Union Jack, since they were aiming at local autonomy, not complete independence. 'The people, however, did not take kindly to it'! Finally, partly on Mahatma Gandhi's suggestion, a tricolour was accepted, of saffron above, green below, with white in the middle, in which was set a spinning-wheel sign of navy-blue. With the coming of Independence in 1947 it was felt necessary to modify the spinning wheel for the sake of simplicity, to avoid directional confusion; if the symbol appeared identically on both sides of the flag it would be pointing different ways. So, on a resolution moved by Pandit Sri Jawaharlal Nehru, a simple wheel was substituted. He described the flag as 'a flag of freedom and symbol of freedom'. He pointed out that in the white previously there was the *chakra* which symbolized the common man in India, which symbolized the masses of people, which symbolized their industry. But in considering a simplified revision, minds went to the wheel of the Asokan column. 'That wheel is a symbol of India's ancient culture; it is a symbol of the many things that India had stood for throughout the ages. . . .' The theme of the symbolic significance of the wheel in Indian history was elaborated by others also, and the wheel was described as the Wheel of the Law of Dharma, denoting motion, representing life, symbolizing righteousness, etc. (Vasudeva, 1964; Y. G. Naik, 1957). So here a contemporary symbol, the spinning wheel, associated with the mass of the peasantry, and with Gandhi's simplicist but powerfully appealing mode of life, was converted to the historic symbol, the wheel of Asoka, associated with much more complex religious sentiment, at a deeper level. Though motivated by expediency, the translation gave an increment of symbolic power.

The circumstances of the decision on the symbolism of the Indian

what it means to be black in this country today'. (See for example *New York Times*, 13–19 September 1971; 17 November 1971.) For action in schools see later.

flag appear quite clear. But as with the national flag of the United States, establishing the origin of some other national flags has been a subject of some controversy, often of political significance. This seems to have been the case in Argentina, where the history of the precise colours of the national flag has been open to debate, and where a military circular was issued on the antecedents of the 'national symbols' (no. 635/41; cf. Luis Cánepa, 1943, 1953).

MORAL SIGNIFICANCE OF FLAG COLOURS

Running all through discussion of the symbolism of national flags is the vague but persistent theme that not only the design but also the colours of the particular flag of a country may have more than an accidental significance. It is often held that irrespective of the circumstances of their selection to compose the national flag they represent objects or qualities of significance to the nation, or to mankind more generally. These are always of a positive, morally approved character.* I give only a few examples. The flag of the Republic of Eire has green and orange, to represent the two major religious components of its population, with a band of white, representing peace, in between. The white and gold of the Vatican City are likewise symbolic of peace; here the avoidance of 'strong' colours has led to a breach of the heraldic rule of not ordinarily juxtaposing 'metals' – the white being equivalent to silver. In the flag of Afghanistan the royal colour, red, is stated to symbolize wars fought against aggressors, while the bordering strips of black and green stand for the dark past and the bright future of the country. Such moral overtones of colour symbolism appear especially in the newly-created African states. In the flag of Kenya, which attained independence only after a bitter struggle, black is said to stand for the people, red for their blood, green for their land, and white for unity. In the Dahomey flag, which has a common African colour combination of green, red and yellow, the green stands for palm groves, the yellow is for the northern savannah, and the red represents the struggle for freedom. But in Chad, which has a tricolour with blue not green, the blue stands for agriculture, the yellow for its

* The statistical survey by Sasha Weitman (1971) examines the meanings officially assigned to the major colours occurring in about seventy national flags.

deserts, and red for unity between the regions. Of the Nigerian flag, decided upon after a competition, the designer himself spoke of the green as a symbol of agriculture and the white as the sign of amity and peace. Some of these attributions are of a fairly obviously descriptive kind – red for blood, green for agriculture. Others are more abstract, as red for unity, overlapping with white in this respect. In some of these newer flags the symbolic meaning has been conceived in terms of a combination of colours, such as green and yellow representing the different regions of the country and their juxtaposition, national unity. But while there is a common thread running through many of these colour symbolisms, there is no clear predictive value to be seen in the use of any particular colour.

The arbitrary nature of flag colour symbolism appears even more clearly with national flags of long-standing where usually there is no official interpretation of meaning by colour. Among the many accounts of the origin and development of the national flag of the United States, some severely scholarly, others more popular and a few apocryphal, there are various statements of the positive moral values attaching to this symbol. In one straightforward eulogy: 'The three colours used in our flag, of which we lustily shout our approval when we sing "Columbia's the gem of the ocean – three cheers for the red, white and blue" – mean something. The red signifies valour, the white purity and the blue truth. . . . The flag is the symbol of our national sovereignty and of the union of the states, and the birth, progress and growth of the nation are told upon its folds. There is perhaps no national flag more beautiful, and none other can be so beautiful in the eyes of a true American.'

NATIONAL FLAGS AS SYMBOLS OF STATUS AND POWER

So far the poetic statements, the speeches, the histories of these national symbols all seem to speak the same language – and rather surprisingly, to speak the same language as the sociologists and anthropologists. Carlyle, Durkheim, Sapir, Nehru, Honigman all emphasize the significance of flags as reinforcing solidarity, having power to evoke sentiment and lead to self-sacrificing action. Such moral attitudes evidently persist in contemporary society.

National flags are prominently displayed on national holidays and special occasions of public rejoicing, by ordinary citizens as well as by public offices. In some countries government offices regularly fly the national flag – a useful mark of identification – and as a token of loyalty, some private establishments may also fly the flag. In the United States such enthusiastic use of the national flag is common. The *Chicago Tribune*, a newspaper long noted for its strident Americanism (it describes itself as 'The American Paper for Americans') bears the device of a United States flag waving (now in colour) over its headline, on every issue. Every day, for nearly a decade this newspaper published a photograph of 'Today's Flag' flying outside a commercial office or private residence. Towards the end of 1970 it had been calculated that 3,000 such photographs had so far been published, of 2,300 separate flags, and that the items of print, placed end to end, would be more than 1,000 ft high! This kind of patriotic obsession may have no direct parallel elsewhere, but the attitudes it expresses can be found in many other contexts and countries. The value of a national flag as symbol is evidenced by the discreet use of it in political campaigning in many countries. Its solemn associations are brought home by its use as a shroud for a coffin or bier of a soldier killed in the course of military duty, or as a memorial sign in a military cemetery, or as borne in procession on a national memorial day.

The significance of the flag as a symbol of solidarity and national virtues may be indoctrinated through the educational system. In the United States, Flag Day Assembly and similar patriotic occasions intensify attitudes of respect inculcated by daily pledges of allegiance to the flag. Teachers and athletic coaches may have the obligation specifically laid upon them to instruct their pupils appropriately. (A handbook of the Inter-Suburban Association of a number of schools near Chicago 'tells the coach to instruct players in the proper method of paying respect to the colors' – *Chicago Tribune*, 10 October 1970). Unofficial pressures such as neighbours' gossip or remarks of business colleagues can help to reinforce conformity to the conventional attitudes towards the national symbol.*

But there is another side to the picture. A national flag, as a sym-

* Cf. the *New Yorker* cartoon of a business executive addressing an employee: 'Naturally, X, the company doesn't care whether its employees have little flags on their desks or not. It's purely a voluntary thing. We just wondered why you happen to be the only person here who hasn't got one!' (24 October 1970).

bol of state power, has its composition and internal use in the society controlled by authority. By legal prescription the shape, size, cloth and design of most national flags are controlled. A citizen's error in such detail may be ignored by the state or left to the informal control of public opinion in which some citizens score off others by display of expertise. But there is sometimes an uneasy balance between official authority and private initiative in the public display of national flags. When a foreign dignitary arrives in the more democratic countries the display of flags is left primarily to the spontaneous feelings of the citizens, over and above the official decking of buildings. The quantity of flags shown is some measure of the popular respect and support the visitor enjoys. (When the Emperor Hirohito visited the Netherlands during his world tour the lack of flags in display was remarked upon in the press, as indicative of the resentment still felt by many Dutch people against the war conduct of the Japanese – *New York Times*, 9 October 1971.) Under a dictatorship, however, explicit or implicit orders for display of national flags means that the amount of display is a direct reflection of the official view of the occasion.

Externally, display of a national flag on vessels of war, on aircraft of a national airline, on embassies and other representative buildings, symbolizes the status of the country concerned. Hence the 'protocol' involved in the use of national flags at the United Nations. (When the People's Republic of China became a member of the United Nations great care was taken to obtain the correct placing of the flag at the front of the U.N. building – after ascertaining the government's wishes it was inserted at C (for China) and not at P.) This external status is linked with power, in that the presence of the flag symbol implies a direct possibility of action to enforce compliance with the policy of the state concerned. Internationally, a national flag can be used as a warning of armed force to follow, and in effect as a substitute for armed force. But a national flag may have a rather different function in symbolizing rights conceded by international convention, without reference to powers of enforcement. The 'flags of convenience' adopted by some shipping lines are legal symbols, internationally recognized as entitling the carrier, if properly endowed, to very definite rights and privileges pertaining to the country whose flag is carried, irrespective of the national status of the owner of the vessels. Countries such as Liberia and Panama, who are prepared to register vessels under their jurisdiction but who are less concerned than many other countries about regulation of crew wages and employment conditions, standards of seaworthiness and taxation levels, present operating advantage to shipping companies which some regard as more than offsetting protection from their own national flag. The system has been shown to have advantages too at a national level for a country such as the United States, which wishes for strategic reasons to keep in being a considerable merchant fleet but finds difficulty in manning it on American standards.*

Such a device of transfer of status involves much more than merely flying an appropriate national flag; complex legal instruments are necessary to secure and implement the status which the flag symbol indicates. In other conditions the use of a national flag may be a more formal device to indicate not so much temporary transfer of sovereignty as a claim to privilege or an avoidance of responsibility, with the implied consent of the countries concerned. In the field of international relations some national vessels engaged on United Nations business, as F.A.O. fishing research vessels, may fly a United Nations flag in addition to or as substitute for their own flag. A practice, which has as much an element of disclaimer as of claim in it, is that reported of submarines in the Adriatic manned by Chinese crews but flying the Albanian flag – though Albania was not known to possess submarines.

In these examples the national flag is a symbol of the political entity, and it is displayed officially as a symbol of the status, often also of the power, of the nation concerned. By implication too it is expected that the symbol will receive the respect ordinarily paid to more substantial tokens of the nation's strength. So, the expression 'showing the flag', even if metaphorical, means staking a claim to national interest. So when a Soviet ship opened a passenger run between South-East Asia and Australia, this new development was interpreted by foreign diplomats as a matter of Russian policy – 'another Russian step to show her flag in a new area'. When the United States acquired a naval base on Bahrain this was treated as

* For brief discussion of economic and political questions raised by 'flags of convenience', see Roger Eglin, *Observer*, 7 March 1971; Michael Baily, *Times*, 3 June 1972. Official disregard of a 'flag of convenience' by Cuba was reported in tension with the United States (*New York Times*, 19 December 1971).

'a flag-showing operation to manifest United States interests in the area'. That a physical flag was flown in such circumstances was almost irrelevant; in each case the political implications of the physical operations were indicated by the verbal use of the symbol of the flag. So when the President or Prime Minister of a country makes an official visit abroad he may be said to be 'showing the flag' merely by advancing his country's interests.

STATUS SYMBOLS IN REVERSE

But the symbolism of national flags also operates in reverse. If the flag represents its country's interests, it can be used as a concrete instrument of protest against these interests or against conduct related to them. The symbolic significance of the national flag is dramatically demonstrated by treatment in which it is physically maltreated and defiled. When in mid-1970 the British Conservative government moved towards the sale of arms to South Africa, amid the many protests from the Commonwealth was one from Malaysian students in Kuala Lumpur. The British union flag was laid down in a street and a motor-car forced to drive over it; the flag was later burnt, together with an effigy of the British Prime Minister. When President Nixon announced that he was sending American combat troops into Cambodia, demonstrations against the United States in many foreign cities included the burning of the Stars and Stripes. A leftist Filipino demonstration against the government of President Marcos was also against the influence of the United States in the Philippines, and ended by burning an American flag. Later in 1970 the United States Embassy in Sierra Leone was stoned and the American flag ripped from its staff, in a demonstration against the alleged involvement of a member of the embassy unit in a plot to overthrow the Sierra Leone government. In September 1971 militant Jewish youths in protest against the Soviet Union's refusal to let Jews migrate to Israel stole a Soviet flag from an international display, diverting police by burning a Soviet plastic flag a short distance away. In Amsterdam Dutch demonstrators burned Japanese paper flags in protest against the visit of the Emperor Hirohito. In New York Nationalist Chinese burned a Chinese People's Republic flag in front of the hotel of the first communist delegation from

Peking to the United Nations. (For some details see: *Times*, 24 July 1970; *New York Times*, 25 May 1970; 15 September 1971; *Time Magazine*, 18 May 1970; *Chicago Tribune*, 16 October 1970.) The major point about such demonstrations is that while they show resentment against a national power, they substitute action against the symbol for action against more integral constituents of the nation such as the person of its citizens. So, an American report on the Filipino incident of burning the Stars and Stripes described the demonstration as 'noisy but peaceful' since no one was assaulted. It is noteworthy that such incidents have now come to be accepted as part of the modern way of life by the powers whose flag symbols are maltreated. Assuming that formal diplomatic protest is lodged, there nevertheless seems to be tacit recognition that in the prevailing climate of criticism of economic and political power as exercised by the larger nations, these had better tolerate abuse of their symbols than threaten reprisals. In this sense the symbol is treated as a surrogate, on which moral and physical force can be allowed to spend itself with minimal harm.*

FLAGS IN DECORATION AND DESECRATION

The symbolism of national flags is not completely covered by the conventional treatment of essayists, politicians and sociologists. It is not correct that in all cases a national flag is reverenced by its citizens, and intensifies their solidarity. There are discordant notes. Not only do Malaysians run automobiles over the Union Jack or

* But the formal destruction of a flag of political significance has more gravity. Historically, flags captured from an enemy in battle have been preserved as trophies – which in itself indicated a kind of respect for the symbols so acquired. But in the Jacobite struggle against the English Hanoverian kings, after the battle of Culloden, which effectively ended the Highland resistance in 1746, the rebel standards captured were treated with ignominy. They were carried by the chief hangman of Edinburgh and by chimneysweeps, with an escort, and laid in the dust, while a proclamation was read explaining why they were to be burnt by the public hangman. Each standard was then held over the flames, while the senior herald named the Scottish clan that had marched behind it to battle. This was deliberate disrespect, with symbolic modes of contempt: trailing in the dust; handling by executioners and men associated with black soot; consumption by fire. Yet when standards were preserved in what might seem superficially to be analogous conditions of disrespect, the interpretation was very different. The standards of the Appin Stewarts and of Clan Chattan were torn from their poles by clan members, who wrapped them round their bodies, ran from the battlefield and saved them. While intentional contact with dirt and fire was regarded as degrading to the symbols, contact with sweaty human bodies was regarded as meritorious, or at least as not defiling (see John Prebble, *Culloden*, Pelican, 1967, 93, 99, 190–1).

Filipinos burn the Stars and Stripes – some British citizens use the image of their national flag on their shopping bags, and some United States citizens have worn images of their own flag on their trousers. Such acts imply lack of reverence, and some of them have indubitably provoked dissension rather than solidarity among citizens. Has something gone wrong with the argument? If the flag is a rallying point for the unity of all members of the society, how is it there can be internal as well as external maltreatment of it? Clearly the stock Durkheimian view can only be regarded as a statement of a majority position or a general tendency; the image of society as something that is revered, with symbols respected and held sacred, is incomplete. I would suggest indeed that while the national flag is generally recognized as the symbol of the society, the sentiment postulated towards the symbol may be more complex and have a much wider range of variation than the Durkheimian position allows.

There can be variation in intensity of appreciation of such national symbols. In both Britain and the United States, for instance, there are opinions which are highly critical of the state of the society, and which protest against what they regard as its oppressive character. But on the whole in the British scene there has been much less focus on the national flag as an instrument of protest. In Britain the national flag as symbol of the society is held in looser association than in the United States. I would argue that one of the mechanisms by which the United States authorities have helped to identify symbol and society very closely, the enactment of laws which set out in detail how the national flag should be treated and how offenders should be punished, has to some extent backfired. In Britain an alternative symbol, the Monarchy, has been available to take some of the pressure of protest off the flag.

In Britain until recently the Union Jack was used in sober fashion by ordinary citizens, for holiday and memorial display and occasional discreet commercial advertisement. The commercial aspect has continued, as when one of our major airlines has displayed the flag on books of matches, ashtrays and cushions. The Apple and Pear Development Council illustrate the union flag in colour on paper bags to hold fruit, with the encouraging injunction 'Pick an English pear'. In recent years, with the development of freer English fashion and the influence of Carnaby Street, the Union Jack has been seen not only on shopping bags but also on some items of clothing. In mid-1970 newspapers had illustrations of exuberant women with dresses, hats and umbrellas made from Union Jacks cheering a Protestant parade in Belfast; and of hostesses for a world cycling championship in Leicester with the design of the Union Jack on the fronts of their skirts and their umbrellas. (See *The Times*, 14 July 1970; 7 August 1970.) In none of these cases was the use of the national symbol regarded as an offence against the law, though it might have been classed as an offence against taste – vulgar but not illegal.

In the United States the situation has been very different. Towards the end of the nineteenth century the Daughters of the American Revolution advocated a law providing penalties for mutilation, commercial or political use of the national flag, and many states passed such laws. Most states also decreed that the flag should be displayed at all schoolhouses while school was in session and that pupils should pledge allegiance to the flag. Some states also prohibited the display of any red or black flag along with the national flag in any procession or public hall. The Congress of the United States was slower to act, but in 1942 a federal flag code was enacted, becoming public law no. 623. This specified in great detail how the national flag was to be displayed and respected in a variety of circumstances. (*Inter alia*, it was clear that the national flag should never be used on a receptacle, as the Union Jack has been used on British shopping bags.) By a new flag law, which received the presidential signature in 1968, a substantial fine or imprisonment for a year, or both, could be applied for publicly mutilating, defacing, defiling, burning or trampling the national flag. In this way the American national flag has been treated as a sacred symbol much more overtly than has the British national flag.

When the flag of another country is insulted the act is usually brief and violent – trampling, tearing or burning being the most common methods of showing disapproval. Similar methods may be used by protesters who are citizens of the country concerned. When the independence of Bangladesh was being first proclaimed people at a mass rally in (then) East Pakistan burned the Pakistan flag as a symbol of their attitude. In Israel, a group of ultra-Orthodox Jews, Neturei Karta, 'Guardians of the Gate', are reported to hate the

Zionist state, to refuse to carry identity cards issued by the government, and to burn Israeli flags. In the United States in the spring of 1970 a 17-year-old schoolgirl was sentenced to six months in jail in Massachusetts for burning an American flag in a high-school protest; on appeal she was given a lecture on patriotism by the judge and did penance by carrying a large American flag on a three-mile march through the streets of Cambridge. Later in the year two people were arrested for burning an American flag outside a hotel where Vice-President Agnew was making a speech. In riots in Georgia, a peaceful parade culminated in the burning of the Georgia state flag torn from the city hall staff, and of an American flag taken from a nearby funeral home (*New York Post*, 22 September 1971; *New York Times*, 29 May 1971; 3 April 1970; 13 May 1970; *Chicago Tribune*, 7 October 1970; *Time Magazine*, 30 November 1970). But internal protest in the United States has sometimes taken more personal and more subtle forms. Various cases have been reported in the Press over the last few years of men arrested, charged or penalized for using the American flag on their clothing or in other idiosyncratic ways. One wore the flag over his shoulders, another wore a shirt patterned like the flag, another had an American flag upside down on the right leg of his trousers, and still another had a flag sewn to his trouser-seat. Others again were charged with 'contemptuous display' because they had painted their automobiles with stars and stripes of appropriate colour.

On the other hand, while various federal and state laws can be invoked against 'defilement' or 'desecration' of the national flag, it has not always been clear exactly what those terms mean, and whether they can always be applied with certainty to some specific cases. When characters in the anti-Establishment rock musical 'Hair' played with an American national flag on stage, a New York State law official who investigated held that while the conduct of the actors was at times irreverent, there was no violation of the law. (This opinion was hotly contested by the president of the U.S. Flag Foundation, a body formed in 1889 for the purpose of honouring the American flag and preserving it from desecration.) An American magazine once asked the question: 'Does it desecrate the American flag to sit on it?' The answer, in mock solemnity, was – not presumably when the sitter is a famous film-star. This problem arose because some young men, charged in court with having had a picnic on the American flag, defended themselves by producing a photograph of the actress clad rather scantily in some arrangement of the Stars and Stripes. The judge, inquiring rhetorically: 'Is she glamourizing the flag or desecrating it?', dismissed the case. A New York City Transit Authority patrolman, who had been charged with wearing an unauthorized emblem on his uniform, was found not guilty on the grounds that this was done out of patriotism, and that President Nixon himself had supported similar action in another case, writing: 'We need to encourage Americans in pride of country'. From such incidents it may be inferred that associating the national flag with the person in unorthodox ways may be interpreted as decoration or desecration depending on what may be thought as to be the wearer's motivation.* In this context it is significant that the action under scrutiny had a public character – wearing or using the symbol so that it could be seen generally. Whether for patriotic decoration or for protest, the symbol is expressly utilized as a medium of communication of an attitude towards the society it represents.

Other protest methods of handling national flags may be even more open to ambiguity in that it may be hard to say whether they are acts of desecration or respectful usage to express personal views. In the 'hard hat backlash' of May 1970 in New York, when massed building-construction workers demonstrated with Stars and Stripes against the frequent anti-war demonstrations, there was no doubt: they were carrying the national flag in defence of what they regarded as the national interest. The national flag painted on their construction helmets was taken as positive criticism and fully permissible (*New York Times*, 16, 21 and 25 May 1970; *Time Magazine*, 25 May 1970; 1 June 1970). But how about the man who flew the American flag upside down and at half-staff in front of his house, with the flagpole draped in black, in protest against the conviction of an Army lieutenant for murder of civilians in Vietnam? The protester's argument was that such a conviction was not in the best national interest; it was 'killing our flag'. The local police did not accept this attitude,

* For detail, see *Honolulu Star-Bulletin*, 2 September 1968; *New York Times*, 1 February 1970; 24 and 25 February 1970; 16 April 1970; *Chicago Tribune*, 3 December 1970; *Ithaca Journal*, 14 May 1970; *Time Magazine*, 2 November 1970; *The Times*, 25 March 1971.

saying: 'You can't put the flag that way; you're not in distress.' There is also the case of an American housewife who flew the national flag upside down to protest against the involvement of the country in the Vietnam war, and who was arrested and charged with violating a state law which prohibited showing 'contempt, either by word or act, upon the flag'. The judge held that an act of turning a flag upside down did not indicate a dishonourment or defilement of the flag, and that what was being expressed as a personal opinion of distress was a legitimate use of the flag. Yet when a group of high school students petitioned their authorities to allow the school American flag to be lowered to half-staff as a token of mourning for the notorious shooting of Kent State University students, the judge in this case refused the request. His judgement was that to fly the national flag at half-staff was to commemorate the death of a personage of national or state standing or of a contributor to the local community service. It should not be so flown to involve 'an expression of a political concept' (see *New York Times*, 18 March 1970; 2 June 1970; *Chicago Tribune*, 31 March 1971). On the other hand, a group of demonstrators who flew the United States flag upside down from the head of the Statue of Liberty for two days, as a distress signal against the Vietnam war, were allowed to leave with impunity in compliance with a court order for their eviction (*Time Magazine*, 4 January 1972).

Why these differences of treatment? To some extent they were due to differences in state law, and in judicial interpretation. But broadly they indicate that a symbol is essentially not an object but a relationship; that with acceptance of the object goes also acceptance of notions of its 'normal' or 'proper' use. Hanging out or waving – even wearing – of a national flag symbol in normal 'correct' position is a socially acceptable act, irrespective of whether the motivation that inspires it is loyalty and respect or a scornful concession to popular opinion. But to put the symbol in an unusual context causes confusion, and focuses attention on motivation. Yet the situation is ambiguous because most of the evidence about motivation often comes only from the act of flag display itself. Hence the variation in judicial and other public interpretations of 'contempt' towards the symbol – leaving aside the debatable issue of the right of 'free speech' which may be involved in personal use of a national flag. The 'distress issue is especially interesting. The well-known conventional way of expressing 'distress' at sea is to fly a flag upside down. In the language of flag signals the effect is to link disturbance in the order of the symbol with disturbance in the order of the vessel concerned. But the signal refers to disturbance in the physical order – severe damage to structure or equipment – or possibly to such disturbance in the social order as to hamper the functioning of the physical order – sickness or death of crew, mutiny. Any idea of attitude of mind of the signaller is inferential, and on the whole irrelevant to the immediate purpose. But the display of a national flag upside down by an individual citizen belongs to a different order of communication: it refers primarily to his attitude of mind, and not to physical conditions. Hence the analogy claimed is not exact, and the authorities have some basis for intervention on this ground, quite apart from the question of the right of the citizen to use a national symbol on a personal basis.*

A parallel problem of ambiguity arises when the national flag is taken as a basis for modification in pattern or colour. Some of these modifications have been patently of a political order. In mid-1970 a man in upstate New York was sentenced to ten days in jail on a charge of defiling the American flag; he had hung a replica of the flag, with a 'peace' symbol in the blue field, from his front porch. On the other hand, a policeman arrested a university student of Dayton, Ohio, with a United States flag bearing green 'ecology' stripes instead of the normal blue, and charged him with desecrating the flag. When other students complained the head police official (described by one of his aides as 'unbelievably flexible') said 'we were wrong' and returned the banner. (*Post Standard*, Syracuse, 3 June 1970; *Newsweek*, 9 November 1970.) Modifications in the name of art have caused even more difficulty. A painting 'Three Flags' by Jasper Johns in 1958, a simple superimposition of Stars and Stripes, has apparently caused no concern, and so also with wall

* Note that the issue tends to be affected by the design of the flag. British people not uncommonly fly the Union Jack upside down out of ignorance on occasions of public rejoicing, since broad and narrow white stripes are not easily distinguished. But from the position of the stars it is very clear when the United States flag is flown the wrong way up. (Yet the Town Council of Boston, England, proudly displayed an American flag for nine years, presented by an American television company and seen by an estimated 5,000 American tourists, which had white stars on a red, not a blue ground, without its being discovered as an error – *New York Times*, 29 November 1970.)

rugs depicting the American flag with more stripes and fewer stars. But a New York art dealer who exhibited works of art including a phallic symbol wrapped in the American flag was convicted of violating a state law against flag desecration and sentenced to sixty days in jail or $500 fine. The State Court of Appeals upheld this conviction, ruling that the right of free speech did not permit the use of the American flag in 'dishonourable' ways as a form of protest. This particular construction was deemed 'insulting', and several artists who displayed work in a 'People's Flag Show' in support of the dealer were arrested and charged with desecrating the flag on their own account (see *New Yorker*, 14 May 1970; *New York Times*, 19 February, 10 April and 15 November 1970). The majority judicial view on appeal was that while the art dealer may have had a 'sincere ideological' point of view he should have found other ways to express it, and whether he thought so or not, 'a reasonable man' would consider the wrapping of a phallic symbol with the flag an act of dishonour. Yet a minority dissenting opinion, that of the Chief Judge, held that the challenged 'constructions' were in effect only political cartoons, and that they had been singled out for prosecution only because of their political message.

This political element seems to be the nub of the issue in such cases of alleged desecration of the flag in the American scene. The possibility of aesthetic values, personal sentiment, freedom of speech are all admitted, but the flag is not regarded as the appropriate symbol for expressing them if its use can be given a political interpretation which runs counter to established norms. This is one of the dilemmas of democracy: the national flag is a symbol for the society; but it is a symbol for the society in its political as well as its cultural dimension. As such, it can serve as a focus for negative as well as positive sentiment for the political actions of the society. So a question of practical import is: how far can the established organs of society tolerate private idiosyncratic use of national symbols such as the flag to promote ideas which run counter to immediate national policy as expressed by the governing authorities?* In the con-

* This issue was raised in another form in December 1971 by a decision of Newark, New Jersey Board of Education to permit the hanging of the 'Black liberation flag' of red, black and green (cf., above) in every school classroom containing a majority of black students, for example in all but a very few schools. The decision seemed legal, but was strongly resisted by local White citizens and by responsible Black authorities as divisive in nature, likely to arouse

servative view, if flag as symbol represents society, it should express consensus, not dissent.

FLAG AS SYMBOL OF DISSENT

I can now return at a more theoretical level to the incident described at the beginning of this chapter, where the American flag was used to introduce a parody of a courthouse scene. The flag here was not desecrated – it was carried solemnly in procession, and it was the 'victim's' chair that was burned. But the flag was not displayed as a symbols of solidarity, focusing the sentiments of participants and observers in loyalty towards their society. It was used as the representative sign of one of the basic institutions of the society, and so as a symbol of the society itself. But it was used as part of a criticism of the society, as a symbol to mobilize protest against what were regarded by the participants as the injustices of their society. It was used in apparent respect, but in a context of irony which inverted its political meaning. On the other hand, while some of the potential audience seemed impressed, others ignored the proceedings. They reacted neither favourably towards the demonstration which used the flag in protest, nor unfavourably to challenge this unorthodox, critical use of the national symbol. They behaved as a kind of non-Durkheimian body, uninfluenced by the use made of one of their most prestigious national symbols.

From the data I have presented, drawn from the raw noted observation of many scattered instances and not from the introspection of sociologists, it is clear that there are no monolithic sentiments towards flags as national symbols in a modern politically differentiated society. Attitudes towards the symbol can be very flexible, within the structure of authority as well as in the general public body. Durkheim's idea of the essential unity of society and symbol is meaningful only at a very general level of abstraction. I have taken

other partisan activity. The sponsor of the resolution argued that it would stimulate Black consciousness and pride without lessening allegiance to the American flag; but critics held that it was an unwarranted introduction of political symbolism into the educational system. (*New York Times*, 2, 3 and 5 December 1971; *Time Magazine*, 13 December 1971). The issue was high-lighted by an earlier attempt in a Florida school to use a Confederate battle flag pattern as a school banner (*New York Times*, 14 October 1971) which outside observers saw as equally subversive.

the United States flag as a prime example because superficially in the overt sacralization of its national symbol that country has gone further than many others, and so invited more direct challenge by those of its citizens who wished to protest. The United States position in this respect may be a reflection of several circumstances: the initial revolutionary character of the society; its development by federation of a large number of discrete units; and its rapid absorption of many immigrants from diverse linguistic, cultural and national sources. All this would make sense of concentration on some easily identifiable symbols of national unity, and protection of them from abuse. The United States flag has been described as 'a protective symbol' but it has also needed protection.

The Durkheimian type of proposition about national flag as focus for sentiment about society, with sacred character, is valid to only a limited degree. The 'sentiment' has usually been interpreted as positive, involving consensus. But in writing about Australian aboriginal society, with totem as 'flag of the clan', Durkheim omitted the political dimension. For totemic belief and behaviour the assumption of positive sentiment and consensus was reasonable, though not unchallengeable. But to cite as a parallel the national flag, or flag of a military unit, was to ignore the significance of the power component. A national flag of a modern state is an *officially defined symbol*, not simply a symbol of informal public choice or traditional development. As such, its 'sacredness' is an officially imputed quality. Hence 'desecration' becomes a legal matter, to be judged in the light of official pronouncements, either codified or expressed in the common law.

What is at stake in most of these cases of unorthodox use of a national flag is the issue of legitimacy. The national symbol is maltreated as an instrument of protest against authority, to deny the legitimacy of what that authority has done. It may express dissent from a single type of action – such as involvement in overseas conflict – or it may represent basic disagreement with the structure and ideology of the society as at present constituted. But in essence the national symbol is manipulated to assert moral value over existing power value. (That some of the issues may have been misconceived is beside the point.)

Such critical use of national flags as symbols bears also upon the

Durkheimian concept of the sacred. Durkheim has argued that sacred things evoke respect, and are separated from profane things by an opposition which may become antagonism. This division of the world into two domains, as Durkheim has put it, has been shown to be inadequate. In an analysis of Australian aboriginal concepts, W. E. H. Stanner has shown (1967, 217–40) that a concept of an intermediate sphere is needed, the 'mundane', the affairs of the everyday world in which the sacred is not regarded as antagonistic but ignored. But if Durkheim's sphere of the profane needs weakening at one side it needs strengthening at the other. In the use of national flags as symbols, the sphere of the profane is shown in the United States by the interdicted areas of display – commercial advertisement or political ideology. The sphere of the mundane (in Stanner's terms) is shown in Britain by the use of the Union Jack on dresses or umbrellas – they treat the flag neither with reverence nor despite. But the intentional destruction of his national flag by a protester is profaning it in a more intensified way than Durkheim meant. To Durkheim, the sacred thing was *par excellence* that which the profane should not touch and cannot touch with impunity. It is the profane which tends to be punished or damaged by the contact – as a person who touches a sacred relic may be stricken by blindness. But when a Union Jack or a Stars and Stripes is burned, it is the flag not the protester who receives the damage; the sacred is desacralized. And it is the profane, not the sacred, which carries the moral value charge. This is very different from what Durkheim noted as introducing the sacred temporarily to the profane as a means of stimulating its powers – as throwing stones into a sacred pool to rouse the immanent powers or whipping a sacred image to wake it up to perform its duty. The national flag is not symbolically stimulated, not symbolically ignored, not symbolically polluted, but symbolically violated. The sacred representation is not just contaminated by careless contact with non-sacred things; it is actively treated in symbolic fashion as a counter-instrument to what it represents. In the general ritual field the nearest analogy to such symbolism of destructive behaviour is the Black Mass, the significance of which is the inversion of customary procedures with the sacred. So also with the burning of national flags by political dissidents; the flag stands for the political authority of the Establishment, and its destruction has definite symbolic value, of integrating effect for the group concerned.*

Durkheim's use of the term profane incorporated two notions, that of common or secular, and that of defiling or contaminating. But the concept includes also the notion of violating, in contrast to the inviolate. I do not propose another category of phenomena to describe this field of action, but I think it deserves attention. In essence it is an inversion of the sacred, using the symbol in a ritual manner, but in a contrary sense to normal usage, and attaching antithetical values to the referent, in a positive moral way. Durkheim and most other commentators have seen the significance of national flags as symbols in serving as rallying points for social solidarity, as foci and even as generators of sentiments of a positive kind. But a symbol is a double-edged instrument. When as is the case with national flags, it is associated with a structure of power and authority, it becomes an officially defined representation, with the possibility of dissent from the values it is intended to convey. The symbol still stands for the society, or for the controlling power in society, but the 'sentiment' component is diversified, and the controlling power may take steps to try and correct this accordingly. So a society does not merely choose its symbols; it also may choose the level of reaction it will endure against them. This operation of a feed-back principle indicates a complexity in behaviour towards flag symbols which I have not seen examined hitherto in systematic analysis.

* It has been reported (*New York Review of Books*, 22 April 1971) that 'underground' groups in the United States may start their clandestine meetings by burning the American flag, with powerful emotional reaction.

Chapter 11

SYMBOLISM IN GIVING AND GETTING

As we walked down one evening from a little Umbrian hill town to the local railway station my wife gathered some wild-flowers, of which she is very fond. While we waited at the station we passed the time of day with the station master's wife, who was tending her garden, and praised her flowers. Just before the train arrived she came up and smilingly presented my wife with a bunch – unusual behaviour to a couple of complete strangers, passing tourists. As an act of courtesy, a pure gift, it touched us deeply. How far was it a symbolic act?

In ordinary social and economic life in industrial society there is a marked disjunction between two major types of behaviour: that of market operations, of buying and selling; and that of presentation, of making gift of goods or services. These are sharply opposed, structurally, materially and morally. A market sale is a two-way transaction, a gift is one-way. A market sale is for business, impersonal, hoping for profit, competitive, contractual; a gift is friendly, personal, not seeking profit, contributory, free. In both spheres one seeks to hand over what is judged appropriate by the other party. But in the market the giver reckons the acceptable by its reciprocation; in the gift he reckons it by the recipient's satisfaction. In the market sphere behaviour is seen as sensible and careful with resources, while gifts are apt to be thought emotionally dictated and wasteful. In the social sphere outside the market, the market behaviour is often regarded as greedy, sordid; while gift-making is held to be generous and is highly praised. These are the conventional stereotypes.

Yet as anthropologists and sociologists have realized since the work of Thurnwald, Malinowski and Mauss about fifty years ago, the opposition between these two spheres of transaction is by no means so clear-cut. Empirically, in market operations buyer and seller do not always try to exact the last shred of profit. They may use definitely personal trading links, traditionally of long-standing in some businesses. Even the conventions of haggling may involve courtesies of an elaborate social order.* In applying provisions of a contract strong views often exist as to what is ethical, with criticism for a man who is 'too sharp' in taking advantage of the law, and praise for one who is 'fair-minded'. Conversely, the implications of a gift are rarely exhausted by a single transfer; the notion of reciprocity is often near the surface. If there is little calculation of profit to be got from exchange of gifts there is much of estimation of equivalences. Malinowski demonstrated from analysis of the Trobriand *kula* how the elaborate ritualized gifts of these Melanesian valuables were based on a firm code of obligation to make counter-gifts of at least equal value. And he acknowledged a minor criticism from Marcel Mauss, who pointed out that even what Malinowski had called the 'pure gift' from Trobriand husband to his wife was in effect a return for sexual and other domestic services. In more general context Malinowski was fond of asserting that 'reciprocity is the basis of social organization'. Stimulated by such findings, Mauss raised discussion of the gift to a more abstract plane by formulating three neat rules of obligation: the obligation to give; the obligation to receive; and the obligation to repay. Many others, including Karl Polanyi, Barry Schwartz, Marshall Sahlins, Michel Panoff, as well as myself, have taken up these themes and showed how in societies lacking overt market institutions, customs of gift-exchange have served to facilitate transfer of goods and services, as well as to symbolize social relations.†

Identification of relevant process has been carried beyond the traditional field of the primitive. Classical societies of Greece, Rome, India have been shown to have recognized the implications of the gift. As Mauss quoted the *Edda* to the effect that a gift always looks for recompense, so Peter Blau cited Aristotle to the effect that all men or

* See for example the account by T. F. Mitchell (1957) of the language of buying and selling in Cyrenaican shops and markets.

† For a recent study of ceremonial exchange among New Guinea 'big-men' see A. Strathern, 1971.

most men wish what is noble but choose what is profitable; and while it is noble to render a service not with an eye to receiving one in return, it is profitable to receive one (Blau, 1964, 88). It was suggested by Mauss but demonstrated by M. I. Finley (1962, *passim*) that antiquity indeed knew a period when gift-exchange was the dominant mode of transaction. In modern times it has often been pointed out that the tradition of 'one good turn deserves another' underlies many of our social institutions, from sending of Christmas cards to wedding invitations. Manning Nash has even gone so far as to say that middle-class social life in the United States approximates to the reciprocal-exchange systems of the Melanesian archipelago; that among families of equal status, dinner invitations in number and quality have all the essentials of exchange equivalents; and that if the balance gets too badly disturbed there may be some show of aggression or the invitations may cease (Nash, 1966, 31).

In an even broader approach George Homans and Peter Blau have sought to show, not just that giving is a part of exchange but that the structure of social relations in areas right outside the market field is an exchange structure. Homans has seen social behaviour as an economy, with interaction between persons as an exchange of non-material as well as material goods, and a pay-off in terms of cost and reward. Blau is much more concerned with the polity of social life, the status and power differentials which are the object of reciprocal social behaviour. (Cf. Ehrmann, 1970, for a striking analysis in this field.)

In all this the theory of the gift has been brought into line with the theory of market exchange. The gift relationship appears as a kind of market relationship, in that a kind of cost-benefit analysis applies but in different operational channels – less open to alternative offering, a minimum of haggling, and an almost explicit admission of intangible, non-material elements into the exchange situation. From different angles, both Mauss and Homans have indicated this. Mauss has stated (1925, 34) that the market is a human phenomenon familiar to every known society. Primitive societies do not lack the 'economic market' – though their exchange patterns are different from ours. And Homans has argued that his theory of social interaction as exchange is quite compatible with 'the special conditions of exchange that economics chooses to confine itself to' (1961, 79). He has said in his charmingly blunt style that he is out to rehabilitate the 'economic man', and that by broadening the range of values of 'economic man' he gets a greater realism into his propositions; that the new economic man is just 'plain man'.

In the terms of such a theoretical approach the gift of flowers to my wife, which I mentioned earlier, can be regarded as not just a simple expression of goodwill to a stranger, but as an item in an on-going series of social exchanges. My wife and I made the effort to initiate a social contact. We used the occasion for a mild exercise in Italian; and we diverted ourselves during the wait for a train – in a very minor way we obtained social benefit from the encounter. But so also did the station master's wife – she had momentary relief from the fatigue of gardening; a fleeting acquaintance with the world outside to give food for gossip; and praise of her flowers to support her self-esteem. Her present of a bunch of flowers could be seen then as not just a courtesy but also as an acknowledgement of social service. One can even introduce a principle of balanced opposition into the analysis – her gift of garden flowers was the response of culture and nurture to nature and casual exploitation.

Yet while one may have much sympathy with this type of interpretation the monolithic exchange theory seems inadequate. One need not accept the postulate of Karl Polanyi and George Dalton, that the distinction between market behaviour and gift or gift-exchange behaviour is so radical that ordinary concepts of economics are useless in interpretation of 'primitive' economic systems (cf. Firth, 1972). But the patterned differences between market process and the passage of gifts are considerable. Among the criteria generally involved are: a wider field of alternatives in choice in market relations; much less personalized ties as a rule in buying and selling than in gift; a different range of sanctions for reciprocity, with much more specific legal sanctions in the market;* and much more closely specified equivalents in market exchange.

* Legal sanctions have not necessarily been absent from the field of the gift. In Britain formerly it was an implied condition that the gift of an engagement ring was returnable in the event of the marriage not taking place, unless it was the man himself, the giver, who refused to marry. By an Act of January 1971, however, gifts made to each other by engaged persons will normally be returnable only if they were made on the specific assumption that there would be a marriage. A purely personal present such as an engagement ring is therefore not recoverable – though conventional wedding presents are, since they are thought of as made on the condition that the wedding takes place (see *The Times*, 6 June 1970).

CONCEPT OF THE GIFT

The notion of the gift is complex, in several ways. The basic element of a gift is an outgoing from the self, but this implies an input to another. In judging the implications of a gift then, the effect upon the other has to be taken in conjunction with the effect upon the self. So, as F. G. Bailey and others have emphasized (Bailey, 1971, 23–4) all gifts, like all exchanges, have both competitive and co-operative elements. A gift commonly involves the transfer of a material object, or the performance of a service over time which involves the displacement of material objects. But it is also commonly regarded as implying some immaterial quality, of positive sentiment, of goodwill. In many conditions the material good or service is regarded as not only the token but as even the measure of the sentiment. Gifts are often judged not primarily as a contribution to resources, but as an index to the attitude of the giver. In this sense that which is seen, the gift, is a symbol of what is unseen, the concepts and emotions of the giver. But it may not be a reflection of a simple state: the giver may feel he is acting under pressure and react later accordingly; he may be using the gift as a 'sprat to catch a mackerel', to benefit by a larger counter-gift; he may be focusing on the social rather than on the material aspects of the transfer and looking to intangible benefits; he may be concerned with his own reputation and only marginally with the recipient; he may envisage his gift primarily as a statement of a moral position. The donor may even see the gift as just an expression of himself in a general benefactor role. Max Beerbohm's remark that mankind is divisible into two great classes, hosts and guests, might be translated into terms of donors and recipients, and be regarded as valid in some people's conceptualization.

By definition a gift is freely made. Any notion of duress is alien to the concept. As Blackstone put it in his *Commentaries* 200 years ago: 'gifts are always gratuitous; grants are upon some consideration or equivalent'. A gift is a voluntary, non-contractual transfer of property without any valuable consideration – in particular, without any material equivalent being stipulated.

Each of these criteria, however, is capable of further interpretation. The notion of gratuitous transfer may be used as a disguise for what is in effect a contributory factor in an exchange. Examples of such eccentric so-called 'gifts' are the extra merchandise offered to housewives when they buy So-and-so's soap or cereal. Premiums of this kind have now become a vital part of the market philosophy in such fields, and in economic terms have considerable aggregate value – an annual value of £200 million in Britain alone in the last few years has been given as an estimate.* According to market research findings – not necessarily the last word on the subject – the operative word which attracts the housewife, the only word which advertisers find really matters, is the word 'free' and its equivalents. A well-known airline has enticed its customers with: 'Begin your trip to Hawaii aboard a . . . Fan-Jet. There are orchids on every tray; complimentary champagne and steak dinner. For every lady, a beach bag – a gift from. . . .' Yet obviously in such a purely commercial relationship the notion of such items being 'free' gifts can be taken in only a special, fantasy sense; they are part of the service for which a market price is paid. But it is the notion of gift that is thought to bait the market hook. My argument at this stage is not that a gift is not free, but that the illusion of freedom is used to label a market service as a gift because the idea of voluntaristic transfer is attractive.

But the categorization of voluntariness depends upon the sanctions. A transfer of property without equivalent, if done as a result of force, is not a gift: if done under compulsion from a properly constituted authority it is confiscation; if otherwise it is robbery.† In the case of taxation the sanction of force may be remote, but in any case the one-way transfer can be regarded as being ultimately compensated for by diffuse benefits.

In some of the elaborate series of transactions involved in market relationships the criterion of freedom in the gift is sometimes used as a demarcator. Where in the taxation of business firms, certain kinds of business expenses are deductible but contributions to political campaign funds are not, the business company may sometimes represent such contributions as actual ordinary company expenses for services rendered to the company. Effort is made to avoid the

* John Davis (1972) has estimated the economic magnitude of some other categories of gifts in the United Kingdom.

† For relation between gift, taxation and robbery in nineteenth-century African conditions see Speke, 1912, 107–62.

concept 'gift', which would not be tax deductible, in favour of expense, on grounds that the payment was not voluntary and free because it was necessary to meet a service rendered. (Empirically, it is merely a substitution of long-term putative benefit for short-term calculated benefit, with a wider choice for making the payment in the former case.) In a reverse type of instance, a claim to have made a transfer of property by gift is made in order to divest oneself of responsibility for taxation. In countries such as the United States, where genuine gifts of a charitable order can attract tax deductions of considerable magnitude, a person with a high income has actually been able to save money by giving away property to charity. But questions of interpretation have arisen in respect of the 'family foundations' in which rich men or women endowed members of their families with shares of their business. In the ensuing argument it has emerged that the essential feature of true gift in such cases has been a complete relinquishment of rights in the property, including right of future disposal. In discussions about the establishment of such family foundations as a mode of tax avoidance one study commented that such foundations 'lack the finality which characterizes a true parting with property'. But even with final relinquishment of interest in that which is given on the part of the donor, the framework of society may impose restrictions on freedom of gift, as I show later.

The ordinary concept of gift carries with it an association of positive moral value. This is linked with the notion that together with the transfer of the material object or service an element of the self is also offered – not in the rather crude sense put forward by Mauss, of a detachment of part of the donor's personality, which can injure or be injured thereby, but in the more abstract sense of a commitment of a personal kind to the implications of the action. A gift, a relinquishment of rights to another, is a commitment of the self to the interests of another. It is this emphasis which at first sight receives primary attention in the classics of our literature which enshrine and express so many of our values.

The New Testament is outspoken: 'It is more blessed to give than to receive', wrote St Paul (*Acts*, 20: 35). 'Freely ye have received, freely give', wrote St Matthew (10: 8). And as a high-minded Christian moralist, Wordsworth rammed the lesson home: 'Give all thou canst; High Heaven rejects the lore, of nicely calculated less or more' – in the *Ecclesiastical Sonnets* – 'Tax Not the Royal Saint'. But perhaps the best example of poetic expression in this line comes from a confessed pagan, Walt Whitman: 'Behold I do not give lectures or a little charity – When I give, I give myself' (*Song of Myself*).

But commitment of the self is not necessarily without thought. A text in the Douai Bible (*Ecclesiasticus*, 11) is cautious: 'Do good to the just, and thou shalt find great recompense, and if not by him, assuredly of the Lord.' Even in the New Testament there are differences of emphasis. According to St Luke: 'Give and it shall be given unto you; good measure, pressed down and shaken together and running over shall men give into your bosom' (6: 38). So one should give not because one has received, as St Matthew says, but in order to receive – with forethought of the advantage to be gained, which sounds just like the 'nice calculation' which Wordsworth so scorned! Coleridge put it more coolly: 'We receive but what we give' – from a poem perhaps appropriately named *Dejection*. And in his *Complaints* Edmund Spenser listed the results of lack of calculation more sadly – 'to spend, to give, to want, to be undone'.

There is clearly a paradox in this traditional literary field – giving is good, but getting is not to be ignored. I am not concerned to explain discrepancies in Biblical and other standard texts, but literary wisdom, and presumably popular wisdom too, bear out the anthropological conception of reciprocity attaching to a gift. I examine this aspect in more detail later. But if one distinguishes the symbolic quality of a gift from its pragmatic quality, it is evident that insistence on a pragmatic return may detract from the symbolic value of the transfer. Underneath the paradox about giving and receiving, then, may be a dilemma as to how far pragmatic components may be supported, in the light of symbolic aims. This is where the formalism of the gift has an important function.

FORMALITY OF GIFT-MAKING

It is clear that what is important in making a gift is not just the transfer of goods or services in a putatively one-way action, and that the name of the 'gift' or 'present', though significant, is not completely acceptable at face value. The conditions of the gift, the implication of equivalent desired or not, and the attitudes of giver and recipient are all relevant in interpretation.

Sociologically, a striking aspect of gifts of material objects is that they are very rarely just handed over. They are usually given with some formality. Broadly speaking, the degree of formality in gift is commensurate with the degree of publicity, that is with the degree to which the gift is of general social interest. Indeed, the term *presentation*, in contrast to *present* tends to be reserved for gifts made in fairly formal circumstances on public or semi-public occasion. A 'presentation' of a medal to someone for distinguished service implies an assembly and some formal statement; a 'present' of a medal to him might be a private gift. But private gifts too, even in the domestic circle, may have their own formal touches, especially when a number of people are involved. There are families who when their children are young, celebrate Christmas by piling up all their gifts under a Christmas-tree and having some ceremonial distribution of them by some adult disguised as Father Christmas, or some other elder such as a grandfather. Birthday presents are not just put at the disposal of the recipient ('presentee' is apparently a good dictionary term); they are laid beside the plate at the breakfast table on the birthday morning. Christmas and birthday presents are apt to be wrapped in some formal way, perhaps in paper specially bought for the purpose, often with a written message of greeting. Why such formality, when the wrapping paper is immediately torn off, and the last thing one wants in a family usually is to be sending written messages to one another? The reason is well understood – that with family presents as with public presentations, the formality celebrates not so much the gift as the social relationship which the gift symbolizes. The transfer of the material thing is a recognized expression of the importance of the immaterial relationship between the persons, and this is enhanced by removing the gift out of the sphere of everyday transactions by diacritical signs – as by removing the price tag. Such symbolization of intangible social ties by gift seems to be a universal phenomenon.

The formality of gift commonly carries with it a display of positive social interest. The passage of a gift implies that friendly relations should exist between the parties. Even if such do not exist the popular spirit of the gift is that they ought to exist, in a kind of public statement of a viable social relationship. In some circumstances a gift is overtly taken to serve the function of converting a hostile relationship into a friendly one. Marshall Sahlins has said epigrammatically: 'If friends make gifts, gifts make friends' (1965, 139). Yet such display may be at a purely formal level; the parties may hate each other. This too may be well understood by all concerned. What the gift stands for in such a case then is a social relationship at two levels – at a superficial level of amity; and at a deeper level of viability. To paraphrase Sahlins – gifts do not make friends; they make people behave as friends behave, that is maintain an ongoing relationship.

This symbolic significance of the gift is manifested by the common convention of formal physical contact between the parties. The object itself, or a material token of it, should be involved in direct personal relationship. In Western societies, on public occasions of presentation especially, the gift is physically handed over from donor to recipient. This act, often done with the left hand, leaves the right hand free for a handshake. The high point of the ceremony is the hand-to-hand touch, which formally seals the transaction. (A smile by the donor is nearly always obligatory.) Procedures vary according to circumstances. Sometimes the gift is kept in the background until the critical moment arrives, and is then put by others into the donor's hand to make the actual presentation. Sometimes the actual thing never appears, but some token of it is used in the presentation instead – a cheque, some title deeds to land, the key of a building. Status considerations may enter into these more public formal occasions: some gifts are handled by servants or functionaries of lesser status until the moment of actual presentation arrives, when they are passed to the hands of the person of high status who is to be the actual donor; other gifts may not be handled at all by the donor, who involves himself in the presentation act by some word or gesture. But in some societies where there is no full hand-to-hand transfer of objects it is the recipient who signifies his acceptance of the gift by touching it and so linking it with his personality (compare Malinowski, 1922, 352). In Western domestic circles, whether or not a gift formally changes hands, the transfer may be sealed with an even more intimate gesture, a kiss. In all such ways the physical contact – of hand with hand; of hand with object; of lip with cheek – symbolizes a social relationship established or maintained. But it is to be noted that the symbolic pattern varies – according to the particular culture, the nature of the social unit concerned, the relative status positions of the participants. In general we are on the threshold of the kind of primitive thinking to which Mauss was pointing – the relation between physical and conceptual personality, with the latter envisaged in a social dimension.

Another aspect of formality in gift-making is its verbal signalization. The physical transfer of the gift is often accompanied, especially on public occasions, by utterance in a conventional form of words of what the English call rather oddly '*a* speech'. This is often only a duplication in words of what may be seen in deed, but it allows the symbolic character of the transfer to be underlined, through statements as to the value – possibly the emotional meaning – of the relationships involved. But the verbal accompaniment to a gift may be complex in intention. One of its functions may be to avoid embarrassment by disguising the emotional aspects of the transfer. But a contrary function may be to allow the recipient to underline the emotional significance, the bonding value, of what has been presented to him. Superficially, in many societies, there are two sharply contrasting modes of behaviour here, maximization and minimization. In maximization the donor draws attention to the value of his gift, praises its quality and leaves the recipient in no doubt as to his view of the importance of what is being given and, by implication, the importance of the linkage thus effected. We like to think that maximization of a gift is not a British or American habit. Our technique of signalization goes the other way, to under-praise, in order (we say) that the recipient shall not feel embarrassed. But under-praising is just as much a convention as over-praising. It is implied that the gift is so evidently valuable that it can 'speak for itself' as we say. Moreover, the convention prescribes that the more the gift is underplayed by the donor, the more should the recipient make it clear that he is not accepting this statement at face value, but realizes the worth of what he is being given. In effect, the words spoken, casual though they may often seem, are part of the total gift situation, and are taken into account by the recipient in his acknowledgement, which is or is part of his form of reciprocity.

But in some cases the technique of minimization appears to take idiosyncratic forms, as when a donor refuses even to identify himself. This is not a disclaimer of the value of the gift, but an avoidance of public linkage of gift with person of the donor, and so a disclaimer of public credit. This may be no mere subterfuge. In recent years a very generous donor of funds for students' hostels for colleges of the University of London laid it down as a condition that if any attempt were made to find out his identity the gift would be cancelled. One can only speculate on the motivation of such anonymous acts. The desire to do good by stealth may correspond to a noble and selfless devotion to the welfare of others in need. It may indicate a shrinking from the formal conventions of public gift and acceptance in British society. It may be in conformity to another convention, such as the religious maxim of Judaism, that secret charity is a higher form of giving than open charity. But it may arise from a wish to remain free from involvement and responsibility and to avoid further calls upon the donor's wealth. It may even cover a delight in being the unseen object of public attention, all the more to be savoured because only the donor knows to whom it is directed – a kind of voyeur in the field of philanthropy. Such interpretations may sound ungenerous. But part of my analysis in this chapter is to show how complex can be the motivation of much gift-making, and even more, to point out how the accepted social conventions codify and standardize the expression of these motives, so that gifts assume regular symbolic patterns. From this example of the anonymous donor it can be seen how such idiosyncratic behaviour poses problems of interpretation and enforces unfamiliar responses upon recipients. It also raises a more theoretical question about the character of reciprocity when no donor is available to receive recompense.

The formality of gift-making emerges in another way, that of the appropriateness of the gift. Theoretically, the donor decides what to give – his act is free. But in practice most gifts are fairly rigorously circumscribed, by type and amount according to occasion. For this, recognized conventions operate in every society, with associated symbolism at various levels. At a Tikopia funeral there are three main sets of formal participants, each with a service to perform, and each the recipient of gifts. The immediate family of the deceased, with his father's kin, form the chief mourners – with subsets according to whether the deceased was male or female, old or young, married or single. Their prime task is to wail for the dead person for the prescribed period, to celebrate his virtues and mourn his loss. Such wailing, irrespective of its emotional base, is a conventional expression, developing into a funeral dirge of symbolic significance; whether or not a mourner 'feels' grief he must 'utter' grief. The representatives of the mother's family of the deceased are mourners too, but whereas the deceased's father's kin stay secluded in the death house, the job of his mother's kin is to bury him, and as such they are in a separate category. The third main set of participants is made up of neighbours, friends, more distant kin, who are not prime mourners but providers of food for the mourners. They visit the mourning house for three successive evenings, with water bottles and baskets of food, and when all have wailed together, they induce the mourners to eat. And at the end, like the burial party, their services are compensated for by gifts of property (see Firth, 1939, 325–31; and above p. 247). Now at every stage the gifts are specified as to type, and largely also as to amount, by tradition. Cooked food is brought for the household mourners to eat, and the providers are compensated with gifts of wooden bowls and coconut sinnet cord. Pandanus mats and bark-cloth sheets, bowls, sinnet cord and food are presented to the burial party; they must be reciprocated in turn by bowls and sinnet alone, but of the same quality. A great range of subsidiary transactions in raw and cooked food and bark-cloth takes place. Some of the basis for this is utilitarian – food for the hungry mourners, wrappings for the corpse; but much is conventional, its appropriateness being socially not pragmatically dictated. Some of the items are directly, obviously, symbolical – as when raw food from a man's cultivations is stood on his grave to represent the work of his hands and indicate the readiness of his successors to dedicate it spiritually to him (Firth, 1970a, 249). But others are only symbolical in a more general sense, representing social bonds between the parties and not any specific thought. The wooden bowls given to the food providers are overtly intended to express gratitude for the feeding, and recognition of the status factors involved, but not any explicit symbolism of food preparation for which the bowls are used; they are primarily presented as valuable property.

In a Western society, analogous social specification of gifts exists. For a couple who are newly married, a present of kitchenware; for a family member with a birthday, an item of personal clothing; for an anniversary after twenty-five years of marriage, a piece of silver – each of these is appropriate in its context and violently out of place in some other contexts. But the freedom of choice still permissible within such conventional limits has given rise in modern times to a further convention – that for an occasion such as a wedding the projected recipients draw up a list of desirable gifts, from which the donor may choose, so combining utility with symbolic value.

The symbolic value of a gift is particularly attested by the limitations on the disposal of it. A gift may be of small practical use – if, for instance, it is a duplicate of something already owned – and it may have market value; but to sell it may be insulting, or at least wounding.* As Barry Schwartz (1967) has pointed out, to make a gift is self-defining; it is an index to idea of personality of giver and recipient. Hence to sell a gift or even to change it for another item is to reject or modify by implication the donor's conception of the personalities and the relation between them.

EARNEST AND TOKEN

Part of the ordinary convention in many societies is that gifts should be broadly proportionate to resources of donor and recipient, not only as a pragmatic matter but also as an indication of their symbolic significance. Either meanness or ostentation may be equally criticized, in terms of a lack of fit between size and style of gift and quality of social relationship it represents.

But there are circumstances in which a gift is recognized by both donor and recipient to be very disproportionate to the resources which could have been expended – perhaps only a small fraction of what ordinarily might be expected – and yet it is acceptable. Such a gift may have several functions.

It may be an *earnest*, an indication of what is further to come, or

* I have been told that in the United States, Christmas gifts are often taken back to the store where they were originally bought, and exchanged for something more suitable of equivalent value, on the excuse that they are 'wrong size', 'wrong colour', etc. But to treat a family gift in this way may need prior negotiation.

what may further come if certain conditions are met by the recipient. A Trobriand example of this is what Malinowski has described as a 'solicitary gift' (1922, 354), by which a man who hopes to secure a valuable shell ornament in the *kula* distribution tries to make an initial present of some smaller item to the immediate owner, with the implication that he is ready to make the appropriate large gift if he is successful. Interpretation of the donor's attitude may be difficult – he may be supplicating from an inferior position for the grant of the valuable, or he may be virtually issuing a command that he expects it to be given to him. But in terms of socio-economic relationship, the offer of the earnest has set up a bond of obligation which the recipient must take into account even if he does not accede to the donor's request. In Western society a small gift is sometimes made as an earnest because a larger gift which is intended or promised is not yet ready for presentation. Here the accent of the earnest is on maintaining the character of the social relationship, lest the recipient may think the donor promises but does not perform, and modify his attitude accordingly.

Of the same general order as an earnest is a *token* gift. The two terms are often merged, but as I indicate later, the concept of token can also carry a more critical negative connotation. In common usage one function of a token gift is to serve symbolically in overt fashion. A small presentation is made, commensurate neither with the resources of the donor nor with the needs of the recipient, but as index of commitment. In itself this may be encouraging, as support for the recipient's interests or conception of his own personality. But in public affairs in Western society a token gift is often designed as a means to stimulate other gifts, more substantial, or other commitments which can lead to effective action. In a recent election campaign in the state of Michigan, the chairman of a noted automobile firm sent $900 to aid the cause of a Democratic candidate. The amount was small by comparison with other contributions, but it was noted in a New York newspaper with the comment that 'in his case, the symbolism was the main thing' (*New York Times*, 8 November 1970). Looked at as a serious campaign contribution from such a multimillionaire source, the gift was ludicrous; but the knowledge that this particular donor had engaged himself on the candidate's side was presumably of great value to the campaign managers. But it is to be noted that in such circumstances the effect of the token gift is dependent largely upon the publicity it receives; a secret gift of a million dollars without the symbolism would have achieved a different effect.

But a token gift may be symbolic not of commitment but of a wish to avoid commitment. Historically, tokens have been coin-shaped pieces of metal circulating at less than their nominal value, and the notion of token can carry an idea of substitute or inferior counterpart. So the modern colloquial word 'tokenism' has developed, to indicate behaviour which assumes the form of, but falls short of, true commitment. What is symbolized by a token gift in this sense is the handing over of some inconsiderable item in the form of a gift but without intention to follow this up by any substantial action of the kind required by the situation. In the philanthropic climate of modern Western society it is not uncommon to buy a badge or a button in a street or campus campaign, not just from a generous wish to help the cause, but also to make one's sympathy plain to other people, or even to protect one from being troubled further. Such crude 'tokenism' in giving is socially disapproved, though probably many people in modern cities practise it to some degree. But more insidious, and less stigmatized, is the token gift of money as a symbolic substitute for giving one's time, with its commitment of thought and energy.

The idea of the gift as a generous voluntary gesture by which a person divests himself of his rights in something, to transfer them for the benefit of someone else, is description at a superficial level. The gift may be complicated by elements of formality, publicity and appropriateness. It may embody obscure psychological notions of the definition of personality and of the validity of personal contact, and more obvious sociological notions of the symbolic significance of things transferred and contacts made.

GIFT AND COUNTER-GIFT

I now return to the idea of counter-gift, the notion of reciprocity which is recurrent in anthropological literature. It has been simple for anthropologists to demonstrate empirically the prevalence of reciprocity in gifts, in the societies they have studied, and also to draw attention to parallels in Western society, especially in the field of family ceremony. But the treatment has gone much wider than the field of the gift in the strict sense.

The theme of reciprocity has been found in proverbs. Among the Tswana of Botswana traditionally a man had a special relation to some one of his sisters. He had to buy her clothing occasionally and give her other presents. Whenever he slaughtered an ox he had to give her a flank. In turn this sister looked after him before he was married – cooking, washing, mending his clothes – and after he married she helped his wife in domestic tasks. Most of these obligations have not been compulsory in the sense that the courts would not enforce them. But it would be said that an offender did not show his relatives honour and respect. Ill-feeling resulted, and his relatives might refuse to help the offender materially when he needed them. Symbolically, the Tswana put this ideal of mutual help as a proverb: 'Hands, like sheep, bump against each other' – putting their concept of reciprocity in a pastoral idiom (Schapera, 1955, 187). (Note again the image of touching hands as symbolizing co-operation and social ties.)

Myth too has its illustrations of the reciprocity theme. One such touching symbolic form of the representation of implications of gift has been cited by Denise Paulme (1967, 48–61) from West Africa. It concerns the way in which mankind came to die. Originally, Death lived in the bush and did not come into the villages; he killed game and man did not die. One day a hunter went into the bush. He found Death, who gave him some meat. He thanked Death and brought the meat back to the village, but he did not know that he was in debt. One day Death came to the village to ask for his payment. The man said: 'Why, was not the meat a gift?' Death said: 'I was in the bush when you came and collected all my meat. Today, you must repay me.' So the hunter gave him one of his children, whom Death took away, and men then began to die. So symbolically, in this story, if no exchange takes place, no return gift is made, a gift received means death for the debtor or his kin. At the least, a gift made means power, of donor over recipient, and material and immaterial elements are closely interwoven.

In the stimulus to provide counter-gift two main themes may be involved in varying degree. One is the theme of recoupment, of compensating original donor for his loss. The other is the theme of re-assertion, of establishing original recipient once more on a level of equality. Both have material expression, but the latter can more easily assume a symbolic significance, and as such neglect equivalence in favour of over-compensation.

In the anthropological theory of exchange the central notion of reciprocity is still a subject of debate, and I take it up later. But it is convenient to traverse Mauss's initial formulations by the way, since they have been of cardinal importance in the analysis. Loosely phrased and ethnographically inaccurate as some of his generalizations were,* and tinged with almost a mystical flavour, they did bring into sharper focus than before some of the basic features of this aspect of exchange. Mauss showed that a gift is not a free individual act, but is highly institutionalized; that it is not simply a voluntary gesture, but can be a response to firm obligation; that it is not just a one-way transfer, but tends to involve reciprocity, even sometimes by a return-gift of the same form; that it is accordingly in a symbolic way a transfer of personality and a linking of personalities; that it incorporates ideas of relative status, and of power; and that it may be an important mechanism for group action and for linking groups. So, Mauss gave his epitome in terms of: the obligation to give; the obligation to receive; and the obligation to repay.

Mauss's own formulations have not gone unchallenged. C. S. Belshaw, for instance, while acknowledging the significance of the concept of prestation as indicating the contextualization of gift, has argued that Mauss has overstressed the social imperatives in prestation at the expense of individual choice and entrepreneurial elements (1965, 48). Along somewhat similar lines I would argue that though Mauss did introduce some qualification to the precision of

* Michel Panoff (1970, 60–1) concedes that Mauss may have misread ethnographic accounts at some points, but holds that this does not impair the theoretical results of his study of gift-giving. But while it is true that Mauss's most general results are unaffected, his theory of the relation of the gift to the personality of the giver is certainly distorted by his ethnographic errors. Sahlins (1970) traverses Mauss's Maori ethnography and commentaries upon it, and comes up with an ingenious (though I think misconceived) suggestion of his own about the concept of *hau* which is central to this part of Mauss's work. Sahlins's rendering of the *hau* of the forest as its fecundity, in my view, mistakes an indirect expression of a relationship for a direct expression. It reminds me of my own concrete interpretation of the Tikopia concept of *manu*, but the evidence is of a different order (cf. Firth, 1929, 412–15; 1967b, 174–94).

meaning he gave to concepts of obligation, these are by no means as firm or rigorous as he generally maintains.

THE OBLIGATION TO GIVE

In his examination of the obligation to give, Mauss focused largely on the potlatch of north-west Amerindian tribes, stressing in particular the significance of status estimation and rivalry in inducing large-scale presentations.* In a very different context, that of gifts made by anthropologists to people who have been their informants and friends in the field, I have indicated the importance of status considerations, but also the complexity of the situation. Recognition of obligation is by no means rigorous and automatic but on the contrary may involve choices of a meaningful, even painful kind (Firth, 1967c, 11–14). The symbolic significance of a gift is not merely restrained in the interests of a more utilitarian calculus; it must be estimated against other symbolic considerations.

Here I examine how some of the symbolic aspects of gift may be restricted or conditioned by some other types of modern pressure. In his account of the San Blas Cuna Indians of Central America, the late David B. Stout noted a growing conflict between traditional norms of hospitality and sharing patterns, and the new competitive and individualistic values. Anyone with a temporary surplus of food or goods was beset by friends and relatives, wishing him to share out his property. They would make reference to the old precept that a Cuna would give away or share whatever a fellow Indian asked of him. But even a generation ago young Cuna men would make the rationalization that they did not work harder or attempt to accumulate more property because if they did they would only have to give it away. If they did not so give it, they would be labelled as stingy (1947, 77). Here new wants and opportunities, rising expectations and changing values reduced the pressure of obligation to give, and tended accordingly to modify the symbolic patterns of social intercourse. (For analysis of complications in Zaire kin relations see Lux, 1972.)

Limitations upon the obligation to give may be even firmer from a

* For a recent statement on exchange structures of potlatch type see Paula G. Rubel and Abraham Rosman, 1970.

more fully developed legal system, in which control of property in the wider interests of society may be held to supersede the narrower interest of the individual, whether symbolic or not. The simple conventional notion of gift, that a person disposes freely of his own property, is subject in a modern state to various over-riding demands.

The basic notion of gift is the alienation of property from oneself with complete surrender of all rights over it to another person. Yet in the eyes of the law, a man may not be allowed to divest himself at will of all interest in his property. The attempt at surrender may not be recognized as complete. We are familiar with rules whereby gifts *inter vivos* are still reckoned in certain circumstances as being part of a deceased person's estate for death-duty purposes if he had died in less than a given period (earlier five, later seven years) after making his gift. The state, in the form of the law, asserts a right not to limit the gift but to consider the transfer as incomplete for a statutory period. It may be argued that this is simply a device for maintaining revenue. But even so it has the effect of placing an impediment in the way of achieving the symbolic as well as the practical aims of the gift. In some other conditions the law may refuse to recognize the existence of any obligation to give, and may disallow what a person attempts to hand over as a gift. A record of an English law case some twenty years ago notes a challenge to a man's legacy of £1,000 to the vicar and churchwardens of a church, the income to be spent on 'seasonable food and drink' to be distributed by them in the name of the testator among twenty communicants and women of the parish on Christmas Eve. The judge held that the bequest was invalid. Its motive, he said, was vanity, there was no express note of benefit to the deserving poor, it was therefore not charitable and failed accordingly. With regard to the suggestion that this bequest might have been for a religious purpose his lordship said he was not prepared to hold that the provision of plum pudding was for the advancement of religion (*The Times*, 20 March 1954).

Muslim law is particularly revealing on the subject of the obligation to give, and its symbolic implications. Gifts of a charitable nature are expected from Muslims as part of their religious duty. The Koran enjoins believers to give as charity without material return, what they can spare. God knows, and God will repay – in fact, if there be any good deed, He will repay it doubly, says the Koran, provided that it should not be given in order to be seen of men. (Here is one form of reciprocity for an anonymous giver!) Yet while approving gifts in general, Muslim law lays down quite stringent conditions about them, particularly where they affect the family (see Seymour Vesey-Fitzgerald, 1931, 201–2, 206–23).

Although a gift is gratuitous, the Muslim law regards it as always made with an object in view – it is not a simple discard of property. Gifts made to acquire merit in the sight of God have as object a recompense in the next world. Worldly gifts are made to ingratiate oneself with other human beings. A leading Muslim legal treatise says of these that the object of a gift to a stranger is to get a return. (It is lack of *specification* of return, and lack of *contract* for return that makes the transfer a gift.) It is the custom to send presents to a person of high rank that he may protect the donor; to a person of inferior rank that the donor may obtain his services; and to a person of equal rank that the donor may obtain an equivalent. All these gifts are legitimate.

Gifts to acquire merit, if made without thought of worldly recompense, may be given to people of one's own surroundings, even to one's own kin. In fact, it is held that charity literally begins at home, and properly so; gifts to members of one's own family are highly approved by Islam. But here the interest of the law begins to emerge. A gift to acquire merit cannot be used as a cloak for an act unpleasing to God and the Muslim courts will reject it.

Moreover, to support the interests of the family, Muslim law severely restricts freedom of testation. A person can leave by will only one-third of his property, and legacies to heirs are severely restricted in the interests of the equitable division of the property, which is a cardinal principle of Muslim law. On the other hand, Muslim law makes allowance for a special type of religious gift known as *waqf*. In theory, this means putting an object in the category of divine property so that the donor's right in it is extinguished and it becomes the property of God to be used for the advantage of His creatures. Such would be a piece of land donated for a religious foundation. But since marriage and family life are the religious obligation of every adult Muslim, a man's duty to his family takes precedence over all other objects of his generosity. He can then make an endowment for his family, the assumption being that on the failure of his descendants it would go to the poor. To make such an endowment a person must be free, sane and master of his own affairs. He must not make it for anti-social purposes – such as avoiding payment of his just debts. But the contest which goes on continually between the rule of law and the interest of the individual emerges in many such cases. These inalienable family endowments came to be treated in some Muslim countries as opportunities for a man, in effect, to distribute the income among his heirs at his discretion, instead of abiding by the normal legal and religious rules of inheritance. It has been a matter of common knowledge that, as Gibb has said (1947, 91), this practice has been 'the cause of much moral corruption and economic loss'. Hence modernists in Muslim countries have for long agitated to remove such private family provisions from legitimate protection by religion. The reform has distinguished between genuinely charitable *waqf* intended for the endowment of religious and philanthropic institutions, and private endowments intended to benefit a particular family or individual. Their aim was primarily utilitarian, but it was in the direction of protecting the general symbolic values of the gift from financial manipulation. In Egypt and in Syria religiously backed family endowments have now been abolished for some time, and in other Muslim countries they have tended to be more strictly limited.* So Muslim reformers, while not wishing to reject the sacred law, have dared to reinterpret it radically, stripping it of what they have regarded as the human accretions that jurists have put upon it during its long history. In so doing, while not restricting the 'obligation to give' they have channelled it into forms which could be given most broadly-based social approval, and which had most obvious symbolic value in representing the most abstract religious concepts.

THE OBLIGATION TO RECEIVE

The symbolic qualities of the gift come out especially in the obligation to receive it. Even if on the material side a person may not need

* For further details see J. N. D. Anderson, 1959, 78–9; Snouck Hurgronje, 1906, II, 321; J. Schacht, 1955, 82–3; Gibb and Bowen, I, pt 2, 165–78; E. C. C. Howard, *Minhaj et Talibin*, 230–3.

the object given to him, he may be 'constrained', as Mauss puts it, to receive it; to reject it could be considered a refusal of friendship and intercourse. If in Tikopia, a man comes with a basket of food to one's house as a present, one does not think of refusing it though one may have half-a-dozen baskets already, much more than ample for household needs. The correct thing is to accept it with thanks, and then later if need be to avoid waste, give it away to some other household. That the obligation to receive may entail a further obligation to give, in a kind of chain reaction, is quite in accord with Tikopia ideas of hospitality and social linkage. As Mauss has noted, there is an association in Polynesian society between: hospitality, food, communion, peace, exchange, law.

But there is a danger that such statements will be overgeneralized, since Mauss was not careful enought to distinguish the kinds of social situations where they were applicable from others in which they were not. Without undertaking a systematic study I note that the obligation to receive a gift is conditioned by the structure of the society concerned, operating in particular social situations.

In non-industrial societies of type commonly studied by anthropologists, where individual roles tend to be less sharply differentiated than in industrial, more complex societies, the obligation to receive a gift tends to be more general. In the more complex industrial type of society, with high degree of differentiation of role, there are codes of refusal for gifts just as there are codes of acceptance. It may be argued that if giving is part of the nobler side of life, associated with friendliness, generosity, the contribution of the self to society, why this reluctance to receive, this rejection of participation in the philanthropic act? There is sometimes much ambivalence about acceptance of a gift. There may be pragmatic reasons: that the recipient does not think the donor can afford the gift; that he fears he himself cannot easily afford to pay it back. There may be more subtle considerations: in modern society, however much he might wish and be able to repay, the diffuse patterns of occupation and residence might give him no opportunity to do so. Even further, granted that conventionally 'gifts make friends', the intended recipient may not wish to 'make friends'; the diversity of modern society allows people not only to choose their own friends – even a primitive society allows this – but also to refuse social ties with others who might like to be their friends. Hence the various stratagems to evade gifts from people with whom one does not want to intensify social relations. The obligation to receive is inhibited then in the light of the further obligation – the need to repay, it being understood that repayment may involve intangible as well as tangible considerations.

From this point of view quite stringent limitations may arise on the obligation to receive gifts, when differential status of the parties involves the higher status person as recipient. There are two possible interpretations of gift in such circumstances: that it is complimentary, an acknowledgement of status as a kind of return for the general symbolic role of the recipient; or that it is establishing a platform for future benefit in goods, services or reputation from having social contact with the person of high status. When gifts to modern Western heads of state are in question, both interpretations may apply, but it would seem that the danger of the second has led to restriction. It is understood, for example, that presents sent to members of the British Royal Family by private citizens not known to them are normally returned, though presents from other heads of state, public bodies, and their personal friends are not. While no implication of reciprocity may be involved with the act of the private citizen, the acceptance of the gift might be treated as the creation of a personal link which might be invidious as regards other citizens. The obligation to receive is not acknowledged because it runs counter to another type of obligation – not to discriminate among citizens in what should be equality of general relationship to the Sovereign and Royal Family.

With a head of state the status factor is of prime importance, since in modern times no one is likely to think of any service that can be secured by a gift to a member of the Royal Family. But in the broader sphere of public role the obligation *not* to receive a gift may be much more pointed. By the Civil Service regulations of most advanced countries a civil servant is required not to accept gifts from people with whom he may have technical relationships in the course of his duty. Acceptance of a gift, or even of lavish hospitality, has at times imperilled a politician's or a civil servant's reputation, led to his resignation or dismissal from public office, or possibly brought him to the brink of criminal prosecution.

In the United States, allegations of bribery are made from time to time and though usually denied, arouse public disquiet. In 1970, a Federal grand jury investigating reported conflicts of interest by members of Congress indicted a veteran representative on charges that he accepted a bribe of $25,000 in return for seeking to block a Justice Department prosecution of a business firm for irregularities in house improvement proceedings. In the same year, widespread allegations were made against members of the police department of New York, ranging from accusation that gamblers, narcotics dealers and businessmen made illicit payments of millions of dollars to New York policemen, to charges that small weekly payments were made to police by many shopkeepers so that they could operate on Sundays in violation of state regulations. Public officials became greatly concerned. In the middle of the year the state legislature passed new laws tightening up rules about acceptance of gifts by all municipal employees and requiring all local governments to issue a code of ethics prescribing the standards of conduct 'reasonably expected' of employees. The intention was to prohibit the acceptance of gifts to secure governmental favours, and the definition of gift was a broad one, pertaining to 'money, service, loan, travel, entertainment, hospitality, thing or promise, or in any other form. . . .' Later still the New York Police Commissioner proclaimed a stand against the soliciting or receiving of gifts by policemen, in any form, even including externally financed Christmas parties (see, for example *New York Times*, 1 and 25 April 1970; *Post Standard* (Syracuse), 3 June 1970; *New York Post*, 9 December 1971).

In Britain, such corrupt practices are generally regarded as being rare,* partly because of the different structure of national and local government, partly because of more careful public audit, but largely because of a different tradition of public service official behaviour. But allegations of bribery of police are occasionally made, and public concern sometimes arises over payments made to politicians or to public servants, for which no clear legitimate consideration can be shown. Some years ago it was reported that a clerk of works in a Midland county was sentenced to four months' imprisonment under the Prevention of Corruption Act for accepting small sums of money

* That is nowadays; they were common in the seventeenth and eighteenth centuries, for example in the career of Samuel Pepys, or of Robert Walpole.

on a council housing estate. He said rather naively: 'I thought it was perks for the clerk of works' (for some details see *The Times*, 2 July 1967; 13 February 1971; 14 July 1972, *New York Times*, 30 March 1970). In other countries too, periodically, where the Press is allowed to publish details, cases of alleged bribery are reported, though the degree of public anxiety about the probity of bureaucratic and other figures in public life varies considerably. In Mexico, for instance, a group of peasants appealed to the governor of their state to stop illegal depredations by timber merchants upon the forests; they complained that forest guards did nothing to intervene, being silenced by bribes (*The Times*, 7 August 1970). In Zaire the system of bribery has been said to be ubiquitous among government officials, being necessary to expedite most ordinary services, such as passing building materials at reasonable speed through customs formalities (*Newsweek*, 22 November 1971).

The view that private gift does not accord well with public performance seems to have a long ancestry. In sixteenth-century England 'gift' in one sense meant something given with a corrupting intention, a bribe. And the early seventeenth-century Authorised Version of the Old Testament has repeated warning against the acceptance of gifts because of their untoward influence upon judgement. 'Thou shalt take no gift; for the gift blindeth the wise, and perverteth the words of the righteous' (Exodus, 23: 8 and Deuteronomy, 16: 19; cf. II Chronicles, 19: 7; Ecclesiastes, 7: 7). And an Apocrypha version reads: 'Presents and gifts blind the eyes of the wise, and as a muzzle on the mouth, turn away reproofs' (Ecclesiasticus, 20 (Rev. v.)). The 'obligation to receive' is here quite clearly stated in reverse.

The notion of acceptance of a bribe is in some societies associated with eating, often with an unpleasant association. In Malay the expression for taking bribes is *makan duit*, to eat money, or *makan suap*, to eat a mouthful, as in handfeeding (with idea of gobbling). In German a corrupt judge, one that takes bribes, has been termed *Gabenfresser*, an eater of gifts, using the word for eat that is ordinarily applied to eating by animals, devouring.

Yet the economic and moral classification of gift in such contexts is not entirely simple. Anthropologists have long recognized that in some Oriental and African countries there is a thin line between bribe and status-gift. Traditionally, if one appears before a superior one should not go empty-handed; one should acknowledge his rank by a gift of introduction. Muslim law specifically allows this (see above). Many years ago William Robertson Smith noted that: 'It was the rule of antiquity, and still is the rule in the East, that the inferior must not present himself before his superior without a gift "to smooth his face" and "make him gracious"' (1889, 328). To omit such a gift is ill manners. Conversely, superiors or equals may be expected to recognize the social standing and the worth of other people with whom they have business relations, by gifts either unilaterally transferred or exchanged. In Chinese communities payment of small amounts of 'tea money' to inferiors has been common, as also exchange of more substantial gifts of 'lucky money' or analogous articles between friends and relatives before the Chinese Lunar New Year. In the domestic circle and between private citizens such gifts are commonly status indicators and symbolic tokens of social relationship. But from private citizens to public officials they can so easily assume the character of bribes that in recent years the government of Hong Kong specifically forbade its officials to receive 'lucky money' (*Honolulu Star-Bulletin*, 29 January 1969), even though it might be distributed in the red packets which traditionally expressed the symbolism of good fortune.

Disentangling elements in a gift-bribe-corruption syndrome is not an easy task, since a critical issue is how far the mind of the recipient may be thought to have been influenced towards partiality by the gift, and even he himself may not be able clearly to decide. Cyril Belshaw, who has been much concerned with problems arising from adaptation of traditional economic systems to modern conditions, has taken a rather cautious view of this question. He has pointed out that bribery and corruption carry moral connotations in modern Western society which are not necessarily applicable to the contexts of public affairs in developing countries. He uses the criterion of whether or not a gift effects alteration in the recipient's judgements and actions, particularly in the direction of seeking more gifts. He would probably not class the gift as a bribe if it is the material symbol of a relationship, the sealing of a contract, the payment for a service openly rendered, one element in a complex of continuous exchanges, or part of a stock which the recipient uses to maintain further social obligations. He adds very reasonably that 'the accusation of bribery should be used most sparingly in contexts of development, at least until it has been demonstrated without doubt that the transactions were not part of an indigenous exchange network' (1965, 46). This is perhaps in part a counsel of expediency. The fact that a gift was a payment for a service *openly* rendered would not seem to remove it from the category of inducing an official to partiality against other claimants to service. But where all claimants are expected to use similar measures, it could be argued that it is secrecy which destroys at least part of equality of opportunity to obtain service. The humourous gag 'I believe in bribery but not in corruption' covers an ethical notion that it is theoretically possible to separate acceptance of a gift made with intention to get special treatment, from actual furnishing of such special treatment. In such view the element of corruption lies in perversion – in performing for one party a service which would have been performed equally for another party had there been no gift, or would have not been performed for any party with the same speed or energy. An ingenious analyst in Thailand, said to be a senior government economist, has argued that the system of 'under-the-table' payments common throughout Asia is not corruption in the true sense of the word; it is a system of supplementing sub-standard incomes. Granting that realistically the payments can be so viewed, his classification of corruption is somewhat narrow, being restricted to actions outside the law. In this scheme, corruption implies an illegal transaction; and these bribes are not corruption because the officials who take them are being given them to do what they are supposed to do legally, in any case (*Honolulu Star-Bulletin*, 25 March 1969). (This distinction, however, is not supported by the dictionaries.)

In the complex administrative conditions of a modern state it seems hardly possible to make such fine distinctions. To separate status-gift from bribe in public life and avoid bureaucratic corruption seems a counsel of perfection. Hence the great care taken in the scrutiny of any payments to officials personally from private citizens, and the denial of their obligation to receive gifts.

THE OBLIGATION TO REPAY

In so far as a gift in material terms is a one-way transfer, it creates an asymmetrical relationship socially. In general, among those of broadly equal status, the very act of giving is a symbolic enhancement of the status of the donor. This appears in literary form in various contexts. 'They give to get esteem', wrote Goldsmith (in *The Traveller*). The implication here is that something intangible is exacted in return for the gift – an element of social credit is transferred from recipient of the gift back to the donor. In one type of thinking, then, the acceptance of a gift means weakening one's own personality in return. So the hero of a recent novel (Cecil Brown, *The Life and Loves of Mr Jiveass Nigger*) is made to say: 'The only way to keep your strength is to give; never accept anything from anybody'. It is in this field of the symbolic significance of giving and receiving for the personality that some of the most sensitive issues of interpretation appear. So if a recipient cannot refuse a gift because of the social sanctions he may seek for some equivalent to give back and so recover his status. It is not only more blessed to give than to receive – it is also more comfortable!

There is a kind of compensatory principle at work here: material versus immaterial consideration. A gift by itself yields status, or helps to maintain status. But a gift which is followed by or implies a demand for a material return may have to be content with less immaterial return in status, or less of that concession to status which is the social expression of gratitude. This is brought out in tangential fashion by a comment of Graham Greene's about bribery. The point about a bribe is that it is a gift the purpose of which is understood by both parties to be to secure some material service not ordinarily to be expected. In his novel *The Comedians* – concerning Haiti – Greene has one of his characters say: 'I have often noticed that a bribe . . . changes a relation. The man who offers a bribe gives away a little of his own importance; the bribe once accepted, he becomes the inferior, like a man who has paid for a woman.' In other words, by the passage of the bribe, with implicit stipulation of a material favour in return, the giver has traded status for service.

But as I have just indicated, in social relations the acceptance of a gift may be difficult precisely because no material return is envisaged or possible in the circumstances. The hardest of all ways of reciprocating a gift may be for a person to yield up elements of his status, his pride, his personal dignity. The true symbolic concession of the self, the acceptance of another's will or view, can be the most refractory. Here the institutionalized ways of yielding observed by anthropologists in some less complex societies than our own (for example by use of middle-men), with very different social and ritual sanctions, offer interesting contrasts to ours.

An attempt has been made by Wilton Dillon to utilize some of these anthropological findings in an essay on international relations, under the title of *Gifts and Nations: The Obligation to Give, Receive and Repay* (1968). The author has set out to adapt Mauss's concept of reciprocity to an explanation of the strained relations between Gaullist France and the United States: the United States was obliged to assist France with Marshall Aid after the war, and France was obliged to receive it; but inadequate channels were made available by the United States for repayment to be made, hence French concepts of their own status suffered and relations between the two countries worsened. Dillon has couched his argument partly in terms of a somewhat fanciful contrast between *kula* and *potlatch* behaviour. Treating *kula* as alternate giving and receiving in harmonious equalization, and *potlatch* as desperately competitive humiliation of partners by reiterated giving without accepting return, Dillon holds that the relationship between France and the United States developed along *potlatch* instead of *kula* lines. But as Michael Thompson has pointed out, the distinction is not valid: *kula* is as competitive as *potlatch* and a more continuous status struggle. 'In the international *kula* America is the "big-man" and exchange relationships will not normally be balanced. The blocking of counter-gifts from the inferior partners is not so much unfortunate as inevitable' (1969; cf. Berreman, 1970). Dillon's rather simplicist treatment also tends to overlook the significance of the distinction between the circulation of traditional valuables in the *kula*, the 'agonistic' destruction of some types of valuables in the *potlatch*, and the reproductive use of technological resources which was stimulated by Marshall Aid – though some intricate problems of economic relationship are embedded therein.

A complex issue also relates to the moral evaluation of the gift in such situations of greatly disparate resources at the command of the parties. Recognition of the differential may lead to a very different type of reaction than that postulated by Dillon – a claim to *receive* resources which will be *given without reciprocity*. This is in fact the type of demand which is increasingly being put forward by 'Third World' nations in seeking aid from the more developed nations. It is true that reciprocity theory is invoked to some extent in that it is argued that modern aid without repayment would be only a just recompense for former exploitation. But a major basis for the claim is not the equivalence of exchange theory but equalization in the general name of human rights and international viability.

From all this, however, one significant thought emerges – that transactions of the gift order are apt not to stand as single items but to be part of continuing series of relationships of immaterial as well as material kind. This is the kind of phenomenon Mauss indicated by his term *prestations totales*, though the ethnographic code he gave to it was too dogmatic, despite his claim to 'have access to the minds of the societies through documentation and philological research'. But one inference from this continuity is the difficulty of making precise statements about what is reciprocity for what, since each item can be referred forward as well as back. It is a common experience in modern Western society to hear that someone has not expressed 'proper' gratitude for a gift, that is, in the view of the donor the recipient has not provided the immaterial repayment he regards as due to him. But the recipient may argue that no gratitude is due because the gift is itself an equivalent for some earlier service. President Harry S. Truman's pungent philosophy 'There is no gratitude for things past; gratitude is always for what you're going to do for people in future' may be too extreme. But reciprocation of a gift may envisage favours to come as much as favours past. In much of social life it may be convenient to match transfers, to behave as if transactions were one-to-one. But the concept of a flow often guides the behaviour of the participants, and it is their different interpretations of the point which the flow has reached which is responsible for much manipulation and argument.

In line with such thoughts Marshall Sahlins has analysed the concept of reciprocity. He has pointed out that there has been a popular tendency (deriving in part from Mauss) to view reciprocity as balance, as one-to-one exchange, whereas if considered as material transfer, reciprocity is often not that at all. It is through scrutiny of departure from balanced exchange that the interplay between reciprocity, social relations and material circumstances can best be seen. Sahlins has accordingly made a distinction between 'balanced reciprocity' by direct exchange in gift form, with social relations sustained by the material flow; and 'generalized reciprocity', with much less evidence of material recompense, the material flow resting upon prevailing social relations without exactly matching transactions. I would prefer another way of expressing this point – to view transactions of reciprocity in terms of their diffuseness or specificity; their symmetry or asymmetry; and the degree to which they involve elements which can be equated, as being of the same or different orders. The problem of asymmetry and reciprocity has been taken up especially by Takie Sugiyama Lebra, in a sensitive study of the Japanese concept of *on* (1969). She has argued that the concept of reciprocity is powerful as an analytical tool, but difficult to deal with because of the dynamic interlocking between the symmetrical strain in the abstract concept and the general asymmetry manifest in actual social transactions and ideals. Hence in the Japanese field of obligation represented by *on*, balancing mechanisms are continually at work in conditioning and constraining the official, traditionally recognized patterns of asymmetry ascribed to it. It would not be difficult to see a dialectical process in operation in such phenomena. But what is very evident is that the 'obligation to repay' is not an automatic force behind the reception of a gift; it offers a wide range of possible conduct, with very complex factors involved.

It is evident also that the possibilities of combination of different elements of reciprocity – material goods, services, intangible attributions of reputation and prestige – taken in conjunction with variation in the time factor, allow for accumulation and manipulation of power. In the field of politics, reciprocity for a service may come in the form of a tacit influence upon policy – intangible, non-measurable, perhaps almost unidentifiable, yet a most prized asset.

But the idea that the concept of reciprocity is basic to that of gift has not gone unchallenged. That a gift not only evokes reciprocity but may have been made with the notion of reciprocity in mind may seem offensive. There can be revolt against the notion of calculation, of self-interest, and a stress upon the altruistic, voluntary non-contractual, non-reciprocal aspect of the act. From this point of view Richard Titmuss has put forward a powerfully argued case for the provision of blood for medical care as a species of gift not treated as a market consumption good. Calling on Mauss and Lévi-Strauss for evidence on the nature of gift-transactions Titmuss has entitled his book *The Gift Relationship: From Human Blood to Social Policy* (1970). He recognizes the significance of the concept of reciprocity for the gift, but is impressed more by its altruistic character, its moral component. It is the Mauss of the 'moral conclusions' more than the Mauss of the 'obligation to return' who is his model. Unlike the gift-exchange in traditional societies, Titmuss points out, 'there is in the free gift of blood to unnamed strangers no contract of custom, no legal bond, no functional determinism, no situations of discriminatory power, domination, constraint or compulsion, no sense of shame or guilt, no gratitude imperative . . .' (1970, 239; cf. E. R. Leach (review), 1971). But what he also points out is how strongly what one may be tempted to interpret as moral insight and selfless care for one's fellow men is conditioned by the specific structural arrangements of a particular form of society.

The complexity of the issues here was brought home to me by an experience of my own more than forty years ago. On my way through the Solomon islands to Tikopia I had to rely for transport and hospitality on the Melanesian Mission, and for some weeks was the guest of the head of the Mission, Bishop Steward, on the Mission yacht *Southern Cross*. As we travelled together among the islands we discussed many problems of human relationship in the island communities. Malinowski had only recently published his book *Crime and Custom in Savage Society* in which he stressed the importance of reciprocity as a force of binding obligation in Melanesian social organization. He argued that there was an inner symmetry in all social transactions and that this involved a reciprocity of services without which no primitive community – and, he implied, no community at all – could exist. The Bishop borrowed the book from me, read it, and strongly disagreed. He argued vehemently that Melanesians, like other people he said, performed many acts for others freely and without thought for return. Giving, not reciprocity, was the prime motive of service, he held, and he denied the implication of self-interested action in this field. We argued amicably about this and other themes, and I think came to respect each other – partly perhaps because being more detached I could question his views more stoutly than could his clergy. At last the time came for him to land me on the beach of Tikopia and leave me to my fate. He had shown me many kindnesses, which I could not repay. This was his last trip on the *Southern Cross*; he was retiring from the Mission after many years and we both knew it was unlikely we should ever meet again – and we never did. As he said goodbye, leaving me alone in this remote community he shook me firmly by the hand, said gruffly 'No reciprocity!', turned his back and walked off down the beach to the boat. This was his way of hiding his emotions with a joke – but his words were also a reaffirmation of a moral viewpoint.

The Christian ethic in its basic postulates stresses the significance of vicarious giving, of lack of thought for the interest of the self. All major religions indeed include in their precepts some positive approval of giving without thought of return. Of course this may be wishful thinking. Notions of merit so acquired may be built into the ideology. Ideas of reaping after sowing, and casting one's bread upon the waters (or in a new version, shipping one's grain across the sea) suggest fairly direct interest in output-input analysis on a spiritual plane. As I have argued, one counterpart to giving in this sphere is the maintenance of the dignity and integrity of the self. While such compensatory theory may find little backing in modern theology, it is clear that empirically, consistent selfless gift-making is no more of an operative principle than is reciprocity. Moreover, pragmatically, we tend to oppose any attempt to translate the philosophy of complete self-sacrifice into ordinary social terms. Anyone who might try to put into practice the principles of the Sermon on the Mount would be regarded as eccentric; 'sell all you have and give to the poor' is regarded as metaphor, not an injunction to be taken literally. But such principles are not to be completely dismissed from a sociological analysis.

Each society defines differently what acts should conventionally be followed by a 'return'. In the West we have isolated *par excellence* the economic, commercial field of buying and selling, and applied it to most transfers of goods and services. From this range of transactions is normally excluded, and termed gift, those which operate especially in the domestic field, in kinship and friendship relations and in religious behaviour. Yet in such relations there is much half-concealed reciprocity, with subtle compensations.

It might be argued that in such spheres the moral approval to gift-making without repayment is part of the struggle to free the individual from the demands of the pervasive economic system. But also it might be argued that historically, the Western isolation of commerce from moral considerations* is a means of protection of the individual from the logic of the self-effacing Christian principle. The history of attempts by church and state to enforce the anti-usury laws is a comment on this relationship. But while the issues of giving and getting are apt to be presented in Western society in the form of a dialogue between self-interest and religious principle, they can be set in a secular as well as a religious frame, and are so set in many societies. What is clear is that whether the concept of giving and getting be set in a frame of altruism and gratitude, or in a frame of obligation and reciprocity, the procedures in many aspects are symbolic instruments used for maintenance or alteration of social relationships, in the interests of both self and society.

* For example a claim that the law of supply and demand ignores and (by implication should ignore) morality, as made by Lord Cole, Chairman of Unilever in an annual report address (*The Times*, 3 May 1967).

Chapter 12

SYMBOL AND SUBSTANCE

In this book I have been examining some of the general ideas about symbols held by anthropologists, or held by others and of possible use to anthropologists. I have exemplified this examination by a series of illustrations from some fields where public and private symbolism seems to be closely inter-related: food; hair; flags; giving and getting; greeting and parting. Each of these objects and actions is meaningful symbolically to individuals personally as well as collectively and socially. Unlike some of my colleagues, I argue that important problems of interpretation and clues to understanding lie in analysis of such intricate conjunction between the individual and the collective symbolization.

The kind of illustrations I have taken bear for the most part on issues of status. This was deliberate because I am convinced that what I have called status-involvement is basic in a large number of social arrangements, and comes to expression in highly sensitive, elaborately patterned symbolic forms which are both individually meaningful and socially validated. It has been said often enough that the nature of life in society can be grasped only in symbolic forms, and that people must use symbols to handle their problems of relationship with one another. For their actions to be effective, that is for them to lead a viable social existence, the symbols they use must be individually meaningful as well as collectively recognized. But differences of interest lead to lack of agreement on symbolic meanings as well as to manipulation of symbols in partisan fashion.

Broadly speaking, all the symbols of the kinds I have considered may be said to represent the social order and the individual's place in it. Food exchanges symbolize basic social relationships; mode of wearing the hair makes a statement about the wearer's personality and his attitude to established authority; hanging out a national flag symbolizes identity with the political community; a particular pattern of greeting expresses a view about relative social position . . . and so on. The fundamental question of 'symbols of what?' is fairly easily answered: these are all symbols of social living – of society in relation to its members and their relation to one another. But there are other fields of symbolism where the answer is more open, among anthropologists themselves as well as between anthropologists and users of the symbols. This is so with many religious symbols, which represent not simply sets of social relationships of people, but also relationships of the people to mystical entities and forces removed from everyday experience. Some political symbols such as national flags may have sacred quality attributed to them; but the political community to which they refer and whose authority they legitimize, however abstractly conceived, is grounded in a body of people. But a religious symbol such as the Cross stands not only for the Christian community, the church, with its doctrine and ritual, but also for the concept of the redeeming sacrifice of Christ, with its ultimate referent in the person of God himself. And whereas the church has various manifestations of empirical existence, God, a concept of another order, can be regarded in many ways, from a very real Supreme Being and controller of the universe to an imaginative human construct of a set of ideal values.

In the interpretation of any kind of symbols there is always room for difference of view on the theoretical framework adopted to express the relationships. But with religious symbols there may be basic disagreement even among anthropological interpreters about what is being comprehended by the symbols, where is the true locus of the power claimed to give significance to the symbols. It may be argued that this is not a problem about which anthropologists should be concerned – that their job is to make clear what the people who use the symbols think they mean, and how they use the symbols, and not to try and identify the referent as such. Granted that for the most part this is so, there are still two reasons which draw the attention of anthropologists to the question – 'symbols of what?'. One reason is that, if somewhat obscurely, the question is being put to anthropologists as a general issue. In considering problems of African conversion to Islam and Christianity Robin Horton refers to what he terms the 'symbolist' orthodoxy – the view that the spiritual beings of the African cosmologies can be understood only if they are seen as symbols. Regarding this as barren, he argues for an intellectualist position which takes traditional systems of religious belief 'at their face value', as theoretical systems intended for the explanation, prediction, and control of space-time events. Horton's complaint is that anthropologists – even Victor Turner – have not dealt with the problem of why men should have felt constrained to have invented symbols with such attributes as unobservableness and omnipresence, that is spiritual beings. What lies behind the symbols? The other reason is that the anthropologist's view of what the symbols actually represent may affect his whole treatment of the problem. A generation ago Sir Hamilton Gibb, a noted Islamic scholar, opened a discussion of modern trends in Islam with the statement that 'the metaphors in which Christian doctrine is traditionally enshrined satisfy me intellectually as expressing symbolically the highest range of spiritual truth which I can conceive, provided that they are interpreted not in terms of anthropomorphic dogma but as general concepts, related to our changing views of the nature of the universe' (1947, xi). Obviously, his view of meaning of the symbols of Islam would not be identical with that of a Muslim of parallel scholarly interests.

The problem of the 'inner reality' to which religious symbols correspond has been approached from another angle, that of the principles according to which the relations of the symbols to one another are organized. In terms of such 'structuralist' analysis, of which the most distinguished modern exponent is Claude Lévi-Strauss, the symbols of any religious system conform to a grand logical design, of which those who use and believe in the symbols are unaware, and which cannot be perceived by ordinary observational methods of anthropology alone. In such a theoretical scheme the 'power' of the symbols lies in the basic determinate structure of their relationships, irrespective of what may be thought about their generation from a mystical source.

It is clear that heuristically, structural analyses of this kind have great force. But methodologically they depend upon assumptions about identity and difference of human verbal and non-verbal behaviour, which are not always made explicit, and which are sometimes open to question. At times they are apt to denigrate less highly abstract constructions as lacking an appreciation of 'inner reality'. With the less sophisticated exponents of the structuralist method this view is rather like the attitude of a Malay magical practitioner towards the 'secret', the knowledge of the principles of the inner processes of nature which gives him superiority over his rivals.

My aim in this chapter is less ambitious. Various anthropologists have suggested that as part of investigation of religious symbolism, Christian belief and practice are appropriate for scrutiny, and I myself have given attention to them in brief studies of religious mysticism and concepts of God (Firth, 1964, 1968). Here I consider what kind of statement is being made in a series of Christian symbolic usages of a descriptive and ritual order: the concepts of the ethnicity of Jesus; of the 'Sacred Heart' of Jesus (already referred to in Chapter 6); and of the Eucharist. My prime concern in such inquiry is the substance of the symbolic expression – what is overtly asserted by the description of the event or situation in a symbolic way; the logical implications of this kind of assertion compared with other assertions of a non-symbolic kind within the same general context; the patterning of behaviour in respect of the symbolic frame; and the sociological inferences that can be drawn from what is said and done.

ETHNICITY OF JESUS

The problem of what I have called the ethnicity of Jesus is not simply modern, though it has received most explicit attention in modern times. It is essentially this: Jesus, as Saviour and Redeemer of all mankind, according to the Christian statement, may be regarded as in some sense sharing in the characteristics of every different kind of man. Symbolically, He is the conceptual representation of every individual's humanity, with its fleshly weaknesses and lusts, transmuted into a spiritual nature and so rendered capable of participating in salvation through God's mercy. Jesus as God symbolizes anthropomorphically the love, compassion and mercy which man feels to be necessary to save him from his baser self; He also symbolizes the protection against Divine judgement – which in turn symbolizes the verdict of man's own inner logic in reflecting on his shortcomings. But Jesus as Man represents the object of these emotional and moral attentions. So, many times in the history of Christianity there have been tendencies to portray Jesus as man of a kind like unto those men who worshipped Him.

In the attempt to establish as direct a relation as possible between Jesus and individual men, the language in which He is held to have spoken is rendered into the vernacular. This was so even before the Catholic church allowed the vernacular Mass; there was exposition in the local languages. It is intelligible then that the physical form in which Jesus is conceived to have lived should also have been rendered into local ethnic terms.

In the West, for much more than 1,000 years, from early Christian Roman mosaics to Manet's *Mocking of Christ*, Jesus has been depicted as Caucasian in physical type. The problem of His actual physical semblance has been learnedly debated – was He fair or dark, or as some would have it, red-haired? Was He bearded?* Serious scholarship does not claim any authentic portraits of Christ, and an ingenious suggestion by Sir Wyke Bayliss reinforces the cogent reasons for the lack. Bayliss argued that in the days of persecution in the early Christian church it was not safe for Christians to declare their faith openly by bearing upon their persons the portrait of their Master. So 'the natural alternative was symbol'. A picture of a youth carrying a lamb across a stream represented Christ the Good Shepherd; a beardless Orpheus playing a lyre in the midst of wild beasts and attracting them was a reminiscence of the power of Christ to sustain the martyrs in the arena. 'These were the symbols – safe yet intelligible. But the essential condition of them was that they should not bear the Likeness' (1905, 68). However that may be, artists were free to symbolize Jesus in human form as in other forms, and conventionalized Him in vaguely Mediterranean or even northern European type, with pale skin colour, straight or wavy hair and thin nose and lips.

This seems to have been the image which pictorially and otherwise Christian missionaries offered to Asiatic, African and other populations distant from the Mediterranean. But this image has been if not rejected at least supplemented by artists working in such dis-

* Considerable literature has accumulated on this problem: for example P. Doncoeur, *Le Christ dans l'Art Français*, 1939–1948; E. Senior, *Portraits of Christ*, Harmondsworth, 1940; Engelbert Kirschbaum, S.J., Christus, Christusbild, in *Lexikon der Christlichen Ikonographie*, 1, 355–454, Rome, 1968.

tant lands and striving to express in representations of Jesus some basic principles of common humanity, by giving them local facial features. So, in fifteenth- or sixteenth-century bronzes of the Crucifixion from the lower Congo, it is said that 'the face of the Christ generally presents the negroid type'. Pictures and carvings of the Son of Man by Indian, Chinese and African artists often show Jesus with ethnic features appropriate to the artist's own group. A well-known East African Crucifixion by Job Kekana depicts the Christ with African features; a Chinese picture of Jesus as shepherd by Tsui Hung-I shows Him with Chinese features. Of the painter Lu Hung Nien it was said that his 'desire as a Christian artist has been to depict our Lord as a Chinese Saviour surrounded by Chinese people', when with those of other Chinese artists, his pictures were shown at a pre-war exhibition at the Roman Catholic University of Fu-jên in Peking. The justification for such treatment of Jesus in portraiture is clearly its symbolic value. In a general defence of Chinese form in Christian religious art Cardinal Faulhaber cited the action of the eighth-century (Second) Council of Nicaea providing that images should be venerated though not adored. Since it is the spirit and not the appearance that is significant in Catholic ideology, by implication the visage of the Christ may 'speak the language of the time' provided that it expresses a genuine religious faith. In analogous style Bishop Carey, introducing a volume of illustrations of such portrayals, stated that the Incarnate Christ 'is ever expressing Himself in beauty, truth, goodness and love, in human apprehensions and hearts. He is expressing himself from within . . . Artists pierce through incidents and trappings to the soul underneath . . . In portraying incidents they catch a glimpse of Him who underlies all. In this book they reveal Him, and we understand and adore'.* But if Jesus was ever actually a human being, He cannot have displayed the physical traits of all races; He cannot have been both yellow-skinned and black-skinned, had straight as well as frizzly hair. Some of the portrayals must be metaphorical, representing Jesus conceptually but not naturalistically; they cannot all at the same time pretend to show what He actually looked like.

If it is only symbols that are being dealt in, then the ethnic image

* For material and opinions see: Cardinal Faulhaber, 1932; Walter J. Carey, 1939; S.P.G., *The Life of Christ by Chinese Artists*, 1948; Rob. L. Wanijn, 195ↄ, 45.

of Christ may be allowed to vary according to the audience by whom the representation is needed. But Western Christians, as indeed the church itself after the Council of Nicaea, have been slow to admit Christ-figures of all ethnic types to the same level of iconic authenticity. Hence as well as aesthetic and religious statements of Christ with the lineaments of Oriental or African Man but the representative of common humanity, there has arisen the political statement of an ethnic Christ. What may be called religious nationalists, stringently determined to insist on the immediate relevance of Jesus to their lives in a physical as well as a metaphorical sense, have developed the 'Black Jesus' thesis, which rejects the validity of any other ethnic type of Saviour for Blacks.

To many Christians in the Western world – black as well as white – the assertion that Jesus is black has seemed naive, absurd, perhaps shocking. It contravenes not only the pictures of Christ traditionally available in mosaic, fresco, oils, etc.; it also is incongruent with the setting of Christ's life given in the New Testament story.* Granted the debatable nature of the evidence, assuming that Jesus was an historical figure He must have been a Jew – though Wagner in his *Heldentum* tract seems to have denied that Jesus was of Jewish stock and claimed Him as a kind of archetypal Aryan. If Jesus had been a Roman citizen it is presumably faintly possible that He could have been of negroid stock, but most unlikely. So the choice is between ethnicity and historicity: if Jesus is to be black, then it is the metaphorical, symbolical Jesus, not the actual historical Jesus who is being portrayed. But if Jesus is simply a conceptual figure – as many people would maintain – then white Christians have no monopoly in His physical type. The problem is much simplified if Jesus is recognized as a symbolic figure who can be given any complexion desired. This is what the black poet Countee Cullen did forty years ago in his poem *The Black Christ*: he represented Jesus taking the place of his brother at a lynching, assuming the form of the threatened man as part of His Saviour's role in His daily Crucifixion. In this moving poem it makes much more sense indeed for Jesus,

* The parallel problem has not arisen in Islam, as far as I know. Not only has religious iconography, including portrayals of the Prophet, been severely restricted by Muslim theology; the few paintings depicting the Prophet show him as of broadly Arab or Persian type, whereas a black face is given to Bilal (the first of the Muslims appointed to give the call to prayer) because of his Abyssinian birth (T. W. Arnold, 1928, 97 and pl. XXII).

the representative of suffering humanity, to be black than white. It would be logical too for this theme to be projected further, and Jesus to be accepted as black in the modern Christology, since over the last few centuries it is probably Blacks who might claim to have endured more of human suffering than have Whites.* Unless of course the Crucifixion should be regarded as a kind of spiritual tokenism, a sacrifice on account of those who have sinned on an ethnic basis. Then Blacks might think that since Whites have sinned most, as their representative, Jesus should properly be white!

Leaving aside aesthetic representations, cults of Black Jesus have taken two main forms. One is the quasi-historical assertion that Jesus Himself, the original founder of the cult, was black. In the early 1920s under Bishop McGuire, colleague of Marcus Garvey, the African Orthodox church had Black Madonna and child as a standard picture in the homes. The worship of a Black Christ was openly advocated, and that of a White Christ spurned (C. Eric Lincoln, 1961, 62). In a recent version, that of the Black Christian Nationalists, it is held that the original Israelites were also black. With this provocative view has been linked the idea of Jesus as the Black Messiah, sent by God as a revolutionary leader to rebuild the black nation Israel and liberate black people from white exploitation. Shrines of the Black Madonna serve as temples for the cult (*New York Times*, 6 April 1970). The other form of the cult is a more mystical one, of identifying a present-day black religious leader as Jesus Himself. The former thesis conserves the historical dimension at the expense of spiritual immediacy; the latter thesis is timeless and ahistorical, but brings godhead into the midst of the congregation. Each in a different way is a statement of need – that the religious inspiration and fount of morality should be symbolically expressed in a human form near to that of the worshippers.

But this perpetuates a dilemma for white Christians. God the Father might conceivably materialize in any colour. But fixed into humanity as God the Son, it is more difficult to admit alternatives to Him. So orthodox Christians, assuming they believe in the historicity

* This seems to have been a line along which the thought of some black artists has developed. Since Christ symbolically represents the sufferings of mankind, he must have been black to have had the qualities attributed to him. Hence in the attempt to create images with which black people can identify, artists have included portrayals of Christ as a black man. To some, 'Christ is a purely symbolic black voice'.

of Jesus, have a delicate choice: they might like to acquiesce on symbolic and sympathetic grounds in the blackness of Jesus, but this would mean flying in the face of tradition and the environmental features as they are known; but if they stick to the whiteness of Jesus all they can do is to understand the blackness of Jesus as metaphorical, non-historical, a kind of amiable concession to rising black nationalism. This can be even more exasperating as patronage to earnest Christian Blacks, who may feel it intolerable to have to accept a white Saviour – 'an effeminate white Christ'. In practice, presumably many white Christians do not accept the blackness of Jesus as either literal or metaphorical, and are shocked by the claim.

This example illustrates two important points. Historically, many religious symbols have been selected, consciously or not, for political reasons. And the question whether something is to be classed as a symbol or not is not just an academic one, but can be a matter of great practical concern. The Black Christian Nationalists, it appears, do not believe that Christ was black metaphorically, but literally; for them His blackness was real, not just symbolic. I would argue that some of the highest emotional loading can occur not where a thing is admittedly only symbolic, but where its symbolism is either denied or believed to be shared with a real participation in the thing symbolized.

THE SACRED HEART

A most interesting example of merging of literal and metaphorical in a religious symbolic presentation is in the so-called 'Sacred Heart of Jesus' cult (for general description see Chapter 6). Here is a case where something essentially personal, an intimate internal organ of someone believed once to have lived as a man, has been given worldwide currency as a symbol of love.

For a long while in the history of the cult a question of critical significance was the exact nature of the organ to which devotion was to be paid. The official view of the church at first was that it was the symbolic character only of the Heart to which reverence should be paid, not its physical character. The *Cordicolism* of those attached to this cult of the physical Heart was attacked, especially by the

Jansenists, and defended, especially by the Jesuits. Special confraternities arose, mainly in France, Germany and Poland to propagate the cult of adoration of the actual heart of the Saviour. As the iconography depicting the physical heart in various forms continued to develop, Pius XII clarified the issue by pronouncing the physical heart to be authoritatively included in the object of the cult. So conceptual or metaphorical heart and physical heart – usually shown as a red pear-shaped object – were worshipped together as symbolic objects, symbolic of the redemptive love of Christ, both human and divine.

But a further issue is also of anthropological interest – the concern of theologians for the appropriateness of the heart as a symbol for this love. We know nowadays that the heart is not the seat of the emotions. But there is little doubt that in the seventeenth century Marie Alacoque believed that it was, and the cult grew up on this assumption. Yet within the church there were doubts about accepting this widening gap between physiology and faith. At an early date a liturgical feast proposed in Rome failed to gain acceptance because the devotion was presented as based upon the heart as the principle and organ of love. A petition of 1765 was accepted only after it omitted what was termed the 'objectionable explanation'. In the end faith – and the cumulative force of popular enthusiasm – won out over physiology. The physical heart of Christ was not only accepted as the symbol of his love, but also accepted as the proper symbol. The *New Catholic Encyclopaedia* states authoritatively: 'Although every part of Christ's sacred humanity is worthy of the strict adoration due to God alone, the heart is singled out for a special devotion because of its inherent symbolism'. The natural fleshly heart of Jesus is the 'true natural symbol' of his love.

The authorities do seem a bit uneasy on this point. It is recognized that intellectually and emotionally, as distinct from blood circulation, the heart no longer is correctly regarded as the seat of the inner life of man. Yet it is still held that the special object involved in every form of cult rendered to Christ's humanity has somehow a correspondence on the spiritual side which is 'proper' to it – a sensible element that has some intelligible connection with the psychological element, as the *Encyclopaedia* puts it. So Pius XII called the physical heart of Christ a 'natural symbol' of His threefold love. And to the adoration of this redemptive love are added devotional acts that it is said 'spring from the character of this special object: imitation of the virtues of Christ's heart . . .'. The argument is in fact a bit apologetic. It is admitted that neither the Scriptures nor the Fathers of the church expressly refer to the physical heart of Jesus as the symbol of his love. But, it is argued, they do explicitly declare that Christ has a true and integral human nature, and hence (presumably by implication) a heart upon which his entire affective life exercises a real physical influence. 'This real connection between the physical heart and the affective life provides the basis for the natural symbolism of the heart in respect to love.' But as anthropologists we should notice that this is really a reversal of the classical view of the relationship: the symbolism is treated as natural not because the heart is the seat of the emotions, but because emotions affect the heart.

But this form of argument could have unexpected results if logically pursued. In effect what we are seeing is the momentum of a symbolic recognition* – the Catholic church has been unable to make the switch from heart to brain as symbol, as physiological knowledge has altered, so it is still the Sacred Heart and not the Sacred Head that is worshipped. (Polynesians have been more discerning; they have made the head and not the heart taboo.) What we really have is a case of concordance between liturgy and popular thought – the church's symbolism of the Sacred Heart of Jesus is in line with the popular metaphors which still talk of hearts aching and hearts breaking, and loving people with all one's heart. It is in line with Western popular distribution of symbolic meanings attaching to the body, that other organs of Christ have gone uncelebrated.† There is no cult of the Holy Tongue, though this was the organ chiefly responsible for proclamation of Jesus's message. If Christ really had a 'true and integral human nature' there are other organs as well as his heart upon which his affective life might have exercised a real physical influence. One commentator (A. D. Howell-Smith, 1950, 542) has bluntly observed that Catholics would be horrified at the adoration of the divine genitals; but notes that the worship of

* For analogy in the field of emotional relations see D. M. Schneider, 1968, 115.

† Otherwise too, considering the value placed upon Mary's virginity, one might have expected a cult of adoration of the Holy Womb – the Holy Hymen could perhaps be symbolized by the veil.

the *lingam*, the conventionalized symbol of the phallus of Shiva, by pious Hindus is deemed perfectly natural. I think one can detect in some recent Catholic writings a move to make sex more religiously respectable, as part of a general 'with-it' trend in the church. (It has been suggested, for instance, that nuns, in their physical purity, might serve as sex symbols of an idealized kind. But a recent Vatican decision to allow lay Catholic women not only to take a vow of virginity but also to be consecrated as virgins by a bishop in the same way as cloistered nuns, if they wish to dedicate their lives to God, has been described as a re-affirmation of the significance of chastity in a world obsessed with sex.) But so far neither tongue nor phallus have appeared overtly in the Christian iconography; the church has chosen to locate the sympathetic life of the Saviour in His Heart alone. It is a clear demonstration of the social character of a religious symbol, even when it is put forward as a 'natural' representation. There is a definite element of arbitrariness in the selection of religious symbols, but their arbitrariness is part of a system, within which the operations of individuals may have galvanizing force, and may be determined in part by relation to a wider, secular symbolic system. Moreover, in the selection of themes for symbolic representation, in an elaborately organized institution such as the Catholic church, the emergence of a symbol into liturgical use is by no means only a 'natural' process but a matter of prolonged consideration, including manipulation by pressure groups, using strategies akin to those in vogue in the secular world of politics.

THE SYMBOLIC RITE OF 'GIVING THANKS'

Before turning to the symbolism of the Christian Eucharist I consider briefly a parallel from a more conventional ethnographic field. The Tikopia in pagan times had a communion feast, known as the 'Sacred Food' – a term which nowadays they apply as Christians to the Holy Communion. Male members of the clan assembled in their temple, led by their chief, and celebrated their yam harvest by each man eating ritually a cooked yam tuber straight from the oven. The rite was also called the Hot Food because it was in part a competitive display to see who would be the first to bite off and swallow a piping hot morsel of the vegetable. The rite had peculiar significance for two reasons. One was that the yam tubers were regarded in totemic alignment as symbolizing the supreme god of the clan – indeed, the vegetable was termed the 'body' of the god. The other reason was that the god himself was believed to attend the rite in person, to be actually present in the body of the presiding chief – looking out through human eyes at the performance which he was believed to have instituted in times long past. The man who first swallowed the scalding hot morsel of yam was thought in a vague way to stand well in the graces of the god for the ensuing season (see Firth, 1967a, 152–60; 1971 (1951a), 227–32).

The physical act of eating the yam was regarded as consuming the body of the god in the presence of the god himself, and this was regarded as symbolical of a wider set of relationships between man and the forces and objects of nature. The Tikopia did not engage in any elaborate analysis of the exact processes thought to be involved in consuming both the yam and the body of their god. They regarded identification of yam with god's body, and chief with god's presence, as conforming to what they believed were the capacities of their deities, not calling for searching explanation. Questions of timing – when the god actually entered or left the chief's body – or of distribution of qualities – how god and vegetable could co-exist in the same material form – did not seem to worry the Tikopia.

Some exploration of this problem in another context has been given in an inquiry of mine into problems of identification in primitive religious thought (Firth, 1966a); and also by Audrey Hayley (1968) in an examination of the 'symbolic equation' in the Nuer substitution of a cucumber for an ox in sacrifice – which I have also referred to in a study of organizational problems of offering and sacrifice (Firth, 1963). In the course of her analysis Audrey Hayley has distinguished two meanings of symbol: as 'standing for', 'being a representation of'; and as equivalent to the concept of 'is', and identified with the referent. As an example of the latter is taken Evans-Pritchard's citation of the Nuer view that the crocodile is not just a representation of God; the creature *is* God. As he put it, 'symbol and what it symbolizes are fused'. But if to the Nuer the crocodile *was* a god, or a portion of the personality of God, in all circumstances, then it was not a symbol. It was the anthropologist who by classing it as a symbol, invented the fusion. But if, as seems plausible, the Nuer believed the crocodile to be God in some circumstances and not in others, or God in some respects or qualities and not in others, symbol and object were conjoined, and fused in only a limited sense. That a symbol comes to take on some of the qualities of what it symbolizes – for example sacredness – is a common phenomenon, as also is the attribution to a material object of being both itself in physical qualities and something else in spiritual qualities. Leaving aside the question of whether we should best speak of such phenomena as identification, conjunction, fusion or (in Lévy-Bruhl's term) as mystic participation, I would argue that these do not constitute a logically different class from those of symbolic representation – that the differences are those of degree and aspect of identification.

Neither Tikopia nor Nuer intellectualized such a symbolic equation process. But we do have a more intellectualized parallel in the Christian religious rite of Communion, the sacrament of the Eucharist. The name Eucharist applied to the consecration and distribution of the elements of bread and wine in the Christian rite refers to a thanksgiving, an acknowledgement of favour, which was also the Tikopia attitude in their pagan rite of consuming the body of their god in the yam festival. Anthropologists and psychologists, for example B. Malinowski, E. O. James, C. G. Jung, Lloyd Warner, Mary Douglas, have already examined various aspects of the Eucharistic ritual and concepts. But I want to focus particularly on the ideas about relation of symbol to substance found therein. In the development of the cult of the Sacred Heart of Jesus, Pope Pius XII was at some pains to stress that the faithful should pay their devotions to the physical as well as to the metaphysical organ – or since no physical heart of Jesus exists, to the idea of the physical organ. In some ways a parallel concern with the physical has marked the Catholic theory of the Eucharist in the Mass, though in this case the material substances exist and are of human manufacture. In both cases it would seem that the material symbol is retained in the interests of emotional involvement in the cult or rite, and related by an elaborate analytical construction to the spiritual referent, in the interests of intellectual demands for an acceptable reasoned statement on the phenomenon.

In the Catholic Mass, as is well known, the overt rite includes the offering of bread (the 'Host', from *hostia*, a sacrificial victim) and wine (in the chalice) at the altar, purification of them with incense, and consecration of them with appropriate invocations. Since the later Middle Ages in the Roman Catholic church, those of the congregation who are ritually entitled to do so then partake of the bread, the priest alone drinking the wine. (Other Christian churches have modified forms of this Holy Communion service; in most the congregation as well as the priest partake of the wine.) The ritual paradigm for this communion is the Last Supper of Jesus with his disciples. As recorded in the Scriptures (for example John, vi; I Corinthians, xi) on the night before he was betrayed, Jesus took bread, gave thanks, broke it and said 'This is my body for you; do this in remembrance of me', and took winc likewise, describing it metaphorically as his blood, and gave both to the disciples to be consumed. There seems to be some doubt whether Jesus's words as reported should include the actual injunction 'do this in remembrance of me' (cf. E. O. James, 1937, 127). But for all Christians the general symbolism of the communion rite is the same: it commemorates the Last Supper; and it symbolizes the sacrifice of Christ, His death on the Cross as the representative of humanity in the person of God the Son, His redemptive love, and the personal link of every Christian with Him, periodically renewed in solemn gathering of the faithful. The symbolic interpretation of specific parts of the rite varies considerably in the different sectors of Christianity, and in the more liturgical-minded groups can be very elaborate indeed. So, the breaking of the bread (*Fractio*) can be interpreted as symbolic of Christ's death on the Cross; the mixing of water with the wine can be seen as the symbolic commingling of divinity and humanity in Christ's nature. The conjunction of elements, the *Commixtio*, when bread is dipped in the wine, has been interpreted as a symbolical representation of the Resurrection, when body and blood were again reunited – or in another symbolism, the congregation, the body of Christ, as the bread, is infused with the spirit of Christ, the wine. Almost any action in the rite can be turned to use in the symbolic system.

For many Christians the Eucharistic rite is primarily a commemorative one; it is done in memory of Jesus, on whom they think solemnly and with gratitude while they are partaking of the communion elements. For many others it is not only commemorative but also symbolic, in that the elements themselves stand for the bodily substances of Jesus and therefore allow the congregation to absorb metaphorically part of the person of their Saviour and therefore to share in his sacrifice and in His eternal life. For them, the words of the Gospel of St John are very meaningful, when Jesus said that he was the 'living bread' that came down from heaven, and if any man eat of this bread he shall live for ever. William Tyndale's translation, now more than 400 years old, gives the sense of the passage very vividly, as very many Christians have known it, as it continues: 'And the breed that I will geve, is my flesshe, which I will geve for the lyfe of the worlde. And the Iewes strove among them selves sayinge: How can this felowe geve vs his flesshe to eate? Then Jesus sayde vnto them: Verely, verely I saye vnto you, except ye eate the flesshe of the sonne of man, and drinke his bloude, ye shall not have lyfe in you. . . . For my flesshe is meate in dede; and my bloude is drynke in dede. He that eateth my flesshe and drynketh my bloude, dwelleth in me and I in him . . .' (1534, Cambridge edn, 1938, 200). Protestants generally leave the matter at this level: when Jesus died, his body was broken and his blood was shed; by eating the bread and drinking the wine of the Communion they both re-enact the Lord's Supper, and in simulacrum make contact with his body and blood from the Crucifixion, with its spiritual implications. Many of them are aware of the more general ritual significance in other contexts of breaking of bread and eating together as a sign of friendship, and of mutual drinking of wine as a pledge. Some too may know that the realism of the Gospel language of eating probably refers to early ideas of flesh and blood as vitalizing agents in mystery cults, to ideas of feeding upon Christ as a necessary means of union with the substance of the Saviour as a means of escape from the material world (cf. James, 1937, 126 ff.; McGiffert, 1932, 32, 47; Loisy, 1948, 251–2; Warner, 1961, 314–39).

CONCEPT OF SACRAMENTAL SUBSTANCE

But for Catholics the interpretation is more complex, and for anthropologists even more interesting. Catholics believe, and by the rules of their church are bound to believe, that the Mass is not simply a memorial, not simply a symbol, but a divinely efficacious sacrament. The elements of bread and wine do not remain unchanged throughout the rite, as Protestants hold, but are changed at the moment of consecration into the actual flesh and blood of Christ – 'the sacramental presence of Our Lord's Body with Its natural dimensions in the Holy Eucharist'. This transubstantiation, or change from one substance into another, of the Eucharistic elements has been part of Catholic belief for about 1,000 years, though a subject of bitter controversy until made an article of faith in 1215, and re-affirmed against Protestant heterodoxy by the Council of Trent three centuries later. Moreover, it is the teaching of the church that not merely parts of Christ's bodily substance thus appear at the Mass – His body and blood under the species of bread and wine – but Christ Himself is involved as a whole personality, renewing His sacrifice on the Cross, hence the doctrine of the 'Real Presence'. 'The same Christ is contained and is immolated in an unbloody manner, who, on the altar of the Cross, offered Himself once in a bloody manner' – in the words of the Council of Trent.

All this has been the subject of a great deal of subtle metaphysical and mystical interpretation by Catholic theologians and apologists. It has also been given more sociological study, as I noted earlier. E. O. James interpreted the Eucharistic mystery as a primitive life-giving rite of sacrifice, akin in its basic notion of a dying to live, to the pagan mysteries which preceded it. As part of the 'age-long struggle for eternal life by sacramental means' he saw the Eucharist in St Ignatius's terms as 'a medicine of immortality', parallel to the conception of the Vedic sacred beverage *soma* (James, 1937, 149–52; cf. McGiffert, 1932, 43). C. G. Jung (1958) saw the Mass as anthropomorphic symbol of a mystery which relates the human spirit to the eternal; wherein nature, man and God are all sacrificed in the unity of symbolic gift under the forms of bread and wine. The sacrifice of God was seen by Jung as a kind of punishment. Ruthlessly pushing his argument beneath the surface of the church's explanations, Jung saw the 'natural logic' of the punishment in guilt, and God's guilt in the fact that as creator of the world he was inadequate and therefore had to transform himself by ritual slaying from a concrete to a spiritual lord. Malinowski used the Mass (1936, 47–50) as an illustration of the relation between myth and miracle. In the transubstantiation of the sacrament, the miracle, supernatural realities are created by ritual acts. In the stories of the origin of the Mass, the myth, there is the affirmation of primeval miracles. For Mary Douglas, too, the doctrine of the Eucharist is a demonstration of belief in efficacious power, the rite is an effective field of change and instrument of change (Douglas, 1970, 46–9). The crux of the doctrine is that a real, invisible transformation has occurred when the priest has recited the sacred words, and that the eating of the consecrated host, in which Christ the Lord is present, has saving efficacy, a redemptive force as a channel of grace. But whereas Malinowski despite his Catholic upbringing, was discussing the Eucharist as an external observer, Douglas, seemingly as a matter of personal conviction, holds that its full meaning involves magical and sacramental efficacy, and is scornful of her co-religionists who are insensitive to this meaning.

I am not here concerned with these problems. What I want to do is to consider particularly some aspects of the logical forms in which the symbolism is couched, and what in effect is being asserted by what is being said.

In the traditional Catholic doctrine, the Mass is a true sacrifice of Christ which performed once in blood on the Cross, is perpetuated without blood in mystical manner on the altar, and communicated to the faithful under the appearance of bread and wine. Anthropologically, the use of bread and wine is intelligible as it was to John of Damascus in the eighth century – that familiar objects give reassurance, whereas the unfamiliar and unusual would be repellent (see McGiffert, 1932, 324). And from the point of view of the solemnity of the rite, the Catholic doctrine of transubstantiation and the Real Presence may be more telling than the Protestant idea of simple analogy. To imagine that one has on one's tongue a portion, however minute, of the flesh of the living God, who is present at the rite, is an awful thought, which should have its effect upon conduct. As a matter of ritual organization, then, the transubstantiation doctrine makes good sense; it aims at bringing the sacred home personally to every worshipper. With Catholic Christian as with pagan Tikopia, the belief in ingestion of sacred substance reinforces the respect for the rite.

But the traditional Catholic doctrine has certain logical implications to which theologians have given attention. To assert that bread becomes flesh, and wine becomes blood, not by digestive process slowly but by ritual process instantly, when a rite of sacralization is performed by a priest, calls for explanation by any thoughtful person. That symbol has become referent introduces a concept which has to be fitted into the system of ideas. Malinowski implied that the Eucharistic explanation of identity of symbol and referent is a case of inference from general assumption, and not of a separate mode of thought. He has pointed out that a theologian would not give the title of miracle to this process, since it is regarded as falling under the law of the nature of the supernatural, and not occurring in terms of a tangible, concrete sensuously appreciable working of supernatural force. The theological explanation indeed tries very carefully to distinguish what it is that actually alters, in order to present a plausible form of argument to the faithful who may question the meaning of the rite. So a popular exposition of the mystery of the Eucharist by a Dominican (traditionally, guardians of doctrine) states: 'As God, Christ is everywhere; but His Sacred Body and precious Blood are not everywhere. They are in the Blessed Sacrament under the phenomena of bread and wine.... But the phenomena or sensible qualities of bread and wine undergo no intrinsic change when the substances underlying them pass, at the words of consecration, into the Body and Blood of Christ. They remain as they were before consecration' (O'Neill, 1933, 64–5). So, the communicant does not feel the taste of blood and meat upon the tongue. Hence, the accusation of cannibalism, with analogies of totemic feasting, is rejected as superficial. So too are notions of aesthetic shock avoided. This is done by drawing a distinction between *accident*, the external appearance and properties, and *substance*, the inner part. This distinction between externals and inner reality is of course common in many contexts, and in Western religious and philosophical thought has been identified going back through Thomas Aquinas to Aristotle. But what is uncommon, said to be unique, is that the inner conceptual reality should suffer a physical and not merely a conceptual change. Transformation is indeed not the correct word, since it is substance and not form which is believed to alter. And Catholic theologians insist on the completeness of the change. 'Transubstantiation means the conversion of the bread and wine into the Body and Blood of Christ, in such a complete manner that none of the substance of the bread or wine remains, but only the species thereof ... It implies that ... Our Lord's Sacred Body comes, and is truly and really there ...' (compare O'Neill, 39–40). The concept means basically that the accidents or qualities of the bread and wine, which are perceptible to the senses, continue to exist apart from, and without the support of, the substance of the bread and wine, which ceases and is replaced by the substance (but not the sensory qualities) of Christ's body and blood.

Various anthropological issues of interest arise from this concept. It has certain parallels over a wide ethnographic field. Pagan Tikopia, for instance, believed that every religious offering had in addition to its material stuff, visible and palpable, an immaterial counterpart, invisible and impalpable. They regarded this as in part a matter of demonstration, as when fresh taro plants set out as offering on a grave wilted; they argued that the immaterial counterpart of the plants had been taken away by the spirits, leaving the solid part of the offering behind. In ordinary terminology one might speak, as I have been accustomed to do, of the visible part of the offering as the substance, and the invisible counterpart as the essence. But in Catholic terminology one might speak of the visible part as the appearances (or accidents or species) and the invisible part as the substance. Now both the pagan Tikopia and the Catholic theologians have been faced by the same problem: how if the substance (essence) be withdrawn can the appearance sustain itself? The Tikopia view was less abstract – the material stuff suffers – but they bothered little about the problem, attributing the whole phenomenon to the work of spirits. The Catholic view has been to regard the persistence of the bread and wine when deprived of their essential substance as a matter altogether above the order of nature – 'part of the mystery of the Real Presence which we do not pretend to fathom', as our popular account puts it. The explanations are very similar.

In keeping with the sacred character of the Eucharistic rite, a number of ritual precautions have been traditionally observed in regard to it. The fitness of the priest to consecrate the Host, and the fitness of the celebrant to receive it have been naturally the subject of considerable regulation. And since partaking of the Eucharist means communing not only with Christ but also with fellow Christians in a common body, views have been expressed on who should be allowed to share in the celebration. More specific ritual procedures have also been closely specified. Traditionally, the wafer of unleavened bread has been placed by the priest on the tongue of the celebrant; it has been taboo for the celebrant to touch it with his hand. In some modern Catholic churches it has now been allowed for a celebrant to take the host in his hand and place it in his mouth, and an apostolic constitution issued by the Pope in 1953 relaxed some of the rules for fasting before Communion. But while the sacred proprieties seem capable of modification, an attempt is made to preserve the sensory message of the Eucharist. Some modern Catholic circles find it very important that celebrants shall still feel, taste and smell bread and wine; that no violence be done to the senses. A recommendation in a new Roman Catholic missal was that the Host received by laymen during Holy Communion should 'really appear to be food'. In the New York metropolitan area in 1970 a new order of the Mass tried to bring the sacred rite closer to the people *inter alia* by using real unleavened bread instead of the former round small communion wafers that quickly dissolved on the tongue without chewing. The idea of the real bread was to emphasize that the rite was not only a memorial to the sacrifice of Christ but also a communal meal. But there were technical difficulties. The church requires the bread to be unleavened, and without yeast it is hard to get the bread to rise. A suggestion to use Jewish matzoth as in Passover, understandably, met with little favour. For some time convents which made communion host experimented. Wafers made from whole-wheat flour were found to be more tasty, but to crumble easily; and the production change-over required to make them needed new equipment that could be expensive for convents on tight budgets. A large commercial concern in this field began marketing 'unleavened altar bread', tiny baked cubes that could be chewed; but some priests complained that these 'looked like breakfast food' (patent commercial cereal). (See *New York Times*, 23 March 1970; *Chicago Daily News*, 16 November 1970.) So the search for new recipes may still proceed. In parallel style, outside the Catholic range, another concession to sensory elements occurred in some Nonconformist circles which stressed teetotalism. Spurred on by tales of reformed alcoholics who relapsed at their first sip of communion wine, some generations ago Methodists and others began to use unfermented grape juice to symbolize the blood of the Saviour.

With all such attention to pragmatic detail, as part of sacred ritual, anthropologists are quite familiar. The exegetical apparatus of the Catholic Eucharist is, however, rather special in its care for the logical proprieties. The doctrine of the sacramental presence of Jesus 'under the veils of bread and wine' has produced not merely a distinction between two kinds of reality – that which is superficial and that which is underneath – but also between two kinds of perception corresponding to these. Moreover, the validity of the thesis of transformation of inner substance, while held to rest ultimately on faith and revelation, is defended vigorously by reason as far as possible. It is argued: that the doctrine of transubstantiation has foundation in Scripture; that the church, divinely endowed, has the hereditary title, which she can prove, to pronounce authoritatively upon the subject; that those who question the doctrine are trying to measure Christ by a human standard, and cannot see that they are substituting their individual judgment for His; that it is ludicrous to suppose that the whole Christian world has erred for 2,000 years in the interpretation of what Christ meant. It is claimed not only that the doctrine is true, but that it is also reasonable and consistent; that Catholic philosophers and theologians have subjected it to tests of severe intellectual analysis in order to discover its relation to the eternal principles of thought reflected in the human mind. So Catholic theologians draw as legitimate the conclusion that 'the actual separation of an existing material thing from the phenomena which naturally accompany it, is neither contradictory in conception nor impossible in fact'. Though it may be difficult to conceive just how the processes take place, the mind can conceive of the substantial presence of a material thing in a place without being subject to the conditions of place. As imaginative constructs, such assertions about the independent nature of 'substance' and 'accidents' are of great interest. But to translate them into statements of fact requires assumptions about divine power of another order of reality, acceptance of which requires faith and not simply an appeal to reason.

I now summarize the position of the symbolism of the Eucharist, as seen by an anthropologist not a participant believer in the cult.

It is clear, from historical research, by E. O. James and others, and from comparative ethnographical evidence, that the Eucharistic ideas of a communion obtained by partaking of the bodily substance of the god are in conformity with a wide range of symbolic concepts which unite sacred with secular in food, as it is consumed (cf. Fortes, 1966b, 21). They belong too to that sector of concepts in which it is not the food which becomes sanctified, but the sanctified which becomes food. The special ritual values attaching to blood are important here, in line with the magical significance of blood in many religious systems.* But the blood and the body of Christ are presented in the Catholic Eucharist in an unusual way, as part of a very complex and intricately organized symbolic system. They are presented as occurring without sensory evidence, in invisible, impalpable 'substance' (in another context one might have said 'essence') only, beneath the 'veils' of bread and wine – that is, empirically, simply as assertion. The assertion is defended elaborately, by appeal to reason as well as to faith and authority. It is offered also, however, as a challenge to reason, a demand for faith, as a mystery which is not and cannot be fully comprehended. But by its very form, by maintaining the continuity of appearance of bread and wine to the senses, it avoids the more blatant contradiction of the senses, as well as the aesthetic shock of oral confrontation with flesh and blood. The Eucharistic doctrine gives an example of what may be called a super-symbol. The wafer and the wine symbolize Jesus and the Crucifixion, atonement and redemption, the union of the faithful in the body of the church. But as Mary Douglas has maintained, symbolizing is not understood in the Catholic tradition to have exhausted the meaning of the Eucharist, which also is believed to have sacramental efficacy, providing a channel of grace for redemption. The doctrine of the Eucharist is then a statement about power and the source of power. It is an assertion that the symbol is not merely about power, but in its inner substance *is* power.

Propositions of this kind are not capable of proof or disproof.

* Cf. the notion of the redemptive power of Christ's blood. Also the Church of England prayer 'Almighty God, our heavenly Father, who hast purchased to thyself a universal church by the precious blood of thy dear Son . . .' (Communion Collect in Ember Week, *Book of Common Prayer*).

But they have sociological implications, including those of defining group allegiance. The doctrine of transubstantiation has served the Catholic church as a critical indicator of definition on various occasions. So Berengar of Tours had to do penance for the scandal of his heresy in the eleventh century after he had stressed the symbolism of the Eucharist in his attempt to submit the mysteries of faith to logical treatment by dialectic (Knowles, 1962, 94–5). And the Council of Trent in the sixteenth century reasserted an earlier article of faith about transubstantiation, and redefined the term, in its effort to support the church in the Counter-Reformation. So statements purportedly about bread and wine in their symbolic relationships are also statements about social structures and institutions. They are assertions in defence of established positions or claims to attain such positions, on a pragmatic social level as well as on a conceptual level. Primitive societies have such symbol markers too, but are commonly less dogmatic about them; their critical tests are more pragmatic.

CONCLUSION

For a variety of reasons anthropologists have recently become very interested in symbolism. One of our major jobs has been identification of alien symbols and interpretation of them. We have tried to show the coherence, the 'logic' of such symbol systems, as conceptual entities, as systems of thought. I have followed this line, but only part way. I have tried to show also how symbol systems are not always monolithic, not always uniformly coherent; how thinking about them is often inconsistent; how it may be personal as well as conventional, fiercely defensive or experimental and progressive, with new implications being seen and faced, and new attempts at definition being made. An institution such as the Catholic church, with nearly 2,000 years of history offers a most interesting field for study of such processes.

In such symbol systems a lack of coherence, with gaps, modifications and inconsistencies, can occur because of the continual intrusion of pragmatic issues into the kinds of functions symbols are made to serve. Despite the metaphorical language of some commentators I do not think symbols can rightfully be described as actors, operating in their own right; I think people invent them, acquire them by learning, adapt them, use them for their own purposes. And there tends to arise a gap between the results of symbolic action and those of pragmatic or empirical action. It is not a matter of which is real; it is a matter of sorting out the different implications of each. In a New Guinea cargo cult, for instance, people may build an airstrip, or an aeroplane, as a symbolic means of obtaining the desired goods, the 'cargo' from the white man's world. Their activity may be classed as no less real to them than is our technological construction to us. But the results are of different order. To expect a material aeroplane to land on a symbolic airstrip, or material rice and calico to come out of a symbolic aeroplane, is a confusion of implications. But such confusion of implications of symbolic action can occur, and out of it can come much dissatisfaction and disturbance of social relations.

Symbolic thought offers great advantages in speed and ease of communication. And because of the allusiveness and indefiniteness of symbols, possibly their ambiguity, they allow some greater understanding of complex entities and action with them. Symbols also allow flexibility in individual handling and interpretation. But they may also have liabilities. The ambiguity of a symbol can be made part of a defence mechanism, to support an argument about the quality of knowledge it conveys. By allowing a range of alternatives, a symbolic form of statement may inhibit thought about the implications of what is being said. The operation of relationships at symbolic level can lead to an avoidance of decision on a pragmatic level. (It may be simpler to burn the national flag – or to charge someone with desecrating the national flag – than to think out and act upon the substantive issues at stake.)

This seems particularly so with political and religious symbols, which tend to be credited with absolute value, to be treated as if they were empirical referents. Symbolic relationships have sometimes been described as having truth of value if not truth in fact. This is a distinction which may not be capable of being maintained in metaphysical analysis, and it is often denied by those who believe in the significance of the symbols. But the attempt to claim a physical, pragmatic reality for things which an outside observer would regard as only symbols not only blurs relationships in the orders of reality;

it also has historically been a potent trigger for social conflict. To put the point from another angle, problems arise not merely in the vagueness of symbols but also in the denial of symbolic quality, or claim of more than symbolic quality, to what is claimed as substance.

Symbolic concepts merit respect as a framework for organizing experience, as a way of apprehending the world around one, especially the world of human relations. Whether or not the assertion that symbolism constitutes a unique and verifiable mode of perception is justified (a claim I myself am not prepared to concede), symbolism surely yields results that are aesthetically satisfying and often operationally viable. To criticize a symbolic mode of approach as 'unreal', 'unverifiable', seems to me then to be beside the point. But what does seem extremely relevant and to be criticized, is the demand often made for acknowledgement of a symbolism as uniquely real. Such a demand for acquiescence in the absolute validity of the symbol is a political demand, even when it speaks in the name of a religious system. In all such contexts the primary problem for an anthropologist is not to pronounce on 'ultimate reality'. It is to examine the forms of symbolic statement, to try and understand the system of ideas they express, the order of that system, and the effects associated with the use of such symbolic concepts.

References

AIYAPPAN, A. 1944 *Iravas and Social Change*, Bull. Madras Gov. Museum, n.s. gen. sec. V, 1. Madras: Government Press

AJISAFE, A. K. 1924 *The Laws and Customs of the Yoruba People*. London: Routledge

ALLPORT, GORDON W. 1950 *The Individual and His Religion*. New York: Macmillan

ANDERSON, J. N. D. 1959 *Islamic Law in the Modern World*. New York: Universities Press

ANDERSON, M. D. 1938 *Animal Carvings in British Churches*. Cambridge: University Press

ARNOLD, SIR THOMAS W. 1938 *Painting in Islam*. Oxford: Clarendon Press

ATTWATER, DONALD 1965 *The Penguin Dictionary of Saints*. Harmondsworth: Penguin

AUBER, L'ABBÉ C. A. 1884 *Histoire et Théorie du Symbolisme Religieux*. 4 v. Paris: Féchoz and Letouzey

AYER, ALFRED JULES 1946 *Language, Truth and Logic*, 2nd edn. London: Gollancz

BACHOFEN, J. J. 1897 *Das Mutterrecht. Eine Untersuchüng über die Gynaikokratie der alten Welt nach ihrer religiösen und rechtlichen Natur* (1861), 2nd edn. Basel: Benno Schwabe

—— 1925 *Versuch über die Gräbersymbolik der Alten* (1859), 2nd edn, foreword C. A. Bernoulli; appreciation Ludwig Klages. Basel: Helding & Lichtenhahn

—— (See also Campbell, Joseph)

BAEUMLER, ALFRED 1965 *Das Mythische Weltalter: Bachofens Romantische Deutung des Altertums*. München: C. H. Beck

BAILEY, F. G. (ed.) 1971 *Gifts and Poison: The Politics of Reputation*. Oxford: Basil Blackwell

BATESON, GREGORY 1936 *Naven: A Survey of the Problems suggested by a Composite Picture of the Culture of a New Guinea Tribe Drawn from Three Points of View*. Cambridge: University Press (2nd edn with Epilogue, 1958)

—— (ed., introd.) 1961 *Perceval's Narrative: A Patient's Account of his Psychosis 1830–1832*. Stanford: University Press

BAYLISS, SIR WYKE 1905 *Rex Regum: A Painter's Study of the Likeness of Christ from the Time of the Apostles to the Present Day*. London: S.P.C.K.

BEATTIE, JOHN 1966 'Ritual and Social Change,' *Man*, 1, 60–74

—— 1968 'Aspects of Nyoro Symbolism,' *Africa*, 38, 413–42

BEATTIE, JOHN and MIDDLETON, JOHN 1969 *Spirit Mediumship and Society in Africa*. London: Routledge & Kegan Paul

BÉGUIN, ALBERT 1939 *L'Âme Romantique et le Rêve*, 2nd edn. Paris: José Corti

BEIDELMAN, T. O. 1966 'The Ox and Nuer Sacrifice: Some Freudian Hypotheses,' *Man*, 1, 453–67

BELL, SIR CHARLES 1928 *The People of Tibet*. Oxford: Clarendon Press

BELSHAW, CYRIL S. 1965 *Traditional Exchange and Modern Markets*. Englewood Cliffs, N.J.: Prentice-Hall

BENT, CHARLES N., S.J. 1967 *The Death-of-God Movement*. Westminster, Md: Paulist Press

BERNDT, RONALD M. 1951 *Kunapipi: A Study of an Australian Aboriginal Religious Cult*. Melbourne: F. W. Cheshire

—— 1952 *Djanggawul: An Aboriginal Religious Cult of North-Eastern Arnhem Land*. London: Routledge & Kegan Paul

BERNOULLI, C. A. 1924 *Johann Jakob Bachofen und das Natursymbol*. Basel: Benno Schwabe

—— 1925 *Die Psychologie von Carl Gustav Carus und deren geistesgeschichtliche Bedeutung*. Jena: Eugen Diederichs

BERREMAN, GERALD 1970 Review of Dillon, op. cit., *American Anthropologist*, 72, 867–9

BERRY, JACK 1965 Intro. to B. Malinowski, *Coral Gardens and their Magic*, 2, vii–xiii. Bloomington: Indiana University Press

BIRDWHISTELL, RAY 1952 *Introduction to Kinesics*. Louisville: University of Louisville Press

—— 1970 *Kinesics and Context*. Philadelphia: University of Pennsylvania Press

BIRNBAUM, NORMAN 1955 'Monarchs and Sociologists: A Reply to Professor Shils and Mr Young,' *Sociological Review*, n.s. 3, 5–23

BLAU, PETER 1964 *Exchange and Power in Social Life*. New York: Wiley

BLYTHE, WILFRED 1969 *The Impact of Chinese Secret Societies in Malaya*. London: Oxford University Press

BOAS, FRANZ 1927 *Primitive Art*, Inst. for Samm. Kulturforskning, ser. B., viii. Oslo: H. Aschehong

BOHANNAN, P. 1964 Intro. to Tylor, *Researches into the Early History of Mankind* (1865), abr. from 3rd edn. Chicago: University Press

BOTT, ELIZABETH 1971 'Psychoanalysis and Ceremony' (1968), in *The Interpretation of Ritual*, ed. J. S. LaFontaine. London: Tavistock, 205–37

BOUDET, MARCELLIN 1874 *Les Conventionnels d'Auvergne: Dulaure*. Paris: Auby

BOUTEILLER, MARCELLE 1950 *Chamanisme et Guérison Magique*. Paris: Presses Universitaires

BOWRA, B. M. 1943 *The Heritage of Symbolism*. London: Macmillan

BRANTL, GEORGE (ed.) 1967 *Catholicism*. New York: Washington Square Press

BRETON, ANDRÉ 1936 *What is Surrealism!* London: Faber

BROWN, J. A. C. 1961 *Freud and the Post-Freudians*. Harmondsworth: Pelican

BURKS, ARTHUR W. 1949 'Icon, Index and Symbol,' *Philosophy and Phenomenonological Research*, 9, 673–89

BURRIDGE, K. O. L. 1960 *Mambu: A Melanesian Millennium*. London: Methuen

—— 1969 *New Heaven New Earth: A Study of Millenarian Activities*. Oxford: Basil Blackwell

CAMERARIUS, JOACHIM (YOUNGER) 1668 *Symbolorum et Emblematum Centuriae Tres*. Moguntiae: L. Bourgeat

CAMPBELL, JOSEPH 1967 Intro. to *Myth, Religion and Mother Right. Selected Writings of J. J. Bachofen*, trans. Ralph Manheim, Bollingen ser. 84. Princeton: University Press

CÁNEPA, LUIS 1943 *Antecedentes Hisótricos y Tradicionales de los Símbolos Argentinos*. Buenos Aires: Talleres Graficos Linari

—— 1953 *Historia de los Símbolos Nationales Argentinos*. Buenos Aires: Albatross

CAREY, BISHOP WALTER J. 1939 Intro. to *Son of Man: Pictures and Carvings by Indian, African and Chinese Artists*. London: S.P.G.

CARUS, CARL GUSTAV 1846 *Psyche: Zur Entwicklungsgeschichte der Seele*. Pforzheim: Flammer & Hoffman

—— 1853 *Symbolik der Menschlichen Gestalt: Ein Handbuch zur Menschenerkenntnis*. Leipzig: Brockhaus

—— 1857 *Ueber Lebensmagnetismus und über die magischen Wirkungen überhaupt*. Leipzig: Brockhaus

CASSIRER, ERNST 1953–7 *Philosophy of Symbolic Forms*, 3 v., trans. Ralph Manheim. New Haven: Yale University Press

—— 1944 *An Essay on Man: An Introduction to a Philosophy of Human Culture*. New Haven: Yale University Press

CASTANEDA, CARLOS 1969 *The Teaching of Don Juan: A Yaqui Way of Knowledge*. New York: Ballantine

CATHOLIC UNIVERSITY OF AMERICA 1967 *New Catholic Encyclopaedia*. New York: McGraw-Hill

CHARBONNIER, G. (ed.) 1969 *Conversations with Claude Lévi-Strauss*, trans. John & Doreen Weightman. London: Cape

CLAPHAM, A. W. 1934 *English Romanesque Architecture after the Conquest*. Oxford: Clarendon Press

COHEN, ABNER 1969 'The Analysis of the Symbolism of Power Relations,' *Man*, 4, 215–35

—— 1971 'The Politics of Ritual Secrecy,' *Man*, 6, 427–48

COLANGELI, ORANZO 1965 *Simboli e Bandieri nella Storia del Risorgimento Italiano*. Bologna: Patron

COLLINGWOOD, R. G. 1925 *Outlines of a Philosophy of Art*. London: Oxford University Press

COPLESTON, F. C. 1961 *Mediaeval Philosophy* (1952). New York: Harper

COULTON, G. G. 1958 *Mediaeval Faith and Symbolism* (1928). New York: Harper

CRAWLEY, ERNEST 1902 *The Mystic Rose: A Study of Primitive Marriage*. London: Macmillan

CREUZER (GEORG) FRIEDRICH 1806 *Idee und Probe alter Symbolik*.

—— 1810 *Symbolik und Mythologie der alten Völker besonders der Griechen* (2nd edn, 2 v. 1819–22; 3rd edn, 4 v. 1837–43). Leipzig: C. W. Leske

CRITCHLEY, MACDONALD 1939 *The Language of Gesture*. London: Edward Arnold

DANBY, HERBERT 1933 *The Mishnah*. London: Oxford University Press

DARWIN, CHARLES 1872 *The Expression of the Emotions in Man and Animals*. London: Murray

DAVIS, JOHN 1972 'Gifts and the U.K. Economy,' *Man*, n.s. 7, 408–29

DE RAEDT, JULES 1964 'Religious Representations in Northern Luzon,' *St Louis Quarterly*, 2, 315

DESHEN, SCHLOMO 1970 'On Religious Change: The Situational Analysis of Symbolic Action,' *Comparative Studies in Society and History*, 12, 260–74

DILLON, WILTON S. 1968 *Gifts and Nations: The Obligation to Give, Receive and Repay*. Hague: Mouton

DODGE, COL. R. I. 1883 *Our Wild Indians*. Hartford, Conn.: A. D. Worthington

DONCOEUR, P. 1939–48 *Le Christ dans L'Art Français*. Paris: Plon

DOOLITTLE, REV. JUSTUS 1876 *Social Life of the Chinese*, 2 v. New York: Harper Brothers

DOUGLAS, MARY 1966 *Purity and Danger*. London: Routledge & Kegan Paul

—— 1970 *Natural Symbols*. London: Cresset

—— 1972 'Deciphering a Meal', in Myth, Symbol and Culture, *Daedalus*, Winter 1972, 61–81

DOUGLAS, MARY (ed.) 1970 *Witchcraft Confessions and Accusations*, A.S.A. Mon. 9. London: Tavistock

[DULAURE, J. A.] 1786 *Pogonologia: or a Philosophical and Historical Essay on Beards*, trans. from Fr. Exeter: R. Thorn

DULAURE, J.-A. 1805 *Des Divinités Génératrices ou du Culte du Phallus*. Paris: Dentu

—— 1805 *Des Cultes qui ont Précédé et Amené l'Idolatrie ou l'Adoration des Figures Humaines*. Paris: Fournier

—— 1825 *Histoire Abrégée de Differens Cultes*, 2 v. (combined 2nd ed. reissue from 1805). Paris: Guillaume

—— 1905 *Des Divinités Génératrices chez les Anciens et les Modernes* – avec un chapitre complémentaires par A. van Gennep. Paris: Société de Mercure de France [A privately printed Eng. trans. (by A.F.N.) was issued by Panurge in New York, 1933.]

DUNBAR, HELEN FLANDERS 1929 *Symbolism in Mediaeval Thought*. New Haven: Yale University Press

DURKHEIM, ÉMILE 1912 *Les Formes Elémentaires de la Vie Religieuse*. Paris: Alcan

—— 1926 *The Elementary Forms of the Religious Life*. trans. J. W. Swain. London: Allen & Unwin

DURLIAT, MARCEL 1952 *La Sculpture Romane en Rousillon*, 2nd edn, 1. Perpignan: La Tramontane

EFRON, D. 1941 *Gesture and Environment*. New York: King's Crown Press

EGGAN, FRED and PACYAYA, ALFREDO 1962 'The Sapilada Religion: Reformation and Accommodation among the Igorots of Northern Luzon,' *Southwestern J. of Anthrop.*, 18, 95–113

EHRMANN, JACQUES 1970 'Structures of Exchange in *Cinna*,' in *Introduction to Structuralism*, ed. Michael Lane. New York: Basic Books, 223–47

ELIADE, MIRCEA 1964 *Shamanism: Archaic Techniques of Ecstasy*, Bollingen ser. 76, trans. Willard R. Trask. New York: Pantheon

—— 1969 *Images and Symbols* (1952), trans. P. Mairet. New York: Sheed & Ward

ELKIN, A. P. 1954 *The Australian Aborigines*, 3rd edn. Sydney: Angus & Robertson

EMBREE, JOHN F. 1946 *A Japanese Village: Suye Mura*. London: Kegan Paul

ÉTIEMBLE, RENÉ 1961 *Le Mythe de Rimbaud*, 2: *Structure du Mythe*, new edn. Paris: Gallimard

EVANS-PRITCHARD, E. E. 1937 *Witchcraft, Oracles and Magic among the Azande*. Oxford: Clarendon Press
—— 1948 *The Divine Kingship of the Shilluk of the Nilotic Sudan*. Cambridge: University Press
—— 1956 *Nuer Religion*. Oxford: Clarendon Press
—— 1962 *Essays in Social Anthropology*. London: Faber
—— 1965a *The Position of Women in Primitive Society...* London: Faber
—— 1965b *Theories of Primitive Religion*. Oxford: Clarendon Press

FAIRCHILD, HOXIE NEALE 1928 *The Noble Savage: A Study in Romantic Naturalism*. New York: Russell & Russell
FARBENSTEIN, WOLF 1955 *Romantische Einflüsse in der Geschichte Psychologie im deuthschen Sprachgebiet: Carl Gustav Carus und die neuere Psychologie*. Zürich: Kammerdruck
FAULHABER, CARDINAL 1932 'L'Eglise et L'Art Religieux. Art Chrétien Chinois,' *Collectanea Commissionis Synodalis*, 5, Peiping, 496–508
FEIDELSON, CHARLES JR 1953 *Symbolism and American Literature*. Chicago: University Press
FERGUSON, ADAM 1767 *An Essay on the History of Civil Society*. Edinburgh: Kincaid & Bell
FERGUSON, GEORGE 1961 *Signs and Symbols in Christian Art*. London: Oxford University Press
FIELD, MARGARET J. 1960 *Search for Security: An Ethno-psychiatric study of Rural Ghana*. London: Faber
FINDLAY, J. N. 1963 *Language, Mind and Value*. London: Allen & Unwin
FINGESTEN, PETER 1970 *The Eclipse of Symbolism*. Columbia, S.C.: University of S. Carolina Press
FINLEY, M. I. 1962 *The World of Odysseus*. Harmondsworth: Pelican
FIRTH, J. R. 1957 'Ethnographic Analysis and Language with reference to Malinowski's Views,' in Firth, Raymond (ed.), 1957 93–118
FIRTH, RAYMOND 1929 *Primitive Economics of the New Zealand*

Maori. London: Routledge (2nd edn, 1959. Wellington: Govt Printer)

—— 1936 *We, The Tikopia: A Sociological Study of Kinship in Primitive Polynesia*. London: Allen & Unwin (repr. 1957)

—— 1939 *Primitive Polynesian Economy*. London: Routledge (2nd edn, 1965)

—— 1943 'The Coastal People of Kelantan and Trengganu', *Geographical J.*, 101, 193–205

—— 1951a *Elements of Social Organization*. London: Watts (3rd edn, 1971, Tavistock)

—— 1951b 'Contemporary British Social Anthropology', *American Anthropologist*, 53, 474–89

—— 1954 'Anuta and Tikopia: Symbiotic Elements in Social Organization,' *J. Polynesian Society*, 63, 87–131

—— 1959 *Social Change in Tikopia*. London: Allen & Unwin

—— 1963 'Offering and Sacrifice: Problems of Organization,' *J. Royal Anthrop. Inst.*, 93, 12–24

—— 1964 *Essays on Social Organization and Values*, L.S.E. Mon. Soc. Anthrop., 28. London: Athlone

—— 1966a 'Twins, Birds and Vegetables: Problems of Identification in Primitive Religious Thought,' *Man*, n.s. 1, 1–17

—— 1966b 'The Meaning of Pali in Tikopia,' in *In Memory of J. R. Firth*, ed. C. E. Bazell *et al.*, 1966, 96–115. London: Longmans

—— 1967a *The Work of the Gods in Tikopia* (1940), L.S.E. Mon. Soc. Anthrop. 1 and 2. London: Athlone

—— 1967b *Tikopia Ritual and Belief*. London: Allen & Unwin

—— 1967c 'Themes in Economic Anthropology: A General Comment,' in A.S.A. Mon. 6, 1–28. London: Tavistock

—— 1967d 'Ritual and Drama in Malay Spirit Mediumship,' *Comp. Studies in Society and History*, 9, 190–207

—— 1968 'Gods and God: An Anthropologist's Standpoint,' in *The Humanist Outlook*, ed. A. J. Ayer. London: Pemberton, 31–44

—— 1969 'Tikopia Social Space,' *Bijdragen, tot de Taal-*..., 125, 64–70.

—— 1970a *Rank and Religion in Tikopia*. London: Allen & Unwin

—— 1970b 'Reflections on Tikopia "Totemism",' *Oceania*, 40, 280–95

—— 1970c 'Postures and Gestures of Respect,' in *Échanges et Communications: Mélanges offerts à Claude Lévi-Strauss*, ed. Jean Pouillon and Pierre Maranda. Hague: Mouton, 188–209

—— 1972 'Methodological Issues in Economic Anthropology,' *Man*, n.s., 7, 467–75

FIRTH, RAYMOND (ed.) 1957 *Man and Culture: An Evaluation of the Work of Bronislaw Malinowski.* London: Routledge

FIRTH, RAYMOND and SPILLIUS, JAMES 1963 *A Study of Ritual Modification*, Occ. Paper 19. London: Royal Anthrop. Inst.

FORGE, ANTHONY 1965 'Art and Environment in the Sepik,' *Proc. Royal Anthrop. Inst.*, 23–31

FORTES, MEYER 1945 *The Dynamics of Clanship among the Tallensi.* London: Oxford University Press

—— 1957 'Malinowski and the Study of Kinship,' in Raymond Firth (ed.), 1957, 157–88; repr. as 'Malinowski and Freud', *Psychoanalysis and the Psychoanalytic Review*, 1958, 45, 127–45

—— 1966a 'Religious Premisses and Logical Technique in Divinatory Ritual,' *Philosoph. Trans. Royal Soc.*, B, 251, 409–22

—— 1966b 'Totem and Taboo,' *Proc. Royal Anthrop. Inst.*, 5–22

—— 1970 'Ritual Festivals and Social Cohesion in the Hinterland of the Gold Coast' (1936), *Time and Social Structure . . .* L.S.E. Mon. Soc. Anthrop., 40, 147–63. London: Athlone

FORTES, M. and EVANS-PRITCHARD, E. E. (eds) 1940 *African Political Systems.* London: Oxford University Press

FORTUNE, R. F. 1932 *Sorcerers of Dobu.* London: Routledge

FRANKL, PAUL 1960 *The Gothic: Literary Sources and Interpretations through Eight Centuries.* Princeton: University Press

FREUD, SIGMUND 1937 *The Interpretation of Dreams*, trans. A. A. Brill, 8th German edn. London: Allen & Unwin

—— 1952 *A General Introduction to Psychoanalysis*, trans. Joan Riviere, intro. Ernest Jones. New York: Liveright

—— 1963 *The History of the Psychoanalytic Movement* (1914), intro. Philip Rieff. New York: Macmillan

—— 1964 *New Introductory Lectures on Psychoanalysis*, trans., ed. James Strachey. New York: Norton

—— 1965 *Group Psychology and the Analysis of the Ego* (1921), trans. James Strachey; intro. Franz Alexander. New York: Bantam

FRIEDL, ALOIS 1968 *Deutsche Staatssymbole.* Frankfurt: Athenäum

FRIEDRICH, PAUL 1966 'Revolutionary Politics and Communal Ritual,' in *Political Anthropology*, ed. M. J. Schwartz *et al.* Chicago: Aldine, 191–220

FRY, ROGER 1928 *Vision and Design.* London: Chatto & Windus

FRYKE, CHRISTOPHER 1929 *Voyages to the East Indies*, intro. C. Ernest Fayle. London: Cassell

FUSTEL DE COULANGES [1955] *The Ancient City* (1864). Garden City, N.Y.: Doubleday

GANTNER, JOSEPH and POBÉ, MARCEL 1956 *Romanesque Art in France.* London: Thames and Hudson

GAUNT, WILLIAM 1962 *Dictionary of Pictorial Art.* London: Dent

GELLNER, ERNEST 1969 *Saints of the Atlas.* London: Weidenfeld & Nicholson

GENNEP, ARNOLD VAN 1960 *The Rites of Passage* (1909), trans. Manika B. Vizedom and Gabrielle L. Caffee, intro. Solon T. Kimball. London: Routledge & Kegan Paul

GIBB, H. A. R. 1947 *Modern Trends in Islam.* Chicago: University Press

GIBB, H. A. R. and BOWEN, H. 1950–7 *Islamic Society and the West*, 1 and 2. London: Oxford University Press

GLUCKMAN, MAX 1963 *Order and Rebellion in Tribal Africa.* London: Cohen & West

GLUCKMAN, MAX (ed.) 1962 *Essays on the Ritual of Social Relations.* Manchester: University Press

GODELIER, MAURICE 1971 'Myth and History,' *New Left Review*, 69, 93–112

GOFFMAN, ERVING 1967 *Interaction Ritual.* Garden City, N.Y.: Doubleday

GOMBRICH, E. H. 1966 'Ritualized Gesture and Expression in Art,' see Huxley, 393–401

—— 1968 *Art and Illusion*, 3rd edn. London: Phaidon

GOODY, JACK 1962 *Death, Property and the Ancestors.* London: Tavistock

GORE, CHARLES 1901 *The Body of Christ: An Inquiry into the Institution and Doctrine of Holy Communion*, 2nd edn. London: Murray

GRENZMANN, WILHELM (ed.) 1949 *G. Chr. Lichtenberg: Gesammelte Werke*, 2 v. Frankfurt a/M: Holle

GRIVOT, DENIS and ZARNECKI, GEORGE 1961 *Gislebertus Sculptor of Autun*. London: Trianon

GUIGNIAUT, J. D. 1825–41 *Religions de l'Antiquité Considérées Principalement dans leurs formes symboliques et Mythologiques* (trans. F. Creuzer, *Symbolik und Mythologie*, 2nd edn, rearranged, developed and clarified). Paris: Treuttel & Würtz

HALL, EDWARD T. 1961 *The Silent Language* (1951). Greenwich, Conn.: Fawcett

—— 1968 'Proxemics,' *Current Anthropology*, 9, 83–95

HALLPIKE, C. R. 1969 'Social Hair,' *Man*, n.s. 4, 256–64

—— 1971 *The Konso of Ethiopia: A Study of the Values of a Cushitic People*. Oxford: Clarendon Press

HALSTED, JOHN B. (ed.) 1965 *Romanticism: Problems of Definition, Explanation and Evaluation*. Boston: D. C. Heath

HARRÉ, JOHN 1968 'A Matter of the Length of Hair: Beliefs and Symbols in Social Studies,' *National Education* [New Zealand]

HASKINS, CHARLES HOMER 1958 *The Renaissance of the Twelfth Century* (1927). New York: Meridian

HAUSER, ARNOLD 1952 *The Social History of Art*, 2 v. New York: Knopf

HAYLEY, AUDREY 1968 'Symbolic Equations: The Ox and the Cucumber,' *Man*, n.s. 3, 262–71

HEER, FRIEDRICH 1962 *The Mediaeval World*, trans. Janet Sondheimer. New York: Mentor

HERBART, J. F. 1824 *Psychologie als Wissenschaft*. Königsberg

HERTZ, ROBERT 1960 'The Pre-eminence of the Right Hand: A Study in Religious Polarity,' in *Death and the Right Hand*, trans. Rodney and Claudia Needham. London: Cohen & West

HIATT, L. R. 1967 'Nabokov's Lolita: A "Freudian" Cryptic Crossword,' *American Imago*, 24, 360–70

HIRN, YRJÖ 1912 *The Sacred Shrine: A Study of Poetry and Art of the Catholic Church*. London: Macmillan

HOCART, A. M. 1970 *Kings and Councillors*, new edn, intro. Rodney Needham. Chicago: University Press

HOEBEL, E. ADAMSON 1966 *Anthropology: The Study of Man*. New York: McGraw-Hill

HOGBIN, H. IAN 1940–1 'The Father Chooses His Heir: A Family Dispute over Succession in Wogeo,' *Oceania*, 11, 1–39

HOMANS, GEORGE C. 1950 *The Human Group*. New York: Harcourt Brace

—— 1961 *Social Behaviour: Its Elementary Forms*. New York: Harcourt Brace

HONIGMAN, J. J. 1959 *The World of Man*. New York: Harper

HOOTON, E. A. 1946 *Up From the Ape*, rev. edn. New York: Macmillan

HORTON, ROBIN 1971 'African Conversion,' *Africa*, 41, 85–108

HOSTETLER, JOHN A. 1964 'The Amish Use of Symbols and their Function in Bonding the Community,' *J. Royal Anthrop. Inst.*, 94, 11–22

HOTOMAN, ANTONIUS 1628 *Pogonias Sive De Barba* ... (1586). Rostochii: ex officina Ferberiana

HOWALD, ERNST 1926 *Der Kampf um Creuzer's Symbolik: Eine Auswahl von Dokumenten*. Tübingen: J. C. B. Mohr

HOWARD, E. C. C. 1914 *Minhaj et Talibin: A Manual of Muhammedan Law according to the School of Shafi*, by Mahiudin Abu Zakaria Yahya ibn Sharif en Nawawi, trans. from Fr. of L. W. C. Van den Berg. London: Thacker

HOWELL-SMITH, A. D. 1950 *Thou Art Peter: A History of Roman Catholic Doctrine and Practice*. London: Watts

HOWELLS, WILLIAM 1947 *Mankind So Far*. New York: Doubleday

HULL, L. W. H. 1959 *History and Philosophy of Science*. London: Longmans

HULME, F. E. n.d. *The Flags of the World: Their History, Blazonry and Associations*. London: Frederick Warne

—— 1891 *The History, Principles and Practice of Symbolism in Christian Art*. London: Swan Sonnenschein

HURGRONJE, C. SNOUCK 1906 *The Achehnese*, 2 v. Leyden: Brill

HUXLEY, SIR JULIAN 1966 'A Discussion on Ritualization of Behaviour in Animals and Man,' *Philosoph. Trans. Royal Soc.*, B, No. 772, vol. 251, 247–526

JAMES, E. O. 1937 *Christian Myth and Ritual.* London: Murray

JAMESON, MRS 1900 *Legends of the Monastic Orders as represented in the Fine Arts.* London: Longmans

JARVIE, I. C. 1967 *The Revolution in Social Anthropology.* London: Routledge & Kegan Paul

JENYNS, SOAME 1935 *A Background to Chinese Painting.* London: Sidgwick & Jackson

JUNG, C. G. 1926 *Psychological Types*, trans. H. Gordon Baynes. London: Kegan Paul

—— 1958 *Psyche and Symbol*, ed. Violet S. de Laszlo. New York: Doubleday

JUNOD, H. A. 1927 *The Life of a South African Tribe*, 2 v. London: Macmillan

KANDINSKY, V. 1946 *On the Spiritual in Art* (1912), trans. Hilla Rebay. New York: Guggenheim Foundation.

KATTENBUSCH, F. 1894–1900 *Das Apostolische Symbol*, 2 v. Leipzig: Hinruchs

KEYSER, C. E. 1927 *A List of Norman Tympana and Lintels*, 2nd edn. London: Elliot Stock

KIRSCHBAUM, ENGELBERT, S.J. 1968–71 *Lexikon der Christlichen Ikonographie*, 3v. Rome: Herder

KNOWLES, DAVID 1962 *The Evolution of Mediaeval Thought.* London: Longmans

KRETZMANN, NORMAN 1967 'Semantics, History of,' *Encyclopaedia of Philosophy*, 7. New York: Macmillan

KREWALD, ARTUR 1939 *Carl Gustav Carus seine philosophischen psychologischen und characterologischen Grundgedanken* (Die Lehre von der praktischen Menschenerkenntnis, 3, 2). Berlin: Bernard & Graefe

KROEBER, A. L. 1901 'Arapaho Decorative Art,' *American Anthropologist*, n.s. 3, 308–36

KÜNSTLE, KARL 1928–36 *Ikonographie der Christlichen Kunst*, 2 v. Freiburg i.B.: Herder

KUPER, HILDA 1947 *An African Aristocracy: Rank among the Swazi.* London: Oxford University Press

LA BARRE, WESTON 1969 *The Peyote Cult* (enlarged edn). New York: Schocken

LA FONTAINE, J. S. 1963 'Witchcraft in Bugisu,' in *Witchcraft and Sorcery in East Africa*, ed. John Middleton and E. H. Winter. London: Routledge & Kegan Paul

LANGEN, AUGUST 1962 K. Ph. Moritz 'Weg zur symbolischen Dichtung,' *Z. f. dt. Philologie*, 81, 169–218, 402–40

LANGENDOEN, TERENCE D. 1968 *The London School of Linguistics: A Study of the Linguistic Theories of B. Malinowski and J. R. Firth*. Cambridge, Mass.: M.I.T. Press

LANGER, SUSANNE K. 1953 *Feeling and Form: A Theory of Art*. New York: Scribner

LATTIMORE, OWEN S. 1934 *The Mongols of Manchuria*. New York: John Day

—— 1941 *Mongol Journeys*. New York: Doubleday

LAWRENCE, PETER 1964 *Road Belong Cargo*. Manchester: University Press

LAYARD, JOHN W. 1942 *Stone Men of Malekula*, I. *Vao*. London: Chatto & Windus

—— 1944 *The Lady of the Hare*. London: Faber

LEACH, E. R. 1954 *Political Systems of Highland Burma*. London: Bell

—— 1957 'The Epistemological Background to Malinowski's Empiricism,' in Firth (ed.), 1957, 119–38

—— 1958 'Magical Hair,' *J. Royal Anthrop. Inst.*, 88, 147–64

—— 1961a *Rethinking Anthropology*, L.S.E. Mon. Soc. Anthrop. 22. London: Athlone

—— 1961b 'Lévi-Strauss in the Garden of Eden: An Examination of Some Recent Developments in the Analysis of Myth,' *Trans. New York Acad. Sciences*, ser. II, 23, 386–96

—— 1965 'Frazer and Malinowski,' *Encounter*, Nov., 24–36

—— 1966a 'The Legitimacy of Solomon: Some Structural Aspects of Old Testament History,' *European J. Sociology*, 7, 58—101

—— 1966b 'Ritualization in Man in Relation to Conceptual and Social Development,' *Philosophical Trans. Royal Soc.*, B, 251, 403–8

—— 1971 'The Heart of the Matter' (review of Titmuss, op. cit.), *New Society*, 23 December

—— 1972 'The Structure of Symbolism,' in *The Interpretation of Ritual: Essays in Honour of A. I. Richards*, ed. J. S. La Fontaine. London: Tavistock, 239–75

LEBRA, TAKIE SUGIYAMA 1969 'Reciprocity and the Asymmetric Principle: An Analytical Reappraisal of the Japanese Concept of "On",' *Psychologia*, 12, 129–38

LEE, DOROTHY 1959 *Freedom and Culture*. Englewood Cliffs, N.J.: Prentice-Hall

LEIRIS, MICHEL 1948 *La Langue Secrète des Dogons de Sanga (Soudan Français)*. Trav. et Mem. Inst. d'Ethnologié, L. Paris: Institut d'Ethnologie

—— 1958 *La Possession et Ses Aspects Théatraux chez les Ethiopiens de Gondar*. Paris: Plon

LEISINGER, HERMANN 1957 *Romanesque Bronzes*. New York: Praeger

LÉVI-STRAUSS, CLAUDE 1948 'La Vie Familiale et Sociale des Indiens Nambikwara,' *J. Soc. des Americanistes*, n.s. 1, 37, 1–132

—— 1949 *Les Structures Eléméntaires de la Parenté*. Paris: Presses Universitaires

—— 1950 'Introduction à l'Oeuvre de Marcel Mauss,' *Sociologie et Anthropologie par Marcel Mauss*. Paris: Presses Universitaires, ix–lii

—— 1957 'The Principle of Reciprocity,' in *Sociological Theory*, ed. L. A. Coser and B. Rosenberg. New York: Macmillan, 74–84.

—— 1958 *Anthropologie Structurale*. Paris: Plon

—— 1962a *Le Totemisme Aujourd'hui*. Paris: Presses Universitaires

—— 1962b *La Pensée Sauvage*. Paris: Plon

—— 1963 'The Efficacy of Symbols,' *Structural Anthropology*. New York: Basic Books

—— 1964 *Le Cru et Le Cuit. Mythologiques*, I. Paris: Plon

—— 1969 *The Elementary Structures of Kinship*, ed. Rodney Needham, trans. J. H. Bell, R. H. von Sturmer, rev. edn. Boston: Beacon

—— 1971 *L'Homme Nu: Mythologiques*, IV. Paris: Plon

LÉVY-BRUHL, L. 1938 *L'Expérience Mystique et les Symboles chez les Primitifs*. Paris: Alcan

—— 1949 *Les Carnets de Lucien Lévy-Bruhl*, pref. Maurice Leenhardt. Paris: Presses Universitaires

LEWIS, I. M. 1971 *Ecstatic Religion: An Anthropological Study of Spirit Possession and Shamanism*. Harmondsworth: Penguin

LEWIS, M. M. 1947 *Language and Society*. London: Nelson

LICHTENBERG, GEORG CHRISTOPH (*see Grenzmann, Mautner*)

LIENHARDT, GODFREY 1961 *Divinity and Experience: The Religion of the Dinka*. Oxford: Clarendon Press.

LINCOLN, C. ERIC 1961 *The Black Muslims in America*. Boston: Beacon

LINCOLN, JACKSON STEWARD 1935 *The Dream in Primitive Cultures*. London: Cresset

LINTON, RALPH 1936 *The Study of Man*. New York: Appleton-Century

—— 1939 Intro. to *The Individual and His Society* (with Abraham Kardiner). New York: Columbia University Press

LLOYD, P. C. 1967 *Africa in Social Change*. Baltimore: Penguin

LOISY, ALFRED 1948 *The Birth of the Christian Religion*, trans. L. P. Jacks. London: Allen & Unwin

LOUDON, J. B. 1965 'Social Aspects of Ideas about Treatment,' in *Transcultural Psychiatry*, ed. A. V. S. de Reuck and Ruth Porter. Ciba. London: J. & A. Churchill, 137–60

LOWIE, ROBERT 1924 *Primitive Religion*. New York: Boni & Liveright

—— 1937 *History of Ethnological Theory*. London: Harrap

LUX, ANDRÉ 1972 'Gift Exchange and Income Redistribution . . . Yombe Rural Wage-Earners,' *Africa*, 42, 173–91

MCGIFFERT, ARTHUR CUSHMAN 1953 *A History of Christian Thought*, I. New York: Scribner

MCLENNAN, J. F. 1865 *Primitive Marriage*, repr. in *Studies in Ancient History*. London: Quaritch

M'MILLAN, WILLIAM n.d. *Scottish Symbols: Royal, National and Ecclesiastical* . . . Paisley: Alexander Gardner

MAIR, LUCY P. 1934 *An African People in the Twentieth Century*. London: Routledge

MÂLE, ÉMILE 1947 *L'Art Religieux du XIIe Siècle en France.* Paris: Armand Colin

MALINOWSKI, BRONISLAW 1922 *Argonauts of the Western Pacific.* London: Routledge

—— 1926 *Myth in Primitive Psychology.* London: Kegan Paul

—— 1927a *The Father in Primitive Psychology.* London: Kegan Paul

—— 1927b *Sex and Repression in Savage Society.* London: Kegan Paul

—— 1932 *The Sexual Life of Savages in North-Western Melanesia*, 3rd edn. London: Routledge

—— 1935 *Coral Gardens and Their Magic*, 2 v. London: Allen & Unwin

—— 1936 *The Foundations of Faith and Morals*, Riddell Mem. Lectures, 7th ser. London: Oxford University Press

—— 1939 'The Group and the Individual in Functional Analysis,' *Amer. J. Sociology*, 44, 938–64

—— 1944 *A Scientific Theory of Culture.* Chapel Hill: Univ. of N. Carolina Press

—— 1948 *Magic, Science and Religion . . .*, intro. Robert Redfield. Glencoe, Ill.: Free Press

MANGIN, EUGENE 1921 *Les Mossi.* Paris: Auguste Challamel

MANNHARDT, WILHELM 1875–7 *Antike Wald- und Feldkulte . . .* Berlin: Gebrüder Borntraeger

MARETT, R. R. 1933 *Sacraments of Simple Folk.* Oxford: Clarendon Press

—— 1935 *Head, Heart and Hands in Human Evolution.* London: Hutchinson

MARTIN, KINGSLEY 1963 *The Crown and the Establishment.* Harmondsworth: Penguin

MASCALL, E. L. 1949 *Existence and Analogy.* London: Longmans

MAUSS, MARCEL 1925 'Essai sur le Don, Forme Archaique de l'Echange,' *L'Année Sociologique*, n.s. 1 (trans. Ian Cunnison, *The Gift.* London: Cohen & West, 1954)

—— 1900–1 Review of Kattenbusch, *L'Année Sociologique*, v, 298–301

MAUTNER, FRANZ and HATFIELD, HENRY 1969 *Lichtenberg: Aphorisms and Letters.* London: Cape

MEAD, MARGARET 1963 *Sex and Temperament in Three Savage Societies* (1935). New York: Morrow

MELVILLE, HERMAN 1938 (1846) *Typee: Narrative of a Four Months Residence* ... Harmondsworth: Penguin

MÉNÉGOZ, EUGENE n.d. 'Symbolo-Fideism,' *Hastings Encyclopaedia of Religion and Ethics*. New York: Scribner

MÉTRAUX, ALFRED 1959 *Voodoo in Haiti*, trans. Hugh Charteris. London: Deutsch

MEYER, PETER 1945 *Schweizerische Münster u. Kathedralen des Mittelalters*. Zürich: Atlantis

MICHAUD, GUY 1947 *Message Poétique du Symbolisme*. Paris: Nizet

MIDDLETON, JOHN 1960 *Lugbara Religion*. London: Oxford University Press

MILLS, C. WRIGHT 1961 *The Sociological Imagination*. New York: Grove

MITCHELL, T. F. 1957 'The Language of Buying and Selling in Cyrenaica: A Situational Statement,' *Hespéris: Archives Berbères* ... 32–71

MOMIGLIANO, ARNALDO 1946 'Friedrich Creuzer and Greek Historiography,' *J. Warburg and Courtauld Inst.*, 9, 152–63

MOONEY, JAMES 1965 *The Ghost Dance Religion* (1896), intro. A. F. C. Wallace. Chicago: University Press

MORGAN, LEWIS H. 1851 *League of the Ho-dé-no-sau-nee, Iroquois*. Rochester N. Y.: Sage [reprod. with introd. William N. Fenton 1962, New York: Corinth]

MORITZ, KARL PHILIPP 1830 *Mythological Fictions of the Greeks and Romans*, trans from 5th edn, with improvements, by Charles Frederick William Jaeger. New York: A. & C. & H. Carvill

—— 1861 *Götterlehre oder Mythologische Dichtungen der Alten*. 10th edn, intro. Dr Friedrichs. Berlin: F. A. Herbig

—— 1968 *Andreas Hartknopf eine allegorie* 1786; *Andreas Hartknopfs predigerjahre* 1790; *Fragment aus dem Tagebuche eines geistersehers*, 1787 (facs). Stuttgart: J. B. Metzler

MORRIS, CHARLES 1945 *Signs, Language and Behavior*. Chicago: University Press

MUNN, NANCY 1969 'The Effectiveness of Symbols in Murngin Rite and Myth,' in *Forms of Symbolic Action*, ed. Robert F.

Spencer, Amer. Ethnological Society. University Washington Press, 178–207

MURPHY, ROBERT E. 1971 *The Dialectics of Social Life*. New York: Basic Books

MYERS, A. R. 1966 *England in the Late Middle Ages*, rev. edn. Harmondsworth: Pelican

NADEL, S. F. 1942 *A Black Byzantium: The Kingdom of Nupe in Nigeria*. London: Oxford University Press

—— 1951 *Foundations of Social Anthropology*. London: Cohen & West

—— 1954 *Nupe Religion*. London: Routledge

NAIK, Y. G. [1957] *Indian National Emblems: Their Significance*. Bombay: Visual Education Society

NASH, MANNING 1966 *Primitive and Peasant Economic Systems*. San Francisco: Chandler

NEEDHAM, RODNEY 1967a 'Right and Left in Nyoro Symbolic Classification,' *Africa*, 37, 425–52

—— 1967b 'Percussion and Transition,' *Man*, n.s. 2, 606–14

NOVOTNY, FRITZ 1930 *Romanische Bauplastik in Österreich*. Vienna: Benno Filser

OGDEN, C. K. and RICHARDS, I. A. 1923 *The Meaning of Meaning*. London: Kegan Paul

O'MALLEY, L. S. S. 1935 *Popular Hinduism – The Religion of the Masses*. Cambridge: University Press

O'NEILL, A. M., O.P. 1933 *The Mystery of the Eucharist*. Dublin: M. H. Gill

PALMER, L. F. JR 1970 'Black America's Other National Anthem,' *Chicago Daily News*, 26–27 August 1970

PALMER, PAUL F., S.J. 1953 *Mary in the Documents of the Church:* London: Burns & Oates

PANOFF, MICHEL 1970 'Marcel Mauss's *The Gift* Revisited,' *Man*, n.s. 5, 60–70

PAQUES, VIVIANA 1954 *Les Bambara*, International African Inst. Survey of Africa, Fr. ser. pt I. Paris: Presses Universitaires

PARSONS, ANNE 1969 *Belief, Magic and Anomie: Essays in Psychosocial Anthropology*. New York: Free Press

PARSONS, ELSIE CLEWS 1916 'Holding Back in Crisis Ceremonialism,' *American Anthropologist*, 18, 41–52

PARSONS, TALCOTT 1949 *The Structure of Social Action* (1937), 2nd edn. Glencoe, Ill.: Free Press

—— 1957 'Malinowski and the Theory of Social Systems,' in Firth (ed.), 1957, 53–70

PAULME, DENISE 1967 'Two Themes on the Origin of Death in West Africa,' *Man*, n.s. 2, 48–61

PEACOCK, JAMES L. 1968 *Rites of Modernization: Symbolic and Social Aspects of Indonesian Proletarian Drama*. Chicago: University Press

PEIRCE, CHARLES S. 1931–5 *Collected Papers of Charles Sanders Peirce*, ed. C. Harteshorne and P. Weiss. Camb., Mass: Harvard U.P.

—— 1958 *Values in a Universe of Chance*, selected writings, ed. P. P. Wiener. New York: Doubleday

PIAGET, JEAN 1971 *Structuralism*, trans. and ed. Chaninah Maschler. London: Routledge

PICKERING, W. A. 1878–9 'Chinese Secret Societies,' *J. Straits Branch Royal Asiatic Soc.*, 1, 63–84; 3, 1–18

POIZAT, ALFRED 1924 *Le Symbolisme, de Baudelaire à Claudel*, 2nd edn. Paris: Bloud & Gay

PORTAL, FRÉDÉRIC 1857 *Des Couleurs Symboliques dans l'Antiquité, le Moyen-Age et les Temps Modernes*. Paris: Treuttel & Würtz

POWDERMAKER, HORTENSE 1950 *Hollywood The Dream Factory: An Anthropologist Looks at the Movie-Makers*. Boston: Little, Brown

PREBBLE, JOHN 1967 *Culloden*. Harmondsworth: Pelican

RADCLIFFE-BROWN, A. R. 1922 *The Andaman Islanders*. Cambridge: University Press

—— 1930–1 'The Social Organization of Australian Tribes,' *Oceania*, Mon. 1. Melbourne: Macmillan

—— 1952 'Taboo,' in *Structure and Function in Primitive Society*. London: Cohen & West

—— 1957 *A Natural Science of Society*, ed. M. N. Srinivas. Glencoe, Ill.: Free Press

RADIN, PAUL 1958 Introduction to E. B. Tylor, *Primitive Culture*

RAPPAPORT, ROY A. 1968 *Pigs for the Ancestors: Ritual in the Ecology of a New Guinea People*. New Haven: Yale University Press

RATTRAY, R. S. 1916 *Ashanti Proverbs (The Primitive Ethics of a Savage People)*. Oxford: Clarendon Press

—— 1929 *Ashanti Law and Constitution*. Oxford: Clarendon Press

READ, HERBERT 1933 *Art Now*. London: Faber

—— 1936 Introduction to *International Surrealist Exhibition Catalogue*. London

—— 1948 Introduction to *Klee (1879–1940)*. London: Faber Gallery

REAY, MARIE 1959 *The Kuma: Freedom and Conformity in the New Guinea Highlands*. Melbourne: University Press

REINACH, SALOMON 1942 *Orpheus, A History of Religions*, new edn, trans. Florence Simmonds. New York: Liveright

RICHARDS, AUDREY I. 1932 *Hunger and Work in a Savage Tribe*. London: Routledge

—— 1956 *Chisungu: A Girl's Initiation Ceremony among the Bemba of Northern Rhodesia*. London: Faber

RIEFF, P. (See Freud, 1963)

RIVERS, W. H. R. 1906 *The Todas*. London: Macmillan

—— 1918 *Dreams and Primitive Culture*, Bull. John Rylands Library (Manchester), 4, nos 3–4

—— 1920 *Instinct and the Unconscious*. Cambridge: University Press

—— 1924 'Mind and Medicine' (1919), in *Medicine, Magic and Religion*. London: Kegan Paul

ROBERTSON, BRYAN 1971 *Bridget Riley, Paintings and Drawings 1951–71*, intro., biographical note. London: Arts Council of Great Britain

ROHEIM, GÉZA 1969a *Psychoanalysis and Anthropology* (1950). New York: Internat. Universities Press

—— 1969b *The Gates of the Dream* (1952). New York: Internat. Universities Press

—— 1971 *The Origin and Function of Culture*. New York: Doubleday

ROSEN, GEORGE 1968 *Madness in Society: Chapters in the Historical Sociology of Mental Illness*. London: Routledge & Kegan Paul

ROSENBERG, HAROLD 1965 *The Anxious Object*. London: Thames & Hudson

ROSENBERG, JAKOB 1967 *On Quality in Art*. London: Phaidon

RÖTHEL, H. K. *Modern German Painting*, trans. Desmond and Louise Clayton. London: Eyre & Spottiswoode

ROUT, ETTIE A. 1927 *Maori Symbolism*. London: Routledge

RUBEL, PAULA and ROSMAN, ABRAHAM 1970 'Potlatch and Sagali: The Structure of Exchange in Haida and Trobriand Societies,' *Trans. New York Academy of Sciences*, ser. II, 32, 732–42

SAHLINS, MARSHALL 1965 'On the Sociology of Primitive Exchange,' in *The Relevance of Models for Social Anthropology*, ed. M. Banton. A.S.A. Mon. 1, London: Tavistock, 139–236

—— 1970 'The Spirit of the Gift' *Échanges et Communications. Mélanges offerts à Claude Lévi-Strauss*, ed. Jean Pouillon and Pierre Maranda. Hague: Mouton, 998–1012

SAPIR, EDWARD 1934 'Symbolism,' *Encyclopaedia of the Social Sciences*, repr. in *Selected Writings of Edward Sapir* . . . ed. David G. Mandelbaum. Berkeley: University California Press, 564–8

SCHACHT, JOSEPH 1955 'The Law,' in *Unity and Variety in Muslim Civilization*, ed. G. E. von Grünebaum. Chicago: University Press, 65–86

SCHAPERA, I. 1955 *A Handbook of Tswana Law and Custom*, 2nd edn. London: Oxford University Press

SCHAUBERG, JOSEPH 1861–3 *Vergleichendes Handbuch der Symbolik der Freimauerei*, 3 v. Basel: Benno Schwabe

SCHENK, H. G. 1969 *The Mind of the European Romantics*. New York: Doubleday

SCHERNER, KARL ALBERT 1861 *Das Leben des Traumes – Entdeckungen auf dem Gebiet der Seele* (Erstes Buch). Berlin: Schindler

SCHLEGEL, GUSTAVE 1866 *Thian Ti Hwui: The Hung-League or Heaven-Earth League*. Batavia: Lange (repr. 1958, Singapore: Govt Printer)

SCHNEIDER, ALBERT 1954 *G.-C. Lichtenberg: Précurseur du Romantisme; L'Homme et l'Oeuvre*. Nancy: Société d'Impressions Typographique

SCHNEIDER, DAVID M. 1968 *American Kinship: A Cultural Account*. Englewood-Cliffs, N.J.: Prentice-Hall

SCHOLEM, GERSHOM 1955 *Major Trends in Jewish Mysticism*, 3rd edn. London: Thames & Hudson

SCHRIMPF, HANS JOACHIM 1968 (See Moritz, 1968)

SCHUBERT, GOTTHILF HEINRICH 1814 *Die Symbolik des Traumes*, Bamberg: C. F. Kunz

SCHWARTZ, BARRY 1967 'The Social Psychology of the Gift,' *American J. Sociology*, 73, 1–11

SCHWENK, KONRAD 1851 *Die Sinn-Bilder der alten Völker*. Frankfurt a/M: Sauerländer

SELIGMAN, C. G. 1932 'Anthropological Perspective and Psychological Theory,' *J. Royal Anthrop. Inst.*, 62, 193–228

SELIGMAN, C. G. and B. Z. 1911 *The Veddas*. Cambridge: University Press

SENIOR, ELIZABETH 1940 *Portraits of Christ*. Harmondsworth: Penguin

SEUPHOR, MICHEL 1962 *Abstract Painting*. London: Prentice-Hall

SHILS, EDWARD and YOUNG, MICHAEL 1953 'The Meaning of the Coronation,' *Sociological Review*, n.s. 1, no. 2, 63–81

SHURMER, PAMELA 1971 'The Gift Game,' *New Society*, 23 December 1971

SKULTANS, VIEDA 1970 'The Symbolic Significance of Menstruation and the Menopause,' *Man*, n.s. 5, 639–51

SLOTKIN, J. S. 1965 *Readings in Early Anthropology*, Viking Fund Pub. Anthrop., 40. Chicago: Aldine

SMITH, MARGARET 1931 *Studies in Early Mysticism in the Near and Middle East*. London: Sheldon

SMITH, M. G. 1962 *Kinship and Community in Carriacou*. New Haven: Yale University Press

SMITH, W. ROBERTSON 1885 *Kinship and Marriage in Early Arabia*. Cambridge: University Press

—— 1889 *Lectures in the Religion of the Semites*. Edinburgh: Black (new edn, 1907)

SOCIETY FOR PROPAGATION OF THE GOSPEL 1948 *The Life of Christ by Chinese Artists*. London: S.P.G.

SOMERVILLE, J. *et al.* 1967 'Symbol,' *New Catholic Encyclopaedia*. New York: McGraw-Hill

SØRENSON, BENGT ALGOT 1963 *Symbol und Symbolismus in den aesthetischen Theorien des 18 Jahrhunderts und der deutschen Romantik*. Kopenhagen: Munksgaard

SPEKE, JOHN HANNING 1912 *Journal of the Discovery of the Source of the Nile*, Everyman edn. London: Dent

SPENCER, ROBERT F. (ed.) 1969 *Forms of Symbolic Action*, Proc. Ann. Spring Meeting, Amer. Ethn. Soc. Seattle: Univ. Washington Press

SPICKER, STUART, F. 1970 *The Philosophy of the Body*. Chicago: Quadrangle

STANNER, W. E. H. 1960 'On Aboriginal Religion,' *Oceania*, 31

—— 1967 'Reflections on Durkheim and Aboriginal Religion,' in *Social Organization: Essays Presented to Raymond Firth*, ed. Maurice Freedman. London: Frank Cass, 217–40

STEBBING, L. S. 1948 *A Modern Introduction to Logic* (1930). London: Methuen

STOUT, DAVID B. 1947 *San Blas Cuna Acculturation: An Introduction*, Viking Fund Pub., 9. New York: Wenner-Gren Foundation.

STRATHERN, ANDREW 1971 *The Rope of Moka: Big Men and Ceremonial Exchange in Mount Hagen New Guinea*. Cambridge: University Press

STRATHERN, ANDREW and MARILYN 1971 *Self-Decoration in Mount Hagen*. London: Duckworth

SUNDKLER, BENGT G. M. 1948 *Bantu Prophets in South Africa*. London: Lutterworth Press

THIERS, JEAN-BAPTISTE 1609 *Histoire des Perruques*. Paris: at author's expense

THOENE, PETER 1938 *Modern German Art*, trans. Charles Fullman. Harmondsworth: Penguin

THOMPSON, MICHAEL 1969 Review of Dillon, op. cit., *Man*, n.s. 4, 664–5

THOULESS, R. 1961 *Psychology of Religion*. New York: Macmillan

TITMUSS, RICHARD M. 1970 *The Gift Relationship: From Human Blood to Social Policy*. London: Allen & Unwin

TRUMBULL, HENRY CLAY 1885 *The Blood Covenant*. New York: Scribner

—— 1894 *Studies in Oriental Social Life*. Philadelphia: John D. Watts

—— 1896 *The Threshold Covenant or the Beginning of Religious Rites*. New York: Scribner

—— 1899 *The Covenant of Salt*. New York: Scribner

TUREL, ADRIEN 1938 Introduction to J. J. Bachofen, *Règne de la Mère au Patriarcat*, pages choisis. Paris: Alcan

—— 1939 *Bachofen-Freud: Zur Emanzipation des Mannes von Reich der Mütter*. Bern: Huber

TURNER, TERENCE S. 1969a 'Tchrikin: A Central Brazilian Tribe and its Symbolic Language of Bodily Adornment,' *Natural History*, 78, 50–70

—— 1969b 'Oedipus: Time and Structure in Narrative Form,' in *Forms of Symbolic Action*, ed. Robert F. Spencer. American Ethnological Society: Univ. Washington Press, 26–68

TURNER, VICTOR W. 1957 *Schism and Continuity in an African Society*. Manchester: University Press

—— 1962 *Chihamba, The White Spirit* (Rhodes-Livingstone Paper 33). Manchester: University Press

—— 1966 'The Syntax of Symbolism in an African Religion,' see Huxley, 295–304

—— 1967 *The Forest of Symbols: Aspects of Ndembu Ritual*. Ithaca: Cornell University Press

—— 1969 *The Ritual Process: Structure and Anti-Structure*. Chicago: Aldine

TURNEY-HIGH, H. H. 1949 *General Anthropology*. New York: Thomas Y. Crowell

TYLOR, EDWARD BURNETT 1873 *Primitive Culture*, 2 v., 2nd edn. London: John Murray

—— 1878 *Researches into the Early History of Mankind and the Development of Civilization*. 3rd edn. London: John Murray

URBAN, WALTER MARSHALL 1939 *Language and Reality: The Philosophy of Language and the Principles of Symbolism*. London: Allen & Unwin

VALERIAN, JOHAN PIERIUS 1533 *A Treatise written by Johan Valerian a greatte clerke of Italie, which is intitled in latin Pro*

Sacerdotum barbis translated into Englysshe. London: Tho. Berthelet (orig. pub. 1533; Paris: Christianus Wechelus)

VASUDEVA, S. AGARVALA (AGRAWALA) 1964 *The Wheel Flag of India: Chakra-Dhvaja*. Varanasi: Prithivi Prakashan

VERLAINE, PAUL 1884 *Les Poètes Maudits*. Paris: Leon Vanier

—— 1939 *Poèmes Saturniens*. Paris: Editions de Cluny

VESEY-FITZGERALD, SEYMOUR 1931 *Mohammedan Law: An Abridgement*. London: Oxford University Press

VOLKELT, JOHANNES 1873 *Das Unbewusste und der Pessimismus*. Berlin: F. Henschel

—— 1875 *Die Traum-Phantasie*. Stuttgart: Meyer & Zeller

—— 1876 *Der Symbol-Begriff in der neuesten Aesthetik*. Jena: Hermann Dufft

VOSS, JOHANN HEINRICH 1824–26 *Antisymbolik*, 2 v. Stuttgart: Metzler

WAKE, CHARLES STANILAND and WESTROPP, HODDER M. 1875 *Ancient Symbol Worship. Influence of the Phallic Idea in the Religions of Antiquity*, 2nd edn, intro., notes, app. Alexander Wilder. New York: J. W. Bouton

WALLACE, ANTHONY F. C. 1958 'Dreams and the Wishes of the Soul,' *American Anthropologist*, 60, 234–48

WALLACE-HADRILL, J. M. W. 1962 *The Long-Haired Kings and Other Studies in Frankish History*. London: Methuen

WANIJN, ROB. L. 1950 'Ancient Religious Insigniae in Bas-Congo,' in *Arts in Belgian Congo and Ruanda-Urundi* [Vatican Exhibition]. Brussels: C.I.D., 41–55

WARD, J. S. M. and STIRLING, W. G. 1925 *The Hung Society or the Society of Heaven and Earth*, 3 v. London: Baskerville

WARNER, W. LLOYD 1961 *The Family of God: A Symbolic Study of Christian Life in America*. New Haven: Yale University Press

WÄSCHE, ERWIN 1933 *Carl Gustav Carus und die romantische Weltanschauung*. Düsseldorf: G. H. Nolte

WEITMAN, SASHA R. 1971 'The Flags of All Nations: First Results of a World-Wide Statistical Survey,' Paper presented to the 66th annual meeting of the American Sociological Assn, 2 September 1971

WERBNER, RICHARD P. 1971 'Symbolic Dialogue and Personal

Transactions among the Kalanga and Ndembu,' *Ethnology*, 10, 311–28

WESTERMARCK, E. A. 1891 *The History of Human Marriage*. London: Macmillan (subsequent edns, for example, 5th edn, 3 v., 1921)

—— 1914 *Marriage Ceremonies in Morocco*. London: Macmillan

—— 1926 *Ritual and Belief in Morocco*, 2 v. London: Macmillan

—— 1930 *Wit and Wisdom in Morocco: A Study of Native Proverbs*. London: Routledge

WHATMOUGH, JOSHUA 1956 *Language: A Modern Synthesis*. New York: Mentor

WHITE, T. H. (ed.) 1960 *The Bestiary: A Book of Beasts* (1954). New York: Capricorn

WHITEHEAD, A. N. 1927 *Symbolism, Its Meaning and Effect*. New York: Macmillan

WILSON, EDMUND 1962 *The Triple Thinkers*. Harmondsworth: Pelican

WILSON, MONICA 1957 *Rituals of Kinship among the Nyakyusa*. London: Oxford University Press

—— 1959 *Communal Rituals of the Nyakyusa*. London: Oxford University Press

WILSON, THOMAS 1894 *The Swastika*, report of the U.S. National Museum, 757–1030

WINTER, E. K. 1928 'Bachofen-Renaissance,' *Z. f. die gesamte Staatswissenschaft*, 85, 316–42. Tübingen

WINZEN, DAMASUS 1957 *Symbols of Christ*. London: Longmans Green

WOLF, ARTHUR P. 1970 'Chinese Kinship and Mourning Dress,' in *Family and Kinship in Chinese Society*, ed. Maurice Freedman. Stanford: University Press, 189–207

YALMAN, NUR 1969 'On the Meaning of Food Offerings in Ceylon,' in *Forms of Symbolic Action*, ed. Robert F. Spencer. American Ethnological Assn: University of Washington Press, 81–96

YANG, MARTIN C. 1947 *A Chinese Village: Taitou, Shantung Province*. London: Kegan Paul

YONGE, CHARLOTTE M. 1889 *Womankind*, new edn. London: Walter Smith & Innes

YOUNG, MICHAEL D. 1971 *Fighting with Food: Leadership, Values and Social Control in a Massim Society.* Cambridge: University Press

ZAINAL-'ABIDIN BIN AHMAD 1950 'Malay Manners and Etiquette,' *J. Royal Asiatic Society, Malayan Branch*, 23, 43–74

ZIMMER, HEINRICH 1946 *Myths and Symbols in Indian Art and Civilization*, Bollingen, 6. Washington, D.C.: Pantheon

Addenda (for chs. 8 and 9):

DÉMEUNIER, J. N. 1776 *L'Esprit des Usages et des Coutumes des différens peuples.* 3 v. London/Paris: Pissot

TEGG, WILLIAM 1877 *Meetings and Greetings: The Salutations, Obeisances and Courtesies of Nations.* London: William Tegg & Co. (This compendium, for notice of which I am indebted to T. M. Ciołek, covers a wide range of ethnographic data. Though superficial, it is apparently the first general work in the field.)

INDEX